ALIVE IN CHRIST

GRADE 1 CATECHIST EDITION

Jesus Christ

aliveinchrist.osv.com

OurSundayVisitor

The Subcommittee on the Catechism, United States Conference of Catholic Bishops, has found the doctrinal content of this manual, copyright 2014, to be in conformity with the *Catechism of the Catholic Church*.

Nihil Obstat
Rev. Fr. Jeremiah L. Payne, S.Th.L.
Censor Librorum, Diocese of Orlando

Imprimatur
✠ Most Rev. John Noonan
Bishop of Orlando
April 30, 2013

For permission to reprint copyrighted materials, grateful acknowledgment is made to the following sources:

English translation of the *Catechism of the Catholic Church for the United States of America* copyright © 1994, United States Catholic Conference, Inc.—Libreria Editrice Vaticana. English translation of the *Catechism of the Catholic Church: Modifications from the Editio Typica* copyright © 1997, United States Catholic Conference, Inc.—Libreria Editrice Vaticana. Used by permission. All rights reserved.

Scripture selections taken from the *New American Bible, revised edition* © 2010, 1991, 1986, 1970 by the Confraternity of Christian Doctrine, Washington, D.C., and are used by license of the copyright owner. All rights reserved. No part of the *New American Bible* may be reproduced in any form without permission in writing from the copyright owner.

English translation of the *Catechism of the Catholic Church for the United States of America* copyright © 1994, United States Catholic Conference, Inc.—Libreria Editrice Vaticana. English translation of the *Catechism of the Catholic Church: Modifications from the Editio Typica* copyright © 1997, United States Catholic Conference, Inc.—Libreria Editrice Vaticana. Used by permission. All rights reserved.

Alive in Christ Parish Grade 1 Catechist Edition
ISBN: 978-1-61278-021-4
Item Number: CU5111
2 3 4 5 6 7 8   015016   18 17 16 15 14
Webcrafters, Inc.; Madison, WI; USA; September 2014; Job# 118184

Vision and Philosophy

❝ I am the way and the truth* and the life… I am the resurrection and the life. ❞

John 14:6, 11:25

❝ Jesus Christ not only transmits the word of God: he is the Word of God. Catechesis is therefore completely tied to him. Thus what must characterize the message transmitted by catechesis is, above all, its 'christocentricity'. ❞[1]

General Directory for Catechesis, 98

Jesus Christ at the Center

Welcome to *Alive in Christ*. Christ is at the center of our faith, our Church, our catechesis. *Alive in Christ* is intentional in its focus on the life, mission, and saving work of Jesus Christ. This lays a foundation for a relationship with Jesus, who continually leads us to his Father's love and calls us through the Spirit to share in the divine life through his Church (see *Catechism of the Catholic Church*, 426).

Mirroring the Divine Pedagogy

The catechetical process of *Alive in Christ* mirrors the divine pedagogy—the gradual and relational way God teaches us so that we can know him and his truth, be guided by the Holy Spirit to respond with faith and love, and accept the gift of new life in Christ.

In this unique and effective pedagogy, each lesson encourages a personal and ongoing relationship with God, beginning with God's invitation through Sacred Scripture and leading children to reflect on his Word, deepen their understanding of our Sacred Tradition, and respond with a lived faith within the home and among friends, within the Church and in the community.

Building Knowledge of, and Reverence for, Sacred Scripture

Sacred Scripture from the *New American Bible Revised Edition* is foundational to every lesson in *Alive in Christ*. Scripture from both the Old Testament and New Testament is presented in a variety of ways that encourage children to listen to the voice of God in his written Word and learn about the people and stories of the Bible. Each lesson offers several distinct encounters with Sacred Scripture, giving children the opportunity to pray with, reflect on, study, and apply God's Word to their lives.

Comprehensive Presentation of Catholic Teaching

Alive in Christ provides an authentic and comprehensive presentation of the essentials of the Catholic faith and has been found by the United States Conference of Catholic Bishops' Subcommittee on the Catechism to be in conformity with the *Catechism of the Catholic Church.*

Following a systematically organized scope and sequence, key themes of Catholic teaching are repeated each year, through a grade-level focus, building on the child's knowledge of the faith at each developmental stage. This presentation of Catholic teaching—coupled with a purposeful emphasis on Catholic practices, images, and models of faith—promotes a common language of faith and builds a vibrant Catholic identity.

Developmentally Responsive and Appropriate

Created by a team of experts in catechesis, theology, and child psychology, *Alive in Christ* incorporates the most trusted research on how children learn and communicate. Definitions, activities, questions, and reading passages have been reviewed for developmental appropriateness. Targeted on-page interactions help children more effectively learn or reinforce lesson content.

Topics are presented at important developmental "windows"—ages when research in child development tells us that learning about a particular topic would be most effective. Illustrations, Catholic art, and photos emphasize Scripture and visually present the chapter objectives in ways children can understand and relate to.

Complete and Purposeful Approach to Prayer and Worship

Every grade level intentionally incorporates each of the five forms of prayer mentioned in the *Catechism*—blessing and adoration, petition, intercession, thanksgiving, and praise (see CCC, 2626–2643). Children learn about and pray these basic prayer forms and are introduced to traditional prayers and devotions of the Church. They are taught how to talk with God in their own words and listen silently as he speaks to them. Each grade level also presents many opportunities to deepen children's understanding of the feasts and seasons of the Church year and how we celebrate the Paschal Mystery through them.

Putting Faith into Practice

Alive in Christ presents and effectively implements the six fundamental tasks of catechesis (see *General Directory for Catechesis*, 84–85). Exercises, features, and questions throughout the text prompt children to relate knowledge of our Catholic faith with their life experience. Every chapter has on-page activities for immediate application as well as concrete suggestions for children to live out the faith at school, at their parish, and in their homes, and communities.

Each lesson's Our Catholic Life section provides practical examples of the ways we worship, live, pray, and serve together as Catholics. It introduces children to Catholic figures who stand as models of heroic virtue in everyday life. Every lesson has connections to the Catholic social tradition, and each grade level provides catechesis on the seven major themes of the Church's Social Teaching.

Practical Ways to Involve Families in Their Children's Faith Formation

The "Family + Faith" page and an extensive website give parents the tools they need to know what their children are learning, talk about the faith, and recognize how they can more consciously live the faith in their daily family life.

On each lesson's take home page, parents will find information about children's developmental understanding, discussion prompts, and resources for family prayer. Taking into consideration the aims of the New Evangelization, each page includes an opportunity for adult reflection on their own relationship with Jesus and the Church.

Online resources offer multimedia tools to foster family interaction and reinforce the lesson at home.

A Commitment to Support Both New and Experienced Catechists

Alive in Christ Catechist Editions empower catechists with easy-to-use and effective tools for lesson planning, teaching and reinforcing faith concepts, and growing in their own relationship with Christ and his Church.

The key concepts and chapter objectives are fully explained and conveniently located at the beginning of each lesson along with background information to strengthen catechist understanding and nurture personal faith. A clear, concise, wraparound lesson plan leads the catechist page-by-page through the effective three-step process with integrated background on Sacred Scripture and doctrine, teaching tips, and connections to music, liturgy, and Catholic Social Teaching.

Extensive Online Resources for Catechists and Families

Alive in Christ provides catechists and leaders comprehensive program level resources and unit, chapter, and seasonal specific tools and activities. Online support includes lesson planning tools, catechist formation, custom test building and eAssessments, connections to the Sunday readings, and the option to share lesson plans via social media.

This extensive site provides children and families access to web-based assessments, interactive games and reviews, and articles and resources targeted specifically to adults—all to support faith sharing and continued learning in the home.

Age-Appropriate Music that Enhances Learning

With the knowledge that music is a means for forming children in Sacred Scripture, Church teachings, and Catholic Identity, *Alive in Christ* integrates multiple music options into every lesson. A variety of music from OCP (Oregon Catholic Press), John Burland, Dr. Jo Ann Paradise, and other sources is tied to chapter objectives and themes.

Music is suggested at point-of-use in the Catechist Edition, with multiple song suggestions for each chapter. Many prayer pages feature a song to be used within the prayer service. Music can be sampled and downloaded.

Also, we now have an all-new music component, *Songs of Scripture: Deepening Children's Understanding of the Word of God*, which features songs that teach, reinforce, and unfold the meaning of Scripture stories presented in the Student Book.

Alive in Christ Development Team

Greg Erlandson
President and Publisher

Beth McNamara
General Manager

Sabrina Magnuson
Associate Publisher

Dr. Jo Ann Paradise   Dr. Joseph White

Ana Arista   Heidi Busse   David Dziena   Dr. Hosffman Ospino   Denise Utter

Alive in Christ Structural Framework

Alive in Christ follows a systematic Scope and Sequence organized around key themes of Catholic teaching that repeat each year within a grade-level focus, building on the child's knowledge of the faith at each developmental stage.

This organizational structure takes into account research in child development that tells us at which age learning about a particular topic is most effective. These developmental "windows" help us to understand when the spiritual, cognitive, emotional, sociological, moral, and physical abilities of a child are "ripe" for learning. Included in the sequence, then, is a sensitivity to when children are ready to learn. A grade-level focus based within the structural framework of the seven essential themes allows for optimal learning.

The seven essential, foundational themes of the faith—Revelation, Trinity, Jesus Christ, The Church, Morality, Sacraments, and Kingdom of God—provide the structural framework that organizes the content of the grade. Progressing from first to sixth grade, the child deepens understanding as he or she is presented content that is theologically precise and developmentally appropriate.

As you study the Scope and Sequence, you will see how the objectives across grades move the learner to examine and appropriate a greater knowledge of our Catholic faith and how those objectives help to form a vibrant Catholic Identity.

Grade Level Focus	
1: Jesus Christ	"For through faith you are all children of God in Christ Jesus." **Galatians 3:26**
2: Sacraments of Penance and the Eucharist	"This is my body, which will be given for you; do this in memory of me." **Luke 22:19**
3: The Church	"I am the vine, you are the branches. Whoever remains in me and I in him will bear much fruit…" **John 15:5**
4: The Moral Life	"This is my commandment: love one another as I love you." **John 15:12**
5: The Seven Sacraments	"The water I shall give will become in him a spring of water welling up to eternal life." **John 4:14**
6: The Word of God in the Old Testament	"Your word is a lamp for my feet, / a light for my path." **Psalm 119:105**

 Go to **aliveinchrist.osv.com** for an overview of the developmental windows for each grade level focus and full program Scope and Sequence.

Program Scope and Sequence

This graphic gives a visual image of the scope and sequence as a first grader in your group will experience it. The circles on the outside name the foundational themes that are the framework (unit structure) for every grade level. The child is holding key developmental factors or "windows" that lead to the grade level focus (for more on this, see page CE29). No matter what unit you are teaching, some component of the grade level focus is being treated.

Unit 1
Revelation

Unit 2
Trinity

Unit 3
Jesus
Christ

Unit 4
The
Church

Unit 5
Morality

Unit 6
Sacraments

Unit 7
Kingdom
of God

Snapshot of Developmental Factors First Grade—Jesus Christ

- Because this is the beginning of formal religious education for many children, and because the aim of catechesis is communion with Christ, it is logical to focus first grade catechesis around the person of Jesus.

- Children this age are just beginning to move beyond the developmental self-focus of the preschool years, so an introduction to a relationship with Jesus and the Church community is appropriate.

- First graders are beginning to move into a cognitive stage of rule-based thinking, so this is a great opportunity to provide them with the basic teachings of the faith.

Alive in Christ Parish Edition Program Components

Student Books Grades 1–6

Student Books follow a seven unit structure with a grade level focus on a foundational topic in our Catholic faith. They are the perfect tool to teach children to know, love, and live their Catholic faith through Sacred Scripture, doctrine, prayer, practices of the faith, and seasonal celebrations.

Catechist Editions Grades 1–6

The Catechist Editions help to build confident, capable, and successful catechists with comprehensive background and lesson preparation pages, timed wrap around lesson plans, optional activities, and point of use information. They are spiral bound and conveniently sized to match the Student Book.

People of Faith Collection Grades 1–6

This beautifully illustrated collection of Saints, Blesseds, and Venerables are connected to specific chapters. Children will learn about models of our Catholic faith while deepening their relationship with God and the Church.

Music Resources

Catechists are provided options for developmentally appropriate music that enhances learning. *Alive in Christ* integrates music into each step of the lesson. A variety of music from Oregon Catholic Press is tied to chapter objectives and themes.

A unique, all new music component, *Songs of Scripture: Deepening Children's Understanding of God's Word*, features songs by John Burland and Dr. Jo Ann Paradise that teach, reinforce, and unfold the meaning of Scripture stories presented in the Student Book.

Go to **aliveinchrist.osv.com** to find comprehensive online support with lesson planning tools, electronic assessments, and a variety of helpful resources for catechists, administrators, parents, and children.

Online Resources for the Catechist

- Online lesson planning helps catechists to plan using chapter, seasonal, or Catholic Social Teaching lessons
- Share lesson plans via social media such as Facebook & Twitter
- Unit- and chapter-specific tools, assessments, activities, and multimedia resources
- Build a Custom Test allows catechists to build, print, and distribute tests using a bank of multiple choice, matching, fill in the blank, and long answer questions
- Assign eAssessments to children for completion online
- Catechetical formation and professional development tools are designed to help catechists hone their skills and grow in the knowledge of God's love
- Sample and download chapter-specific music to enhance catechetical learning or for prayer

Online Resources for the Student & Family

- Interactive Reviews offer children an opportunity for web-based assessment, preparation, and practice
- At-home faith formation resources for all ages help reinforce Catholic identity
- Faith-sharing features and resources geared to parents, children, and families encourage continued learning at home via games, multimedia activities, Lectionary-connected resources, social media interaction, and topical articles
- Sample and download chapter-specific music to enhance catechetical learning or for prayer

Online Resources for the Leader

- Program-level tools and resources provide directors, administrators, and leaders with higher-level materials from correlations to in-service models
- Sample and download chapter-specific music to enhance catechetical learning or for prayer

Responding to Your Vocation

> " Give thanks to the Lord for the gift of your vocation, through which Christ has called you from among other men and women to be instruments of his salvation. Respond with generosity to your vocation and your names will be written in heaven. "
>
> — Pope Saint John Paul II, *Guide for Catechists*, 37

These words, taken from a talk by Pope Saint John Paul II to the catechists of Angola, are both awe inspiring and challenging! You have been called, he said, called by Christ from among other men and women. Have you ever wondered why you responded to the talk of the pastor or DRE that spoke about the need for catechists? Why did the bulletin article that outlined the responsibilities of a catechist stir your heart and prompt you to respond? Who gave your name to the catechetical leader in your parish?

No matter how the invitation came, it was Christ who called you. And by the power of the Holy Spirit, you, like Mary, responded, "Yes!" The vocation to catechesis, like all vocations, first comes from the grace of Baptism,

is strengthened in Confirmation, and is sustained by the Eucharist and Penance. "The Church awakens and discerns this divine vocation and confers the mission to catechize….This personal call of Jesus Christ and its relationship to him are the true moving forces of catechetical activity. 'From this loving knowledge of Christ springs the desire to proclaim him, to "evangelize," and to lead others to the "Yes" of faith in Jesus Christ'[2]" (GDC, 231).

You have been called by Christ and been given the mission by his Church to be instruments of his work. Take a moment and ponder that statement. With so many responsibilities and demands on our time, we might sometimes lose sight of this, and being a catechist becomes just one of the many things we must do each week. This cannot be so. Every time you gather with your children, you take your place in the long line of those who have for 2,000 years held the sacred duty of bringing others into "communion, in intimacy, with Jesus Christ" (*Catechesi Tradendae*, 5).

Your Role as Catechist

To support and nurture children in their baptismal call to a lifetime of growing closer to and more like Jesus, the Church sets out some essential instructions. In order to provide a presentation of the "entire treasure of the Christian message" while adapting it to the "capacity of those being catechized" (GDC, 112), a catechist must do several things.

Teach the comprehensive course of study outlined by the United States Conference of Catholic Bishops' Subcommittee on the Catechism. In *Alive in Christ*, you find these doctrines and practices presented in the objectives of the lesson. (See GDC, 112.)

Respect the developmental level of your children by understanding how they learn. (See GDC, 112.)

Use various methods as they are a "sign of life and richness" that will address multiple learning styles and special needs (GDC, 148).

Model a Catholic life through your own behaviors and practices, for the "charism given to [the catechist] by the Spirit, a solid spirituality and transparent witness of life constitutes the soul of every method" (GDC, 156).

Proclaim with joy and enthusiasm that "God so loved the world he sent his only Son" (John 3:16). In the words of Pope Benedict XVI, "Today too, there is a need… to rediscover the joy of believing and the enthusiasm for communicating the faith" (*Porta Fidei*, 7).

As you accept this sacred and challenging vocation, be assured, that the Holy Spirit will lead and guide you in handing on our Catholic faith to the next generation. Let the love of God pour through so that they see in you the image and heart of our loving God.

As Jesus Formed His Disciples

There are six fundamental tasks in the ministry of catechesis. These six tasks are named and treated in the *General Directory for Catechesis* (see GDC , 85), and later in the *National Directory for Catechesis* (see NDC, 20). Each of these tasks corresponds to an aspect of faith in Jesus. The following are the six tasks of catechesis.

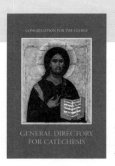

General Directory for Catechesis

Promoting Knowledge of the Faith

We cannot live a faith we do not know. For this reason, studying the teachings of Jesus and his Church is an essential task of catechesis. The U.S. Bishops' Subcommittee on the Catechism and the conformity review process direct what is to be contained in this comprehensive presentation of the faith. According to the *National Directory for Catechesis*, this task of catechesis is a response to the individual's desire that God plants in the heart of every person to know. This desire comes naturally when individuals have had opportunities to encounter Christ and his message and have experienced an initial conversion. *Alive in Christ* begins each lesson by giving children an opportunity to meet God in his Word and to wonder about his life and love, followed by a process of helping them to know more about him through Sacred Tradition—the teaching of the Church. In this way, we help children frame questions that drive their desire to know more.

Liturgical Education

This task relates to learning about the ways in which the Church worships and celebrates, including the Seven Sacraments, the Order of Mass, and the liturgical year. According to the *General Directory for Catechesis*, liturgical education includes teaching about the form and the meaning of liturgical celebrations, but also means helping individuals prepare their minds and hearts to enter into these mysteries of our faith. As you use *Alive in Christ*, you will teach your students about the liturgy both through the doctrine presented in the core chapters as well as through seasonal activities and prayerful experiences that echo the words and rhythms of our liturgical celebrations.

Moral Formation

This task of catechesis involves forming the consciences of learners through the moral teachings of Jesus and his Church and fostering understanding of what it means to live these teachings in one's daily life. Morality in the Christian life involves standards and guidelines, but it is more than learning a list of rules. Morality is about discipleship. As you use *Alive in Christ*, you will find opportunities to challenge children to apply what they have learned about the Ten Commandments, Jesus' command to love as he has loved, and the Beatitudes to situations at home and school and in the community.

Teaching to Pray

"When catechesis is permeated by a climate of prayer, the assimilation of the entire Christian life reaches its summit" (GDC, 85). The "climate of prayer" in catechesis invites individuals into an ever deeper relationship with God. Teaching to pray is more than merely "teaching prayers"; it involves fostering an understanding of prayer as conversation with God—helping children learn how to talk with God in their own words as well as how to listen to God.

This task of catechesis involves teaching the traditional prayers of the Church and the various forms and expressions of prayer mentioned in the *Catechism of the Catholic Church*. *Alive in Christ* incorporates experiences of all five forms of prayer. You will also have opportunities to help children speak to God in their own words.

Education for Community Life

This task of catechesis relates to developing an understanding of what it means to be a part of the Christian community, including respecting the authority and structure of the Church as well as living out Jesus' New Commandment to love one another as he has loved us. "Catechesis prepares the Christian to live in community and to participate actively in the life and mission of the Church" (GDC, 86). Catechesis should prepare us to live and work with one another, both within the Church and in society as a whole. The

bishops write that catechesis should encourage a spirit of simplicity and humility, a special concern for the poor, particular care for the alienated, a sense of fraternal correction, common prayer, mutual forgiveness, and a fraternal love that embraces all these attitudes. (See GDC, 86.) Various chapter features, as well as the "Live Your Faith" sections on Catholic Social Teaching will assist you in this task of catechesis.

Missionary Initiation

While only some may be called to other lands to minister in Christ's name, by Baptism, all are called to live in such a way that we serve as witnesses of the faith to those who are around us. This task of catechesis prepares the learner to share his or her faith with others. *Alive in Christ* helps to form children in the language of the Catholic faith and the behaviors and practices of the faith. Forming them in a vibrant Catholic identity gives them the skills necessary to be strong witnesses of the faith. This is reinforced in the tools we provide the parents in the Family + Faith page, as it equips the parents to talk about faith with their children.

Our bishops state, "all efforts in evangelization and catechesis should incorporate these tasks" (NDC, 20). In this way, we pay attention to several different dimensions of faith, with the ultimate goal of helping children grow into deeper communion with Christ so that they live as disciples in faith, word, and deed.

The Divine Pedagogy

As catechists, we always hold two realities: the "what" and the "how" of catechesis. What do we want our children to know and love about our faith and how do we best communicate the treasure of our faith?

We use the word *pedagogy* to speak about the art, science, or profession of teaching. In other words, pedagogy is the "how" of faith formation. We are called to hand on the truths of our faith by echoing God's own way of teaching us his truths. The *General Directory for Catechesis* tells us that,

66 Catechesis, as communication of divine Revelation, is radically inspired by the pedagogy of God, as displayed in Christ and in the Church. [It is the Church's mission to be] a visible and actual continuation of the pedagogy of the Father and of the Son. 99

GDC, 143, 141

Jesus the Teacher

Each lesson in *Alive in Christ* mirrors the divine pedagogy—the gradual and relational way God teaches us so that we can know him and his truth, be guided by the Holy Spirit to respond with faith and love, and accept the gift of new life in Christ. Even as we teach others, God remains active in their hearts, bringing growth to the seeds of faith that are planted there.

Here are five important characteristics of the divine pedagogy that are at the heart of each lesson of *Alive in Christ*.

The pedagogy of God is invitational and person-centered.

God initiates a relationship with each person. He does so by first creating us with a desire to know him and the capacity to respond to him. The ultimate invitation to relationship comes in Jesus. Pope Saint John Paul II tells us that the purpose of all catechesis is to bring people into intimacy with Jesus.

As God enters into dialogue with us, we are called to follow this example by providing catechesis that it is rooted in interpersonal relationships and involves a process of dialogue. (See GDC, 143.) God also meets us where we are and accommodates for our particular needs. Therefore, effective catechesis should be developmentally appropriate and should make allowances for adapting to special needs.

God's pedagogy is incarnational.

Dei Verbum points out the "inner unity" of deeds and words in God's plan of revelation: "the deeds wrought by God in the history of salvation manifest and confirm the teaching and realities signified by the words, while the words proclaim the deeds and clarify the mystery contained in them" (2).

From speaking the universe into existence, to his promise to Noah and his covenants with Abraham and Moses, to the Word made flesh in Jesus Christ, it is evident that God's Word becomes action.

An effective pedagogy should make the faith come to life through hands-on activities and applications and multisensory teaching methodologies. It should give learners clear ways to go out and live the Gospel they have received.

The pedagogy of God is familial and communal.

God reveals himself as a communion of persons—Father, Son, and Holy Spirit—and creates human beings to be in communion with one another.

Effective catechesis should build community among the children, involve parents and families as primary catechists, and connect children to the larger parish community. Connecting the families to the life of the parish, particularly through participation in the Sunday Eucharist, is vital in building up the Body of Christ.

God's pedagogy is structured and comprehensive.

In salvation history, God reveals himself to humanity gradually as people are able to understand. One revelation builds upon the next, until Revelation reaches its fullness in the Person of Jesus Christ. Effective catechesis also presents key truths of the faith gradually as the learner is able to receive them.

The pedagogy of God is perpetual.

We read in **Isaiah 55:11**, "So shall my word be / that goes forth from my mouth; / It shall not return to me empty, / but shall do what pleases me, / achieving the end for which I sent it." God's truths are handed on through the generations in the forms of Sacred Scripture and Sacred Tradition, which is the living memory of the Church. God's covenants do not end, but come to greater fulfillment and realization.

A catechesis based on the divine pedagogy prepares the learner to share the Gospel with others, in word and deed, so that the Good News of salvation is handed on to others and to future generations.

Three-Step Catechetical Process

Alive in Christ's catechetical methodology mirrors the divine pedagogy by following a three-step process of **Invite**, **Discover**, and **Live**. This process encourages a personal and ongoing relationship with the Holy Trinity.

1. **The Invite Step** begins the lesson with God's invitation through Sacred Scripture. Children open their minds and hearts to what God is saying to them in Scripture, reflect on it, and transition to the Discover step and chapter objectives.

2. **The Discover Step** helps form Catholic identity through the study of Scripture, knowledge of Church teaching, and an understanding of Catholic practices. It presents the doctrine of the lesson in developmentally appropriate language and images. Charts, on-page questions, and gold star activities prompt children to interact directly with the page, and aid in understanding and retention. With large on page activities, children are given the opportunity to process and reinforce what they have learned and apply it to their own lives and the experience of the Church.

3. **The Live Step** helps children relate knowledge of the faith and the ways we worship, live, pray, and serve together as Catholics. Children are given the tools to connect their faith to everyday life and to deepen their relationship with God and the Church through the prayer experiences at the end of each lesson.

If you follow this three-step process, you will in fact mirror the divine pedagogy by offering children the opportunity to know God and his truth through Sacred Scripture and Sacred Tradition. You will inspire them to be open to the Holy Spirit so that they will respond in faith and love and accept the gift of new life in Christ!

As a catechist, during the **Invite** step you:

- Call the children together to begin in **prayer**.
- Prepare the children to hear the **Word of God**.
- Guide the children through the **Scripture reflection** process, proclaiming God's Word and inviting quiet thought. (See CE22 for a full description of the Scripture reflection process.)
- After proclamation of the Scripture, allow time (governed by what is developmentally appropriate) for sacred **silence**.
- Invite children **to share** what they have experienced, what they felt God was saying to them or what he wanted them to know in a special way today. Assure them sharing is voluntary.
- Prompt continued thought about God's Word and move to chapter objectives by using the "**What Do You Wonder**" questions.

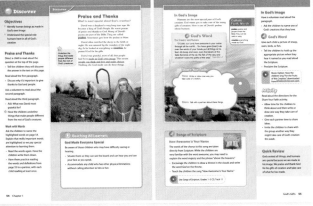

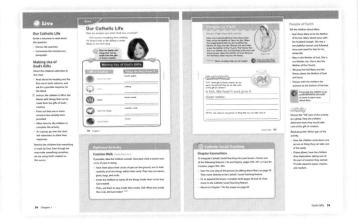

As a catechist, during the **Discover** step you:

- Teach the **objectives** of the lesson, which are identified in the Catechist Edition in two places: the overview Lesson Plan in the catechist background section and in the top left-hand corner of each Discover spread. The Quick Review, highlighted in the bottom right hand corner of the Discover spread, allows you to check that you have fully covered the objectives.

- Follow the **instruction** in the vertical side columns, which walks you through the entire lesson. Note that the activities are an integral part of the lesson. They emphasize the essential elements of Church teaching and help the children apply those truths to worship, prayer, and daily life.

- Present the **Catholic Faith Words**, which are highlighted in the text and called out in the side boxes. These words build a common language of faith and are explained with precise theological language that is developmentally appropriate.

- Use the **boxes** framed in green at the bottom of the page that provide additional Scripture and doctrinal background, optional activities, quick tips, ways to adapt for special needs, suggestions for including music, and more.

As a catechist, during the **Live** step you:

- Guide the children through a graphic organizer, chart, or reflection activity to **synthesize** what they have learned in the chapter.

- Hold up the Communion of Saints, and introduce the children to a **Saint**, **Blessed**, or **Venerable** whose life exemplifies the content of the lesson. What better way to encourage faith-filled living than through Catholic heroines and heroes?

- Give the children the opportunity through a closing **activity** to relate their knowledge of the faith to their lives, and invite them to commit themselves more deeply to what it means to be Catholic with concrete action and future steps.

- Conclude with a **prayer celebration**. Make sure to leave time at the end of the lesson to pray with the children. If the prayer calls for it, you may want to assign parts a week ahead of time.

- Send home the **Family + Faith** page. As the children live their faith primarily in the circle of their families, this page is an excellent resource to connect the children's learning with their home and to form their parents in faith.

Lesson Preparation

Alive in Christ Catechist Editions give you everything you need for lesson planning, teaching and reinforcing faith concepts, and growing in your own relationship with Christ and his Church.

Each chapter has catechist-specific content provided in the planning and background pages. These are the five pages that provide scriptural, doctrinal, and methodological background and formation. You will also find pages that address the different ways children process, understand, and learn lesson content at any given grade level.

Catechist Background easy-to-understand theological background on the chapter content. The Reflect questions help connect faith concepts with the catechist's own life experience.

Key Concept for each lesson is clearly stated at the start of each chapter.

Doctrinal Content correlates to paragraphs from the *Catechism of the Catholic Church.*

Tasks of Catechesis relate lesson components to one of the six Tasks of Catechesis as outlined in the *National Directory for Catechesis.*

Catechist's Prayer offers a moment of reflection for the catechist before planning each lesson.

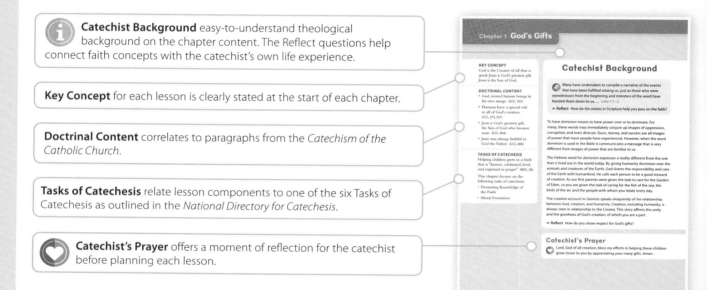

Timed Lesson Plan clearly stated chapter objectives, step-by-step instructions, and a suggested time frame to complete each step of the lesson.

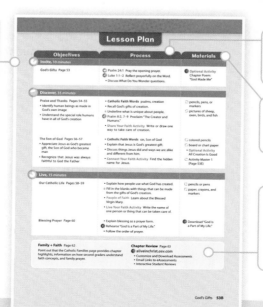

Process Column notes prayer, Scripture, activities, and Catholic Faith Words in each step.

Materials Column materials and online resources needed for the lesson.

Family + Faith / Chapter Review reminders to share chapter content with families and directs catechists to various opportunities for review and assessment.

Sharing the Message offers insight on the relationship between the lesson objectives and the child's developmental level of understanding of those topics.

How Grade Level Children Understand provides background on where children this age typically are in terms of cognitive, social, spiritual, and emotional development.

Online Resources are clearly labeled throughout the Catechist Edition and direct you to downloads, lesson planning tools, interactive reviews, eAssessments, and more.

Chapter Story or poem provides an opportunity to extend the Invite step of the process with additional life experience connections.

NCEA IFG: ACRE Edition correlates the lesson objectives to the domains of *NCEA Information for Growth: Assessment of Children/Youth Religious Education* (2013) and helps catechists measure children's understanding and appropriation of lesson content.

Catholic Social Teaching identifies which principles of Catholic Social Teaching/Live Your Faith pieces connect to this chapter and provides direction for how to integrate them into the Live step of the process. These connections are also noted at point of use in the bottom band of the lesson plan.

Music Options are provided to enhance catechetical learning and the prayer celebration. These options are also called out at point of use in the wraparound lesson plan.

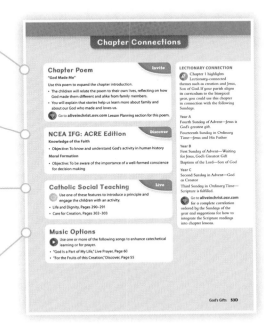

Sacred Scripture

"For in the sacred books, the Father who is in heaven meets His children with great love and speaks with them; and the force and power in the word of God is so great that it stands as the support and energy of the Church...."

Dei Verbum, 21

Catholic Bible

NABRE

New American Bible Revised Edition

Sacred Scripture from both the Old Testament and New Testament is at the heart of *Alive in Christ*. The children are invited to understand the importance of Sacred Scripture, as a font of Divine Revelation and the guide for their lives. The Word is always given prominent visual importance to highlight its significance, with a parchment background, an icon, and a logo. Children are led to know, love, and be formed by God's Word.

Scripture in the Catechetical Process

The children always **pray** with Scripture in the opening prayer of the Invite step and often in the prayer experience in the Live step.

The practice of Scripture **reflection** is an essential element in the Invite step of every lesson and the means by which we enter into the divine pedagogy.

Children are formed by this practice of reflecting on Scripture and being open to the Word of God personally speaking to them. Listening with the ear of the heart and reflecting on Scripture prepares children for practices such as *Lectio Divina*.

Sacred Scripture is **studied** in the Discover step as children learn about God's action throughout salvation history and see how Scripture is a source of Church teaching. Key Scripture accounts are presented in multiple grade levels to encourage biblical literacy, familiarity, and understanding.

Throughout the Discover and Live steps, the children **apply** the Word of God to their lived experience and acquire the behaviors and practices of a Catholic life.

Scripture Reflection

CHAPTER 3

God's Commandments

Let Us Pray

Leader: Loving Father, you made us to know you and your desire for us.

"I delight to do your will, my God;
your law is in my inner being!" **Psalm 40:9**

All: O God, help us to learn how to listen for your voice so that we will know how to follow you. Amen.

Scripture

"When [Moses] looked, although the bush was on fire, it was not being consumed.... When the LORD saw that he had turned aside to look, God called out to him from the bush: Moses! Moses! He answered, 'Here I am.' God said: Do not come near! Remove your sandals from your feet, for the place where you stand is holy ground." **Exodus 3:2b, 4–5**

What Do You Wonder?

• How does God speak to people today?

• How do the Ten Commandments help you to know God and what he wants for you?

Invite

Let Us Pray

Invite children to gather in the [...] prayer space and make the Sign [...] the Cross. Begin with leader's p[...] and have a volunteer pray alou[...] psalm verse from a Bible. Pron[...] the group's response.

Have the children move out o[...] prayer space and back to thei[...]

Say: God wanted Moses to lead [...] People, who were slaves, to freedom. The Word of God we will hear [...] of Moses' journey of faith.

Scripture

Guide the children through [...] process of Scripture reflection.

• Invite them to close their eyes and open their minds and hearts to what God is saying to them by being silent and still.

• Proclaim the Scripture.

[...] several moments of

Step 1: Begin by using the directions provided on the Invite page of the lesson or you may use the recorded preparation titled, "Mantra," included in both the *Songs of Scripture* CDs.

Step 2: Help the children enter into sacred space by prominently displaying the Bible, lighting or turning on a candle, and guiding them to become quiet and still.

Step 3: Read the passage in a slow and steady voice, one complete sentence at a time.

Step 4: Ask the question, "What did you hear God say to you today?" This reflection is critical in providing the children an opportunity to encounter God through his Word. It prepares the child to receive and respond in faith to God's personal invitation.

Sacred Tradition

What is necessary for the children to know so that they will develop a vibrant Catholic identity and be able to express their faith with competence, understanding, and love?

The Church guides us, teaching that the catechetical message has "a 'comprehensive hierarchical character'[3] which constitutes a vital synthesis of the faith" (GDC, 114). The truths of the faith are organized in a hierarchy around the mystery of the most Holy Trinity, in a Christ-centered (or *Christocentric*) perspective.

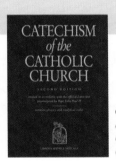

Catechism of the Catholic Church

> " The mutual connections between dogmas, and their coherence, can be found in the whole of the Revelation of the mystery of Christ.[4] 'In Catholic doctrine there exists an order or "hierarchy" of truths, since they vary in their relation to the foundation of the Christian faith.'[5] "
>
> CCC, 90

In other words, some truths are so basic and foundational to what we believe as Catholics that they must be presented first, and then other related truths can be better understood.

To help us know what is basic and foundational, the USCCB's Subcommittee on the Catechism has identified the truths of the faith deemed essential to the formation of children. *Alive in Christ* has been found to be in conformity with the *Catechism of the Catholic Church*.

In salvation history, God has revealed himself to people in a systematic and gradual way, showing us more of himself as we are capable of understanding. (See GDC, 38 and CCC 54–65.) Our catechesis models this divine pedagogy and includes all of the foundational elements of the faith, presenting them in a gradual and systematic way as the learner is ready to hear them.

Alive in Christ organizes the foundational truths around seven key themes of Catholic teaching that repeat each year within a grade level focus.

Systematic and Comprehensive

The content of Sacred Scripture and Sacred Tradition are systematically presented in precise theological language in the **lesson objectives** of each lesson. The objectives are found on your Lesson Plan and at point of use where they are presented to the children.

Important **Catholic Faith Words** are highlighted in every chapter with definitions that grow as children's understanding does, and their repetition across grades helps to promote the common language of faith.

Each **Unit Opener** summarizes key concepts being presented and identifies *Catechism of the Catholic Church* references for each of these faith statements.

At the back of each Student Book, the **Our Catholic Tradition** reference section reinforces the faith basics presented in the lessons. It is referenced in your lesson plan with specific instructions on how to integrate the content into the lesson.

The Theory Behind It

At one point or another in your family life and your ministry as a catechist, you've likely found yourself explaining to a child, "It's not just what you say, it's how you say it." The message is as important as the delivery. You can't separate the *what* from the *how*. Similarly, doctrine and method are not two ends of a spectrum. They are interdependent. In catechesis, you can't have one without the other. And it goes a step further, for it's not just *what* we teach, and how we teach it, but *how* the learner receives it.

"Consequently catechesis starts out with…the integral structure of the Christian message, and proceeds to explain it in a manner adapted to the capacity of those being catechized" (GDC, 112).

When we teach things in a theologically accurate way, and in a manner sensitive to where the children are developmentally, we provide the best chance that they will appropriate the content—process and understand it in a way that has meaning to them and that they can then apply to their own lives.

According to the National Association for the Education of Young Children (NAEYC), *developmental appropriateness* includes multiple components.

1. It is important to know how children develop and learn at particular ages and stages and to create learning environments that are responsive to these general needs.

2. Because every child is unique, knowing the individual children and how they learn best is essential.

3. It is important to know what is culturally appropriate for different ages and stages of development.

The Practice of It

Alive in Christ provides you with carefully selected topics and activities that meet the developmental level of the children you are teaching as well as tips for addressing individual needs. The program includes prayers, Saints, activities, and stories that represent the

Presentation of Text

- Information is sequenced and organized in smaller "chunks" to make reading and understanding faster and easier.

- Sentences are shorter in length for younger grades.

- Fonts and type sizes are set with consideration given to the reading level of the child.

- Words are defined consistently at point-of-use and highlighted for easy identification.

- Terms and concepts are introduced, reinforced, and then further defined in advanced ways as they develop across grades.

diversity of cultures found in our Church and introduces these traditions at developmentally-appropriate times.

Alive in Christ takes into account the experience level of today's children with various topics and how they are used to receiving and processing those topics. So, the series is developmentally appropriate not just in what kids learn at particular ages, but how they learn it.

As a catechist, you can feel confident that you are giving the children the most precise presentation of Church teaching in the most developmentally appropriate way. That's what excellent catechesis is all about.

Use of Visuals

- Fine art, illustrations, and photos advance in detail and sophistication as grades progress.

- Graphic organizers, charts, and callouts are used to present content in easy to track and access formats.

- Captions are used to aid in learning, and the content and purpose of captions advance as the grades do.

- The text-to-art ratio is intentional and customized for each grade level.

Teaching Strategies

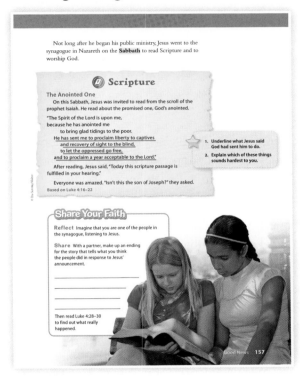

- Questions focus reading, prompt reflection, and reinforce learning.

- On-page activities and teaching strategies incorporate dynamic, interactive learning methods.

- Chapter Reviews use multiple formats to accommodate different learning styles.

- The Catechist Edition includes a Teaching This Grade page that gives details on how children at this age might understand lesson objectives.

- Ideas for customizing content are found in the Reaching All Learners boxes in some chapters.

The Use of Images

" In order to communicate the message entrusted to her by Christ, the Church needs art. "

—*Letter of Pope Saint John Paul II to Artist* (1999), 12

While educational research assures us that children make meaning through the interplay of text and images (Carney and Levine, 2002), any adult who has spent time with a young child knows that verbal and visual both tell the story. For hundreds of years, the Church has used sacred art and stained glass windows to teach Catholic doctrine and provide a physical presentation of the truths of our faith. Jesus often used images when he preached, giving his disciples a glimpse into his Father's mystery and the Kingdom.

Alive in Christ mirrors the divine pedagogy through its use of photos, illustrations, and images of fine art, stained glass, and statues—each one specifically selected for this program.

Educational research (Carney and Levine, 2002) and our own experience tell us that photos, illustrations, and art closely tied to text

- improve the reader's learning and recall
- direct the child's attention to what's most important on the page
- make the text more understandable and memorable
- help the child connect and apply what's been learned to their lived experience.

In *Alive in Christ* lessons, developmentally appropriate visuals—Scripture illustration, fine art, stained glass, statues, icons, photos, and accompanying captions—meet lesson objectives and build Catholic identity.

You will find historically accurate, child friendly Scripture and Saint illustrations that grow in sophistication and detail as grades advance. This promotes a common visual language of faith and builds a vibrant Catholic identity.

Grade 2   Grade 6
Saints Thérèse of Lisieux and Teresa of Ávila

Grade 1   Grade 3
The Sacred Heart of Jesus in statue and fine art

Grade 2   Grade 5
The Parable of the Good Samaritan

The Role of Music

The use of music in *Alive in Christ* is both intentional and purposeful. The music has been chosen to form children in the lesson content and Catholic identity. It is age appropriate and includes children's voices. It has both a formative and an informative purpose.

Long-term Retention

It has been demonstrated that the repeated rehearsal of information has a positive effect on long-term retention. Activities from the arts, such as music integrated into classroom content, can be used as prompts to recall information. Combining music with movement further enhances a child's learning. We "encode" information through both verbal and motor activity. In other words, when we sing and move, we are learning in both our bodies and our minds.

Sustain Attention

Music and movement also sustain attention. Translating material into actions (role-playing a song) helps learners not only recall a story but can also help them connect that story to a concept they have learned. Besides, moving to music is a universal response, and, with the proper disposition, can enhance prayer.

Emotional and Spiritual Connection

Music can also affect us on an emotional level. Who of us has not been moved by a song to feel something deep within our hearts? Music has helped form us as Catholics throughout the ages and has enabled us to both experience God's presence and respond to him from the depths of our being.

Moral Formation
- Objective: To be aware of the importance of a well-formed conscience for decision making

Catholic Social Teaching — Live

Use one of these features to introduce a principle and engage the children with an activity.
- Life and Dignity, Pages 290–291
- Care for Creation, Pages 302–303

Music Options

Use one or more of the following songs to enhance catechetical learning or for prayer.
- "God Is a Part of My Life," Live Prayer, Page 60
- "For the Fruits of this Creation," Discover, Page 55

First Sunday of Advent—Waiting for Jesus, God's Greatest Gift
Baptism of the Lord—Son of Go...

Year C
Second Sunday in Advent—God as Creator
Third Sunday in Ordinary Time—Scripture is fulfilled.

Go to **aliveinchrist.osv.com** for a complete correlation ordered by the Sundays of the year and suggestions for how to integrate the Scripture readings into chapter lessons.

Music options are integrated into every lesson and can be used to celebrate prayer or enhance learning. You will find these options both at point of use in the wraparound and on the Chapter Connections page in the box titled, "Music Options."

 Play chapter-specific music to enhance catechetical learning or for prayer. Go to **aliveinchrist.osv.com** to sample and download.

Songs of Scripture Music CDs

To support the commitment to Sacred Scripture, an all-new, original resource, *Songs of Scripture Deepening Children's Understanding of God's Word*, by John Burland and Jo Ann Paradise, unfolds one of the Scripture passages in each unit. Activities for these songs are found in bottom-band boxes in the Catechist Edition.

 Go to **aliveinchrist.osv.com** to order the *Songs of Scripture* CDs and for more information.

Reaching All Learners

66 Growth in faith is related to human development and passes through stages. Individuals develop as human beings and faithful followers of Christ in different ways and according to their own pace…The Church's catechesis—and even more so, the catechist—must take into consideration all the human factors of a particular age level in order to present the Gospel message in a vital and compelling way. 99

NDC, 48

Benefitting from the work of educators in the past decades, religious educators now have new tools in providing children the fullness of the faith in developmentally appropriate ways.

Not only must we teach the faith related to children's level of human development, we must also meet the individual needs of our children. When working with any group of children, it does not take long to realize that they learn in different ways. Many have written about how to best provide strategies to address different learning styles. Dr. Howard Gardner's research on Multiple Intelligences provides particular insight. His theory looks at eight different ways people learn. Applying his theory to your planning will help you reach each child with the Good News of salvation.

Throughout *Alive in Christ*, a variety of teaching strategies are employed within the lesson process. Working with words and reading Scripture (Verbal/ Linguistic), using photos and illustrations to prompt discussion (Visual/Spatial), and listening to, singing, and reflecting on songs (Musical) are just a few examples. Additional features, such as Reaching All Learners and Optional Activities, address various methods to help students with different learning styles and abilities connect with the lesson.

Multiple Intelligences	
Verbal/ Linguistic	This learning occurs best through reading, writing, telling stories, and discussing ideas.
Logical/ Mathematical	This learning occurs best through problem solving, analyzing, and applying logic.
Musical	This learning occurs best through singing, listening to music, and remembering melodies.
Bodily/ Kinesthetic	This learning occurs best through physically moving, dancing, acting, and making things.
Visual/Spatial	This learning occurs best through looking at pictures, drawing, and creating.
Interpersonal	This learning occurs best through sharing about one's feelings, talking with others, and collaborating with others on tasks.
Intrapersonal	This learning occurs best through working alone and reflecting.
Naturalist	This learning occurs best through exploring nature and living things.

 Go to **aliveinchrist.osv.com** for additional resources on meeting the challenges of providing for special needs in your faith formation sessions.

Teaching First Graders

Getting to Know Jesus

For some children, the first grade is their first experience of learning about God in a group of peers. It's important that we create an atmosphere of welcome and excitement. Because this is the beginning of formal religious education for many children, and because the aim of catechesis is to help others develop a relationship with Jesus Christ (see GDC, 80), it is logical to focus first grade catechesis around the person of Jesus.

We want first graders to get to know Jesus, as Lord and King but also as a friend who knows and loves each person. The catechist is essential in this understanding of the relational nature of our faith. Your first graders need to see you as a friend of Jesus and also as a friend of theirs.

Moving Beyond the Self

First graders are just beginning to move beyond the developmental self-focus of the preschool years, so an introduction to a relationship with Jesus and the Church community is appropriate as they begin to gain more perspective about the world around them. They are still growing in their understanding that other people might have different ideas and experiences than they do.

Sometimes children this age will need help to understand someone else's opinions or feelings. The catechist can serve as a "coach" in these situations, encouraging children to dialogue with one another and asking relevant questions of one child so that another child can listen and understand (e.g., "How did you feel when Matthew said that to you?").

Organizing Their Understanding of the World

Intellectually, first graders are beginning to understand that the world works according to certain "rules." This can make them notorious "tattletales." Because they organize their understanding of the world according to the rules they learn, when someone isn't following the rules (even when it doesn't seem to directly affect them), they can feel threatened. If someone isn't following the rules, they may feel like their own world is coming apart!

First graders are concrete thinkers. They learn best when they can see, hear, and touch what they are learning about. Be sure to give them multisensory, active learning experiences to make lessons come alive.

The rule-based thinking of first graders presents us with a great opportunity to provide them with the basic teachings of the faith. Their memory and understanding of these basics will be better than before, and an overview of the faith will lay the foundation for faith formation in the years to come.

Living and Learning Together

In the *General Directory for Catechesis* we are told that the "childhood religious awakening which takes place in the family is irreplaceable"[6] (226). The role of the catechetical leader and the catechist in the parish is to help form and support families in this sacred journey.

The Family + Faith page gives families the tools they need to talk about faith and more consciously live the faith in their homes and daily lives. The resources on this page are invaluable in providing adults the practical help they need to grow in faith themselves and to nurture the faith of their children.

Your Child Learned
This section summarizes key Catholic teaching covered in the chapter and introduces families to the Scripture and Person of Faith presented.

Children at This Age
This feature helps families understand the relationship between the content presented and the child's developmental level of understanding. It provides a look at the content through the eyes of the child and equips parents with a perspective that is necessary in order to nurture their child's faith.

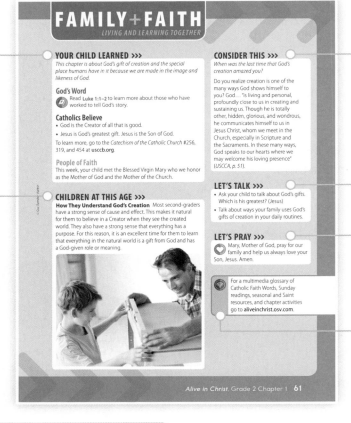

FAMILY + FAITH
LIVING AND LEARNING TOGETHER

YOUR CHILD LEARNED >>>
This chapter is about God's gift of creation and the special place humans have in it because we are made in the image and likeness of God.

God's Word
Read **Luke 1:1–2** to learn more about those who have worked to tell God's story.

Catholics Believe
• God is the Creator of all that is good.
• Jesus is God's greatest gift. Jesus is the Son of God.
To learn more, go to the *Catechism of the Catholic Church* #256, 319, and 454 at **usccb.org**.

People of Faith
This week, your child met the Blessed Virgin Mary who we honor as the Mother of God and the Mother of the Church.

CHILDREN AT THIS AGE >>>
How They Understand God's Creation Most second-graders have a strong sense of cause and effect. This makes it natural for them to believe in a Creator when they see the created world. They also have a strong sense that everything has a purpose. For this reason, it is an excellent time for them to learn that everything in the natural world is a gift from God and has a God-given role or meaning.

CONSIDER THIS >>>
When was the last time that God's creation amazed you?

Do you realize creation is one of the many ways God shows himself to you? God... "is living and personal, profoundly close to us in creating and sustaining us. Though he is totally other, hidden, glorious, and wondrous, he communicates himself to us in Jesus Christ, whom we meet in the Church, especially in Scripture and the Sacraments. In these many ways, God speaks to our hearts where we may welcome his loving presence" (USCCA, p. 51).

LET'S TALK >>>
• Ask your child to talk about God's gifts. Which is his greatest? (Jesus)
• Talk about ways your family uses God's gifts of creation in your daily routines.

LET'S PRAY >>>
Mary, Mother of God, pray for our family and help us always love your Son, Jesus. Amen.

For a multimedia glossary of Catholic Faith Words, Sunday readings, seasonal and Saint resources, and chapter activities go to **aliveinchrist.osv.com**.

Alive in Christ, Grade 2 Chapter 1 **61**

Consider This Through the use of targeted questions that encourage reflection, adults are given the opportunity to reflect on their experience and inform that experience with the teaching of the Church.

Let's Talk Adult-specific questions or directions help to facilitate discussion with the child about the lesson content.

Let's Pray This provides families with a short prayer that incorporates the key concept of the lesson.

Go to **aliveinchrist.osv.com**. The Family + Faith page sends adults to aliveinchrist.osv.com so that families can reinforce and assess their learning, as well as find suggestions for family discussions and ways to apply faith to family life.

The **aliveinchrist.osv.com** Student/Family pages extend learning, foster family faith sharing, and provide session plans and tools for home-based catechesis.

Catholic Social Teaching

Pope Saint John Paul II reminded us that one of the fundamental tasks of the Christian family is to remember that the family is always at the service of God's Kingdom. While the family is to "guard, reveal, and communicate love," it does so knowing that their love is not only to be shared within itself, but meant to be shared with the world (*Familiaris Consortio*, 17). We are called to reach out past our family to build relationships of love and justice in our neighborhoods, communities, and beyond.

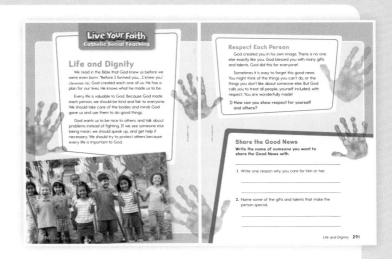

Each grade level of *Alive in Christ*, presents the seven principles of Catholic Social Teaching, articulated by the United States Conference of Catholic Bishops. In this **Live Your Faith** component, the scriptural and doctrinal foundations of the principles help the children connect their faith to a life of peace and justice. While peace and justice are taught in many of the core chapters, the seven principles are intentionally treated in Live Your Faith.

You can use these Catholic Social Teaching features in a variety of ways. Every core chapter and seasonal lesson has a Catholic Social Teaching connection integrated into the lesson plan. A **bottom band box** will provide you with suggestions on how to incorporate the Live Your Faith component with the lesson. Combining these components with the seasonal lessons can help your children connect how Catholics worship with how Catholics live.

Your catechetical leader may choose to schedule these components so that all the children will be focusing on the same principle at the same time. If you schedule your own sessions, you may choose to combine several of the principles and present them at one time.

This presentation of Catholic teaching builds a vibrant Catholic identity and prepares us to evangelize the world through faith and action as we work in service of God's Kingdom.

🌐 Using This Feature

Lesson Connection

Use this feature to enhance, or in place of, the Live section of the following chapters:

Chapter 1, page 53   **Chapter 5**, page 97

Chapter 3, page 73   **Chapter 12**, page 175

Chapter 4, page 87   **Chapter 20**, page 267

Use this feature after the Discover section, before the Live prayer begins in the following seasonal lessons:

Ordinary Time: All Saints, page 15

Christmas, page 25   **Easter, We Rejoice**, page 43

Scope and Sequence

Unit		Chapter	Lesson Concepts
1 REVELATION	CHAPTER 1	Created By God	• The Bible is God's Word written by humans. We learn about God from the Bible. • God made humans to be his friends, to know and love him. • God made everything. All of his creation is good.
	CHAPTER 2	God's Gifts for Us	• God created the world to show his love. • All of creation is God's gift to us, and his Son, Jesus, is his greatest gift. • People use God's gifts in the world to make things we need. • Thanksgiving is showing God we are grateful for all that he's given us.
	CHAPTER 3	Made to Care	• The image of God is the likeness of God that is in all human beings because we are created by him. • Humans are the most special part of creation. God gave us the ability to think and make choices. • God gave Adam and Eve the responsibility to be caretakers of his creation. • Each of us is responsible for treating all of creation with care and respect.
2 TRINITY	CHAPTER 4	The Holy Trinity	• God asks us to be friends with one another, to be nice, and to help each other when in need. • Jesus is the Son of God who shows us the way to his Father. • God the Father loves us so much he sent his only Son to be with us. • The Holy Trinity is God the Father, God the Son, and God the Holy Spirit, the one God in three Divine Persons.
	CHAPTER 5	The Holy Family	• Signs of love are expressed in families. • Jesus is the Son of God and a human being. • The Holy Family is the name of the human family of Jesus, Mary, and Joseph. • Jesus grew up with Mary and Joseph in Nazareth, praying and learning.
	CHAPTER 6	About the Bible	• Jesus told stories like the Lost Sheep to show us how God watches over and guides us, always welcoming us back. • A parable is a short story Jesus told about everyday life to teach something about God. • The Bible is the Church's holy book. • The two parts of the Bible are the Old Testament and the New Testament.
3 JESUS CHRIST	CHAPTER 7	Jesus the Healer	• Blessed Mother Teresa is an example of how we are to share God's love by caring for the sick. • Jesus' healings showed God the Father's power and love. • Faith is the gift of believing and trusting in God so much that we do what he asks us to do.
	CHAPTER 8	Jesus Teaches Love	• A Commandment is a law that God made for people to obey. • Jesus taught the Great Commandment to love God above all else and to love others the way you love yourself.
	CHAPTER 9	Jesus Teaches Us to Pray	• Prayer is talking to and listening to God. • We need prayer to get close to God. • The Lord's Prayer is the prayer Jesus taught his followers to pray to God the Father.
4 THE CHURCH	CHAPTER 10	Responding to God	• Noah said "yes" to God, and God promised to always keep him safe. The rainbow is a sign of that promise. • Jesus invites everyone to God's Kingdom—the world of love, peace, and justice that is in Heaven and is still being built on Earth. • The Church shares Jesus' message about God's love. • The Church is a community of baptized people who believe in God and follow Jesus.
	CHAPTER 11	The Church's Guide	• A guide helps us and shows us the way. • The Holy Spirit is the Third Divine Person of the Holy Trinity. • Jesus promised us that the Holy Spirit would guide the Church. • Saint Thérèse loved God very much and worked for him through her little jobs. She called this "The Little Way."

Sacred Scripture	Catechism of the Catholic Church	Tasks of Catechesis	Catholic Faith Words	People of Faith	Catholic Social Teaching
You Created Me Psalm 139:13–15; The Garden of Eden Genesis 2:7–22	105–106, 355, 299	Promoting Knowledge of the Faith, Education for Community Life	Bible, creation	Bl. Fra Angelico	Life and Dignity, Care for Creation
God Was Pleased Genesis 1:11–31; The Story of Creation Genesis 1:6–25	293–294, 299, 312, 2402, 2637	Promoting Knowledge of the Faith, Teaching to Pray	Jesus, praise, thanksgiving	St. Nicholas	Dignity of Work, Care for Creation
Humans in Charge Genesis 1:27–31; Take Care of What I've Given You Genesis 1:26–30	357, 356, 373, 2415	Promoting Knowledge of the Faith, Education for Community Life	image of God	St. Albert the Great	Life and Dignity, Care for Creation
Go and Make Disciples Matthew 28:19–20; The Way to the Father John 14:8–9	1822, 1844, 426, 1698, 422, 253–254	Promoting Knowledge of the Faith, Education for Community Life	God the Father, Son of God, Holy Trinity	St. Patrick	Life and Dignity, Rights and Responsibilities
Joseph's Dream Matthew 2:19–23; The Boy Jesus Luke 2:51–52	1656–1657, 423, 1655, 532–533	Promoting Knowledge of the Faith, Education for Community Life	Mary, Holy Family	Sts. Zechariah, Elizabeth, and John	Life and Dignity, Call to Community
Jesus' Parables Matthew 13:34–35; The Parable of the Lost Sheep Luke 15:3–6; The Good Shepherd John 10:14–15	605, 546, 104, 138, 120	Promoting Knowledge of the Faith, Moral Formation	Old Testament, New Testament	St. Paul of the Cross	Life and Dignity, Option for the Poor
Jesus Preached and Healed Matthew 9:35; Have Faith Luke 8:40–56	2447, 1503, 1814	Promoting Knowledge of the Faith, Education for Community Life	faith	St. Louise de Marillac	Option for the Poor, Human Solidarity
The Most Important Commandment Mark 12:28–31; The Greatest Commandment Luke 10:25–28	2056, 2055	Moral Formation, Education for Community Life	Commandment, Great Commandment	St. Thomas of Villanova	Life and Dignity, Dignity of Work
When You Pray Matthew 6:6–8; How to Pray Ephesians 5:18–20	2559, 2565, 2759	Promoting Knowledge of the Faith, Teaching to Pray	prayer, Lord's Prayer	St. Ephrem the Hymnist	Life and Dignity, Call to Community
Noah Built an Ark Hebrews 11:7; Noah Says "Yes" Genesis 6:14–22, 7:1–10, 9:17; The Parable of the Great Feast Luke 14:16–23	2569, 543, 737, 782	Promoting Knowledge of the Faith, Education for Community Life	Kingdom of God, Church	Bl. Mary Theresa of Jesus	Call to Community, Rights and Responsibilities
Live in and Follow the Spirit Galatians 5:22–23, 25; Jesus Promises the Holy Spirit John 14:26	729, 243, 747, 1477	Promoting Knowledge of the Faith, Education for Community Life	Holy Spirit	St. Rose of Lima	Rights and Responsibilities, Dignity of Work

Grade 1 Scope and Sequence

Unit	Chapter		Lesson Concepts
4	CHAPTER 12	Friends of God	• Saints are heroes of the Church who loved God very much, did his work on Earth, and are now with him in Heaven. • Holy means unique and pure; set apart for God and his purposes. • We are part of the family of Saints, connected to the Saints who lived before us and to those who believe in Jesus now.
5 MORALITY	CHAPTER 13	Disciples Serve	• Jesus washed his disciples' feet to show us how to serve and love one another. • Jesus asks us to have a kind, giving heart when we serve and help others. • A disciple is a follower of Jesus who believes in him and lives by his teachings. • Serving others is a way to serve God.
	CHAPTER 14	Making Choices	• The Ten Commandments are God's laws that tell people how to love him and others. • Free will is being able to choose whether to obey God or disobey God. • God created us with free will because he wants us to make good choices. • All choices have consequences, or results, that can show love and respect or hurt others.
	CHAPTER 15	Showing Sorrow	• Sin is the choice to disobey God on purpose and do what you know is wrong. It is not an accident or a mistake. • The consequences of sin are hurting your friendship with God and others. • God wants us to be close to him and will always forgive us when we say we are sorry. • Jesus wants us to be sorry for our sins and turn to God our forgiving Father.
6 SACRAMENTS	CHAPTER 16	Jesus the Savior	• Adam and Eve chose to bring sin into the world. Their disobedience is called Original Sin. • God did not stop loving people because of their sin. • God sent his Son, Jesus, to be our Savior and bring people back to him. • Jesus died for all people to save them, giving his life so that people could have new life with God.
	CHAPTER 17	Holy Signs	• The Seven Sacraments are special signs and celebrations that Jesus gave his Church. • The Sacraments celebrate that Jesus is still with us, sharing his life and love. • Every Sacrament has words and actions we do and things God does that we can't see that bring us life.
	CHAPTER 18	We Are Welcomed	• Baptism is the Sacrament that brings new life in God and makes the person a member of the Church. • Grace is God's gift of sharing in his life and help. • In Baptism, a person is immersed, or has water poured over him or her in the name of the Father, Son, and Holy Spirit. • The baptized person is anointed, receives a white garment, and is given the light of Christ.
7 KINGDOM OF GOD	CHAPTER 19	We Give Thanks	• The Last Supper is the meal Jesus shared with his disciples the night before he died. • The Eucharist is the Sacrament in which Jesus himself, and the bread and wine become his Body and Blood. • The Mass is the gathering of Catholics to worship God and celebrate the Eucharist. • In the Mass we hear God's Word, give thanks for his gifts, and receive Jesus in Holy Communion.
	CHAPTER 20	Forever with God	• Heaven is living and being happy with God forever. • God desires for everyone to be happy with him forever. • Following Jesus and obeying God's laws are how we live in love now and forever.
	CHAPTER 21	God's Kingdom	• We pray for the coming of God's Kingdom, working together with God as he builds his Kingdom. • By being forgiving, treating others with respect, and helping those who are hungry and in need, Jesus showed us how to work for the Kingdom. • When we are kind, share, play fair, and include others, we are spreading peace.

Sacred Scripture	Catechism of the Catholic Church	Tasks of Catechesis	Catholic Faith Words	People of Faith	Catholic Social Teaching
Love Your Enemies Matthew 5:44–45; Martha and Mary Luke 10:38–42	823, 228, 825, 946–948	Promoting Knowledge of the Faith, Missionary Initiation	Saint, angel, holy	St. Dominic	Call to Community, Rights and Responsibilities
The Greatest Among You Matthew 23:11–12; The Washing of the Disciples' Feet John 13:2–17	1337, 1823, 618, 1816	Education for Community Life, Missionary Initiation	serve, disciple	V. Fr. Solanus Casey	Option for the Poor, The Dignity of Work
Do This and You Will Live Luke 10:25–28; God's Commandments Deuteronomy 10:12–13	2067, 1731, 1743, 1739	Promoting Knowledge of the Faith, Moral Formation	Ten Commandments, obey, free will	St. Frances Cabrini	Call to Community, Rights and Responsibilities
Seventy-Seven Times Matthew 18:21–22; The Forgiving Father Luke 15:11–32	1850, 1849, 1431–1432, 1427	Promoting Knowledge of the Faith, Moral Formation	sin	St. Dismas	Rights and Responsibilities, Option for the Poor
Do Not Be Afraid Matthew 28:5–6; Jesus Lives Luke 23–24	402–404, 410, 457, 613	Promoting Knowledge of the Faith, Moral Formation	Original Sin, Resurrection	St. Josephine Bakhita	Option for the Poor, Human Solidarity
I Am in My Father John 14:20; The Advocate John 14:18–19	1084, 1131, 1123	Promoting Knowledge of the Faith, Liturgical Education	Seven Sacraments	Mary	Human Solidarity, Care for Creation
Go Into the Whole World Mark 16:15–16; People Everywhere Believe Acts 8:4–12	1213, 1996, 1239, 1241	Promoting Knowledge of the Faith, Liturgical Education	Baptism, grace, godparents	St. Moses the Black	Rights and Responsibilities, Human Solidarity
For the Forgiveness of Sins Matthew 26:26–28; The Last Supper 1 Corinthians 11:23–25	610, 1333, 1329–1330, 1346–1347	Promoting Knowledge of the Faith, Liturgical Education	Last Supper, Eucharist, Mass, Holy Communion	Pope Saint John XXIII	Call to Community, Human Solidarity
God's Kingdom Is Not Something You Can See Luke 17:20–21; Together Always John 14:1–3	1024, 1045, 1693	Moral Formation, Teaching to Pray	Heaven	St. Emily de Vialar	Option for the Poor, Human Solidarity
Do Justice, Love Goodness, and Walk Humbly Micah 6:8; Starting Small Matthew 13:31–32	2818, 2831–2832, 2304	Moral Formation, Education for Community Life	peace	St. Pedro Calungsod	Call to Community, Option for the Poor

Unit	Chapter	Lesson Concepts
1 **REVELATION**	**CHAPTER 1** God's Gifts	• God created human beings in his own image. • Humans have a special role in all of God's creation. • Jesus is God's greatest gift, the Son of God who became man. He is always faithful to God the Father.
	CHAPTER 2 God's Promise	• God gives all people the ability to choose. • Original Sin is the first sin committed by Adam and Eve. • Jesus is the Savior because he led people who were lost through sin back to God; Jesus is the Good Shepherd.
	CHAPTER 3 The Word of God	• God tells us about himself through the Bible. • The Bible is God's Word written down by humans. • Jesus tells stories that help us know and love God the Father. • The Old and New Testaments are the two parts of the Bible, also called Scripture.
2 **TRINITY**	**CHAPTER 4** God the Father	• God the Father is the First Divine Person of the Holy Trinity. • Jesus taught us that God the Father loves and cares for us. • We rely on God the Father, praying to him and trusting he will provide what we need.
	CHAPTER 5 God the Son	• The Angel Gabriel announced to Mary that she would be the Mother of the Son of God, the Savior, Jesus. • The Holy Family of Jesus, Mary, and Joseph lived in Nazareth where Jesus grew up, learning and praying. • Jesus is both the Son of God and a human being. • The Baptism of the adult Jesus by John the Baptist was the beginning of his public teaching.
	CHAPTER 6 God the Holy Spirit	• The Holy Trinity is one God in three Divine Persons. • The Holy Spirit is the Third Divine Person of the Holy Trinity who helps and guides us as Jesus promised. • Jesus is the Son of God who became man, the Second Divine Person of the Holy Trinity. • The Holy Spirit helped the Apostles understand and spread Jesus' teachings and he remains with the Church today.
3 **JESUS CHRIST**	**CHAPTER 7** God's Commandments	• The Ten Commandments are God's laws that teach us to love him and others. • The Great Commandment sums up all of God's laws, telling us to love God above all else and others the way you love yourself. • Jesus told the parable of the Good Samaritan to help us understand that loving God means loving our neighbor. • Jesus gave us a New Commandment to teach us to love as he loves.
	CHAPTER 8 Choose to Do Good	• When we make bad choices that hurt our relationship with God and others, God forgives us if we are truly sorry. • Sin is a free choice to do what we know is wrong. Mistakes and accidents are not sins. • Both venial and mortal sins harm our relationship with God, but in different ways. • Conscience is an ability given to us by God that helps us make choices about right and wrong.
	CHAPTER 9 God's Mercy	• We learn about God's mercy in the story of the Prodigal Son. • The virtues can help us say no to temptation and choose what is good. • Mercy is kindness and concern for those who are suffering; God has mercy on us even though we are sinners. • It's important to ask God and others for forgiveness, and to be forgiving.
4 **THE CHURCH**	**CHAPTER 10** The Sacraments	• The Seven Sacraments are special signs and celebrations that Jesus gave his Church that allow us to share in God's life and work. • Jesus continues to share his life and love with us in the Sacraments. • Baptism, the first Sacrament received, makes a person a child of God and member of the Church, taking away Original Sin and all personal sin. • The Sacraments of Initiation—Baptism, Confirmation, Eucharist—celebrate our membership into the Catholic Church.
	CHAPTER 11 Seek Forgiveness	• An examination of conscience is a prayerful way of thinking about how we have followed the Ten Commandments, Beatitudes, and Church teachings. • Contrition is being sorry for your sins and wanting to live better. • In the Sacrament of Penance and Reconciliation, God's forgiveness for sin is given through the Church. • The Sacrament includes confession, penance, contrition, and absolution.

Sacred Scripture	Catechism of the Catholic Church	Tasks of Catechesis	Catholic Faith Words	People of Faith	Catholic Social Teaching
Handing Down the Stories Luke 1:1–2; The Creator and Humans Psalms 8:2, 7–9	355, 373, 357, 464, 606	Promoting Knowledge of the Faith, Moral Formation	psalms, creation, sin, Son of God	Blessed Virgin Mary	Life and Dignity, Care for Creation
The Sinner Who Repents Luke 15:7; The Garden of Eden Genesis 2:15–17; 3:1–6, 23; The Good Shepherd John 10:11–14	1730–1731, 389, 397, 457, 754	Promoting Knowledge of the Faith, Moral Formation	Original Sin, Savior	St. Cristóbal Magallanes Jara	Call to Community, Human Solidarity
Jesus Among the Crowds Luke 6:17–18; The Great Flood Genesis 6–9; Jesus Teaches Matthew 4:23–25	104, 105, 546, 120	Promoting Knowledge of the Faith, Missionary Initiation	Bible, Old Testament, New Testament	St. Luke	Life and Dignity, Rights and Responsibilities
Trust in the Father Luke 12:29–31; Rely on God Matthew 6:25–32	254, 322, 2779–2781, 2590	Promoting Knowledge of the Faith, Teaching to Pray	Saint, God the Father, prayer, trust	Bl. Julian of Norwich	Life and Dignity, Care for Creation
My Beloved Son Luke 3:21–22; Announcing Jesus' Birth Luke 1:26–38; 2:1–11; The Boy Jesus in the Temple Luke 2:41–52; Baptism of Jesus Matthew 3:13–17	430, 514–515, 723–724, 535	Promoting Knowledge of the Faith, Liturgical Education	Mary, angel, Holy Family	St. Peter	Life and Dignity, Human Solidarity
Risen Jesus Appears to Disciples Luke 24:49; The Promise John 14:15–26; The Spirit Comes Acts 1:4–5, 8; 2:2–3	683–684, 258–259, 253–255, 767–768	Promoting Knowledge of the Faith, Liturgical Education	Holy Spirit, Holy Trinity, disciples, Pentecost, Apostles	St. Arnold Janssen	Call to Community, Rights and Responsibilities
Moses on the Mountain Exodus 24:12; Love the Lord Your God Luke 10:27; The Parable of the Good Samaritan Luke 10:29–37	1962, 2055, 1465, 546, 1970	Promoting Knowledge of the Faith, Moral Formation	Ten Commandments, Great Commandment, parable, New Commandment	St. Elizabeth of Hungary	Rights and Responsibilities, Option for the Poor
Peter Hears the Rooster Mark 14:69–72; Peter Denies Jesus John 18:17–18, 25–27	1441, 1849, 1777–1778, 1854–1855	Promoting Knowledge of the Faith, Moral Formation	free will, mortal sin, venial sin, conscience	St. Thérèse of Lisieux	Rights and Responsibilities, The Dignity of Work
Forgive Seventy-Seven Times Matthew 18:21–22; The Prodigal Son Luke 15:11–32	1439, 270, 2447, 1810, 1459	Moral Formation, Education for Community Life	virtues, temptation, mercy	St. Jane de Chantal	Call to Community, Human Solidarity
Jesus Heals a Blind Man Luke 18:35–43; The Commissioning of the Apostles Matthew 28:19–20	1113, 1116, 1127–1128, 1212, 1213	Promoting Knowledge of the Faith, Liturgical Education	Seven Sacraments, Baptism, grace, Sacraments of Initiation	St. Pius X	Option for the Poor, Care for Creation
Whose Sins You Forgive John 20:21, 23; The Woman Who Was Forgiven Luke 7:36–39, 44–50	1779, 1432, 1422, 1423–1424	Liturgical Education, Moral Formation	examination of conscience, contrition, Sacrament of Penance and Reconciliation, confession, penance, absolution	St. Benedict-Joseph Labre	Call to Community, Human Solidarity

Unit	Chapter	Lesson Concepts
4	CHAPTER 12 The Church Year	• The liturgy is the public prayer of the Church. • The Church year celebrates the life, Death, Resurrection, and Ascension of Jesus. • The seasons of the Church year are Advent, Christmas, Ordinary Time, Lent, The Three Days (Triduum), and Easter. • Easter celebrates Christ's Resurrection and is the greatest feast of the Church year.
5 MORALITY	CHAPTER 13 Welcome in the Kingdom	• By the things he said and did, Jesus included those often left out and showed that God welcomes everyone. • The story of Zacchaeus is an example of Jesus welcoming someone who had faith and was willing to repent. • Jesus has a great love for children, and welcomed them along with all others into his Kingdom. • The Kingdom of God is the world of love, peace, and justice that God has in Heaven and wants for us on Earth.
	CHAPTER 14 Share the Good News	• The Gospel message is the Good News of God's Kingdom and his saving love. • In his parable of the Vine and Branches, Jesus teaches us that we need to stay connected to him in order to have life. • The Holy Spirit strengthened the Apostles to share what Jesus had taught them. • Many people in our parish share Jesus' message and work together with God as he builds his Kingdom.
	CHAPTER 15 Ways to Pray	• Jesus taught us to pray the Lord's Prayer, which we also call the Our Father. • There are five basic forms of prayer: blessing, petition, intercession, thanksgiving, and praise. • Prayer is important to deepen our friendship with God, and we can pray in many ways and at different times. • Sacramentals are blessings, objects, and actions that remind you of God and are made sacred through the prayers of the Church.
6 SACRAMENTS	CHAPTER 16 Gather to Worship	• The Eucharist is the Sacrament in which Jesus Christ shares himself and the bread and wine become his Body and Blood. • The Mass is another name for the celebration of the Eucharist. • The assembly is all those gathered for Mass. We take part by praying, singing, and using actions to worship God. • The Introductory Rites gather and unite us, preparing our hearts to hear God's Word.
	CHAPTER 17 Listen to God's Word	• Jesus used stories as a way to help us understand more about God and his Kingdom. • The first main part of the Mass is the Liturgy of the Word during which we hear readings from both the Old and New Testaments. • We listen to the deacon or priest proclaim the Gospel reading and give a homily to help us understand and apply God's Word. • This part of the Mass ends with the Creed and Prayer of the Faithful.
	CHAPTER 18 Remembering Jesus' Sacrifice	• The Mass is a memorial celebration of Jesus' Death, Resurrection, and Ascension. • Jesus' Death on the Cross is a sacrifice and gift that saves all people from the power of sin and everlasting death. • The Liturgy of the Eucharist is the second main part of the Mass in which Jesus Christ gives us the gift of himself, and we receive his Body and Blood in Holy Communion. • In the consecration, through the power of the Holy Spirit and the words and actions of the priest, the gifts of bread and wine become the Body and Blood of Jesus Christ.
7 KINGDOM OF GOD	CHAPTER 19 Supper of the Lamb	• The story of the Loaves and the Fish helps us understand what Jesus gives us in Holy Communion. • Before receiving Communion, we pray together the Lord's Prayer and offer each other a sign of peace. • Through the Eucharist, Jesus' followers are united with him and one another. • Jesus Christ is really and truly present with us in the Eucharist, so we receive Holy Communion with reverence and adore him in the reserved Blessed Sacrament.
	CHAPTER 20 Go Forth!	• In the Concluding Rites of the Mass, we are blessed and sent out to proclaim the Good News and give honor to God by the way we live. • As the Apostles were called to share the Good News, the Church's mission is to share Jesus' message of love and the Kingdom. • All members of the Church share in her mission, and some serve as missionaries who travel far away to spread the Good News.
	CHAPTER 21 A Feast for Everyone	• Heaven is life and happiness forever with God. • The story of the Wedding Feast is compared to God's invitation and our response. • The Eucharist is spiritual food that helps us to live with Jesus forever. • We are called to say "yes" daily to God.

Sacred Scripture	Catechism of the Catholic Church	Tasks of Catechesis	Catholic Faith Words	People of Faith	Catholic Social Teaching
The Holy Family Celebrates Passover Luke 2:41–42	1069–1070, 1171, 1163–1164, 1169	Liturgical Education, Education for Community Life	liturgy, worship, Resurrection	Pope Saint Victor	Life and Dignity, Human Solidarity
Let the Children Come Luke 18:15–17; Zacchaeus the Tax Collector Luke 19:1–10; Blessing of the Children Matthew 19:13–15	542–543, 2412, 526, 559, 2818–2819	Promoting Knowledge of the Faith, Education for Community Life	faith, peace, Kingdom of God	St. Brigid of Kildare	Option for the Poor, The Dignity of Work
Jesus' Disciples Receive a Mission Mark 16:15–16; The Vine and the Branches John 15:4–5	541, 787, 746–747, 941–942	Education for Community Life, Missionary Initiation	Gospel, proclaim, parish	Bl. Mother Teresa of Calcutta	Rights and Responsibilities, The Dignity of Work
The Lord's Prayer Luke 11:1–4; How to Pray Matthew 6:5–9	2759, 2644, 2565, 1668, 1671	Liturgical Education, Teaching to Pray	Lord's Prayer, blessing, petition, intercession, thanksgiving, praise, sacramentals	St. Alphonsus Liguori	Human Solidarity, Care for Creation
The Road to Emmaus Luke 24:30–32; The Community Gathers Acts 2:42–47	1323–1324, 1382, 1346, 1348–1349	Education for Community Life, Liturgical Education	Eucharist, Mass, assembly	St. Tarcisius	Call to Community, The Dignity of Work
The Parable of the Yeast Luke 13:18–21; The Mustard Seed Matthew 13:31–32	2613, 1154, 131–132, 1349, 1184, 1346	Promoting Knowledge of the Faith, Liturgical Education	Liturgy of the Word, homily, creed, Prayer of the Faithful	St. Paul	Call to Community, Care for Creation
Give God His Due Matthew 6:24; The Rich Young Man Matthew 19:21–22	1330, 616–617, 1408, 1142, 1411	Liturgical Education, Education for Community Life	sacrifice, Last Supper, Liturgy of the Eucharist, consecration	Bl. Imelda Lambertini	Option for the Poor, Human Solidarity
The Bread of Life John 6:30–35; The Feeding of the Five Thousand Luke 9:10–17	1335,1365, 1369–1370, 1374	Liturgical Education, Moral Formation	Holy Communion, Real Presence, reverence, Blessed Sacrament, Tabernacle	V. Pierre Toussaint	Call to Community, Option for the Poor
Paul Proclaims the Kingdom Acts 28:30–31; Peter Preaches Acts 10:42–48	1332, 849, 851–852	Missionary Initiation, Education for Community Life	mission, missionaries	St. Anthony Claret	Life and Dignity, The Dignity of Work
Jesus Knocks Revelation 3:20; The Wedding Feast Matthew 22:2–10 and Luke 14:16–23	326, 1329, 1391, 143	Promoting Knowledge of the Faith, Moral Formation	Heaven	St. Mary Magdalen de Pazzi	Option for the Poor, The Dignity of Work

Endnotes:

1. Cf. CCC 426-429; CT 5-6; DCG (1971) 40.

2. CCC 429.

3. Cf. CT, 31; CT 31 which expounds the integrity and organization of the message; cf. DCG (1971) 39 and 43.

4. Cf. Vatican Council I: DS 3016: *nexus mysteriorum*; LG 25.

5. UR 11.

6. CT 68.

Opening Lesson
&
Church Year Feasts and Seasons

Opening Lesson

The Church Year Feasts and Seasons

KEY CONCEPT

The key concept for each lesson is clearly stated at the start of each chapter.

DOCTRINAL CONTENT

- The doctrinal content for each chapter will be found in this section. It will show how the chapter correlates to paragraphs from the *Catechism of the Catholic Church.*

TASKS OF CATECHESIS

The six tasks of catechesis are outlined in the *National Directory for Catechesis.* The relevant tasks of catechesis for a chapter will be found in this section.

Catechist Background

Thomas said to him, "Master, we do not know where you are going; how can we know the way?" Jesus said to him, "I am the way and the truth and the life. No one comes to the Father except through me. If you know me, then you will also know my Father. From now on you do know him and have seen him." John 14:5–7

→ **Reflect** In what ways do I see myself as a child of God?

The Catechist Background includes a short essay that provides easy-to-understand theological background on the chapter content for both novice and experienced catechists.

The catechetical process of **Alive in Christ** mirrors the divine pedagogy—the gradual and relational way God teaches us so that we can know him in his truth, be guided by the Holy Spirit to respond with faith and love, and accept the gift of new life in Christ. Each lesson encourages this personal and ongoing relationship, beginning with God's invitation through Sacred Scripture. This leads children to reflect on his Word, deepen their understanding of our Sacred Tradition, and respond with a lived faith within the home and in the community.

Alive in Christ incorporates the most trusted research on how children learn and communicate. Topics are presented at important developmental "windows"—ages when research in child development tells us that learning about a particular topic would be most effective. For example, first graders are just beginning to move beyond the developmental self-focus of the preschool years, so an introduction to a relationship with Jesus and the Church community is appropriate. In Chapter 11, they will learn that Jesus promised us that the Holy Spirit would guide the Church.

→ **Reflect** Throughout your life, how has God invited you to know him and love him?

Catechist's Prayer

Lord, thank you for calling me to the ministry of catechesis. Draw me closer to you, so that I may teach by word and example.

A New Year

Let Us Pray

Leader: We shout joyfully to you, God.

"Know that the LORD is God,
    he made us, we belong to him,
    we are his people, the flock he
    shepherds." Psalm 100:3

All: Thank you, God, for guiding and loving us.
Amen.

God's Word

Thomas said to him, "Master, we do not know where you are going; how can we know the way?"

Jesus said to him, "I am the way and the truth and the life. No one comes to the Father except through me. If you know me, then you will also know my Father. From now on you do know him and have seen him." John 14:5–7

What Do You Wonder?

- What does it mean to be a child of God?
- How does God invite us to know and love him?

A New Year **1**

Catechist Background

Reflecting on Scripture

Each chapter in *Alive in Christ* begins with a focus on Sacred Scripture. On the *Invite* page, the children are called to open their minds and hearts to God's message.

- The Psalm verse and New Testament excerpt set the theme for the chapter. The passage from John is especially appropriate for this opening lesson, as it relates to Jesus' role in teaching us about God the Father.

- For more information on the use of Sacred Scripture throughout the chapters, refer to page CE22.

 Invite

Ask the children how they feel when they are invited somewhere. Point out the *Invite* heading on the page and explain that every lesson will begin with an invitation.

Let Us Pray

Introduce the children to the prayer space and invite them into it. Lead them in the Sign of the Cross. Read aloud the leader's prayer and the Psalm verse. Prompt the children's response.

Have the children move from the prayer space back to their seats.

 God's Word

Explain that you will read something that Jesus told his friends. Guide the children in reflecting on Scripture.

- Invite them to close their eyes and concentrate on the message in this passage.
- Proclaim the Scripture.
- Pause for several moments.
- *Ask:* What message did you hear?
- Invite volunteers to share.

What Do You Wonder?

Point out the picture and ask why the children are happy. Explain that following Jesus makes people happy.

Invite the children to respond to the questions. Ask what else they might wonder about God.

Discover

Objectives

- Chapter objectives relating to this Discover section are clearly stated here
- Begin to understand what is going to be learned this year, especially about Jesus and God's love for us

First Grade

Ask the children to tell you what the word *discover* means. Point out that the Discover pages in this book will help them find out important things about their faith.

Explain that the children will use this book to learn about Jesus and his Father.

- Help the children investigate the book by reading them titles from the table of contents.
- Let them preview the illustrations.
- Ask the children to report on what they will learn.
- Point out the icons on the page and invite the children to speculate on what they signal. Use the text to expand on their responses.
- As you define the icons, reinforce the importance of Scripture, prayer, and songs in learning about God.
⭐ Call attention to the photograph.
- Explain that the gold stars in the book will give them directions.
- Invite the children to underline one thing that they will do this year.

First Grade

What's the year going to be like?

This year you will learn many new things about our Catholic faith. You will learn bout God's love for you. You will grow as Jesus' friend.

🔲 means the story or reading is from the Bible. Through Bible stories you will meet Jesus.

💙 let's you know it's time to pray. You will grow closer to Jesus as you pray and get to know his teachings.

▶️ tells you to sing songs to praise God and celebrate our faith.

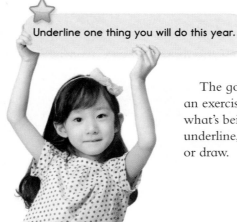

Underline one thing you will do this year.

The gold star above begins an exercise to help you learn what's being taught. You may underline, circle, write, match, or draw.

2

© Our Sunday Visitor

✓ Quick Tip

Lesson Structure

The chapters in this book will all follow the same three-step process:
- *Invite* begins with a prayer that includes Sacred Scripture and calls the children to be open to God's Word.
- *Discover* presents Scripture, Church teachings, and Catholic practices with developmentally appropriate language and art and contains activities to reinforce and apply learning.
- *Live* connects the children's faith knowledge with the ways that Catholics worship, live, pray, and serve in their community. It also contains the concluding prayer for the chapter.
- For more information on the lesson process, see pages CE18–CE19.

Ways to Know God

During this year, you'll discover how we are made by God. He gives us the gifts of his creation. You can know God through his Son, Jesus, and the Bible.

Jesus is the **Son of God** who loves you and shows you how to love the Father and one another.

We also know God through our families and the Church. Jesus is with his Church always, and the Holy Spirit is always guiding and helping us.

© Our Sunday Visitor

Catholic Faith Words

In this box you will see the highlighted words and their definitions.

Son of God a name for Jesus that tells you God is his Father. The Son of God is the Second Divine Person of the Holy Trinity.

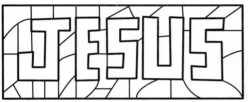

Share Your Faith

When you see these fun green words, you know it's time for an activity!

Think Who is the Son of God? Color in his name.

JESUS

Share Share your work with a partner.

Ways to Know God

Read aloud the first two paragraphs to explain what the children will learn about this year. Emphasize that they will learn about Jesus, who is God's Son.

Read aloud the third paragraph.

- *Ask:* How do you learn about God?
- Encourage them to add any ways that are not in the text.

Work with Words

Call attention to the term *Son of God* in the second paragraph and the Catholic Faith Words definition on the side of the page. Tell the children that they will learn many new words this year.

Activity

Point out the Share Your Faith feature.

- Point out that this feature and others like it will help them think about their faith and share it.
- Read aloud the directions.
- Allow time for the children to complete the activity.
- Have them share their work with a partner.

Quick Review

This book will teach about Jesus and how to follow him. It contains Scripture, prayers, songs, and activities to help us learn.

(i) Catechist Background

Focus on First Graders

Alive in Christ presents key themes of Catholic teaching in a developmentally appropriate sequence. For more information on how the series framework supports faith development, see pages CE8–CE9.

- The Grade 1 Focus is Jesus Christ.
- This year's lessons have been designed to address the children's growing awareness of relationships with others, so focusing on a relationship with Jesus and the Church community is appropriate.
- For more information on the abilities and perspectives of the children you are teaching, see pages CE9 and CE29.

Objectives

- Learn that the Bible is the inspired Word of God written by humans
- Be able to explain the nature of the Gospels

God's Word

Explain that we use words to teach important ideas. God also uses words to teach us.

Read aloud the first two paragraphs to explain the contents of the Bible.

Call attention to the Old Testament illustration.

- Elicit from the children that God made the world for us to enjoy.

Point out the New Testament illustration.

- *Ask:* What is happening in this picture?
- Have the children name the people in the picture.

Explain that the Creation story and the Nativity story are both in the Bible.

God's Word

What can we learn from the Bible?

The **Bible** is the Word of God.

The Bible has two parts. The first part is the Old Testament. It is about the times before Jesus was born. The second part is the New Testament. It tells about Jesus and his followers.

In the Bible there are many kinds of stories. From these stories we learn about God and his love. We hear about how God wants us to live.

Catholic Faith Words

Bible the Word of God written in human words. The Bible is the holy book of the Church.

4   Opening Lesson

✓ Quick Tip

Sacred Tradition

Part of the richness of the Catholic faith resides in Sacred Tradition, accrued through two millennia of Church history.

- Every lesson in this book presents truths of the faith.
- At the back of the Student Book, the Our Catholic Tradition reference section expands on the lesson contents. Your lesson plans will contain specific references to this reference section when appropriate.
- You may want to have the children explore this section. For more on Sacred Tradition, see page CE23.

The Gospels

Some of the most important Bible stories are about Jesus. We find these stories in the Gospels, the first four books of the New Testament.

We learn about Jesus' birth and life. We hear stories Jesus used to help us understand he is the Son of God who leads us to God the Father.

Connect Your Faith

Draw a Bible Story
Draw your favorite story from the Bible.

A New Year **5**

The Gospels

Read aloud the text. Emphasize that the Gospels tell the story of Jesus' life on earth.

- Tell the children that the word *Gospel* means "good news."
- Reinforce that the Gospels are so important that we hear their message every time we go to Mass.
- Encourage the children to listen for the Gospel when they go to Mass.

Discuss what is happening in the picture.

- Encourage the children to share Bible stories with family members.

Activity

Elicit from the children what their favorite Bible stories are. If necessary, remind them of other stories, such as Noah's Ark.

- Allow time for the children to complete the activity and share their work.

Liturgy Link

Bible Readings

The Old Testament and New Testament are the core of the Liturgy of the Word. However, the priests, deacons, and readers do not read directly from the Bible. They read from the Lectionary, which contains passages from the Bible.

- Typically, the first reading on a Sunday is from the Old Testament, followed by a responsorial Psalm. The next reading is usually from a New Testament Epistle, and the last is always from the Gospels.

 Go to **aliveinchrist.osv.com** for Sunday readings, Scripture background, questions of the week, and seasonal resources.

Quick Review

The Bible has many stories that tell about God's love. The Gospels are part of the Bible and tell about Jesus' life.

Our Catholic Life

Point out the Live heading on the page.

- Explain that each chapter in this book has a part that will help the children live as good Catholics. Read the text to further explain this.

Read aloud the boxed text to share the different ways to grow as a follower of Jesus.

People of Faith

Read aloud this paragraph. Tell the children that they will learn about Saints and other holy people in this part of the lesson.

Activity

Have the children complete the activity. When all are finished, emphasize that the children are all friends of Jesus.

Our Catholic Life

What does it mean to be Catholic?

Each chapter in your book has an Our Catholic Life section with activities that help us grow closer to Jesus and the Church.

Grow as a Follower of Jesus

- know more about our faith
- learn about the Sacraments
- live as Jesus calls us to
- talk and listen to God in prayer
- take part in Church life
- help others know about Jesus

© Our Sunday Visitor

People of Faith

Look for this box, where you will meet People of Faith, holy women and men who loved God very much and did his work on Earth.

Live Your Faith

Friend of Jesus You are a friend of Jesus. Write your name.

_____

- -

_____

6 Opening Lesson

 Catechist Background

Six Tasks of Catechesis

As a catechist, you are charged with six fundamental tasks as contained in the *National Directory for Catechesis*.

- Each of these tasks corresponds to an aspect of faith in Jesus. They are: Promoting Knowledge of the Faith, Liturgical Education, Moral Formation, Teaching to Pray, Education for Community Life, and Missionary Initiation.

- For more information on these tasks, refer to pages CE14–CE15.

 Let Us Pray

Pray Together

Every chapter has a prayer. You may ask God for help, thank him, pray for others, and praise him with songs.

Gather and begin with the Sign of the Cross.

All: In the name of the Father and of the Son and of the Holy Spirit. Amen.

Leader: Let us pray.

Bow your heads as the leader prays.

All: Amen.

Leader: A reading from the holy Gospel according to John.

Read John 6:12.

The Gospel of the Lord.

All: Praise to you, Lord Jesus Christ.

 Sing "Alive in Christ"

We are Alive in Christ
We are Alive in Christ
He came to set us free
We are Alive in Christ
We are Alive in Christ
He gave his life for me
We are Alive in Christ
We are Alive in Christ

The Trinity **7**

 Let Us Pray
Pray Together
Read the first paragraph aloud to the children.

- Explain that every chapter will end with prayer.

Prepare
Assume the role of leader.

Teach the children their responses.

> Rehearse "Alive in Christ," downloaded from **aliveinchrist.osv.com**.

Gather
Lead the children into the prayer space.

- Begin with the Sign of the Cross.
- Invite the children to be still and listen to the reading.

Pray
Follow the order of prayer on the student page.

> Conclude by processing around the room with the children singing "Alive in Christ."

 ## Songs of Scripture

Songs for Deepening Children's Understanding of God's Word

In addition to all of the chapter-specific songs available for download, a program component, Songs of Scripture: *Songs for Deepening Children's Understanding of God's Word* by John Burland and Dr. Jo Ann Paradise helps celebrate faith and support catechesis.

- Two CDs, Grades 1–3 and Grades 4–6, offer songs that teach, reinforce, or unfold the meaning of Scripture stories.
- These and other songs are available through **aliveinchrist.osv.com** and searchable by grade and chapter level.

Family + Faith

Distribute the page to the children or parents/adult family members.

Point out the chapter highlights, insights on how first graders understand concepts, the opportunity for the adults to reflect on their own experience and faith journey, and the family prayer.

Your Child Learned is a summary of the Catholic teaching that was covered in the chapter and introduces families to the Scripture and the Person of Faith that was presented.

Children At This Age helps parents become aware of how their child comprehends what was taught and suggests ways to help the child gain a deeper understanding of the material.

Consider This invites parents to ponder some of their own experiences and listen as the Church speaks to their personal journey of faith.

Let's Talk offers parents developmentally appropriate questions that lead to discussion of the week's lesson.

Let's Pray provides a short family prayer based on the Person of Faith featured in the lesson.

Online Resources offers multimedia tools to encourage family interaction and reinforce the lesson at home.

FAMILY+FAITH
LIVING AND LEARNING TOGETHER

YOUR CHILD LEARNED >>>

This page is for you, the parent, to encourage you to talk about your faith and see the many ways you already live your faith in daily family life.

God's Word
In this section, you will find a Scripture citation and a summary of what your child has learned in the chapter.

Catholics Believe
• Bulleted information highlights the main points of doctrine of the chapter.

People of Faith
Here you meet the holy person featured in People of Faith.

CHILDREN AT THIS AGE >>>

This feature gives you a sense of how your child, at this particular age, will likely understand what is being taught. It suggests ways you can help your child better understand, live, and love their faith.

How They Understand the Lessons Your first-grader is making an important transition from your family circle into the wider world. Making friends is important for them. It is common for them to feel intense but brief attachments. They may have a new best friend every few days. While they are still somewhat gracefully self-centered, they like helping others and need opportunities to do so.

Children this age think and learn concretely. When talking about God with your child, use concrete images and experiences.

Repetition and recognition work well with the first-grader. Say the same prayers together often. Determine what religious rituals will be consistently used in your home.

For most young children praying is as natural as talking and listening to a family member or friend. Encourage your child to spontaneously pray aloud at meals or when preparing to go to bed.

CONSIDER THIS >>>

This section includes a question that invites you to reflect on your own experience and consider how the Church speaks to you on your own faith journey.

LET'S TALK >>>

• Here you will find some practical questions that prompt discussion about the lesson's content, faith sharing, and making connections with your family life.

• Ask your child to name one thing they've learned about their book.

LET'S PRAY >>>

 This section encourages family prayer connected to the example of our People of Faith.

Holy men and women, pray for us. Amen.

 For a multimedia glossary of Catholic Faith Words, Sunday readings, seasonal and Saint resources, and chapter activities go to **aliveinchrist.osv.com**.

Optional Activity

Explore the Student Book

In addition to what is presented in this opening lesson, there are many other features that help you present the Catholic faith to the children. Ask them to find the following features in their books.

• The Church Year: Children learn about Church feasts and seasons.

• Unit Openers: Preview the doctrinal theme with photos and art that convey the richness of our Catholic Tradition.

• Catholic Social Teaching/Live Your Faith: Introduce the children to important teachings of Jesus and the Church that help us live Jesus' New Commandment to love as he loved.

The Church Year Overview

Ordinary Time: Mary's Birthday **9A**

The children will:

- identify Mary as the Mother of Jesus and Mother of God
- discuss ways of honoring Mary

Catholic Social Teaching: Live Your Faith

- Call to Community
- Human Solidarity

Ordinary Time: All Saints Day **15A**

The children will:

- celebrate the holiness of everyone in Heaven
- learn about Saints and Heaven

Catholic Social Teaching: Live Your Faith

- Call to Community
- Human Solidarity

Advent: Waiting for Jesus **19A**

The children will:

- recognize that Advent is a time of waiting and preparing our hearts

Catholic Social Teaching: Live Your Faith

- Call to Community
- Option for the Poor

Christmas: The Light of Christ **23A**

The children will:

- understand how Jesus is the light of the world
- explain how we bring Jesus' light to others

Catholic Social Teaching: Live Your Faith

- Life and Dignity
- Rights and Responsibilities

Lent: Time for Change **27A**

The children will:

- recognize that Lent is a time to turn to God
- explore ways to put God first

Catholic Social Teaching: Live Your Faith

- Rights and Responsibilities
- Option for the Poor

Lent: Holy Week **33A**

The children will:

- learn that Holy Week is the holiest week of the Church year
- understand the season of the Triduum
- appreciate that the Easter Triduum of the Passion and Resurrection of Christ is the culmination of the entire liturgical year

Catholic Social Teaching: Live Your Faith

- Call to Community
- Option for the Poor

Easter: He Is Risen. **37A**

The children will:

- remember that God raised Jesus from the dead
- discuss Easter joy

Catholic Social Teaching: Live Your Faith

- Life and Dignity
- Care for Creation

Easter: Pentecost **41A**

The children will:

- understand that we are temples of the Holy Spirit
- appreciate that the Holy Spirit is always with us, especially during Pentecost

Catholic Social Teaching: Live Your Faith

- Life and Dignity
- The Dignity of Work

Check out the activities and resources available for the seasons of the Church Year at the following websites.
Go to **aliveinchrist.osv.com** and click on the Resource Library tab and select a season.
Go to **teachingcatholickids.com** and click on the current month's newsletter.

LESSON OBJECTIVES

- Identify Mary as the Mother of Jesus and Mother of God
- Discuss ways of honoring Mary

ENVIRONMENT

Prayer table
White cloth
Bible
Statue of Mary
Candle or battery-operated candle
Crayons

- Place the prayer table in the center of the prayer space, and cover it with the white cloth.
- Place the statue of Mary on the table, and light the candle.

 MUSIC OPTIONS
Go to **aliveinchrist.osv.com** to sample and download,
"Immaculate Mary"
"Mary, Our Mother"

 CATHOLIC SOCIAL TEACHING

- **Call to Community**, Pages 286–287
- **Human Solidarity**, Pages 294–295

Catechist Background

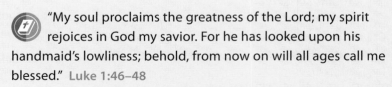 "My soul proclaims the greatness of the Lord; my spirit rejoices in God my savior. For he has looked upon his handmaid's lowliness; behold, from now on will all ages call me blessed." Luke 1:46–48

➜ **Reflect** What does it mean to be blessed?

At the birth of their child most Christian parents share their delight with family and friends. Parents also proudly give their child a name. It was really no different in first century Palestine. Mary, a variation of Miriam, was born to Jewish parents, Joachim and Anne. Although we have no record of her childhood, we assume she grew up participating in all the Jewish customs and laws of her time.

Through the Scripture stories, we know that God found favor with Mary and asked her to be the Mother of his Son, Jesus (Luke 1:26–38). It is her willingness to say "yes" to God that Catholics continue to celebrate today.

Throughout the liturgical year, there are many feasts honoring Mary. In all of them the Church celebrates Mary's favor with God and her willingness to become the Mother of God, and an instrument in our salvation. Mary's birth is celebrated on September 8, nine months following the Church's celebration of her Immaculate Conception on December 8. The celebration of Mary's birthday in the Church calendar is unusual. In most cases the Church celebrates a Saint's feast on the date of their death, which is seen as their birth into eternal life. Mary and Saint John the Baptist are the only two people whose human births are celebrated in the liturgical year. In celebrating Mary's birthday, the Church gives expression to her birth as a special moment in salvation history. She would give birth to Jesus, the Savior.

➜ **Reflect** Which qualities of Mary do you most admire?

Catechist's Prayer

 Dear Mother Mary, help me to serve God and the children with joy in my heart, so that the children will want to say "yes" to God. Amen.

Mary's Birthday

 Let Us Pray

Leader: Dear Mother Mary,
Happy Birthday! Thank you for being
Jesus' Mother. Help us to be like him.

"Most blessed are you among women."
Luke 1:42

All: Amen.

 **God's Word**

My soul proclaims the greatness of the Lord;
my spirit rejoices in God my savior. For he has
looked upon his handmaid's lowliness; behold,
from now on will all ages call me blessed. The
Mighty One has done great things for me, and
holy is his name.   Luke 1:46–49

? What Do You Wonder?

- What did Mary and Elizabeth
do while they were together?
- Was Mary happy all the time?

 © Our Sunday Visitor

9

 Lectionary Connection

Luke 1:46–49

The story of the Annunciation in the Gospel according to Luke is
proclaimed on the Fourth Sunday of Advent, Year C of the Lectionary
cycle.

- The Annunciation is immediately followed by Mary's visit to
Elizabeth. The Hail Mary recalls Elizabeth's words of recognition.
- Mary's response is the Magnificat, which is included in the Church's
evening prayer.
- Elizabeth recognizes that Mary's child will be the promised Savior.

Invite

Let Us Pray

Invite the children to gather in the
prayer space and make the Sign of
the Cross. Choose a child to be the
leader. Read aloud the verse from a
Bible. Prompt the children's
response.

Have the children move out of the
prayer space and back to their seats.

Say: When Mary found out she was
to be the Mother of God's Son she
went to see her cousin Elizabeth.
She was so happy when she and
Elizabeth were talking about it, she
sang a song. This is part of the song.

God's Word

Guide the children through the
process of Scripture reflection.

- Invite them to close their eyes, be
still and open their minds and
hearts to what God is saying to
them in this passage.
- Proclaim the Scripture.
- Maintain several moments of
silence.
- *Ask:* What did you hear God say
to you today?
- Invite volunteers to share.

What Do You Wonder?

Say: Mary knew God had given her
a great gift. How might you feel if
you were there and heard Mary's
song?

Invite the children to respond to the
questions. Ask what else they might
wonder about Mary and Elizabeth,
or how Mary felt about being the
Mother of Jesus.

Mother Mary

Ask: Why does the Church honor Mary?

- Write the children's responses on the board or on chart paper.

Ask the children what they know about Mary. Possible response: She is the Mother of Jesus.

Invite the children to study the picture on page 10.

- Ask them to tell what they see happening in the picture. The angel is asking Mary to be Jesus' Mother.

- Elicit what feelings Mary might have had when the angel asked her to be Jesus' Mother. Possible responses: happy, afraid

Read aloud the three paragraphs.

- Invite the children to draw a face that shows how they feel about what you just read.
- Invite volunteers to share their drawings with the group.
- Point out that white is the color for the feasts of Mary.

Read aloud the text in the box.

- Explain that Ordinary Time celebrates the words and works of Jesus, what Jesus taught and did.
- *Ask:* What is the color for Ordinary Time? green

Discover

Mother Mary

Why does the Church honor Mary?

You are God's child. Because God is your Father, Jesus is your Brother.

The Mother of Jesus is Mary. Mary is your mother, too. Mary said "yes" to God's plan for her, and the Son of God became man.

We celebrate Mary's birthday on September 8. The color for the feasts of Mary is white.

Ordinary Time
- Ordinary time celebrates the words and works of Jesus.
- This season is marked by the color green.
- There are many feasts of Mary in this season.

10   The Church Year

ⓘ Catechist Background

Mary's Birthday

Mary and Saint John the Baptist are the only two people whose human births are celebrated in the liturgical year. The Church celebrates Mary's birthday on September 8.

- By celebrating Mary's birthday, we rejoice that she was open to God's invitation to become the Mother of Jesus.
- We rejoice that through her, Jesus came into the world, and she continues to be our Mother today.

Ordinary Time

Ordinary Time is a season of the Church year that comes twice, once after Christmas and for a longer time after Easter. During this time we learn more about Jesus' teachings so we can grow as his disciples. We also honor Mary and many of the Saints.

 Underline when Ordinary Time comes during the Church year.

➤ **Why do we honor Mary?**

Activity

Honor Mary You honor Mary when you say "yes" to God. Color in the picture of Mary and Jesus.

© Our Sunday Visitor

Ordinary Time

Read aloud the paragraph.

 Have the children underline when Ordinary Time comes during the Church year.

- Emphasize that as we celebrate Jesus' teachings during Ordinary Time, we can grow as his disciples.
- *Ask:* Why do we honor Mary?

Refer to pages 301–303 in the Our Catholic Tradition reference section of the Student Book to find out more about Mary and how the Church honors her.

 Music Option: Have the children sing, "Mary, Our Mother," downloaded from **aliveinchrist.osv.com**.

Activity

Read aloud the directions for the activity.

- Have the children work independently.
- Invite volunteers to share their pictures with the group.

(i) Catechist Background

Marian Devotions

Many of today's popular devotions to Mary have grown over the years and enhanced people's faith.

- Devotion to the Rosary was spread by Saint Dominic in the thirteenth century.
- Devotion to the Miraculous Medal was initiated by Saint Catherine Labouré, a Daughter of Charity of Saint Vincent in the nineteenth century.

Discover

People of Faith

Point out the chart.

- Explain to the children that each chapter of their book teaches about a Saint or person of faith.
- The left column shows the chapter number of the book.
- The middle column shows who is taught in each chapter.
- The right column shows the feast day for the person.
- Draw attention to Mary's name on the chart. Explain that the Church honors Mary more than once during the year.

Read through the names of the People of Faith one at a time.

- As you read, pause after each name and invite the children to raise their hands if they have heard of the person.
- Encourage those who raise their hands to share what they remember about the person.
- Summarize by telling the children that throughout the year, they will be learning about each of these holy people.

 Encourage the children to go to **aliveinchrist.osv.com** at home to learn more about Mary and the other Saints.

People of Faith

Chapter	Person	Feast Day
1	Blessed Fra Angelico	February 18
2	Saint Nicholas	December 6
3	Saint Albert the Great	November 15
4	Saint Patrick	March 17
5	Zechariah, Elizabeth & John	November 15 and June 24
6	Saint Paul of the Cross	October 19
7	Saint Louise de Marillac	March 15
8	Saint Thomas of Villanova	September 8
9	Saint Ephrem the Hymnist	June 9
10	Blessed Mary Theresa of the Child Jesus	May 9
11	Saint Rose of Lima	August 23
12	Saint Dominic	August 8
13	Venerable Father Solanus Casey	November 3
14	Saint Frances Cabrini	November 18
15	Saint Dismas	March 25
16	Saint Giuseppina Bakhita	February 8
17	Mary	Jan 1, Aug 15, Dec 8
18	Saint Moses the Black	August 28
19	Blessed Pope John XXIII	October 11
20	Saint Emily de Vialar	June 17
21	Saint Pedro Calungsod	April 12

Saint Patrick

Saint Rose of Lima

Saint Moses the Black

© Our Sunday Visitor

12   The Church Year

 ## Catholic Social Teaching

Chapter Connections

To integrate Catholic Social Teaching into your lesson, choose one of the following features: Call to Community, pages 286–287; or Human Solidarity, pages 294–295.

- To expand the lesson, move to the Catholic Social Teaching feature after completing page 12.
- Return to the prayer on page 13.

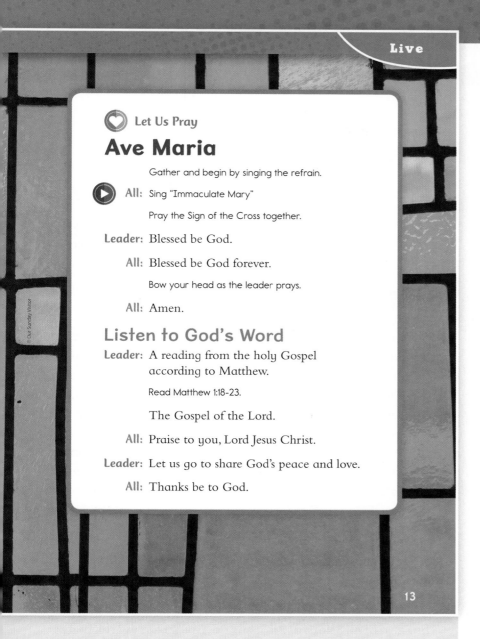

Let Us Pray

Ave Maria

Gather and begin by singing the refrain.

All: Sing "Immaculate Mary"

Pray the Sign of the Cross together.

Leader: Blessed be God.

All: Blessed be God forever.

Bow your head as the leader prays.

All: Amen.

Listen to God's Word

Leader: A reading from the holy Gospel according to Matthew.

Read Matthew 1:18-23.

The Gospel of the Lord.

All: Praise to you, Lord Jesus Christ.

Leader: Let us go to share God's peace and love.

All: Thanks be to God.

13

Let Us Pray

Ave Maria

Invite the children to process to the prayer space. Have each child bring their book.

Rehearse "Immaculate Mary," downloaded from **aliveinchrist.osv.com**.

Follow the order of prayer on the student page.

Begin by singing together "Immaculate Mary."

- *Leader's prayer:* O God, we thank you and we praise you for giving us Mary, Our Mother.
- Invite the children to remain standing for the Gospel.
- Proclaim the Gospel.
- After the Gospel, have the children kneel and pray together the Hail Mary.

Liturgy Link

Kneeling

This is one of the postures of prayer. It expresses submission, adoration, reverence, and humility.

- It is a deep posture of penitential character.
- It is also an expression of devotional piety and the posture of the individual engaged in private prayer.
- During the celebration, it is an expression of reverence and honor of Mary.

Distribute this page to the children or parents/adult family members.

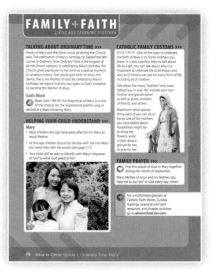

LESSON OBJECTIVES

- Celebrate the holiness of everyone in Heaven
- Learn about Saints and Heaven

ENVIRONMENT

Prayer table
White cloth
Bible
Statue, icon, or picture of any Saint
Candle, or battery-operated candle
Bowl of holy water
Pencils

- Place the prayer table in the center of the prayer space, and cover it with the white cloth.
- Place the bowl of holy water, icon or picture of a Saint on the table, and light the candle.

 MUSIC OPTIONS
Go to **aliveinchrist.osv.com** to sample and download,
"Sing a Song to the Saints"
"Litany of Saints"
"Psalm 98: All the Ends of the Earth"
"When the Saints Go Marching In"

 CATHOLIC SOCIAL TEACHING

- **Call to Community**, Pages 286–287
- **Human Solidarity**, Pages 294–295

Catechist Background

 "As the Father loves me, so I also love you. Remain in my love. If you keep my commandments, you will remain in my love." John 15:9–10a

→ **Reflect** What helps you stay close to Jesus?

Ordinary Time is the longest portion of the Church year. It is divided into two parts. The first begins immediately after the Christmas season and continues until Ash Wednesday, when Lent begins. The second begins immediately after Pentecost and continues until the first Sunday of Advent. The word *ordinary* in Ordinary Time does not mean "as usual" or "common." Rather, it comes from the word *ordinal*, which simply means "counted time" (12th Sunday in . . .). While Ordinary Time does not celebrate a specific aspect of the mystery of Christ as Christmas and Easter do, it is devoted to the mystery of Christ in all its aspects.

The Church year is also structured in two major cycles: the temporal cycle and the sanctoral cycle. The temporal cycle refers to "time" and is the recurring series of the main *times* or *seasons* of the Church year. The sanctoral cycle refers to "Saints" and is the recurring series of the *feasts of the Saints*.

The Feast of All Saints, or All Saints Day, is a solemnity celebrated on November 1. It celebrates all the Saints, known and unknown, especially those with no particular feast day of their own. It is a surprisingly old feast. It was Christian tradition to honor the martyrdom of Saints on the anniversary of their martyrdom. However, when martyrdoms increased during the persecutions of the late Roman Empire, dioceses instituted a common feast day in order to properly honor all martyrs.

→ **Reflect** Which Saints are your favorites?

Catechist's Prayer

 Loving God, may the example of the Saints inspire me to proclaim the Faith in both word and deed. Amen.

All Saints Day

 Let Us Pray

Leader: Dear God, our Father, we are your children. We love you. We want to stay close to you always.

"I am the light of the world. Whoever follows me will not walk in darkness, but will have the light of life." John 8:12

All: Amen.

God's Word

As the Father loves me, so I also love you. Remain in my love. If you keep my commandments, you will remain in my love.... I have told you this so that my joy may be in you and your joy may be complete.
John 15:9–11

? What Do You Wonder?

- How long is forever?
- How can you stay close to Jesus?

15

© Our Sunday Visitor

 Lectionary Connection

John 15:9–11

This Gospel passage comes at the end of Jesus' discourse on the Vine and the Branches. It is part of the Gospel that is proclaimed on the Sixth Sunday of Easter, Year B of the Lectionary cycle.

- Jesus told the disciples that they needed to love one another.
- Have the children take turns telling another child one thing about Jesus. Tell them they are sharing the Good News.

 Let Us Pray

Invite the children to gather in the prayer space and make the Sign of the Cross. Choose a child to be the leader. Read aloud the verse from a Bible. Prompt the children's response.

Have the children move out of the prayer space and back to their seats.

Explain that we are God's children.

Say: God has made us his children. We show we are God's children through prayer and worship and by loving others as he loves us.

 God's Word

Guide the children through the process of Scripture reflection.

- Invite them to close their eyes, be still and open their minds and hearts to what God is saying to them in this passage.
- Proclaim the Scripture.
- Maintain several moments of silence.
- *Ask:* What did you hear God say to you today?
- Invite volunteers to share.

What Do You Wonder?

Say: Jesus gives us a message about how to be happy with God forever.

Invite the children to respond to the questions. Ask what else they might wonder about the Saints and staying close to Jesus.

Holy Lives

Ask: Why does the Church honor Saints?

- Write the children's responses on the board or on chart paper.

Read aloud the first paragraph.

 Direct the children to circle the date that we honor all of the Saints in Heaven.

- Emphasize that All Saints Day is a Holy Day of Obligation and Catholics must attend Mass.

- Explain that the feast of All Saints honors everyone in Heaven.

A Feast for Everyone

Read aloud both paragraphs.

- *Ask:* Do you know the name of someone who is a Saint in Heaven?

Read aloud the caption.

- Ask the children to name any Saints' feast days they may know. Remind the children that the Feast of Saint Patrick is March 17, and the Feast of Saint Nicholas is December 6.

Refer to page 313 in the Our Catholic Tradition reference section of the Student Book for more about Ordinary Time.

> Music Option: Have the children sing, "Litany of Saints," "Psalm 98: All the Ends of the Earth" or "When the Saints Go Marching In," downloaded from **aliveinchrist.osv.com**.

Holy Lives

Why does the Church honor Saints?

> Circle the date that we honor all of the Saints in Heaven.

All Saints Day is celebrated on November 1 It is a Holy Day of Obligation, which means that Catholics must attend Mass. The feast honors everyone who is in Heaven.

A Feast for Everyone

When people who love God very much and lead a holy life die, they go to Heaven to live forever with God. These heroes of the Church are called Saints. They are examples of how to live our faith.

We don't know the name of everyone in Heaven. On All Saints Day, Catholics also honor the Saints we can't name. On that day, we remember everyone in Heaven. We also honor Saints on feast days during the year.

In April, we celebrate the Feast of Saint Joseph.

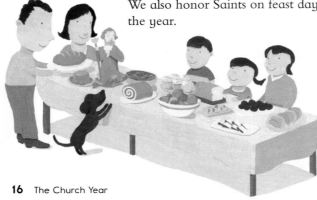

© Our Sunday Visitor

16 The Church Year

🌐 Catholic Social Teaching

Chapter Connections

To integrate Catholic Social Teaching into your lesson, choose one of the following features: Call to Community, pages 286–287; or Human Solidarity, pages 294–295.

- To expand the lesson move to the Catholic Social Teaching feature after completing page 16.

- Return to the prayer on page 17.

Let Us Pray

Celebrate Holy Lives

Gather and begin with the Sign of the Cross.

Leader: Blessed be God.

All: Blessed be God forever.

Leader: Let us pray.

Bow your heads as the leader prays.

All: Amen.

Listen to God's Word

Leader: A reading from the holy Gospel according to Luke.

Read John 6:40.

The Gospel of the Lord.

All: Praise to you, Lord Jesus Christ.

Leader: Like the Saints, let us go out to serve the Lord.

All: Thanks be to God.

 Sing "Sing a Song to the Saints"

17

 ©Our Sunday Visitor

 Liturgy Link

Signing

Signing the children with the Sign of the Cross is a multi-layered ritual.

- It is a reminder of their Baptism.
- It recalls the Cross of Christ and the call to discipleship and service.
- It is also a form of blessing.

 Let Us Pray

Celebrate Holy Lives

Invite the children to process to the prayer space. Have each child bring their book.

> Rehearse "Sing a Song to the Saints," downloaded from **aliveinchrist.osv.com**.

- *Leader's prayer:* God, our Father, we praise and thank you for the lives of the Saints who show us how to live humbly as your children.
- Invite the children to stand for the Gospel.
- After the Gospel, have the children gather around the prayer table.
- *Using holy water, sign each child on their hands with the Sign of the Cross and say:* (Child's name), In Baptism, you are called to serve others.

 Sing together the song refrain.

Distribute this page to the children or parents/adult family members.

LESSON OBJECTIVE

- Recognize that Advent is a time of waiting and preparing our hearts

ENVIRONMENT

Prayer table
Purple cloth
Advent wreath and candles
Bible
Pencils

- Cover the prayer table with the purple cloth.
- Place the Advent wreath in the center of the prayer table.
- Obtain necessary permission to light the candles on the wreath (or use battery-operated candles).

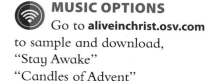

MUSIC OPTIONS

Go to **aliveinchrist.osv.com** to sample and download, "Stay Awake" "Candles of Advent"

CATHOLIC SOCIAL TEACHING

- **Call to Community**, Pages 286–287
- **Option for the Poor**, Pages 296–297

Catechist Background

The wilderness and the parched land will exult…. Like the crocus it shall bloom abundantly…. They will see the glory of the LORD, the splendor of our God. **Isaiah 35:1–2**

→ **Reflect** What do you do to get ready for important events?

Expecting a child takes much preparation and energy. Time is spent preparing a space for a new baby. Parents and siblings dream about what this new child will bring and how their lives will be changed by his or her coming. For centuries the People of God waited for the coming of a Savior. They, too, wondered about what this Savior would bring and how they might be changed by his coming. In the years leading up to the birth of Christ, God prepared his People through the ministry of the prophets, who heralded his coming and awakened expectation in their hearts.

Each year, the Church prepares to celebrate Christ's coming in Advent—the four weeks before Christmas. The Advent season also marks the beginning of the liturgical year. Through Scripture, music, and ritual actions, the worshipping assembly renews the ancient expectations and promises of the Messiah. The color purple, which symbolizes that the hearts of the gathered community are in preparation, adorns the sanctuary and is the color of the vestments worn by the priest. By sharing in Advent celebrations, the faithful renew their sense of desire to see and know Christ when he comes again.

The celebration of Advent takes place both communally and in people's hearts. It is a time for reflection and preparation not only remembering Christ's first coming, but preparing for Christ's Second Coming at the end of time.

→ **Reflect** How will you prepare your heart for Christ's coming this Advent?

Catechist's Prayer

Loving God, during these Advent weeks of anticipation, nurture in me joyful hope and help me to prepare a place in my heart for Jesus. Amen.

Waiting for Jesus

 Let Us Pray

Leader: Lord Jesus, we are waiting for you. Show us what to do to get our hearts ready.

"To you, O LORD, I lift up my soul."
Psalm 25:1

All: Amen.

 God's Word

The wilderness and the parched land will exult…. Like the crocus it shall bloom abundantly…. They will see the glory of the LORD, the splendor of our God.   Isaiah 35:1–2

What Do You Wonder?

- Why do we need to get ready for important events?
- What does it mean to see God's glory?

© Our Sunday Visitor

19

Lectionary Connection

Isaiah 35:1–2

This passage from Isaiah is part of the first reading on the Third Sunday of Advent, Year A of the Lectionary cycle.

- These verses proclaim a powerful and strong God.
- These verses were written at a time when Israel was discouraged. Yet, they paint a picture of hope for then and now.

 Let Us Pray

Invite the children to gather in the prayer space and make the Sign of the Cross. Choose a child to be the leader. Read aloud the Psalm verse from a Bible. Prompt the children's response.

Have the children move out of the prayer space and back to their seats.

Explain that God's People were waiting for Jesus for a very long time.

Say: God invites us now to listen carefully to the words Isaiah spoke to the people when they were waiting and waiting for Jesus to come the first time.

God's Word

Guide the children through the process of Scripture reflection.

- Invite them to close their eyes, be still and open their minds and hearts to what God is saying to them in this passage.
- Proclaim the Scripture.
- Maintain several moments of silence.
- *Ask:* What did you hear God say to you today?
- Invite volunteers to share.

What Do You Wonder?

Say: God wants us to be happy. He wants our hearts to be joyful. He wants us to know how wonderful he is.

Invite the children to respond to the questions. Ask what else they might wonder about Advent or getting ready for Jesus.

Get Ready

Ask: What is Advent?

- Write the children's responses on the board or on chart paper.

Read aloud the Advent text box.

- Ask the children to share some experiences of waiting. Possible responses: the birth of a sibling, a parent to come home

- Ask the children what they do and how they feel when they are waiting.

- Emphasize responses which indicate longing or preparation.

- Explore the feelings God's People must have had waiting for the Messiah—tired of waiting, worried, excited. Have the children share their responses.

Read aloud the first paragraph.

- Point out that Advent is the first season of the Church year.

 Direct the children to circle the color that the priest wears during Advent.

- Ask the children to tell what the color purple stands for. royalty as we await the coming of a king, sorrow and feeling sorry

- Read aloud the next two paragraphs.

▶ Music Option: Have the children sing, "Candles of Advent," downloaded from **aliveinchrist.osv.com**.

Refer to page 312 in the Our Catholic Tradition reference section of the Student Book for more about Advent.

Discover

© Our Sunday Visitor

 Circle the color that the priest wears during Advent.

Advent
- The season during the four weeks before Christmas.
- During this time we prepare to celebrate the coming of Jesus.

20 The Church Year

Get Ready

What is Advent?

Advent is the first season of the Church year. The priest wears (purple) colors in Advent. Purple is the color of royalty as we await the coming King. It is also the color for sorrow and feeling sorry.

People waited many years for God to send someone to save us. Finally, Jesus was born in Bethlehem.

Advent is a time to get our hearts ready for Jesus, our King, to return again in glory.

🌐 Catholic Social Teaching

Chapter Connections

To integrate Catholic Social Teaching into your lesson, choose one of the following features: Call to Community, pages 286–287; or Option for the Poor, pages 290–291.

- To expand the lesson move to the Catholic Social Teaching feature after completing page 20.

- Return to the prayer on page 21.

Let Us Pray

Prayer of Praise

Gather and begin with the Sign of the Cross.

Leader: Come, Lord Jesus.

All: Come, Lord Jesus.

Leader: Let us pray.

Bow your heads as the leader prays.

All: Amen.

Listen to God's Word

Leader: A reading from the holy Gospel according to Matthew.

Read Matthew 24:42.

The Gospel of the Lord.

All: Praise to you, Lord Jesus Christ.

 Sing "Stay Awake"

21

Let Us Pray
Prayer of Praise

Have the children gather around the Advent wreath and light the appropriate number of candles.

 Rehearse "Stay Awake," downloaded from **aliveinchrist.osv.com**.

Follow the order of prayer on the student page.

- Lead the children in the Sign of the Cross.

- *Leader's prayer:* God our Father, we wait for Jesus. Help us prepare a place for him in our hearts.

- Invite the children to stand for the Gospel.

Conclude by singing together "Stay Awake."

Liturgy Link

Advent Wreath

The ritual of the Advent wreath began in pre-Christian Germany. In winter, people made wreaths with evergreens and candles as a sign of hope.

- Christians kept this popular tradition alive to symbolize Advent hope in Christ our Light.

- You may wish to repeat this ritual in your session several times during Advent.

Distribute this page to the children or parents/adult family members.

Christmas: The Light of Christ

LESSON OBJECTIVES

- Understand how Jesus is the light of the world
- Explain how we bring Jesus' light to others

ENVIRONMENT

Prayer table
White cloth
Nativity scene
Cutouts of a star, an evergreen branch, and a baby
Evergreens
Lights
Bible
Pencils

- Place the Nativity scene on the prayer table so children can gather around it. Decorate the table with the white cloth, evergreens, and lights.
- Arrange the space so children can process around it.

 MUSIC OPTION
Go to **aliveinchrist.osv.com** to sample and download, "Glory to God"

 CATHOLIC SOCIAL TEACHING

- **Life and Dignity**, Pages 284–285
- **Rights and Responsibilities**, Pages 288–289

Catechist Background

 "I proclaim to you good news of great joy that will be for all people. For today in the city of David a savior has been born for you who is Messiah and Lord." Luke 2:10–11

➜ **Reflect** How do you think the shepherds felt when the angel spoke to them?

The Christmas season begins with the celebration of Christ's birth on December 25th and ends with the celebration of the Baptism of the Lord in January. The Christmas liturgy sings the glory of the night when the angels appeared to the shepherds in the region of Bethlehem and proclaimed the Good News that the Messiah is born.

The gathered assembly meets Christ in the Word of God and, filled with joy, they celebrate the arrival of the Messiah. The People of God go forth from the Christmas liturgy to spread the Good News that God became man. During the Christmas season, several feast days frame the brilliance of the Incarnation, namely the feasts of the Holy Family, Epiphany, and the Baptism of the Lord.

Christ's Incarnation is important to our salvation, for without God's gift of his Son, we would not know redemption. While on Earth, Jesus taught that his Incarnation is embodied in the commandment of love—loving those who are oppressed. Christ is incarnate in the lives of those around us. The Christmas season celebrates the light of Christ found in one another.

➜ **Reflect** How is God made flesh in your actions and words?

Catechist's Prayer

 God our Father, thank you for the gift of your Son, Jesus. Help me to be a light that leads the children to you. Amen.

The Light of Christ

 Let Us Pray

Leader: Dear Jesus,
Thank you for coming into the world.
Thank you for being our light.

"The people who walked in darkness
have seen a great light."   Isaiah 9:1a

All: Amen.

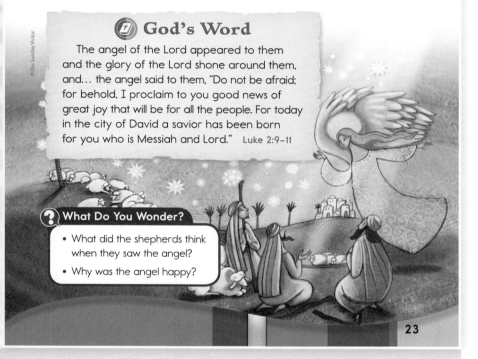

God's Word

The angel of the Lord appeared to them and the glory of the Lord shone around them, and... the angel said to them, "Do not be afraid; for behold, I proclaim to you good news of great joy that will be for all the people. For today in the city of David a savior has been born for you who is Messiah and Lord."   Luke 2:9–11

? What Do You Wonder?

- What did the shepherds think when they saw the angel?
- Why was the angel happy?

23

Lectionary Connection

Luke 2:9–11

This passage is the Second Reading on the Feast of the Nativity of the Lord—Mass at Dawn (Christmas morning).

- The important message of this reading is that God sent his Son, Jesus, to save us, not because we did anything to deserve it, but because God loves us. We have been saved by God's grace.
- When Jesus came to Earth, he came with the message that God's love is for everyone, not just a certain few.

 Let Us Pray

Invite the children to gather in the prayer space and make the Sign of the Cross. Choose a child to be the leader. Read aloud the verse from a Bible. Prompt the children's response.

Have the children move out of the prayer space and back to their seats.

Explain that when Jesus came into the world, he brought God's light to all people.

Say: When Jesus came to the world, he brought God's light of glory to all the people here on Earth. Everyone was happy.

God's Word

Guide the children through the process of Scripture reflection.

- Invite them to close their eyes, be still and open their minds and hearts to what God is saying to them in this passage.
- Proclaim the Scripture.
- Maintain several moments of silence.
- *Ask:* What did you hear God say to you today?
- Invite volunteers to share.

What Do You Wonder?

Say: The shepherds must have been amazed to see all that light and those angels in the middle of the night.

Invite the children to respond to the questions. Ask what else they might wonder about the angels or shepherds.

Discover

A Season of Joy

Ask: How does the Church celebrate the Christmas season?

- Write the children's responses on the board or on chart paper.

Show the children pictures or cutouts of a star, an evergreen, and a baby.

- Ask the children what the symbols have in common. Elicit *Christmas* as a response.

Read the first paragraph aloud.

- Invite the children to tell you what they see at church during the Christmas season. Possible responses: bright decorations, gold or white vestments, a Nativity scene

 Have the children underline what they hear about during the Christmas season.

The Star of Bethlehem

Ask the children to share what they know about the visit of the Magi to the Christ child.

- Emphasize that the Magi followed the star to Jesus.

Read the text aloud.

- Invite children to share ways they can light the way to Jesus for others. Possible response: Be kind to a classmate on the playground.

- Make a list of children's suggestions, and place it in a prominent place.

Refer to page 312 in the Our Catholic Tradition reference section of the Student Book for more about Christmas.

A Season of Joy

How does the Church celebrate the Christmas season?

 Underline what you hear about during the Christmas season.

The Christmas season is more than one day. It is a season that lasts for a few weeks. It is a season of joy. The church is brightly decorated. The priest wears white or gold vestments. We see the Christmas Nativity scene in church for the whole season. During the season you hear about all the things that happened to Jesus as a young child.

The Star of Bethlehem

The star of Bethlehem pointed the way to the Baby Jesus.

When you look at the star on your tree, think of the three wise men.

You will be wise, too, if you look for Jesus.

Are you a star?

One way you can be a star is to light the way to Jesus for others.

 Songs of Scripture

Holy Family

Provide each child with a Christmas card that pictures the Holy Family, and have them create an ornament.

- Have the children cut out the picture of the Holy Family and glue it to a circle of red or green construction paper.
- Punch a hole at the top of the paper and add a loop of ribbon.
- Review or teach the song.

▶ Use *Songs of Scripture*, Grades 1–3 CD, Track 6

Let Us Pray

Celebrate Christmas

Gather and begin with the Sign of the Cross.

Leader: Blessed be the name of the Lord.

All: Now and forever.

Leader: Let us pray.

Bow your heads as the leader prays.

All: Amen.

Listen to God's Word

Leader: A reading from the holy Gospel according to Matthew.

Read Matthew 2:9–11.

The Gospel of the Lord.

All: Praise to you, Lord Jesus Christ.

Leader: Let us rejoice in the birth of Jesus.

All: Thanks be to God.

Sing "Glory to God"

25

Let Us Pray
Celebrate Christmas

Invite the children to process to the prayer space. Have each child bring their book.

> Rehearse "Glory to God," downloaded from **aliveinchrist.osv.com**.

Follow the order of prayer on the student page.

- Lead the children in the Sign of the Cross.
- *Leader's prayer:* God, our Father, we give you thanks for the gift of your Son, Jesus. Help us to follow his light.
- Invite the children to stand for the Gospel.

> While singing the refrain together, lead the children in procession around the room and back to their places.

Catholic Social Teaching

Chapter Connections

To integrate Catholic Social Teaching into your lesson, choose one of the following features: Life and Dignity, pages 284–285; or Rights and Responsibilities, pages 288–289.

- To expand the lesson move to the Catholic Social Teaching feature after completing page 24.
- Return to the prayer on page 25.

Distribute this page to the children or parents/adult family members.

The Light of Christ **25–26**

Lent: **Time for Change**

ENVIRONMENT

Prayer table
Purple cloth
Bible
Crucifix
Markers or crayons

- Place the prayer table in the center of the prayer space, and cover it with the purple cloth.
- Place the crucifix on the prayer table.
- Arrange the prayer space to provide space for the children to kneel.

 MUSIC OPTIONS

Go to **aliveinchrist.osv.com** to sample and download, "God of Mercy" "Lord, Throughout These Holy Days"

 CATHOLIC SOCIAL TEACHING

- **Rights and Responsibilities**, Pages 288–289
- **Option for the Poor**, Pages 290–291

Catechist Background

"You shall not have other gods beside me. You shall not invoke the name of the LORD, your God in vain…. Remember the Sabbath day—keep it holy." Exodus 20:3, 7–8

➜ **Reflect** What can take you away from putting God first?

Lent is a forty-day journey toward conversion and change of heart. The journey includes fasting, prayer, and penance. These practices open you to the presence of God in your life as well as the areas in your life which are in need of conversion. They prepare you to more fully enter into the celebration of Easter when we celebrate that Christ wins our salvation through his Resurrection.

The Church celebrates the forty days of Lent beginning with Ash Wednesday. The signing of a person with ashes with the words "Repent, and believe in the Gospel" is done in the spirit of atonement. The spirit of atonement is reflected in the use of the color purple for church vestments and the stark, desert-like environment created for the liturgy. The *Alleluia* is neither said nor sung during the Lenten season. This practice reminds the community of both their constant need for God and their hunger for the joy of the Risen Christ.

Lent is also a time of intense preparation for those who will receive the Sacraments of Initiation at the Easter Vigil and for the baptized to reflect on their baptismal promises which they will renew at Easter time.

➜ **Reflect** How will you practice atonement during Lent?

Catechist's Prayer

 Loving God, bless my journey through the desert of Lent to the font of rebirth. Amen.

Time for Change

 Let Us Pray

Leader: Lord, God, send your Holy Spirit to guide us to right and loving actions.

"Make known to me your ways, LORD; teach me your paths." Psalm 25:4

All: Amen.

 God's Word

Then God spoke all these words: I am the LORD your God, who brought you out of the land of Egypt, out of the house of slavery. You shall not have other gods beside me.... You shall not invoke the name of the LORD, your God, in vain.... Remember the sabbath day—keep it holy.
Exodus 20:1–3; 7–8

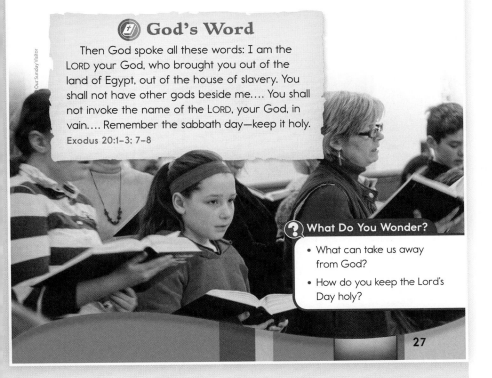

What Do You Wonder?

- What can take us away from God?
- How do you keep the Lord's Day holy?

27

Our Sunday Visitor

 Lectionary Connection

Exodus 20:1–3, 7–8

This Old Testament passage in Exodus is part of a larger passage of God speaking the Ten Commandments, which is proclaimed on the Third Sunday of Lent, Year B of the Lectionary cycle.

- The entire passage is Exodus 20:1–17.
- The form of the Commandments is significant. They are written as laws that impose a command directly on a person obliging that person to perform or not perform a particular action.

 Let Us Pray

Invite the children to gather in the prayer space and make the Sign of the Cross. Choose a child to be the leader. Read aloud the Psalm verse from a Bible. Prompt the children's response.

Have the children move out of the prayer space and back to their seats.

Explain that God asked his Chosen People to do something important.

Say: We ask God to send the Holy Spirit to help us know and remember what God wants us to do. Many years ago God told the Chosen People something very important.

 God's Word

Guide the children through the process of Scripture reflection.

- Invite them to close their eyes, be still and open their minds and hearts to what God is saying to them in this passage.
- Proclaim the Scripture.
- Maintain several moments of silence.
- *Ask:* What did you hear God say to you today?
- Invite volunteers to share.

What Do You Wonder?

Say: God tells us that he wants us to remember he comes first before anything else. He wants us to honor him always.

Invite the children to respond to the questions. Ask what else they might wonder about honoring God and keeping the Lord's Day holy.

Lent

Ask: What do we celebrate during Lent?

- Write the children's responses on the board or on chart paper.

Invite the children to imagine they are going on a trip.

- Ask what they will need to take with them. Possible responses: clothing, water, food

- Brainstorm with the children other things one does to prepare for a trip.

- Compare the journey of Lent to the discussion of the imaginary trip. You may make a chart comparing the two on the board or on chart paper.

Read aloud the text.

- *Ask:* On what day does Lent begin? Ash Wednesday

Draw attention to the pictures.

- Ask the children to tell you what they see happening in each picture.

- *Ask:* How are these people celebrating Lent? Possible responses: they are praying, they are receiving ashes on Ash Wednesday

- Discuss the significance of ashes. They mark the beginning of our Lenten journey. They remind us that we are on a journey to Easter.

Lent

What do we celebrate during Lent?

Lent is a special time. It lasts forty days. The Church is getting ready for Easter!

Lent starts on Ash Wednesday. The ashes on your forehead remind you that Jesus came to save us.

The priest wears purple as a sign of our sorrow for the things that take us away from God.

Lent
- The season of forty days during which the Church gets ready for Easter.

© Our Sunday Visitor

28 The Church Year

ℹ️ Catechist Background

History of Ashes

The Old Testament has references to people covering themselves with ashes as a sign of repentance. (Jonah 3:6; Daniel 9:3)

- In the early Church, sinners seeking reconciliation were signed with ashes at the beginning of Lent.

- In the 11th century, ashes were used for everyone at the beginning of Lent.

Showing Love

Lent is a time when you pay special attention to putting God first. You put God first when you show love to God and others.

You can show love for God by listening to God's Word.

You can show love for God by praying at a special time every day.

You can show love for others by helping out at home.

You can show love for others by saying kind words to them.

➜ **What else can you do to show love during Lent?**

Draw one way you put God first during Lent.

Lent **29**

Showing Love

Tell the children that Lent is a special time of year when we pay special attention to putting God first in our lives.

Read aloud the first paragraph.

Read aloud the second paragraph.

- *Ask:* When do you listen to God's Word?

Read aloud the third paragraph.

- *Ask:* When do you pray every day?

Read aloud the fourth paragraph.

- *Ask:* What do you do at home to be helpful?

Read aloud the fifth paragraph.

- *Ask:* What are some kind words you can say?
- *Ask:* What else can you do to show love during Lent?
- ⭐ Invite the children to draw one way they put God first during Lent. Invite volunteers to share their drawings.

Optional Activity

Make Crosses *Visual/Spatial*

Provide a variety of art supplies and have the children make crosses.

- Possible art supplies might include craft sticks, paints, glitter, construction paper, glue, scissors, or sequins. Use whatever materials are available.
- Tell the children to hang their cross where it can remind them to put God first and show love to God and others.

Put God First

Ask the children to share times that they have been so busy with something they were doing that they forgot about what was going on around them.

- Explain that sometimes we do that to God and others who need our love and attention. The Church gives us Lent to help us pay attention.

Read the paragraph aloud.

Activity

Look at the pictures in the activity together. Talk about what is happening in each picture.

- Read aloud the directions for the activity.
- Have the children work with a partner to complete the activity.

 Music Option: Have the children sing "Lord, Throughout These Holy Days," downloaded from **aliveinchrist.osv.com**.

Refer to page 313 in the Our Catholic Tradition reference section of the Student Book for more about Lent.

Discover

Put God First

Jesus always put his Father first. We put God first in our lives when we show love in our words and actions.

Activity

How can you put God first? Draw a circle around the things you can do to put God first.

© Our Sunday Visitor

30 The Church Year

 ## Catholic Social Teaching

Chapter Connections

To integrate Catholic Social Teaching into your lesson, choose one of the following features: Rights and Responsibilities, pages 288–289; or Option for the Poor, pages 290–291.

- To expand the lesson move to the Catholic Social Teaching feature after completing page 30.
- Return to the prayer on page 31.

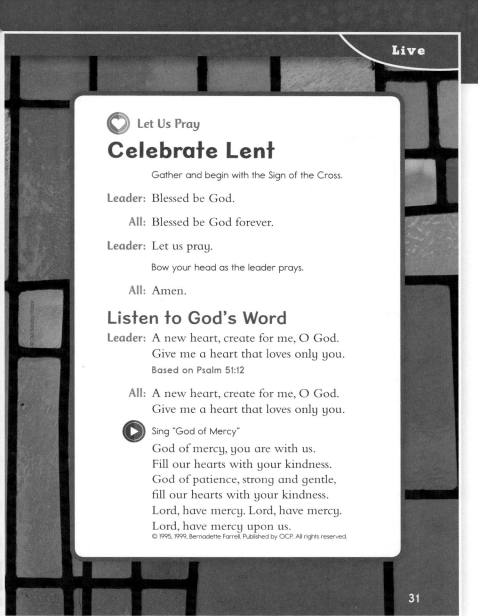

Live

 Let Us Pray

Celebrate Lent

Gather and begin with the Sign of the Cross.

Leader: Blessed be God.

All: Blessed be God forever.

Leader: Let us pray.

Bow your head as the leader prays.

All: Amen.

Listen to God's Word

Leader: A new heart, create for me, O God.
Give me a heart that loves only you.
Based on Psalm 51:12

All: A new heart, create for me, O God.
Give me a heart that loves only you.

Sing "God of Mercy"

God of mercy, you are with us.
Fill our hearts with your kindness.
God of patience, strong and gentle,
fill our hearts with your kindness.
Lord, have mercy. Lord, have mercy.
Lord, have mercy upon us.
© 1995, 1999, Bernadette Farrell. Published by OCP. All rights reserved.

31

 ## Let Us Pray
Celebrate Lent

Invite the children to process to the prayer space. Have each child bring their book.

Rehearse "God of Mercy," downloaded from **aliveinchrist.osv.com**.

Follow the order of prayer on the student page.

- *Leader's prayer:* God, our Father, sometimes we do not act as your children. (*Pause.*) We ask your forgiveness and mercy. (*Pause.*) Lord have mercy, (*pause*) Christ have mercy, (*pause*) Lord have mercy.

Conclude by singing together "God of Mercy."

Distribute this page to the children or parents/adult family members.

 ## Liturgy Link

Lord Have Mercy

This prayer is often prayed at the beginning of the Mass, during the Penitential Act.

- The *Lord Have Mercy* unites the worshipping in asking for God's mercy.
- The *Lord Have Mercy* may be done as a call and response. Pray "Lord have mercy." Have the children respond, "Christ have mercy."

LESSON OBJECTIVES

- Learn that Holy Week is the holiest week of the Church Year
- Understand the purpose of the Triduum
- Appreciate that the Easter Triduum of the Passion and Resurrection of Christ is the culmination of the entire liturgical year

ENVIRONMENT

Prayer table
White cloth
Bible
Glass bowl with holy water
Markers or crayons

- Place the prayer table in the center of the worship space.
- Cover the table with the white cloth.
- Place the glass bowl with holy water in the center of the table. It will be the focal point of the celebration.

 MUSIC OPTIONS
Go to **aliveinchrist.osv.com** to sample and download, "Hosanna" "Sing Hosanna"

 CATHOLIC SOCIAL TEACHING

- **Call to Community**, Pages 286–287
- **Option for the Poor**, Pages 290–291

Catechist Background

"Many people spread… leafy branches that they had cut from fields. They cried out… Hosanna! Blessed is he who comes in the name of the Lord!… Hosanna in the highest!"
Mark 11:8–10

➜ **Reflect** What helps you place your trust in God?

Most Americans are familiar with instant replay—it is very much a part of watching a sporting event on television. With the help of video, one can easily see the best play of a game again and again. The celebration of the Easter Triduum, the three days leading up to Easter, is much more than a replay of historical events leading toward Christ's Resurrection. The liturgical celebration of the Triduum makes real God's accomplishments, allowing the assembly to enter into the lived mystery.

Lent ends and the Triduum begins at sundown on Holy Thursday. It ends with evening prayer on Easter Sunday. During these three days, the whole Church fasts and prays with anticipation and hope. The assembly gathers for the Washing of the Feet and the Mass of the Lord's Supper. They participate in the Adoration of the Cross, and await Christ's Resurrection, which is celebrated in a most solemn way during the Easter Vigil.

Through the symbols of water and the cross, and the liturgical actions of blessing and kissing the foot of the cross, the historical events of Jesus' life, Death, and Resurrection are made real in the here and now. In these liturgical actions, the Triduum is more than a reminder of what God did long ago. Instead, it is a continuous celebration of the Church's salvation today.

➜ **Reflect** What are ways you can participate in the Triduum this year?

Catechist's Prayer

 Loving God, may my faith grow stronger and my eternal salvation be assured. Amen.

Holy Week

 Let Us Pray

Leader: Dear Jesus, help us to grow in trust.
We pray this in your name.

"Blessed is he
who comes in the name of the LORD."
Psalm 118:26

All: Amen.

God's Word

"Many people spread leafy branches that they had cut from the fields. They cried out Hosanna! Blessed is he who comes in the name of the Lord! Hosanna in the highest!" **Based on Mark 11:8–10**

What Do You Wonder?

- Where was Jesus going when the people shouted Hosanna for him?
- How can you trust God more?

Lectionary Connection

Mark 11:8–10

This Gospel passage is part of the story of Jesus' Entry into Jerusalem, which is proclaimed on Palm Sunday.

- In the Gospel according to Mark, Jesus makes arrangements for his entry into Jerusalem. He sends two of his disciples into a village to get a colt.
- Jesus rode on the colt as he entered Jerusalem. People spread their cloaks and leafy branches on the road before him.

Invite

Let Us Pray

Invite the children to gather in the prayer space and make the Sign of the Cross. Choose a child to be the leader. Read aloud the Psalm verse from a Bible. Prompt the children's response.

Have the children move out of the prayer space and back to their seats.

Explain that crowds gathered to praise Jesus as he entered Jerusalem.

Say: We are so grateful that we can trust the Lord Jesus enough to give him our whole life. Let's listen to how the people praise the Lord Jesus.

God's Word

Guide the children through the process of Scripture reflection.

- Invite them to close their eyes, be still and open their minds and hearts to what God is saying to them in this passage.
- Proclaim the Scripture.
- Maintain several moments of silence.
- *Ask:* What did you hear God say to you today?
- Invite volunteers to share.

What Do You Wonder?

Say: At the beginning of the week the people were praising Jesus. At the end of the week many of them were saying "crucify him."

Invite the children to respond to the questions. Ask what else they might wonder about praising Jesus and trusting God.

© Our Sunday Visitor

Time for Remembering

Ask: What special gift did Jesus give us?

- Write the children's responses on the board or on chart paper.

Ask children to share experiences of losing something very important to them and then finding it. Possible responses: a toy, a pet

- Discuss the feelings they had during those experiences. Possible responses: fear, sadness, joy, happiness

- Explain that these feelings are similar to the ones the Apostles felt during the time of Jesus' Death and Resurrection.

- Tell children that we remember these events every year in three special days before Easter Sunday.

Read aloud the text.

- Clarify what Palm Sunday and the events each day of the Triduum remembers.

Activity

Read aloud the directions for the activity.

- Provide time for the children to complete their drawings.

 Music Option: Have the children sing, "Sing Hosanna," downloaded from **aliveinchrist.osv.com**.

Refer to page 313 in the Our Catholic Tradition reference section of the Student Book for more about Lent and Holy Week.

Time for Remembering

What special gift did Jesus give us?

Jesus gave us a special gift. He gave his life for our sins. He died, but he was raised to new life. Palm Sunday marks the beginning of the holiest week of the year. We hear the words of the people to Jesus,

"Hosanna."   Matthew 21:9

During this Holy Week we remember Jesus' dying and rising in a special way, especially on these three holiest days:

- Holy Thursday
- Good Friday
- Holy Saturday

On Palm Sunday, we remember how crowds welcomed Jesus into Jerusalem.

© Our Sunday Visitor

Activity

Draw a Palm Branch Draw yourself welcoming Jesus and waving a palm branch.

34 The Church Year

 Catholic Social Teaching

Chapter Connections

To integrate Catholic Social Teaching into your lesson, choose one of the following features: Option for the Poor, pages 290–291; or Call to Community, page 286–287.

- To expand the lesson move to the Catholic Social Teaching feature after completing page 34.
- Return to the prayer on page 35.

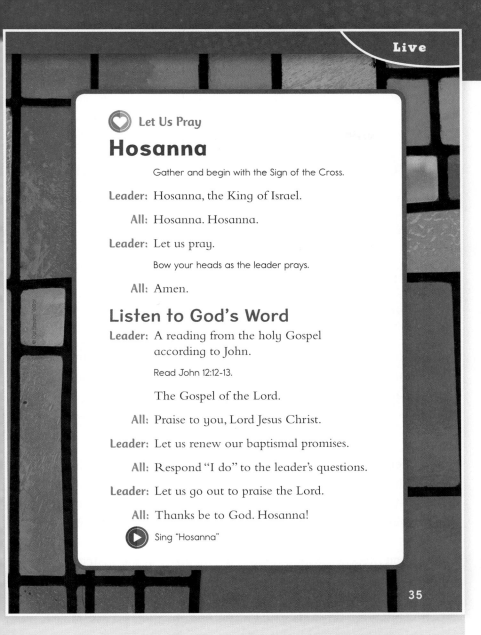

Let Us Pray

Hosanna

Gather and begin with the Sign of the Cross.

Leader: Hosanna, the King of Israel.

All: Hosanna. Hosanna.

Leader: Let us pray.

Bow your heads as the leader prays.

All: Amen.

Listen to God's Word

Leader: A reading from the holy Gospel according to John.

Read John 12:12-13.

The Gospel of the Lord.

All: Praise to you, Lord Jesus Christ.

Leader: Let us renew our baptismal promises.

All: Respond "I do" to the leader's questions.

Leader: Let us go out to praise the Lord.

All: Thanks be to God. Hosanna!

 Sing "Hosanna"

35

Liturgy Link

Baptismal Promises

One of the highlights of the Easter Vigil is the Baptism of the elect and the renewal of baptismal promises by the faithful.

- The sprinkling with holy water is called *asperges*.
- Remind the children that every time they enter the church and bless themselves with holy water, they remember their Baptism.

Let Us Pray
Hosanna

Invite the children to process to the prayer space. Have each child bring their book.

 Rehearse "Hosanna," downloaded from **aliveinchrist.osv.com**.

Follow the order of prayer on the student page.

- *Leader's prayer:* Lord God, we praise and thank you for these holy days.
- Invite the children to stand for the Gospel.
- Invite the children to answer "I do" to the questions you will ask them.
- *Ask:* "Do you believe in God the Father?"; "Do you believe in Jesus, God's Son, who died and rose?"; "Do you believe in the Holy Spirit?"

 Conclude by singing together "Hosanna."

Distribute this page to the children or parents/adult family members.

Holy Week **35–36**

LESSON OBJECTIVES

- Explain that God raised Jesus from the dead
- Discuss Easter joy

ENVIRONMENT

Prayer table
White cloth
Easter lily(s)
Bible
Cross
Crayons or markers

- Cover the prayer table with the white cloth.
- Place the Easter lily in front of the cross and place the Bible in the center of the table on a stand.
- Arrange the space so children can process.

 MUSIC OPTIONS
Go to **aliveinchrist.osv.com**
to sample and download,
"Alleluia"
"This Is the Day"

 CATHOLIC SOCIAL TEACHING

- **Life and Dignity**, Pages 290–291
- **Care for Creation**, Pages 296–297

Catechist Background

> Then the angel said to the women in reply, "Do not be afraid! I know that you are seeking Jesus the crucified. He is not here, for he has been raised…. Go quickly and tell his disciples…."
> Matthew 28:5–7

→ **Reflect** Why would the women be afraid?

The experience of loss is usually a difficult one to overcome. Imagine the elation and even confusion the followers of Christ must have felt after learning that Jesus was alive! On Easter morning, the Church rejoices as disciples of Christ. We celebrate as People of God who have received the extravagant gift of salvation.

The celebration of the Easter season includes the fifty days following the Triduum. The Easter liturgies of these eight weeks reflect the joy of salvation in song and in action. The *Alleluia* not only returns to the repertoire, but also expresses whole-heartedly the joy of the Body of Christ. The Church renews each individual's baptismal vows in the sprinkling rite. The Gospels unpack the meaning of the Easter event and help the assembly to celebrate and remember that what God the Father did in his Son, Jesus, he is doing in the lives of his People. In this period of mystagogy following Christ's Resurrection, the assembly is sent out from the Easter celebration to spread the Good News.

Easter is about the bareness of winter and Lent giving way to Christ's light and life. Jesus' Resurrection is a sign of new life; it is about Christ's triumph over death. Jesus turned the darkness of sin into the light of love. You are called to rejoice and spread the Good News. Allow your Easter joy to translate to action.

→ **Reflect** How do you celebrate the joy and Good News of Easter on a daily basis?

Catechist's Prayer

 Lord Jesus Christ, through your Cross and Resurrection, you share the gift of salvation. Alleluia! Amen.

He is Risen

Let Us Pray

Leader: Lord, God, bless us with Easter joy.

"This is the day that the LORD has made;
let us rejoice in it and be glad."

Psalm 118:24

All: Amen.

God's Word

The angel said to the women, "Do not be afraid! I know that you are seeking Jesus. He is not here, for he has been raised... go quickly and tell his disciples..."

Based on Matthew 28:5–7

? What Do You Wonder?

- Why would the women be afraid?
- Who would you tell first?

37

Lectionary Connection

Matthew 28:5–7

This passage is part of the Gospel according to Matthew proclaimed at the Easter Vigil, Year B of the Lectionary cycle.

- Three days after his Death, Jesus rose from the dead.
- Some faithful women had gone to the tomb, but Jesus was not there.
- The women hurry to tell the disciples. On the way, they encounter the Risen Lord and do him homage.

Invite

Let Us Pray

Invite the children to gather in the prayer space and make the Sign of the Cross. Choose a child to be the leader. Read aloud the Psalm verse from a Bible. Prompt the children's response.

Have the children move out of the prayer space and back to their seats.

Say: On the first Easter morning when the women went to anoint Jesus and he was gone, they were afraid. Listen to what happened.

God's Word

Guide the children through the process of Scripture reflection.

- Invite them to close their eyes, be still and open their minds and hearts to what God is saying to them in this passage.
- Proclaim the Scripture.
- Maintain several moments of silence.
- *Ask:* What did you hear God say to you today?
- Invite volunteers to share.

What Do You Wonder?

Say: In the reading we hear that Jesus is gone from his tomb but he is alive!

Invite the children to respond to the questions. Ask what else they might wonder about the women at the tomb or the Resurrection.

Easter Joy

Ask: Why is Easter a time of joy and happiness?

- Write the children's responses on the board or on chart paper.

Have the children look at the prayer table. Ask them what has changed. Possible responses: color, flowers

- Be sure that the children see that the starkness of the Lenten decorations has turned to joyous abundance.

Read aloud the text with enthusiasm.

- Talk with the children about why Easter is a joyful season. It helps us remember that Jesus is alive. He had power over death. He lives in us.

- Talk about the reasons the Church celebrates Easter and why it is the most important holiday.

- Read aloud the Easter text box.

Activity

Read aloud the directions for the activity.

- Have the children work independently to color the eggs.

- Invite volunteers to share their drawings.

Music Option: Have the children sing, "This Is the Day," downloaded from **aliveinchrist.osv.com**.

Refer to page 313 in the Our Catholic Tradition reference section of the Student Book for more about Easter.

Easter Joy

Why is Easter a time of joy and happiness?

Jesus was dead, but three days later he rose from the dead to new life. Jesus was alive. What great power God showed! Jesus is risen! Now he lives in us!

Easter

The fifty days that the Church celebrates Jesus' Resurrection from the dead.

Activity

Celebrate Easter Color in the Easter egg.

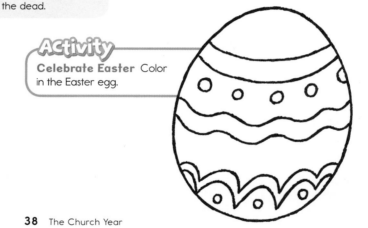

🌐 Catholic Social Teaching

Chapter Connections

To integrate Catholic Social Teaching into your lesson, choose one of the following features: Life and Dignity, pages 284–285; or Care for Creation, pages 296–297.

- To expand the lesson move to the Catholic Social Teaching feature after completing page 38.

- Return to the prayer on page 39.

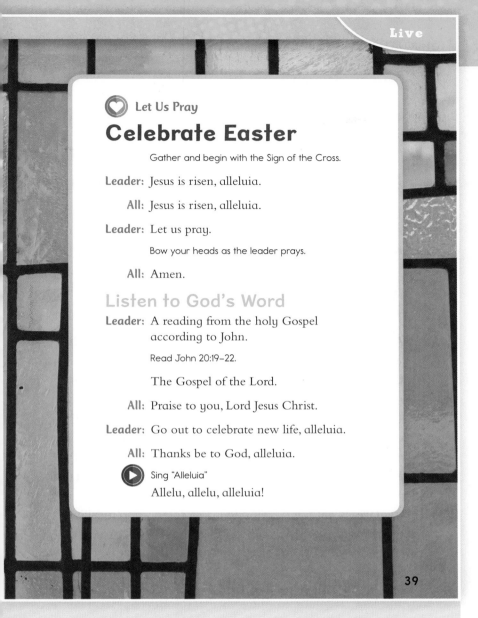

Live

 Let Us Pray

Celebrate Easter

Gather and begin with the Sign of the Cross.

Leader: Jesus is risen, alleluia.

All: Jesus is risen, alleluia.

Leader: Let us pray.

Bow your heads as the leader prays.

All: Amen.

Listen to God's Word

Leader: A reading from the holy Gospel according to John.

Read John 20:19–22.

The Gospel of the Lord.

All: Praise to you, Lord Jesus Christ.

Leader: Go out to celebrate new life, alleluia.

All: Thanks be to God, alleluia.

▶ Sing "Alleluia"

Allelu, allelu, alleluia!

39

Liturgy Link

Alleluia and Processions

The word *Alleluia* comes from a Hebrew word meaning "Praise God!"

- The ritual of processing with the Gospel book and singing the *Alleluia* is a way to honor and praise the Gospel as God's Word.

- After being suppressed during Lent and Holy Week, the *Alleluia* is sung once again beginning at the Easter Vigil. During the Easter season, it can also be sung as part of the Solemn Blessing at the end of Mass.

 Let Us Pray

Celebrate Easter

Invite the children to process to the prayer space. Have each child bring their book.

▶ Rehearse "Alleluia," downloaded from **aliveinchrist.osv.com**.

Follow the order of prayer on the student page.

- Lead the children in the Sign of the Cross.

- *Leader's prayer:* Lord, through your Cross and Resurrection, you have set us free and made us your followers. Thank you.

- Lift up the Bible. Invite the children to follow you in procession around the prayer table singing the refrain.

- Have the children remain standing while you proclaim the Gospel.

▶ Sing together "Alleluia."

Distribute this page to the children or parents/adult family members.

LESSON OBJECTIVES

- Understand that we are temples of the Holy Spirit
- Appreciate that the Holy Spirit is always with us, especially at Pentecost

ENVIRONMENT

Prayer table
Cross
Red cloth
Bible
Symbol of the Holy Spirit
Candle, or battery-operated candle
Bowl of holy water
Pencils

- Cover the table with the red cloth.
- Place the cross, candle, bowl of holy water, opened Bible, and a symbol of the Holy Spirit on the table.

 MUSIC OPTIONS

Go to **aliveinchrist.osv.com** to sample and download,
"The Holy Spirit"
"Come to Us, Holy Spirit"
"I Am with You Always"

 CATHOLIC SOCIAL TEACHING

- **Life and Dignity**, Pages 290–291
- **The Dignity of Work**, Pages 292–293

Catechist Background

 Do you now know that your body is a temple of the holy Spirit within you, whom you have from God, and that you are not your own? …Therefore, glorify God in your body.
1 Corinthians 6:19–20

➜ **Reflect** How is your body a temple of the Holy Spirit?

Jesus' Apostles and disciples were expecting the Holy Spirit. The Risen Lord had told them to remain in Jerusalem to wait for "the promise of the Father about which you have heard me speak; for John baptized with water, but in a few days you will be baptized with the Holy Spirit." (Acts 1:1–5). The disciples gathered in an upper room during the Jewish Feast of Pentecost. There were many people in Jerusalem at that time because for the Jews, this was one of three great feasts that required a pilgrimage to the Temple. Originally, it was an agricultural festival celebrating the "first fruits" of early spring also known as the *Feast of Weeks*. Later it developed into a celebration recalling the making of the covenant, fifty days after Passover. It appears that the Apostles were in the upper room awaiting the end of the festival when the Holy Spirit came to them.

Today the Church celebrates the arrival of the Holy Spirit on Pentecost. This Christian feast celebrates the new covenant of God with his People. Pentecost Sunday is an enthusiastic and uplifting celebration of God's ongoing work in the world. The assembly celebrates an active renewal of the Church's purpose and mission through the renewal of baptismal vows and the dismissal, when they go forth to continue serving as Christ did.

➜ **Reflect** How does the Holy Spirit act in your life?

Catechist's Prayer

 Loving God, help me to use your generous Gifts of the Holy Spirit to share the Good News with the children. Amen.

Pentecost

♡ Let Us Pray

Leader: Come Holy Spirit.
Fill us with your power and love.
Help us follow Jesus.

"Bless the LORD, my soul! Hallelujah!"
Psalm 104:35b

All: Amen.

🔲 God's Word

Do you know that your body is a temple of the holy Spirit within you, whom you have from God, and that you are not your own? For you have been purchased at a price. Therefore glorify God in your body.   1 Corinthians 6:19–20

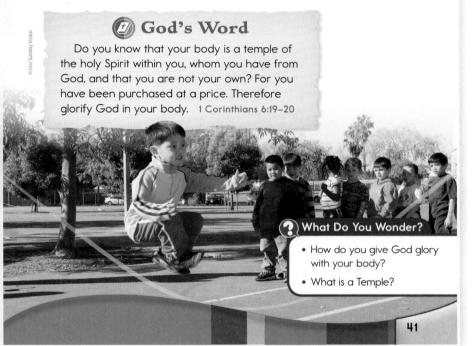

❓ What Do You Wonder?

- How do you give God glory with your body?
- What is a Temple?

41

🔲 Lectionary Connection

1 Corinthians 6:19–20

This passage is part of the second reading proclaimed on the Second Sunday in Ordinary Time, Year B of the Lectionary cycle. Human dignity and respect are common themes throughout the Scriptures.

- In this passage humans are sacred because of God's indwelling Spirit.
- The Book of Genesis teaches that human beings are made in God's image. (See Genesis 1:26–27.)
- The Hebrew prophets spoke out strongly for justice and human rights. (See Amos 5:24.)

Invite

♡ Let Us Pray

Invite the children to gather in the prayer space and make the Sign of the Cross. Choose a child to be the leader. Read aloud the Psalm verse from a Bible. Prompt the children's response.

Have the children move out of the prayer space and back to their seats.

Explain that we are filled with God's love.

Say: Today we prayed asking God to open our hearts to the incredible gift of his love. Now, Saint Paul will speak to us about the love of God that fills our bodies.

🔲 God's Word

Guide the children through the process of Scripture reflection.

- Invite them to close their eyes, be still and open their minds and hearts to what God is saying to them in this passage.
- Proclaim the Scripture.
- Maintain several moments of silence.
- *Ask:* What did you hear God say to you today?
- Invite volunteers to share.

What Do You Wonder?

Say: In the reading we heard that God the Holy Spirit lives in us. Isn't that wonderful?

Invite the children to respond to the questions. Ask what else they might wonder about the Holy Spirit or how to give glory to God.

The Holy Spirit

Ask: How did the Holy Spirit help the Apostles?

- Write the children's responses on the board or on chart paper.

Ask the children about a time they have been lost, perhaps at a store, or at the park or zoo.

- Discuss the feelings that came from that experience. Possible responses: frightened, lonely

- Use this discussion to talk about how the Apostles must have felt after Jesus returned to his Father.

Read aloud the text.

 Have the children underline how the Holy Spirit helped the Apostles.

- Go over some of the Gifts of the Holy Spirit—Wisdom, Courage, Understanding.

- Talk about how the Holy Spirit is always with us.

 Music Option: Have the children sing, "Come to Us, Holy Spirit" or "I am with You Always," downloaded from **aliveinchrist.osv.com**.

Discover

The Holy Spirit

How did the Holy Spirit help the Apostles?

A cheer shows spirit. You cannot see spirit, but you know when people have it. You cannot see the Holy Spirit. The Holy Spirit is always with you.

After Jesus was raised from the dead, he sent the Holy Spirit. The Holy Spirit came to the Apostles in the form of wind and fire and <u>helped them to remember what Jesus told them.</u> This day is called Pentecost.

 Underline how the Holy Spirit helped the Apostles.

42 The Church Year

Songs of Scripture

Holy Spirit

Before teaching the song, play "Pin the Olive Branch on the Dove."

- Place a large paper dove on the wall. Cut out an image of an olive branch and affix tape to the backside.

- Give clues to the blindfolded children to guide them in placing their "olive branch" on the beak of the dove.

- Compare your help to the work of the Holy Spirit in our lives.

Use *Songs of Scripture*, Grades 1–3 CD, Track 12

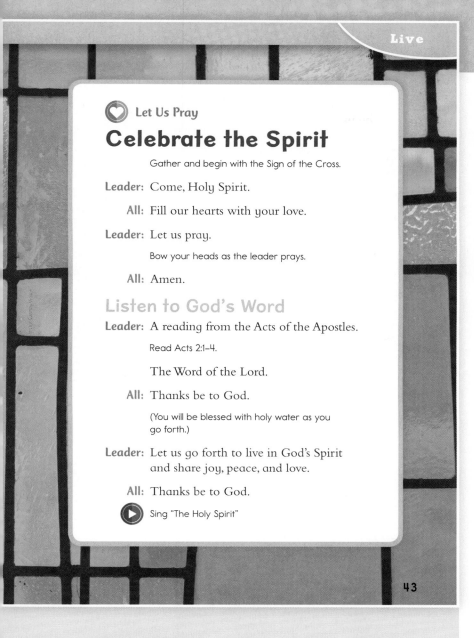

Live

Let Us Pray
Celebrate the Spirit

Gather and begin with the Sign of the Cross.

Leader: Come, Holy Spirit.

All: Fill our hearts with your love.

Leader: Let us pray.

Bow your heads as the leader prays.

All: Amen.

Listen to God's Word

Leader: A reading from the Acts of the Apostles.

Read Acts 2:1–4.

The Word of the Lord.

All: Thanks be to God.

(You will be blessed with holy water as you go forth.)

Leader: Let us go forth to live in God's Spirit and share joy, peace, and love.

All: Thanks be to God.

 Sing "The Holy Spirit"

43

Let Us Pray
Celebrate the Spirit

Invite the children to process to the prayer space. Have each child bring their book.

> As the students process, play "The Holy Spirit," downloaded from **aliveinchrist.osv.com**.

Follow the order of prayer on the student page.

- *Leader's prayer:* Come Holy Spirit, fill us with your gifts.
- After the reading, have the children gather around the prayer table.
- *Using holy water, sign each child on the forehead with the Sign of the Cross and say:* (Child's name), I bless you in the name of God the Father, God the Son, and God the Holy Spirit. (This is appropriately done by a layperson using his or her open right hand, rather than the right thumb as a bishop might do with oil in Confirmation.)

Distribute this page to the children or parents/adult family members.

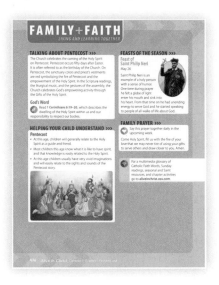

Catholic Social Teaching

Chapter Connections

To integrate Catholic Social Teaching into your lesson, choose one of the following features: Life and Dignity, pages 284–285; or The Dignity of Work, pages 292–293.

- To expand the lesson move to the Catholic Social Teaching feature after completing page 42.
- Return to the prayer on page 43.

Core
Chapters

Units At A Glance

Revelation

Our Catholic Tradition

- God the Father is the Creator. (CCC, 317)

- God tells us about himself in the wonderful world he made. (CCC 319)

- We are God's children, made in his image and likeness. (CCC, 239, 353)

- God gave us life. He wants to be our friend. He wants us to be friends with others. (CCC, 356)

- God asks us to share his love with all people and to take care of his creation. (CCC, 357–358)

What do we know about God?

Unit 1 Overview

Chapter 1

The children will:

- identify the Bible as God's Word written by humans
- appreciate that God made everything and all of creation is good
- understand that God made humans to be his friends, to know him and love him

 Songs of Scripture
"God Created You and Me"

 Catholic Social Teaching: Live Your Faith

- Life and Dignity, Pages 284–285
- Care for Creation, Pages 296–297

Chapter 2

The children will:

- discover that God created the world to show his love
- appreciate that all of creation is God's gift to us, and his Son, Jesus, is his greatest gift
- describe ways that people use God's gifts in the world to make things we need
- understand that thanksgiving is showing God we are grateful for all that he's given us

 Catholic Social Teaching: Live Your Faith

- The Dignity of Work, Pages 292–293
- Care for Creation, Pages 296–297

Chapter 3

The children will:

- define image of God as the likeness of God that is in all humans because we are all created by him
- recognize that humans are the most special part of creation. God gave us the ability to think and make choices
- understand that God gave Adam and Eve the responsibility to be caretakers of his creation
- appreciate that each of us is responsible for treating all of creation with care and respect

 Catholic Social Teaching: Live Your Faith

- Life and Dignity, Pages 284–285
- Care for Creation, Pages 296–297

Preview Unit Theme

Ask: What is the unit theme?

Summarize that the unit focuses on God's Revelation.

Invite volunteers to read aloud each of the bullets in Our Catholic Tradition.

Explain to the children that they will learn about these things in the next three chapters.

Have the children study the photos and images. Invite volunteers to describe what they see. What do these images say about the unit theme?

Ask: What do we know about God?

After some discussion, explain to the children that they will be exploring this question in the next three chapters.

KEY CONCEPT

God created everything. All that he made is good. God knows and loves everyone.

DOCTRINAL CONTENT

- The Bible is God's Word written by humans. We learn about God from the Bible. (CCC, 105–106)

- God made humans to be his friends, to know and love him. (CCC, 355)

- God made everything. All of his creation is good. (CCC, 299)

TASKS OF CATECHESIS

Helping children grow in a faith that is "known, celebrated, lived, and expressed in prayer" (NDC, 20).

This chapter focuses on the following tasks of catechesis:

- Promoting Knowledge of the Faith

- Education for Community Life

Catechist Background

> You formed my inmost being; you knit me in my mother's womb. I praise you, because I am wonderfully made; wonderful are your works! **Psalm 139:13–14**

➡ **Reflect** How did God make every person so unique?

You have had an argument with a friend or spouse; your kids are yelling at one another. When you have one of those days, you may sometimes forget God's infinite love for you. Your path through life can become cluttered with distractions and overshadowed by feelings of resentment, guilt, and loneliness. It can be a difficult task to stay on the path at all.

Focus on the thought that, as a human being, you are created in the image of God. You possess the dignity of a being that mirrors something of God's splendor and his goodness. Remember, too, that no matter what your faults, no matter how difficult your life may be, God's love for you, his child, created in his image, can never fail.

Gazing upon a newborn baby for the first time, a parent falls in love—each tiny feature is an image of himself or herself. With this love comes a parent's great desire to shower this child with tokens of love. A parent wants to give this tiny infant everything needed for survival. So it is with God, the Father of us all. When we were lost, he held out his hand to us, sending us the Savior to show us the way home.

➡ **Reflect** How do you see God's love working in your life right now?

Catechist's Prayer

> God our Creator, I praise you! Thank you for calling me to share my faith with these children. May they know you in the kindness and care I show them. Amen.

Lesson Plan

Objectives	Process	Materials

Invite, 10 minutes

Created By God Page 47

- Psalm 139:1–3 Pray the opening prayer.
- Psalm 139:13–15 Reflect prayerfully on the Word.
- Discuss What Do You Wonder questions.

Optional Activity
Chapter Poem: "Who Made Everyone?"

Discover, 35 minutes

God's Creation Pages 48–49
- Identify the Bible as God's Word written by humans
- Appreciate that God made everything and all of creation is good

- **Catholic Faith Words** Bible, creation
- Explain that the Bible has stories about God's love for us.
- Genesis 2:7–22 Proclaim, "The Garden of Eden."
- Recall that God made everything good.
- ☆ Draw self into creation illustration.
- **Share Your Faith Activity** Name favorite thing in God's creation.

☐ pencils
☐ index cards
☐ crayons or markers
- **Optional Activity** Wonderful Me!
☐ Activity Master 1 (Page 47E)

God Loves You Pages 50–51
- Understand that God made humans to be his friends, to know him and love him

- Explain that we cannot see God but we can know about him from creation and from the Bible.
- ☆ Circle two favorite things in the picture that God made.
- Explain that God created a wonderful world with lots of good things.
- **Connect Your Faith Activity** Trace the word.

☐ pencils
☐ crayons or markers
- **Optional Activity** Sounds of Creation

Live, 15 minutes

Our Catholic Life Pages 52–53

- Explain creation as many gifts from God.
- ☆ Match the pictures of God's gifts to the words.
- **People of Faith** Learn about Blessed Fra Angelico.
- **Live Your Faith Activity** Name gifts of creation in the illustration.

☐ pencils
☐ crayons or markers

Prayer of Praise Page 54

- Teach ASL for *praise*.
- Rehearse "God Is a Part of My Life."
- Follow the order of prayer.

Download "God Is a Part of My Life."

Family + Faith Page 55
Point out that the Catholic Families page provides chapter highlights, information on how first graders understand faith concepts, and family prayer.

Chapter Review Page 56
aliveinchrist.osv.com
- Customize and Download Assessments
- Email Links to eAssessments
- Interactive Student Reviews

ONLINE RESOURCES

 Go to **aliveinchrist.osv.com**

You will find:

- Interactive lesson planning with web specific content and additional activities
- Step by step lesson instruction from printed Catechist Edition for integrated lesson planning
- Custom–built assessments to download and eAssessment links
- Interactive reviews that provide scores and the option to review answers
- Sunday readings with background and questions of the week

 Go to **osvparish.com**

You will find:

- Ask the Experts Q and A
- General Catechist Helps
- Community Connections and Blogs

Sharing the Message with First Graders

Our Creation by God Many first graders have not yet asked themselves how they came to be. They know from photos and stories that they used to be babies, but it is difficult for them to conceive of a time that they did not exist. For this reason, when they are taught that God made them, they might accept this idea without much thought. As they grow and learn more about how new life comes about, they will integrate this information through an understanding that people cooperate with God to bring new life into the world.

Teaching Tip: Create a birthday calendar at the beginning of the catechetical year. Throughout the year, recognize birthdays, talking about how glad you are that God made the birthday boy or birthday girl.

How First Graders Understand

- First graders like being acknowledged. Learn the names of the children in your group as quickly as possible.
- Stories captivate six-year-olds. Add a personal touch, such as gathering the children around you to tell the story. Tell them to listen for something in the story, and they are actively learning.
- First graders are interested in rules. Be sure to make rules clear.

"I have a vivid imagination. Help me use it to learn."

Chapter Poem

"Who Made Everyone?"

Use this poem to expand the chapter introduction.

- The children will relate the poem to their own lives, reflecting on God creating each person.
- Connect to how we learn about God through his creation of people.

 Go to **aliveinchrist.osv.com** Lesson Planning section for this poem.

NCEA IFG: ACRE Edition

Knowledge of the Faith

- Objective: To know and understand God's activity in human history

Communal Life

- Objective: To know the rights and responsibilities of the Christian faithful

Catholic Social Teaching

 Use one of these features to introduce a principle and engage the children with an activity.

- Life and Dignity, Pages 284–285
- Care for Creation, Pages 296–297

Music Options

 Use one or more of the following songs to enhance catechetical learning or for prayer.

- "God Is a Part of My Life," Live Prayer, Page 54
- "Wonderfully Made Parade," Discover, Page 50

LECTIONARY CONNECTION

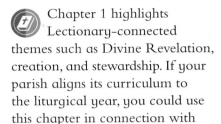 Chapter 1 highlights Lectionary-connected themes such as Divine Revelation, creation, and stewardship. If your parish aligns its curriculum to the liturgical year, you could use this chapter in connection with the following Sundays.

Year A

Twenty-ninth Sunday in Ordinary Time—First Commandment, faith, hope, love

Thirty-third Sunday in Ordinary Time—stewardship, creation, common good

Year B

Fourth Sunday of Easter—Trinity, Divine Revelation

Sixth Sunday of Easter—love, faith

Year C

Second Sunday of Easter—faith, love for God

Twentieth Sunday in Ordinary Time—creation

 Go to **aliveinchrist.osv.com** for a complete correlation ordered by the Sundays of the year and suggestions for how to integrate the Scripture readings into chapter lessons.

Name _____   Date _____

Wonderful Me!

Make the drawing look like you.
Color the things that tell what you can do.
At the bottom of the page,
tell who made you.

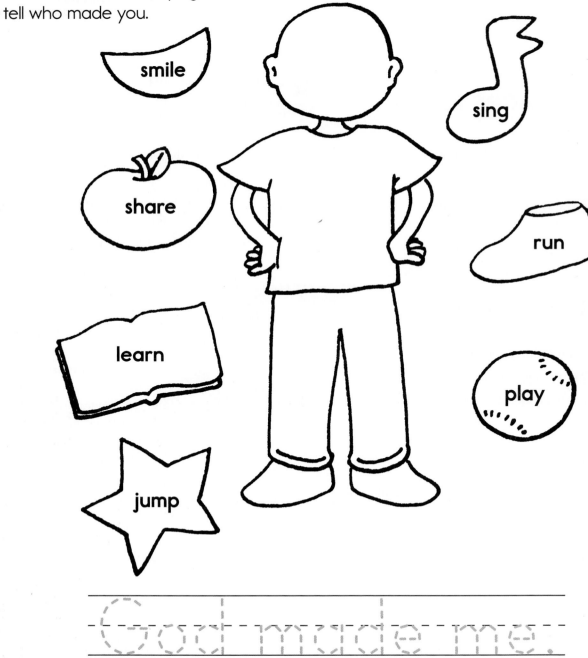

smile

sing

share

run

learn

play

jump

God made me.

Created By God

 Let Us Pray

Leader: Thank you, God, for making each one of us special.

You have examined me and you know me. You know everything I do.
You see me and you know all my actions.
Based on Psalm 139:1–3

All: God, help us know and love you. Amen.

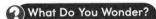 God's Word

God, you created every part of me: you put me together…I praise you…everything you do is wonderful…you saw me before I was born.
Based on Psalm 139:13–15

? What Do You Wonder?

- Why did God create everything?
- How did God make everyone so different?

Created By God **47**

Optional Activity

Chapter Poem: "Who Made Everyone?" *Verbal/Linguistic*

Use this poem after the opening prayer, before explaining that God created the world and everything in it.

- Read the poem aloud as the children follow along.
- Ask each child to stand. One by one, invite each child to say his or her name. After every fourth child, lead everyone in saying, "God made us all!"
- *Say:* Thank you, God, for everyone!

 Go to **aliveinchrist.osv.com** for Chapter Poem.

Invite

 Let Us Pray

Invite the children to gather in the prayer space and make the Sign of the Cross. Invite a child to be the leader. Read aloud the Psalm verse from a Bible. Prompt the children's response.

Have the children move out of the prayer space and back to their seats.

Explain that God created the world and everything in it, including people.

Say: Each one of us is different and special because God made us that way. Now, let's hear how wonderful God is to us.

God's Word

Guide the children through the process of Scripture reflection.

- Invite them to close their eyes, be still and open their minds and hearts to what God is saying to them in this passage.
- Proclaim the Scripture.
- Maintain several moments of silence.
- *Ask:* What did you hear God say to you today?
- Invite volunteers to share.

What Do You Wonder?

Say: God made each of us. Each one of us is created by God to be who we are. God lives in us and asks us to do things that only we can do.

Invite the children to respond to the questions. Ask what else they might wonder about God's creation and how God could make every person unique.

Discover

Objectives

- Identify the Bible as God's Word written by humans
- Appreciate that God made everything and all of creation is good

God's Creation

Ask: Who is the Creator of all things?

- Write the children's responses on the board or on chart paper.

Read aloud the first paragraph.

- Remind the children that God knows and loves them. Emphasize that the Bible has many stories about God's love for all people.
- Show the children a Bible and explain that it is a holy book. It is God's book.
- Hold up an index card with the word *Bible* on it. Have everyone read it.

Read the second paragraph.

 God's Word

Proclaim "The Garden of Eden."

- Invite volunteers to share the names of the first man and woman that God created.
- *Ask:* What else did God create?
- ⭐ Provide time for the children to draw themselves into the picture of creation.

God's Creation

Who is the Creator of all things?

You are God's child. God knows you and loves you. The **Bible** has many stories about God's love for all of us.

Listen to this Bible story. It is about God and how he made Adam and Eve.

 Draw yourself into the picture of the things that God made.

 God's Word

The Garden of Eden

A very long time ago, God created the first man. God breathed into the man, and the man began to live. God loved the man and wanted him to be happy. God created a woman to be the man's partner. The man's name was Adam. The woman's name was Eve.

Based on Genesis 2:7–22

48   Chapter 1

 Songs of Scripture

God Created You and Me

The Scriptures tell us that praising God is such a joy-filled experience that our ancestors in faith both sang and danced to honor God.

- Teach the chorus of the song.
- Have the children form a circle.
- When the chorus is sung, have the children skip together around the circle and sing.

▶ Use *Songs of Scripture*, Grades 1–3 CD, Track 5

God Gives Life

God made everything. All his **creation** is good. God is our Father and the Creator. He gave you life.

Share Your Faith

Think Trace the word that tells what everything that God made is called.

creation

Share Share your answer with a partner.

Catholic Faith Words

Bible the Word of God written in human words. The Bible is the holy book of the Church.

creation everything made by God

Created By God **49**

God Gives Life

Share the information in the paragraph.

- Point to several children at once and ask: "Who made you?"

Work with Words

Hold up an index card with the word *creation* and explain that it is everything that God made.

Explain to the children that we affirm our belief in God the Creator when we pray the Apostles' Creed. Refer the children to page 299 in the Our Catholic Tradition reference section in the back of the Student Book for the Apostles' Creed.

Activity

Read aloud the directions for the Share Your Faith activity.

- Have the children work independently to write their ideas.
- After a short time, have them discuss with a partner.

Quick Review

One place Catholics learn about God is from the Bible. One thing the Bible tells them is that God is the Creator of everything.

Optional Activity

Activity Master 1: Wonderful Me!

Distribute copies of the activity found on catechist page 47E.

- Read aloud the directions. Point out the letter tracing portion of the activity at the bottom of the page.
- As an alternative, you may wish to send this activity home with the children.

Objective

• Understand that God made humans to be his friends, to know him and love him

God Loves You

Ask: Who wants to be your friend?

• Write the children's responses on the board or on chart paper.

Read aloud both paragraphs.

• Explain that humans cannot see God, but they know what he is like from the things that he has made and from the Bible. Explain that God is greater and more wonderful than anything people can imagine about him.

• Emphasize that God loves us very much and that he is our friend.

• Point out the picture of creation. Encourage the children to name what they see and what they like best.

⭐ Invite the children to circle two of their favorite things in the picture that God made.

 Music Option: Have the children sing, "Wonderfully Made Parade," downloaded from **aliveinchrist.osv.com**.

God Loves You

Who wants to be your friend?

Those who love you know you best. God knows you better than anyone knows you. He wants you to know him, too.

God loves you very much. He is your friend. God wants you to be friends with others, too.

➡ **What is one thing you know about God?**

In the picture circle two of your favorite things that God made.

50

 Quick Tip

Celebrating Friendship

Help first graders understand how they can be friends with God by talking about the friendships they enjoy with their peers.

• Explain that the qualities that make them a good friend to other children—loyalty and love for example—can be applied to their friendship with God.

• They can show their loyalty and love to God by praying, treating others with kindness, and behaving well at home, school, and church.

God's World

God created a wonderful
world. It is filled with lots of good things.

There are mountains and rivers,
and fish in the stream,

Birds soaring high and
good things to dream.

There are flowers and
forests and puppy dogs, too,

But the best thing of all is
that God made people, too.

© Our Sunday Visitor

Connect Your Faith

Trace the Word

God loves you!

51

God's World

Ask the children to stand to
celebrate God's wonderful world.

- Invite the children to close their
  eyes as you read the poem. Tell
  them to picture in their mind all
  the wonderful gifts of creation.
- Read aloud the poem.
- Ask the children to raise their
  hands if they saw mountains,
  rivers, fish, birds, flowers, a puppy,
  or people.
- Have the children work together
  to invent gestures to go with each
  line of the poem.
- Read aloud the poem a second
  time while the children use the
  gestures.
- If possible, show the poem with
  gestures to another group of
  children or to the children's
  parents.

Activity

Point out the Connect Your Faith
activity and read aloud the
directions.

- Have the children trace the letters
  to write the word.

Quick Review

No one can see God, but we know a
lot about him through his creation.

Optional Activity

Sounds of Creation *Musical*

Bring in a nature CD or downloads that have the sounds of nature—
birds singing, wind blowing, thunder booming, etc.

- Have the children guess what the sounds are. Tell them God made
  all of these things.
- Or, demonstrate the sounds yourself by using wind chimes, drums,
  or cymbals.

Our Catholic Life

Read aloud the first paragraph.

- *Say:* Name some of God's gifts that you can see. Possible responses: people, animals, trees, rain, lakes, mountains, and so on.

- *Ask:* How do we use some of the things God created? Possible responses: we use trees to build homes, we use people to care for us, we use plants and animals for food.

Gifts God Gives Us

 Read aloud the directions to the activity.

- Encourage the children to work on their own to complete the activity.

- Be sure to help any children who may have difficulty. You may need to read each sentence aloud or help them find the beginning sounds to match the pictures to the words.

- When everyone has finished, read through the puzzle and share the answers together.

Our Catholic Life

How do we use some of the things God created?

God made so many wonderful things. God's gifts are all around you. They help you in many ways.

 Draw a line from the pictures in the sentences to the words they match.

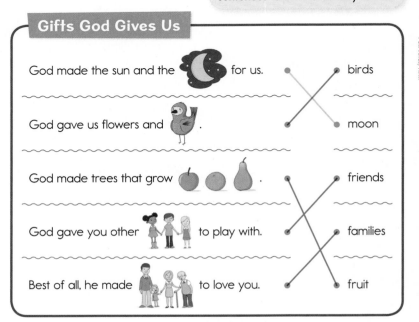

Gifts God Gives Us

God made the sun and the 🌙 for us. — birds

God gave us flowers and 🐦. — moon

God made trees that grow 🍎🍐. — friends

God gave you other 👫 to play with. — families

Best of all, he made 👨‍👩‍👧 to love you. — fruit

© Our Sunday Visitor

52 Chapter 1

✓ Quick Tip

Reverencing the Ordinary

Young children sometimes define a "gift" as something extravagant or costly, given on a rare occasion. Help the children see that their everyday lives are full of simple gifts—the wonders of nature, the joys of time shared with friends, the love shown by family members.

- Invite the children to name a simple blessing. After each child, the group prays together, "We thank you, God."

- Invite the children to thank God for these "ordinary blessings" in their night prayers.

People of Faith

Blessed Fra Angelico, 1387–145

Blessed Fra Angelico was an artist who painted pictures of Jesus, Mary, the Saints, and the angels. One of his most famous paintings shows the Angel Gabriel visiting Mary. Fra Angelico was asked by the Pope to decorate a special little chapel in the Vatican. Even today, many people come to see his paintings.

February 18

Discuss: Where do you see pictures of Jesus?

 Learn more about Blessed Fra Angelico at **aliveinchrist.osv.com**

Live Your Faith

Tell What gifts of creation are the people in the picture enjoying?

Color Finish coloring the picture.

Created By God **53**

 ## Catholic Social Teaching

Chapter Connections

To integrate Catholic Social Teaching into your lesson, choose one of the following features: Life and Dignity, pages 284–285; or Care for Creation, page 296–297.

- Start the Live step of the process by talking about Blessed Fra Angelico on page 53. Then move directly to the Catholic Social Teaching feature.
- Or, to expand the lesson, complete both pages 52 and 53, then move to the Catholic Social Teaching feature.
- Return to Chapter 1 for the prayer on page 54.

People of Faith

Tell the children about Blessed Fra Angelico.

- Invite a volunteer to read aloud the People of Faith story.
- Explain that Fra Angelico was born in Italy more than 600 years ago.
- He was a religious painter even before he joined the Dominican Order as a friar and became a famous religious artist.
- He was known to say that he who lives as a follower of Christ should be with Christ. Therefore he never handled a paint brush without prayer.
- During his life, he was known as Fra Giovanni. It was not until after he died that he came to be known as Fra Angelico, the "Angelic Painter."
- *Ask:* Where do you see pictures of Jesus? Possible responses: at home or at church.

 Encourage the children to go to **aliveinchrist.osv.com** at home to learn more about Blessed Fra Angelico.

Activity

Read aloud the directions for the Live Your Faith Activity. Then as a group, discuss the first part of the activity.

- Allow time for the children to color the picture.
- Invite volunteers to share their drawings.

Live

 Let Us Pray

Prayer of Praise

Explain that *praise* means honoring God for his great kindness and love.

Prepare

Teach the children the American Sign Language (ASL) sign for *praise*—point upward then clap hands twice.

- Have the children practice saying their response while doing the sign for praise.

 Rehearse "God Is a Part of My Life," downloaded from **aliveinchrist.osv.com**.

Gather

Invite the children to process to the prayer space. Have each child bring his or her book.

- Have the children sit in a circle and place their open books on their laps.
- Prompt the children to quiet themselves for prayer.

Pray

Follow the order of prayer on the student page.

 Conclude by singing together "God Is a Part of My Life."

 Let Us Pray

Prayer of Praise

Gather and begin with the Sign of the Cross.

Leader: For the sun and the moon way up in the sky,

All: Praise God!

Leader: For flowers that grow, for birds flying by,

All: Praise God!

Leader: For trees and for fruit that is yummy to share,

All: Praise God!

Leader: For children and families who show love and care,

All: Praise God!

Leader: For all the great things God's love made to be,

All: Praise God!

Leader: For all of creation and that includes me,

All: Praise God!

 Sing "God Is a Part of My Life"

 Liturgy Link

Get Ready to Pray

Explain to the children what they should do whenever they pray together during the session.

- Show them where the prayer space is.
- Tell them to move quietly to that area when you indicate that it is time for prayer.
- Show them how to fold their hands when they pray.

 Go to **aliveinchrist.osv.com** for Sunday readings, Scripture background, questions of the week, and seasonal resources.

FAMILY+FAITH
LIVING AND LEARNING TOGETHER

YOUR CHILD LEARNED >>>
This chapter teaches about God's gift of creation and his love for us. He made us to know and love him.

God's Word
 Read **Psalm 139:13–15** to find out how each one of us is special to God.

Catholics Believe
- God created everything. All that he made is good.
- God knows and loves everyone.

To learn more, go to the *Catechism of the Catholic Church* #295, 299 at **usccb.org.**

People of Faith
This week, your child met Blessed Fra Angelico. He was an innovative painter who used his gifts and talents to honor God.

CHILDREN AT THIS AGE >>>
How They Understand Our Creation by God Many first graders have not yet asked themselves how they came to be. They know from photos and stories that they used to be babies, but it is difficult for them to picture a time that they did not exist. For this reason, when they are taught that God made them, they might accept this idea without much thought. As they grow and learn more about how new life comes about, they will integrate this information through an understanding that people, like their parents, cooperate with God to bring new life into the world.

CONSIDER THIS >>>
Can you ever completely know someone?

No matter how long we know someone it would be foolish to say we know that person completely. God creates each of us with the capacity to know him. When we open our hearts we come to know him in many ways. "In the encounter of God with Moses, God reveals himself as 'I AM WHO I AM.' These words reveal... God...as the source of all that is, but who he is will be revealed still further as he continues his loving work for his people" (*USCCA, p. 13*).

LET'S TALK >>>
- Ask your child to name who made everything in creation.
- Share with your child your favorite part of God's creation.

LET'S PRAY >>>
Dear God, you show us your love when you make beautiful things. Help me to always love you, as Blessed Fra Angelico did. Amen.

 For a multimedia glossary of Catholic Faith Words, Sunday readings, seasonal and Saint resources, and chapter activities go to **aliveinchrist.osv.com.**

Alive in Christ, Grade 1 Chapter 1   **55**

Chapter 1 Review

A **Work with Words** Trace the letters to tell about God's gifts.

1. God made *Adam*

and Eve.

2. God created *everything*.

3. God loves *me*!

B **Check Understanding** Circle the word that finishes the sentence.

4. God is our _____.

(Creator)   pet

Draw your face in the circle. On the line, trace who made you.

5.

6. *God*

 Go to **aliveinchrist.osv.com** for an interactive review.

56 Chapter 1 Review

Family + Faith

Distribute the page to the children or parents/adult family members. Point out the chapter highlights, insights on how first graders understand concepts, the opportunity for the adults to reflect on their own experience and faith journey, and the family prayer.

Chapter Review

Use Catechist Quick Reviews to highlight lesson concepts.

A **Work with Words** Have the children trace the letters to tell about God's gifts.

B **Check Understanding** Have the children circle, draw, and trace to complete each activity.

 Go to **aliveinchrist.osv.com** to prepare customized and downloadable assessments, send eAssessments, and assign interactive reviews.

Created By God   **55–56**

KEY CONCEPT

God's world is a gift to you. You can learn about God and his love by looking at the world he made.

DOCTRINAL CONTENT

- God created the world to show his love. (CCC, 293–294)
- All creation is God's gift to us, and his Son, Jesus, is his greatest gift. (CCC, 299, 312)
- People use God's gifts in the world to make things we need. (CCC, 2402)
- Thanksgiving is showing God we are grateful for all that he's given us. (CCC, 2637)

TASKS OF CATECHESIS

Helping children grow in a faith that is "known, celebrated, lived, and expressed in prayer" (NDC, 20).

This chapter focuses on the following tasks of catechesis:

- Promoting Knowledge of the Faith
- Teaching to Pray

Catechist Background

 God made every kind of wild animal, every kind of tame animal, and every kind of thing that crawls on the ground. God saw that it was good. Genesis 1:25

➜ **Reflect** How did God create such a diverse universe?

Genesis actually begins with two creation accounts. The first creation account (Genesis 1:1–2:4) represents the creation of humanity as the climax of all God's works. According to the second creation account, the first man was created before all the plants and animals, which God subsequently produced for his sustenance, comfort, and delight (Genesis 2:4–25). Common to both stories is the idea that all the other wonders of creation are gifts from God to humanity, gifts that humans have a responsibility to cherish.

Belief in the goodness of creation was one of the most important convictions that the people of ancient Israel bequeathed to the Catholic Church. The Church has defended this doctrine against false teachers who claimed that the physical world was intrinsically evil. Gratitude for creation is a central theme of all Christian prayer. The Seven Sacraments that Christ instituted in his Church employ the good things of the Earth—water, wine, oil, and grain—to bring about human salvation.

When you are working or taking care of children, you may easily overlook the glories of creation. Yet God bestows new gifts on us every day.

➜ **Reflect** Where have you seen the Creator's glory today?

Catechist's Prayer

God our Father and Creator, the world abounds with your wonders. I thank you for the colors, aromas, textures, and tastes that enrich my life. Amen.

Lesson Plan

Objectives	Process	Materials

🕐 Invite, 10 minutes

God's Gifts for Us Page 57

- 💗 **Psalm 8:2** Pray the opening prayer.
- 📖 **Genesis 1:11–31** Reflect prayerfully on the Word.
- Discuss What Do You Wonder questions.

🌐 **Optional Activity** Chapter Poem: "Spring Is Here"

🕐 Discover, 35 minutes

Gifts from God Pages 58–59
- Discover that God created the world to show his love
- Appreciate that all of creation is God's gift to us, and his Son, Jesus, is his greatest gift

- **Catholic Faith Words** Jesus, praise
- Explain that God gives people the world.
- 📖 **Genesis 1:6–25** Proclaim "The Story of Creation."
- Recall that the world is God's gift and everything in it is good.
- **Share Your Faith Activity** Name God's gifts to bring next time.

☐ pencils
☐ index cards
☐ crayons or markers

Made to Help Us Pages 60–61
- Describe ways that people use God's gifts in the world to make things we need
- Understand that thanksgiving is showing God we are grateful for all that he's given us

- **Catholic Faith Words** thanksgiving
- Explain that God gave us everything we need to be happy.
- ☆ Write how God's gift of people helps the world.
- Explain how to show God we are grateful for all he's given us.
- **Connect Your Faith Activity** Solve a message for God.

☐ pencils
☐ index cards
☐ crayons or markers
- **Optional Activity** Gifts from God
☐ Activity Master 2 (Page 57E)

🕐 Live, 15 minutes

Our Catholic Life Pages 62–63

- Explain that God gave people gifts to use.
- **People of Faith** Learn about Saint Nicholas.
- **Live Your Faith Activity** Identify where to say thank you to God this week.

☐ pencils
☐ crayons or markers

Prayer of Thanksgiving Page 64

- Teach ASL for *thank you*.
- ▶ Rehearse "And It Was Good."
- Follow the order of prayer.

🌐 Download "And It Was Good."

Family + Faith Page 65
Point out that the Catholic Families page provides chapter highlights, information on how first graders understand faith concepts, and family prayer.

Chapter Review Page 66
🌐 **aliveinchrist.osv.com**
- Customize and Download Assessments
- Email Links to eAssessments
- Interactive Student Reviews

Teaching This Grade

ONLINE RESOURCES

 Go to **aliveinchrist.osv.com**

You will find:

- Interactive lesson planning with web specific content and additional activities
- Step by step lesson instruction from printed Catechist Edition for integrated lesson planning
- Custom-built assessments to download and eAssessment links
- Interactive reviews that provide scores and the option to review answers
- Sunday readings with background and questions of the week

 Go to **osvparish.com**

You will find:

- Ask the Experts Q and A
- General Catechist Helps
- Community Connections and Blogs

Sharing the Message with First Graders

God's Creation First graders are very concrete thinkers – they know and understand the things they perceive with their senses. For this reason, many children understand God in the context of what he has made. Knowing that God made the trees, flowers, animals, oceans, people and everything in the world teaches them that God is very big and powerful. God's identity is still a mystery for them, but Creation becomes for them the "evidence" that God is real.

Teaching Tip: Make your study of God's creation as concrete as possible. If it's practical to do so, teach a portion of this session outside so you can look around and observe things God has made. If not, be sure to have lots of photos that provide rich visuals of God's creation.

How First Graders Understand

- Lead the children to discover that they are surrounded by gifts from God—in the sky, in the water, on the Earth.
- Praise helps first graders learn what is expected of them. Be generous in your praise.
- First graders like using their whole body—eyes, ears, nose, mouth, and hands—to learn.

"I like to explore God's world. Help me to appreciate what I find."

Chapter Poem

"Spring Is Here"

Use this poem to expand the chapter introduction.

- The children will relate the poem to their own lives, reflecting on God's creation of all things.
- Connect how we learn about God to the diversity of his creation.

 Go to **aliveinchrist.osv.com** Lesson Planning section for this poem.

NCEA IFG: ACRE Edition

Knowledge of the Faith

- Objective: To know and understand God's activity in human history

Prayer

- Objective: To recognize and learn how to engage in Catholic forms of personal and communal prayer and ways of deepening one's spiritual life

Catholic Social Teaching

 Use one of these features to introduce a principle and engage the children with an activity.

- The Dignity of Work, Pages 292–293
- Care for Creation, Pages 296–297

Music Options

 Use the following song to enhance catechetical learning or for prayer.

- "And It Was Good," Live Prayer, Page 64

LECTIONARY CONNECTION

 Chapter 2 highlights Lectionary-connected themes such as stewardship, God's love, and the Kingdom of God. If your parish aligns its curriculum to the liturgical year, you could use this chapter in connection with the following Sundays.

Year A

Third Sunday of Advent—prophecy

First Sunday of Lent—God's chosen

Most Holy Body and Blood of Christ—Eucharist, Real Presence

Year B

Epiphany of the Lord—salvation, Christ the light, mission

Thirty-first Sunday in Ordinary Time—love God and neighbor

Thirty-second Sunday in Ordinary Time—stewardship, Paschal Mystery

Our Lord Jesus Christ, King of the Universe—Kingdom of God

Year C

Epiphany of the Lord—Christ the light, mission

Sixth Sunday of Easter—peace

Twenty-fourth Sunday in Ordinary Time—reconciliation, God's love

Go to **aliveinchrist.osv.com** for a complete correlation ordered by the Sundays of the year and suggestions for how to integrate the Scripture readings into chapter lessons.

Name _____ Date _____

Gifts from God

God gives us a world full of gifts. Circle the hidden food and animals that are gifts from God.

Word Bank

feather
duck
loaf of bread
cat
snake
rabbit
crab
bird
apple
frog
octopus
cow
carrot
turtle
flower

God's Gifts for Us

 Let Us Pray

Leader: God, we thank you for all the wonderful gifts you give to us.

"O LORD our Lord,
how awesome is your name through
all the earth!" Psalm 8:2

All: Help us to see all your gifts. Amen.

 God's Word

God created all the plants and flowers, all the animals that walk on the earth, fly in the sky, and swim in the waters. He said, "I created all kinds of food for you to eat." And God was pleased with what he saw.

Based on Genesis 1:11–31

? What Do You Wonder?

- How did God think of all the things he made?
- Why did God make bugs?

God's Gifts for Us **57**

© Our Sunday Visitor

Optional Activity

Chapter Poem: "Spring Is Here" *Verbal/Linguistic*

Use this poem after the opening prayer, before explaining that God created the entire universe and everything in it.

- Read the poem aloud as the children follow along.
- Invite the children to act out the poem as you read it again.
- *Ask:* What is one thing you like about spring?
- After summarizing that there are so many things to love in creation, transition back to the lesson instruction.

 Go to **aliveinchrist.osv.com** for Chapter Poem.

 Let Us Pray

Invite the children to gather in the prayer space and make the Sign of the Cross. Invite a child to be the leader. Read aloud the Psalm verse from a Bible. Prompt the children's response.

Have the children move out of the prayer space and back to their seats.

Explain that God created the entire universe and everything in it.

Say: God has created so many wonderful gifts for us to enjoy. Let's listen to a reading from the Book of Genesis.

 God's Word

Guide the children through the process of Scripture reflection.

- Invite them to close their eyes, be still and open their minds and hearts to what God is saying to them in this passage.
- Proclaim the Scripture.
- Maintain several moments of silence.
- *Ask:* What did you hear God say to you today?
- Invite volunteers to share.

What Do You Wonder?

Say: God gives us many different kinds of gifts for us to see and to enjoy as well as to give us life.

Invite the children to respond to the questions. Ask what else they might wonder about God's creation and how he thought of so many different things.

Discover

Objectives

- Discover that God created the world to show his love
- Appreciate that all of creation is God's gift to us, and his Son, Jesus, is his greatest gift

Gifts from God

Ask: What gifts has God given to us?

- Write the children's responses on the board or on chart paper.

Read aloud the text on the student page.

Draw the graphic organizer on the board or on chart paper.

- *Ask:* What are some of the gifts in God's world?
- As the children answer, write their responses on the board or chart paper and draw a line connecting it to the world.
- Share that God gives us the gift of the world and all that is good in it.

Work with Words

Using an index card, introduce the words *Jesus* and *praise*.

⭐ Point out the directions to the activity and read them aloud. Have the children work independently to complete the activity. When they have finished, invite them to share with a partner.

Gifts from God

What gifts has God given to us?

God gives you a very, very big gift.

Stretch your arms wide. God's gift is bigger than that!

God's gift is too big to wrap. It is so big that no ribbon can be tied around it.

God gives you the world. He filled the world with many gifts! And his greatest gift is his Son, **Jesus**.

We **praise** God for these gifts.

Catholic Faith Words

Jesus the name of the Son of God who became man

praise giving God honor and thanks because he is God

⭐ Circle some of your favorite gifts in God's world.

58 Chapter 2

✓ Quick Tip

Graphic Organizer

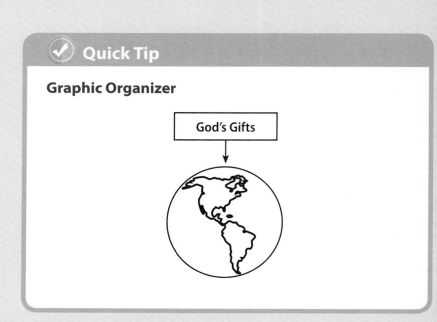

God Made the World

God made many good things. Before God made Adam and Eve, he made the world. He made the world to show his love.

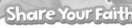 God's Word

The Story of Creation

Long ago, God made the sky, the earth and the seas. But the earth was empty. There were no trees to climb. No flowers swayed in the breeze. No birds to fly in the air.

So the Lord God created a beautiful world. God said: "Let the earth bring forth every kind of living creature: tame animals, crawling things, and every kind of wild animal." Then, birds flew in the sky. Many animals lived on the earth. And fish and whales swam in the seas. God saw that it was good. **Based on Genesis 1:6–25**

Share Your Faith

Think What are some of God's gifts that you would like to bring to your next class?

Share Talk about these gifts in a group.

God's Gifts for Us **59**

Scripture Background

Genesis 1–2:4

The first creation account in the Book of Genesis affirms three vitally important truths.

- God created the Earth and everything in it.
- The world that God created was both orderly and good.
- God created man and woman to be the stewards of his creation and to care for all living things.

God Made the World

Gather the children around you.

Summarize the paragraph to prepare them for the Scripture story they are going to hear.

God's Word

Proclaim "The Story of Creation."

- Read the story a second time, asking the children to raise their hands every time they hear the name of one of God's gifts.
- Tell the children you are going to play a game with them. Tell them that you will point to your eyes, ears, or hands. They should think of something good they can experience in God's world through that sense. For example, as you point to your eyes, a child may say: "clouds."
- Emphasize that the whole world and everything in it is God's gift to us.

Activity

Read aloud the directions for the Share Your Faith activity.

- Organize the children into small groups.
- Tell them they can bring in either a "gift" or a picture of it to the next session.

Quick Review

The whole world and everything in it is God's gift to us.

Discover

Objectives

- Describe ways that people use God's gifts in the world to make things we need
- Understand that thanksgiving is showing God we are grateful for all that he's given us

Made to Help Us

Ask: How do God's gifts help us?

- Write the children's responses on the board or on chart paper.

Read aloud the paragraphs.

- Emphasize that God gave us everything we need to live and be happy.
- Explain that we use these gifts to make things we need, like homes and food.

God's Gifts Help the World

⭐ Read aloud the directions to the activity.

- Read the chart aloud together.
- *Ask:* How do people help us live and be happy? Possible responses: People care for creation, animals, plants, water, air, and people.
- Remind the children that God gives us people to love and care for us and to be our friends.

Discover

Made to Help Us

How do God's gifts help us?

God made people to love. We can learn something about God's love for us by the things he made. He gives us what we need to live and be happy.

We use God's gifts to make other things we need. Wood for houses comes from trees. Food is made from animals or plants.

Trace the words that tell how God's gift of people helps the world.

God's Gifts Help the World

God's Gift	How It Helps
🌙	gives light at night
🌳	we make paper from it
☀️	makes the day bright
👦	we love

Optional Activity

Activity Master 2: Gifts from God

Distribute copies of the activity found on catechist page 57E.

- Tell the children to circle the hidden food and animals.
- As an alternative, you may wish to send this activity home with the children.

Thank God

Everything around you is a gift from God. We can show God we are grateful for all he's given us. We call this **thanksgiving**.

- We can pray to show God thanks.
- We can remember that all we have comes from God.
- We take care of and share these gifts.
- We can tell our family and friends thank you for the things they do.

Catholic Faith Words

thanksgiving giving thanks to God for all he has given us

Connect Your Faith

Give Thanks Color the x's blue and the o's green to tell God something special.

Thank God

Read aloud the first paragraph.

Work with Words

Introduce the word *thanksgiving* using an index card.

Read through the list of ways we can tell God thank you. Pause after each one and affirm the children for how they are already telling God thank you.

- Refer the children to page 319 in the Our Catholic Tradition reference section in the back of the Student Book for Grace After Meals as an example of a prayer of thanksgiving.

Activity

Point out the Connect Your Faith activity.

- Read aloud the directions to the activity.
- When everyone has completed the puzzle, invite the children to quietly say thank you to God.

Quick Review

God gave humans the gifts of creation to both use and care for. People give thanks and praise to God for his wonderful gifts.

✓ Quick Tip

God's Gifts

Children enjoy activities that help illustrate a lesson while allowing them to participate.

- To help them understand the concept of God's intangible gifts, bring a large bow to class.
- Allow each child a turn to place the bow on his or her head while stating one reason why he or she is a gift from God.

Our Catholic Life

Ask: How do people use the things God made?

- Write the children's responses on the board or on chart paper.

Read aloud the first paragraph.

- *Ask:* How do God's gifts help us? Answers may include we use trees to build homes, we use people to care for us, we use plants and animals for food.

- Read the second paragraph aloud. Then read the caption under each picture as the children follow along.

- Pause after each caption to make sure the children understand the sequence of changing natural substances into prepared food.

- *Ask:* What other things can you make from God's gifts?

- Write the children's responses on the board or on chart paper.

- Summarize by pointing out all the wonderful things we can make from God's gifts of creation.

Live

Our Catholic Life

How do people use the things God made?

God gave people many gifts to use. People use God's gifts to make other things they need.

You can use God's gifts to make the food you eat.

Pancake mix is made from flour.

Milk comes from a cow.

Eggs come from a chicken.

All together they make yummy pancakes!

62   Chapter 2

✓ Quick Tip

Giving Thanks

Remind the children that they give thanks for God's gifts that are made into food when they pray grace, or the blessing before meals.

- Teach or review with the children a favorite meal blessing.
- Remind the children that they can thank God by saying grace at family meals or even silently before any meal.

People of Faith

Saint Nicholas, 270–310

Saint Nicholas was a bishop. One night he went to the house of a poor family and threw a bag of gold coins in an open window. The family wanted to thank Nicholas, but he told them to thank God instead. Nicholas liked giving gifts in secret. People still give gifts on his feast day. Saint Nicholas is the patron Saint of children.

December 6

Discuss: What gift can you give to your family and friends today?

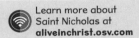 Learn more about Saint Nicholas at **aliveinchrist.osv.com**

Live Your Faith

Thank You God Color the places where you can say thank you to God this week for giving us so many gifts.

God's Gifts for Us **63**

People of Faith

Tell the children about Saint Nicholas.

- Invite a volunteer to read aloud the People of Faith story.

- Explain that Saint Nicholas lived a long time ago, nearly two thousand years ago.

- He was a very kind and generous bishop who especially loved children.

- Most of the time he gave gifts in secret, wanting no thanks or acknowledgment.

- On his feast day, many children still put their shoes out in hopes that Saint Nicholas will leave a treat.

- *Ask:* What gifts can you give to your family and friends today? Answers may include love, friendship, help, or care.

 Encourage the children to go to **aliveinchrist.osv.com** at home to learn more about Saint Nicholas.

Activity

Read aloud the directions for the Live Your Faith activity.

- Talk through the activity together.
- Have the children complete the activity on their own.

Catholic Social Teaching

Chapter Connections

To integrate Catholic Social Teaching into your lesson, choose one of the following features: The Dignity of Work, pages 292–293; or Care for Creation, pages 296–297.

- Start the Live step of the process by talking about Saint Nicholas on page 63. Then move directly to the Catholic Social Teaching feature.

- Or, to expand the lesson, complete both pages 62 and 63, then move to the Catholic Social Teaching feature.

- Return to Chapter 2 for the prayer on page 64.

Live

Live

  Let Us Pray

Prayer of Thanksgiving

Explain to the children that in their prayer today they will be thanking God for all his many gifts to us.

Prepare

Teach the children the American Sign Language (ASL) sign for *thank you*—move right hand from chin out. Or you can choose another gesture.

 Rehearse "And It Was Good," downloaded from **aliveinchrist.osv.com**.

Gather

Gather the children in the prayer space.

- Invite them to quiet themselves for prayer.

Pray

- Begin by leading the children in the Sign of the Cross.
- Follow the order of prayer on the student page.
- Have the children sign *thank you* each time they say the words.

 Conclude by singing together "And It Was Good."

 Let Us Pray

Prayer of Thanksgiving

Gather and begin with the Sign of the Cross.

Leader: Let us give thanks to God for all his gifts.

All: For your gift of the Earth,
Thank you, God.

For your gift of plants and trees,
Thank you, God.

For your gift of animals, Thank you, God.

For your gift of food, Thank you, God.

For your gift of people, Thank you, God.

For your gift of me, Thank you, God.

For your whole-wide-world of gifts,
Thank you, God.

Sing "And It Was Good"

And it was good, good, very, very good,
and it was good, good, very, very good,
and it was good, good, very, very good,
it was very, very, very good.

 Liturgy Link

Music and Prayer

Whenever possible, have the children sing the song or refrain suggested in the prayer for each chapter.

- Children of this age love to sing.
- You will help them discover the Church's treasury of sung prayer.
- You will help build the habit of active liturgical participation.

Go to **aliveinchrist.osv.com** for Sunday readings, Scripture background, questions of the week, and seasonal resources.

FAMILY+FAITH
LIVING AND LEARNING TOGETHER

YOUR CHILD LEARNED >>>

This chapter explores how God gives us what we need to live and be happy. We can thank God for his gifts in many ways.

God's Word

Read **Genesis 1:11–31** to find out about the many gifts God created for us to enjoy

Catholics Believe

- God's world is a gift to you.
- You can learn about God and his love by looking at the world he made.

To learn more, go to the *Catechism of the Catholic Church* #315, 319 at usccb.org.

People of Faith

This week, your child met Saint Nicholas. Saint Nicholas spent his life helping the needy and is the model for our Santa Claus.

CHILDREN AT THIS AGE >>>

How They Understand God's Creation First graders are very concrete thinkers—they know and understand the things they perceive with their senses. For this reason, many children understand God in the context of what he has made. Knowing that God made the trees, flowers, animals, oceans, people, and everything in the world teaches them that God is very big and powerful. God's identity is still a mystery for them, but creation becomes for them the "evidence" that God is real.

CONSIDER THIS >>>

Have you ever had the feeling that someone should be thanked?

There are moments of awe in everyone's life that break through the "ordinary." At these moments we have a sense of the transcendent. "Augustine tells us that God spoke with a vigorous voice. 'You called, you shouted, and you broke through my deafness. You breathed your fragrance on me.... I have tasted you, now I hunger and thirst for more' (The Confessions, bk. 10, no. 27)" (USCCA, p. 346).

LET'S TALK >>>

- Ask your child to name one way we use some of the things God made.
- Talk about a time you were really thankful for God's action in your life. What are some ways people in your family show they are thankful?

LET'S PRAY >>>

Saint Nicholas, help us give generously to the poor like you did. Amen.

For a multimedia glossary of Catholic Faith Words, Sunday readings, seasonal and Saint resources, and chapter activities go to aliveinchrist.osv.com.

Alive in Christ, Grade 1 Chapter 2 **65**

Chapter 2 Review

A **Work with Words** Fill in the circle beside the correct answer.

1. Showing God you are grateful for what he has given us is called ____.

   ● thanksgiving   ○ happiness

2. God created the world to ____.

   ○ do some work   ● show his love

3. The name of the Son of God who became man is ____.

   ● Jesus   ○ John

4. Giving God honor and thanks because he is good is called ____.

   ○ prayer   ● praise

B **Check Understanding** Draw one thing that God created.

5.

Go to aliveinchrist.osv.com for an interactive review.

66 Chapter 2 Review

Family + Faith

Distribute the page to the children or parents/adult family members. Point out the chapter highlights, insights on how first graders understand concepts, the opportunity for the adults to reflect on their own experience and faith journey, and the family prayer.

Chapter Review

Use Catechist Quick Reviews to highlight lesson concepts.

A **Work with Words** Have the children fill in the circle beside the correct answer.

B **Check Understanding** Have the children draw one thing that God created.

 Go to **aliveinchrist.osv.com** to prepare customized and downloadable assessments, send eAssessments, and assign interactive reviews.

God's Gifts for Us **65–66**

Chapter 3 Made to Care

KEY CONCEPT

All creation is a gift from God. Humans are the most special part of creation. Everyone must help care for God's gifts.

DOCTRINAL CONTENT

- The image of God is the likeness of God that is in all human beings because we are created by him. (CCC, 357)
- Humans are the most special part of creation. God gave us the ability to think and make choices. (CCC, 356)
- God gave Adam and Eve the responsibility to be caretakers of his creation. (CCC, 373)
- Each of us is responsible for treating all of creation with care and respect. (CCC, 2415)

TASKS OF CATECHESIS

Helping children grow in a faith that is "known, celebrated, lived, and expressed in prayer" (NDC, 20).

This chapter focuses on the following tasks of catechesis:

- Promoting Knowledge of the Faith
- Education for Community Life

Catechist Background

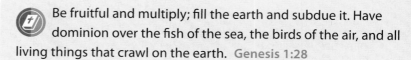 Be fruitful and multiply; fill the earth and subdue it. Have dominion over the fish of the sea, the birds of the air, and all living things that crawl on the earth. Genesis 1:28

➜ **Reflect** How do you care for God's creation?

In the first creation account in the Book of Genesis, God created every living thing and then entrusted all to the care of humans. Only after he had given care of the Earth over to the man and the woman was he able to rest "from all the work he had done in creation" (Genesis 2:3). God gives humans the responsibility and stewardship of his creation.

Called to share in God's power, humans have the ability and responsibility to care for other creatures. Yet, many continue to turn their backs on this responsibility. The repercussions on the rest of creation have been tremendous. The Earth is suffering in many ways today because of human callousness.

As a steward of creation it is important that you take the time to enjoy creation and pass on to future generations this respect for what God has given you. Lead by example. Teach respect by taking time to praise God for the food on the table. Be respectful of the neighbors' garden and lawn. Pick up the paper that litters sidewalks and streets. Take a long walk or hike on a Sunday afternoon. Praise God for flowers, trees, and plants. Show love for him by loving the Earth. Take care of creation as Jesus himself would do.

➜ **Reflect** As a steward of God's creation, what can you do to fulfill your responsibility right now?

Catechist's Prayer

Help me care for the world, O Lord. May I work to repair the damage already done and work to protect that which can be saved. Help me teach the children to be caretakers of your creation. Amen.

Objectives	Process	Materials
Invite, 10 minutes		
Made to Care Page 67	○ Psalm 150:6 Pray the opening prayer. ○ Genesis 1:27–31 Reflect prayerfully on the Word. • Discuss What Do You Wonder questions.	**Optional Activity** Chapter Story: "Sam's Fish"
Discover, 35 minutes		
In God's Image Pages 68–69 • Define image of God as the likeness of God that is in all humans because we are all created by him • Recognize that with the ability to think and make choices, humans are the most special part of creation	• **Catholic Faith Words** image of God • Explain that people were made to be like God. • Explain that people are the most special part of creation. ☆ Underline two gifts that are inside each person. • **Share Your Faith Activity** Draw signs of God's love.	☐ pencils ☐ index cards ☐ crayons or markers • **Optional Activity** Play "What Is It?"
God's Command Pages 70–71 • Understand that God gave Adam and Eve the responsibility to be caretakers of his creation • Appreciate that each of us is responsible for treating all of creation with care and respect	• Explain that God tells humans how to show him love and thanks for creation. ○ Genesis 1:26–30 Proclaim "Take Care of What I've Given You." ☆ Circle what God asked Adam and Eve to do. • Explain that caring for living things shows love for God. • **Connect Your Faith Activity** Complete the sentences.	☐ pencils • **Optional Activity** Be a Caretaker ☐ Activity Master 3 (Page 67E)
Live, 15 minutes		
Our Catholic Life Pages 72–73	• Explain that God wants people to take care of themselves. ☆ Check the things they like best. • **People of Faith** Learn about Saint Albert the Great. • **Live Your Faith Activity** Students will name one way to take care of themselves.	☐ pencils
Prayer of Praise and Thanks Page 74	• Assign lines to small groups. ▶ Rehearse "All Things Bright and Beautiful." • Follow the order of prayer.	Download "All Things Bright and Beautiful."

Family + Faith Page 75
Point out that the Catholic Families page provides chapter highlights, information on how first graders understand faith concepts, and family prayer.

Chapter Review Page 76
aliveinchrist.osv.com
• Customize and Download Assessments
• Email Links to eAssessments
• Interactive Student Reviews

ONLINE RESOURCES

 Go to **aliveinchrist.osv.com**

You will find:

- Interactive lesson planning with web specific content and additional activities
- Step by step lesson instruction from printed Catechist Edition for integrated lesson planning
- Custom-built assessments to download and eAssessment links
- Interactive reviews that provide scores and the option to review answers
- Sunday readings with background and questions of the week

 Go to **osvparish.com**

You will find:

- Ask the Experts Q and A
- General Catechist Helps
- Community Connections and Blogs

Sharing the Message with First Graders

Stewards of God's Creation At the beginning of the school year, many first graders are still in what developmental theorist Jean Piaget described as the "egocentric" stage of development—the time in which they see the world as revolving around them and have difficulty seeing things from the perspective of others. Consequently, they have no difficulty grasping the idea that God made the world for them and that they have some responsibility in caring for what God has given. They may need help, though, to discover practical ways in which they can be good stewards of God's creation.

Teaching Tip: Practice good stewardship of God's creation throughout the year by recycling in your teaching space.

How First Graders Understand

- First graders are beginning to see themselves as part of the world.
- First graders are capable of practicing caring deeds and interactions.
- Connect the theological concepts of the lesson to the children's experience. Most young children naturally delight in the wonders of nature and have an innate attraction to living creatures.

"I need you to affirm and confirm my caring behavior."

Chapter Story

"Sam's Fish"

Use this story to expand the chapter introduction.

- The children will relate the story to their own lives, reflecting on what living thing they take care of.
- Connect how we learn about God to caring for living things.

 Go to **aliveinchrist.osv.com** Lesson Planning section for this story.

NCEA IFG: ACRE Edition

Knowledge of the Faith

- Objective: To know and understand God's activity in human history

Communal Life

- Objective: To know the rights and responsibilities of the Christian faithful

Catholic Social Teaching

 Use one of these features to introduce a principle and engage the children with an activity.

- Life and Dignity, Pages 284–285
- Care for Creation, Pages 296–297

Music Options

 Use one or more of the following songs to enhance catechetical learning or for prayer.

- "All Things Bright and Beautiful," Live Prayer, Page 74
- "Thank You," Discover, Page 71

LECTIONARY CONNECTION

Chapter 3 highlights Lectionary-connected themes such as creation, stewardship, and love for God and neighbor. If your parish aligns its curriculum to the liturgical year, you could use this chapter in connection with the following Sundays.

Year A

Third Sunday of Advent—prophecy

Twenty-ninth Sunday in Ordinary Time—First Commandment, love, neighbor

Year B

First Sunday of Lent—Baptism, Holy Trinity

Thirty-first Sunday in Ordinary Time—love God and neighbor

Thirty-second Sunday in Ordinary Time—stewardship, Paschal Mystery

Year C

Fourth Sunday of Easter—divinity of Christ, Holy Trinity

Twenty-fifth Sunday in Ordinary Time—social justice, dignity of persons, justice

Go to **aliveinchrist.osv.com** for a complete correlation ordered by the Sundays of the year and suggestions for how to integrate the Scripture readings into chapter lessons.

Name _____ Date _____

Be a Caretaker

Color the parts. Then cut them out.
Cut the dotted line in the pot to make a slit.
Tape a straw to the back of the flower.
Pull the flower through the slit and
watch the flower grow.

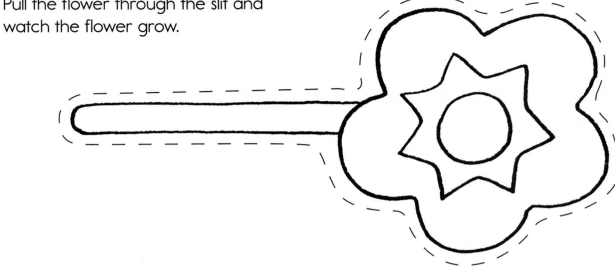

Be a caretaker.

Made to Care

 Let Us Pray

Leader: God, thank you for teaching us how to care for all of creation.

"Let everything that has breath give praise to the LORD!" Psalm 150:6

All: Help us care for the things you have made. Amen.

God's Word

God created human beings and said: "I am putting you in charge to care for all that I created." God looked at everything that he had made, and he found it very good.
Based on Genesis 1:27–31

? What Do You Wonder?

- How can you take care of God's creation?
- Why does God want people to care for what he made?

Made to Care **67**

Optional Activity

Chapter Story: "Sam's Fish" *Verbal/Linguistic*

Use this story after the opening prayer, before explaining that God's gifts are all around them.

- Read aloud "Sam's Fish." Ask the children to search the page for the word *care* and have them circle it.
- *Ask:* What living things do you take care of? Answers may include a pet, a plant or a family member.
- After the discussion, transition back to the lesson instruction.

 Go to **aliveinchrist.osv.com** for Chapter Story.

Invite

Let Us Pray

Invite the children to gather in the prayer space and make the Sign of the Cross. Invite a child to read aloud the Psalm verse from a Bible. Prompt the children's response.

Have the children move out of the prayer space and back to their seats.

Explain to the children that God's gifts are all around them.

Say: God has created so many wonderful gifts for us to enjoy. Now, let's hear who God put in charge to take care of his creation.

God's Word

Guide the children through the process of Scripture reflection.

- Invite them to close their eyes, be still and open their minds and hearts to what God is saying to them in this passage.
- Proclaim the Scripture.
- Maintain several moments of silence.
- *Ask:* What did you hear God say to you today?
- Invite volunteers to share.

What Do You Wonder?

Say: God asks us to take care of everyone and everything that was created.

Invite the children to respond to the questions. Ask what else they might wonder about God's creation and how we can take care of everything God made.

Objectives

- Define image of God as the likeness of God that is in all humans because we are all created by him

- Recognize that with the ability to think and make choices, humans are the most special part of creation

In God's Image

Ask: How are you a part of God's creation?

- Write the children's responses on the board or on chart paper.

Read aloud the paragraph.

Work with Words

Hold up an index card with the term *image of God* written on it.

- Explain that the term *image of God* means that people are made to be like God.

How Are You Special?

Ask the children to discover what Josh made.

- Read aloud the story.
- Ask the children what Josh made.
- Have a few volunteers tell what people can do that cookies cannot do.
- Ask the children what they liked about the story.

Discover

In God's Image

How are you a part of God's creation?

God made people in his image, to be like him. Find out how we are special parts of creation.

How Are You Special?

Josh and his mother were making cookies. Josh held up a piece of dough. "First I want to make a head, then the arms and body…the legs are last. Look! I made a person! He is just like me!"

Josh's mother laughed. "He does look like you, Josh. But he is not just like you. How are you different?"

Catholic Faith Words

image of God the likeness of God that is in all human beings because we are created by him

© Our Sunday Visitor

68 Chapter 3

✓ Quick Tip

Human Dignity

Reinforce the children's understanding of the dignity of each person by creating an atmosphere of care in your room.

- If there are children with special needs in the group, allow them to participate in all activities to the best of their abilities. Model patience and understanding.
- Encourage the children to work together in groups.

Josh thought for a minute. "I am real. I can think, play, learn at school and pray. I can hug you. And you can't eat me!"

"That's right, Josh," his mother said.

Gifts in Creation

Josh made a cookie that looked like him. But it was not really like him. God made all people in his image. We were all made in the **image of God** to be like him. That makes people the most special part of creation. We are each unique but all share God's image. This is why we respect all people of every age.

Creation is full of gifts from God. Some gifts are part of the world. Other gifts are inside of each person. Being able to think and make choices are two of those gifts.

 Underline two gifts that are inside of each person.

Share Your Faith

Think Draw one thing about yourself that shows you are a sign of God's love.

Share Talk about what you like about this gift.

Gifts in Creation

Read the first paragraph aloud.

- Ask the children why people are the most special part of creation.

Read the second paragraph aloud.

- Invite volunteers to share names of gifts from God in the world.
- *Ask:* How are you a part of God's creation? Answers may include God created me, or I can care for creation.
- Discuss how people should share their gifts from God.
- Direct the children to underline two gifts that are inside each person.

Activity

Read aloud the directions for the Share Your Faith activity.

- Set a time limit for the drawing.
- Have each child share his or her picture with someone who sits nearby.

Quick Review

Creation is everything that God made. God made people to be in his image. People are the most special part of creation.

Optional Activity

Play "What Is It?" *Linguistic/Naturalist*

No materials are needed to play "What Is It?"

- Have the children think of gifts from God that are in the world.
- Select a child to start the game. Have this child describe the item.
- When the item is fully described, invite another child to name the item. A child who correctly names the item would then describe another item, and so on.

© Our Sunday Visitor

Objectives

- Understand that God gave Adam and Eve the responsibility to be caretakers of his creation
- Appreciate that each of us is responsible for treating all of creation with care and respect

God's Command

Ask: What does God ask you to do?

- Write the children's responses on the board or on chart paper.

Read aloud the first paragraph.

- Emphasize that only humans were created to be able to do things like make choices and show love.
- Tell the children that God created us to know his love and share in his work.
- Explain that in the following Scripture story, God tells humans how to show him love and thanks for creation.

 God's Word

Proclaim "Take Care of What I've Given You."

⭐ Direct the children to circle what God asked Adam and Eve to do.

- Invite volunteers to share what they circled.

Point out the stained glass window and read the caption aloud.

- Ask the children to share what they see in the window that they have also seen in nature.

God's Command

What does God ask you to do?

Of all God's creatures, only humans can do things like make choices and show love. God created us to know his love and share in his work. Listen to what God asked Adam and Eve to do.

Circle what God asked Adam and Eve to do.

Everything on Earth is part of God's creation.

 God's Word

Take Care of What I've Given You

God made Adam and Eve to be like him. He said to them, "Have children to fill the earth. Use the earth for what you need. Here are plants with seeds, and animals, and birds. Take care of all that I have given you."

Based on Genesis 1:26–30

© Our Sunday Visitor

 Scripture Background

Genesis 1:26–30

This passage comes at the end of the first creation account in the Book of Genesis.

- The Scripture story affirms that humans are the only creatures that God has made in his own image.
- God tells humans to have children and live on the whole earth.
- Everything else was created for humanity's benefit, but God ordered humans to take good care of it all.

Show Love

God told Adam and Eve to care for his creation. God asks you to be a good caretaker, someone who treats his creation with care and respect. When you care for living things, you show your love for God. Caring is a way to thank God for all that he has given you.

Connect Your Faith

Fill it In Trace the words to complete the sentence that tells what God asked Adam and Eve to do.

Take care of __all__ that I have given __you__.

Share Share your answer with a partner.

Show Love

Read aloud the paragraph.

- *Ask:* How can you show your love for God? I can care for living things.
- *Ask:* How can you thank God for all that he has given you? I can be a caretaker.
- Invite the children to name some habits a good caretaker should have.

 Music Option: Have the children sing, "Thank You," downloaded from **aliveinchrist.osv.com**.

Activity

Point out the Connect Your Faith activity and read the directions aloud.

- Have the children trace the letters to complete the sentence.
- Encourage the children to read their answer to a partner.

Quick Review

God put humans in charge of taking care of his creation.

Optional Activity

Activity Master 3: Be a Caretaker

Distribute copies of the activity on catechist page 67E.

- Tell the children they will make a work of art reminding them to be caretakers.
- As an alternative, you may wish to send the activity home with the children.

Live

Our Catholic Life

Ask: How do you help take care of yourself?

- Write the children's responses on the board or on chart paper.

Read aloud the first paragraph.

- Point to the list you just created. Tell the children that these are some ways that they can help take care of themselves.
- Explain to the children that now they are going to talk about other ways they can help take care of themselves.

Take Care of Yourself

Point out the lists of ways to care for the body and mind.

- Have the children follow along as your read the lists aloud.
- Direct attention to the pictures and ask how the children depicted are taking care of themselves.

⭐ Invite the children to place a check mark next to the things they like to do best.

Ask: What other things can you do to take care of yourself? Answers may include read books, dance, play sports, play a musical instrument, and learn a new language

---

Live

Our Catholic Life

How do you help take care of yourself?

You are one of God's greatest gifts! He made your body and your mind. God loves and cares for you very much. He wants you to help take care of yourself.

 Check off the things you like to do best.

Take Care of Yourself

Care for Your Body	Care for Your Mind
☐ Eat good foods.	☐ Listen to stories.
☐ Keep your hair, teeth, and body clean.	☐ Do your best in school.
☐ Play and get exercise.	☐ Make something.
☐ Get enough sleep at night.	☐ Learn to do a new thing.

© Our Sunday Visitor

72 Chapter 3

✓ Quick Tip

Honoring the Body

As Catholics, we are rooted in the incarnational theology that respects the body as the temple of the Holy Spirit.

- Encourage the children to show respect for their own health and safety and that of others.
- Remind the children that God calls us to respect bodies of all sizes, shapes, ages, colors, and levels of ability.

People of Faith

Saint Albert the Great, 1206–1280

Saint Albert was a German priest. He was very smart. He liked to learn about God's world. He looked carefully at spider webs. He studied the stars and the way they move. He spent hours looking at plants and watching animals. He even wrote a book on how to take care of falcons! Because of all the things he knew, he was given the title "the Great." Saint Albert loved all creation because it was made by God.

November 15

Discuss: Name one thing you like to look at when you are outside in God's world.

 Learn more about Saint Albert at **aliveinchrist.osv.com**

Live Your Faith

Tell how you use the objects below to take care of yourself?

Name one way you will take care of yourself this week.

Catholic Social Teaching

Chapter Connections

To integrate Catholic Social Teaching into your lesson, choose one of the following features: Life and Dignity, pages 284–285; or Care for Creation, pages 296–297.

- Start the Live step of the process by talking about Saint Albert the Great on page 73. Then move directly to the Catholic Social Teaching feature.
- Or, to expand the lesson, complete both pages 72 and 73, then move to the Catholic Social Teaching feature.
- Return to Chapter 3 for the prayer on page 74.

People of Faith

Tell the children about Saint Albert the Great.

- Invite a volunteer to read aloud the People of Faith story.
- Explain that Saint Albert loved all creation because it was made by God.
- He hiked for miles just to be around nature. People called Saint Albert "the bishop of the boots."
- *Ask:* What is one thing you like to look at when you go outside in God's world?

Point out that the Church uses many things from nature as sacramentals such as water, oil, and beeswax for candles.

- Reference pages 308–309 in the Our Catholic Tradition reference section in the back of the Student Book for more information on some sacramentals.

 Encourage the children to go to **aliveinchrist.osv.com** at home to learn more about Saint Albert the Great.

Activity

As a group, discuss the first part of the Live Your Faith activity.

- Read aloud the directions and brainstorm together responses to the second part of the activity. Write the children's responses on the board or chart paper.
- Invite the children to choose one of the ideas listed and write it in their book.

Live

 Let Us Pray
Prayer of Praise and Thanks

Tell the children that praise is a form of prayer that lets God know we think he's good and wonderful. We thank God for all he has given us.

Prepare

Have the children run their fingers down the page and notice all the times the words *thank you* are used.

- Arrange the children into small groups, and assign each group a line to remember to say. Everyone should say the "thank you" lines together.

 Rehearse "All Things Bright and Beautiful," downloaded from **aliveinchrist.osv.com**.

Gather

If possible, take the children outdoors for prayer.

- Have the members of each small group stand together to say their lines of the prayer on the student page.

Pray

- Begin the prayer with the Sign of the Cross.
- Follow the order of prayer on the student page.

 Conclude by singing together "All Things Bright and Beautiful."

 Live

 Let Us Pray
Prayer of Praise and Thanks

Gather and begin with the Sign of the Cross.

Leader: God made a wonderful world!
Give thanks to God for his wonderful world.

All: Thank you, thank you, thank you, God.

Leader: For pets and trees and carrots and peas,
And birds that fly and sing.

All: Thank you, thank you, thank you, God.

Leader: We sing our thanks and praise to you,
Every day and night!

We'll care for all that you have made,
We'll try with all our might!

 All: Sing "All Things Bright and Beautiful"
All things bright and beautiful,
all creatures great and small,
all things wise and wonderful:
the Lord God made them all.
Text based on Ecclesiastes 3:11;
Cecil Frances Alexander. Music by ROYAL OAK.

74 Chapter 3

 Liturgy Link

Making Prayer Expressive

Children will naturally respond to some of the words in this prayer, such as *thanks*, *wonderful*, and *praise*. Encourage them to say those words with expression. Invite them to make vigorous arm movements when they pray "Thank you."

Go to **aliveinchrist.osv.com** for Sunday readings, Scripture background, questions of the week, and seasonal resources.

FAMILY+FAITH
LIVING AND LEARNING TOGETHER

YOUR CHILD LEARNED >>>
This chapter explains what it means to be made in God's image and how people have a special role in taking care of creation.

God's Word
 Read **Genesis 1:27–31** to learn about how God asks us to take care of everyone and everything that was created.

Catholics Believe
- All creation is a gift from God. Humans are the most special part of creation.
- Everyone must help care for God's gifts.

To learn more, go to the *Catechism of the Catholic Church* #374–379 at **usccb.org**.

People of Faith
This week, your child met Saint Albert the Great. Albert was one of the world's first scientists.

CHILDREN AT THIS AGE >>>
How They Understand Being Stewards of God's Creation
At the beginning of the school year, many first graders are still very much in what developmental theorists describe as the "egocentric" stage of development. They see the world as revolving around them and have difficulty seeing things from the perspective of others. Consequently, they have no difficulty grasping the idea that God made the world for them and that they have some responsibility in caring for what God has given them. Your child may need help, though, to discover practical ways in which he or she can be a good steward of God's creation.

CONSIDER THIS >>>
How do children distinguish between what they want and what they really need?

This is a serious challenge when outside factors convince them that they need more than they really do. When Jesus proclaimed the eight Beatitudes he stated that "poverty of spirit would enable us to inherit the Kingdom of God. In other words, the first step on the road to joy begins with a healthy detachment from material goods" (*USCCA, p. 449*). If we want our children to know that joy, we must teach detachment to material goods through our own example.

LET'S TALK >>>
- Ask your child to name one thing people can do that the rest of God's creation cannot.
- Tell your child what makes him or her special to you.

LET'S PRAY >>>
Saint Albert, help us take care of all living things in the world, including the plants, the animals, and the people. Amen.

For a multimedia glossary of Catholic Faith Words, Sunday readings, seasonal and Saint resources, and chapter activities go to **aliveinchrist.osv.com**.

Alive in Christ, Grade 1 Chapter 3   **75**

Family + Faith

Distribute the page to the children or parents/adult family members. Point out the chapter highlights, insights on how first graders understand concepts, the opportunity for the adults to reflect on their own experience and faith journey, and the family prayer.

Chapter 3 Review

A **Work with Words** Look at each picture. Draw a line from the word or words to the picture that explains it.

Column A   Column B

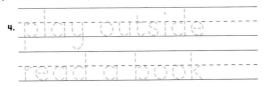

1. Image of God

2. Caretaker

3. Adam and Eve

B **Check Understanding** Trace the words to name one way you can take care of your body and one way you can take care of your mind.

4. play outside
   read a book

 Go to **aliveinchrist.osv.com** for an interactive review.

76   Chapter 3 Review

Chapter Review

Use Catechist Quick Reviews to highlight lesson concepts.

A **Work with Words**
Have the children match the word or words to the picture that explains it.

B **Check Understanding**
Have the children trace the words to name one way to take care of their body and mind.

Go to **aliveinchrist.osv.com** to prepare customized and downloadable assessments, send eAssessments, and assign interactive reviews.

Made to Care   **75–76**

Use Catechist Quick Reviews in each chapter to highlight lesson concepts for this unit and prepare for the Unit Review.

Have the children complete the Review pages. Then discuss the answers as a group. Review any concepts with which the children are having difficulty.

A **Work with Words**
Have the children fill in the circle beside the correct answer.

Unit Review

UNIT
1

A **Work with Words** Fill in the circle beside the correct answer.

1. ____ made the world.
   ● God   ○ You

2. All ____ is a gift from God.
   ○ noise   ● creation

3. The ____ is the Word of God written in human words.
   ● Bible   ○ world

4. God asks ____ to care for his creation.
   ○ animals   ● people

5. All people are made in the image of ____.
   ● God   ○ Adam

Revelation **77**

B Check Understanding Draw a line from each picture to the phrase that best describes it.

Column A   Column B

6.

has stories about God's love

7.

what God created

8.

gifts of creation we use

9.

care for God's creation

C Make Connections Draw a picture of yourself taking care of or using one thing God made.

10.

B Check Understanding
Have the children draw a line to match each picture to the phrase that best describes it.

C Make Connections
Have the children draw a picture of themselves taking care of or using one thing God made.

Go to **aliveinchrist.osv.com** to prepare customized and downloadable assessments, send eAssessments, and assign interactive reviews.

Trinity

Our Catholic Tradition

- The Holy Trinity is one God in three Divine Persons—God the Father, the Son, and the Holy Spirit. (CCC, 234)

- God the Father is the First Divine Person of the Holy Trinity. He loves and takes care of us. (CCC, 239)

- Jesus is the Second Divine Person of the Holy Trinity. He is the Son of God. (CCC, 262)

- The Holy Spirit is the Third Divine Person of the Holy Trinity. He helps us know Jesus and love God the Father. (CCC, 263)

What does the Bible teach us about Jesus?

Unit 2 Overview

Chapter 4
The Holy Trinity
The children will:

- understand that God asks us to be friends with one another, to be nice and help each other when in need
- identify Jesus as the Son of God who shows us the way to his Father
- appreciate that God the Father loves us so much he sent his only Son to be with us
- describe the Holy Trinity as God the Father, God the Son, and God the Holy Spirit, the one God in three Divine Persons

 Catholic Social Teaching: Live Your Faith

- Life and Dignity, Pages 284–285
- Rights and Responsibilities, Pages 288–289

Chapter 5
The Holy Family
The children will:

- identify signs of love expressed in families
- recognize Jesus as the Son of God and a human being
- define the Holy Family as the human family of Jesus, Mary, and Joseph
- appreciate that Jesus grew up with Mary and Joseph in Nazareth, praying in learning

 Songs of Scripture
"The Holy Family"

 Catholic Social Teaching: Live Your Faith

- Life and Dignity, Pages 284–285
- Call to Community, Pages 286–287

Chapter 6
About the Bible
The children will:

- recognize that Jesus told stories like the Lost Sheep to teach us about God's love
- describe a parable as a short story that Jesus told about everyday life to teach something about God
- identify the Bible as the Church's holy book
- name two parts of the Bible as the Old Testament and the New Testament

 **Catholic Social Teaching: Live Your Faith**

- Life and Dignity, Pages 284–285
- Option for the Poor, Pages 290–291

Preview Unit Theme

Ask: What is the unit theme?

Summarize that the unit focuses on the Holy Trinity.

Invite volunteers to read aloud each of the bullets in Our Catholic Tradition.

Explain to the children that they will learn about these things in the next three chapters.

Have the children study the photos and images. Invite volunteers to describe what they see. What do these images say about the unit theme?

Ask: What does the Bible teach us about Jesus?

After some discussion, explain to the children that they will be exploring this question in the next three chapters.

KEY CONCEPT

The Holy Trinity is God the Father, God the Son, and God the Holy Spirit. Jesus is the Son of God, who came to show the Father's love and bring us closer to him.

DOCTRINAL CONTENT

- God asks us to be friends with one another, to be nice and help each other when in need. (CCC, 1822, 1844)

- Jesus is the Son of God who shows us the way to his Father. (CCC, 426, 1698)

- God the Father loves us so much he sent his only Son to be with us. (CCC, 422)

- The Holy Trinity is God the Father, God the Son, and God the Holy Spirit, the one God in three Divine Persons (CCC, 253–254)

TASKS OF CATECHESIS

Helping children grow in a faith that is "known, celebrated, lived, and expressed in prayer" (NDC, 20).

This chapter focuses on the following tasks of catechesis:

- Promoting Knowledge of the Faith

- Education for Community Life

Catechist Background

Jesus said to his disciples: "…Go therefore, and make disciples of all nations, baptizing them in the name of the Father, and of the Son, and of the holy Spirit." Matthew 28:19

➜ **Reflect** Why were you given your name? What does your name mean to you?

The Fatherhood of God is a theme found throughout Scripture. Speaking to Moses, God reveals himself as Father of his Chosen People, and calls Israel his first-born son. (See Exodus 4:22.) Jesus invited his disciples to address God as "Abba," the affectionate Aramaic word for "father." Saint Paul describes how Christians have received a "spirit of adoption" that inspires them to call God by this name. (See Romans 8:15.)

Through his Mother, Jesus Christ belonged to the human family. However, he was God's Son in a unique and privileged sense. He was and is the true and perfect image of his heavenly Father. The works of charity, compassion, and self-sacrifice that he performed on Earth were the works of the Father dwelling in him. For this reason, the life and Death of Jesus are the supreme revelation of the Father's love for humanity. Jesus Christ, God Incarnate, revealed the Father's true nature to humans in a way that no mere prophet or teacher, however wise and good, could have done. Jesus came bearing God the Father's love, and he sends his Church in mission to share this divine love with others.

➜ **Reflect** How can you be God's loving arms for others?

Catechist's Prayer

God the Father, your love for me is greater than that of any parent. Thank you for the gift of all those who helped me grow and taught me about your love. Amen.

Lesson Plan

Objectives	Process	Materials

🕐 Invite, 10 minutes

The Holy Trinity Page 81

- ♥ Psalm 29:2 Pray the opening prayer.
- 📖 Matthew 28:19–20 Reflect prayerfully on the Word.
- Discuss What Do You Wonder questions.

🌐 **Optional Activity**
Chapter Poem: "Nightlight"

🕐 Discover, 35 minutes

Helping Others Pages 82–83
- Understand that God asks us to be friends with one another, to be nice and help each other when in need

- Explain that God wants us to care for others.
- Read "The Lion and the Mouse" and discuss the questions.
- **Share Your Faith Activity** Name what Lion learned.

☐ pencils
- **Optional Activity** Lion and Mouse

God Is Love Pages 84–85
- Identify Jesus as the Son of God who shows us the way to his Father
- Appreciate that God the Father loves us so much he sent his only Son to be with us
- Describe the Holy Trinity as God the Father, God the Son, and God the Holy Spirit, the one God in three Divine Persons

- **Catholic Faith Words** Son of God, God the Father, Holy Trinity
- Explain that God sent Jesus to Earth to show people his love.
- 📖 John 14:8–9 Proclaim "The Way to the Father."
- Explain the Holy Trinity as one God in three Divine Persons.
- **Connect Your Faith Activity** Trace the word *Trinity*.

☐ pencils
☐ index cards
- **Optional Activity** The Holy Trinity
☐ Activity Master 4 (Page 81E)

🕐 Live, 15 minutes

Our Catholic Life Pages 86–87

- Explain that Jesus teaches us about God's love.
- ☆ Circle *Father*, *Son*, and *Holy Spirit* in the text.
- **People of Faith** Learn about Saint Patrick.
- **Live Your Faith Activity** Trace letters to identify each Divine Person of the Holy Trinity.

☐ pencils

Prayer of Praise Page 88

- Practice making the Sign of the Cross with the children.
- ▶ Rehearse "The Sign of the Cross."
- Follow the order of prayer.

🌐 Download "The Sign of the Cross."

Family + Faith Page 89
Point out that the Catholic Families page provides chapter highlights, information on how first graders understand faith concepts, and family prayer.

Chapter Review Page 90
🌐 **aliveinchrist.osv.com**
- Customize and Download Assessments
- Email Links to eAssessments
- Interactive Student Reviews

ONLINE RESOURCES

 Go to **aliveinchrist.osv.com**

You will find:

- Interactive lesson planning with web specific content and additional activities
- Step by step lesson instruction from printed Catechist Edition for integrated lesson planning
- Custom–built assessments to download and eAssessment links
- Interactive reviews that provide scores and the option to review answers
- Sunday readings with background and questions of the week

 Go to **osvparish.com**

You will find:

- Ask the Experts Q and A
- General Catechist Helps
- Community Connections and Blogs

Sharing the Message with First Graders

God as Trinity The Holy Trinity is the most basic mystery of our faith, but it is still a mystery, even for us as adults. Many Catholic first graders have heard (and also said) the words of the Sign of the Cross countless times, so they are accustomed to hearing about God the Father, God the Son, and God the Holy Spirit. Still, they may have particular difficulty understanding how God can be One and yet also Three. This is a mystery that will continue to unfold as they grow in faith and in relationship with God.

Teaching Tip: Use visual images like the shamrock and the triangle to help the children understand that the Holy Trinity is one God in three Divine Persons.

How First Graders Understand

- First graders enjoy listening to stories. Use stories to teach them about God the Father.
- First graders are developing hand-eye coordination. Use this developing skill in activities to help them learn.
- Families are central to the life of first graders, so the image of God as a loving parent is one to which many children can easily connect.

"I like to take things home to share."

Chapter Connections

Chapter Poem

Invite

"Nightlight"

- Use this poem to expand the chapter introduction.
- The children will relate the poem to their own lives, reflecting on how God lights our way.

 Go to **aliveinchrist.osv.com** Lesson Planning section for this poem.

NCEA IFG: ACRE Edition

Discover

Knowledge of the Faith

- Objective: To know and understand basic Catholic teaching about the Incarnate Word Jesus Christ as the way, truth, and life

Communal Life

- Objective: To know the origin, mission, structure, and communal nature of the Church

Catholic Social Teaching

Live

 Use one of these features to introduce a principle and engage the children with an activity.

- Life and Dignity, Pages 284–285
- Rights and Responsibilities, Pages 288–289

Music Options

 Use one or more of the following songs to enhance catechetical learning or for prayer.

- "The Sign of the Cross," Live Prayer, Page 88
- "Glory Be to the Father," Live, Page 86

LECTIONARY CONNECTION

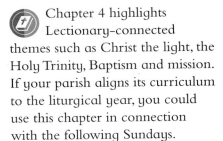 Chapter 4 highlights Lectionary-connected themes such as Christ the light, the Holy Trinity, Baptism and mission. If your parish aligns its curriculum to the liturgical year, you could use this chapter in connection with the following Sundays.

Year A

The Epiphany of the Lord—Christ the Light of all Nations

Palm Sunday of the Passion of the Lord—Paschal Mystery

The Most Holy Trinity—Holy Trinity

Thirty-third Sunday in Ordinary Time—common good

Year B

The Epiphany of the Lord—Christ the Light

The Baptism of the Lord—Baptism, mission

The Most Holy Trinity—Holy Trinity

Twenty-fourth Sunday in Ordinary Time—creed

Year C

The Epiphany of the Lord—Christ the Light

The Baptism of the Lord—Baptism

Second Sunday of Lent—prayer

The Most Holy Trinity—Holy Trinity

Go to **aliveinchrist.osv.com** for a complete correlation ordered by the Sundays of the year and suggestions for how to integrate the Scripture readings into chapter lessons.

Name _____   Date _____

The Holy Trinity

Some people use a three-leaf clover to represent the Holy Trinity. Color and cut out the clover to remind you of the three Divine Persons of the Holy Trinity.

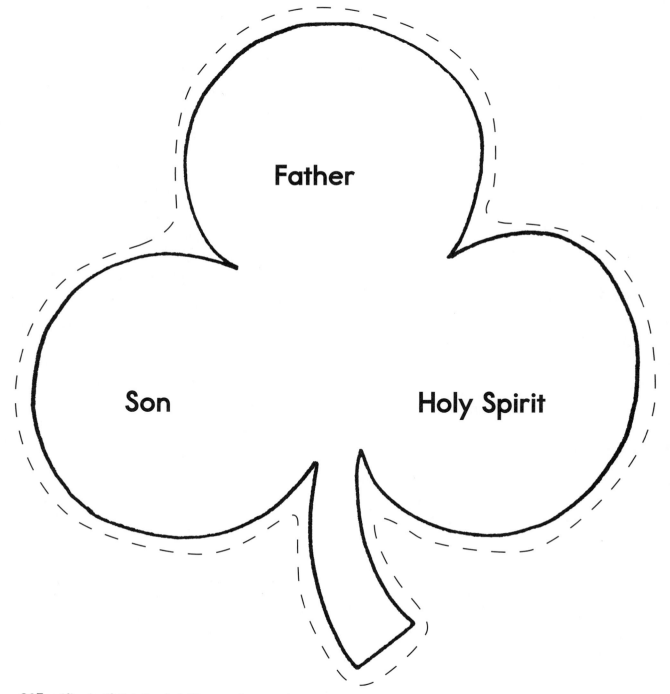

Father

Son

Holy Spirit

The Holy Trinity

 Let Us Pray

Leader: Your name is holy, O Lord our God.

"Give to the LORD the glory due his name.
Bow down before the LORD's holy splendor!" Psalm 29:2

All: May we always remember that your name is holy. And so we pray: In the name of the Father, and the Son, and the Holy Spirit. Amen.

 God's Word

Jesus said to the disciples: "…Go, therefore, and make disciples of all nations, baptizing them in the name of the Father, and of the Son, and of the holy Spirit, teaching them to observe all that I have commanded you."
Matthew 28:19–20

 **What Do You Wonder?**

- Why were you given your name?
- What does your name mean?

81

Optional Activity

Chapter Poem: "Nightlight" *Verbal/Linguistic*

Use this poem after the opening prayer, before explaining that when we pray the Sign of the Cross, we are marking ourselves as belonging to God.

- Read the poem aloud as the children follow along.
- *Ask:* How does a nightlight help people?
- *Ask:* How can you be a light for others?
- When finished, transition back to the lesson instruction.

 Go to **aliveinchrist.osv.com** for Chapter Poem.

Invite

Let Us Pray

Invite the children to gather in the prayer space and make the Sign of the Cross. Choose a child to be the leader. Read aloud the Psalm verse from a Bible. Prompt the children's response.

Have the children move out of the prayer space and back to their seats.

Explain that when we pray the Sign of the Cross, we are showing that we belong to God—the Father, Son, and Holy Spirit.

Say: When we were baptized we were called by name, to show God's great love to everyone. God calls us by name to show his love in this world. Let's listen to a reading from the Gospel of Matthew.

God's Word

Guide the children through the process of Scripture reflection.

- Invite them to close their eyes, be still and open their minds and hearts to what God is saying to them in this passage.
- Proclaim the Scripture.
- *Ask:* What did you hear God say to you today?
- Invite volunteers to share.

What Do You Wonder?

Say: Each of us was given a special name by which we are called.

Invite the children to respond to the questions. Ask what else they might wonder about the importance of their names.

Objective

- Understand that God asks us to be friends with one another, to be nice, and help each other when in need

Helping Others

Ask: How can we be nice to others?

- Write the children's responses on the board or on chart paper.

Read aloud the first paragraph.

The Lion and the Mouse

Ask the children to listen to how the lion and the mouse solve their problem.

- Read aloud the story.
- Cue the children to roar whenever the lion roars.
- *Ask:* Why did the lion think that the mouse could never repay him? Possible response: because the mouse was too small to help a big lion.

Helping Others

How can we be nice to others?

God always wants you to be nice to other people. Lion and Mouse have a problem. Read to find out how they solve the problem.

The Lion and the Mouse

A mighty lion was fast asleep in the woods. Mouse thought Lion was a rock. She ran up his back. Lion woke at once.

He grabbed poor Mouse's tail.

"How dare you wake me up?" he roared. "I am going to eat you!"

"Oh, please," Mouse said. "Let me go. Someday I will repay you."

1. Underline two things Lion did to Mouse.
2. Circle how Mouse helped Lion.

82

© Our Sunday Visitor

✓ Quick Tip

Helping Others

Organize the children in groups of two.

- Have the groups share and discuss the ways they help people and the ways people help them.
- Ask each group to share their responses.
- Have the children tell what they learned about helping others.

"Don't be silly!" Lion roared. "How will you repay me? You are just a little mouse." Then he laughed. "All right, go on," he said.

<u>He put Mouse down</u> and she ran away quickly.

Many days had passed. Mouse ran by that same place. Mouse heard an awful roar. She soon found Lion caught in a net.

Quickly Mouse ran to the net. She chewed through the rope and set Lion free!

"Thank you," roared Lion.

"You are welcome," said Mouse. "Now I hope that you can see what a big help small friends can be!"

Brothers, sisters, and friends can help each other do big things.

Share Your Faith

Think What did Lion learn about being a friend?

<u>Small friends can be a big help.</u>

Share Who has been a good friend to you and why?

The Holy Trinity **83**

Optional Activity

Lion and Mouse *Bodily/Kinesthetic*

Have one or more pairs of children act out the story for the rest of the group.

- You could have the pairs act out the whole story. Or, you might like to have each pair act out the beginning, middle, or end of the story.
- Another option would be for you to read the story aloud again. While you read, some of the pairs could act out the story.

The Lion and the Mouse,
continued

⭐ Have the children underline two things Lion did to Mouse. Then have them circle how Mouse helped Lion.

- *Ask:* What did the lion learn?
- Write responses on the board or on chart paper.

Point out the picture.

- Read aloud the caption.
- Invite the children to share about a time when a brother, sister, or friend helped them to do something.

Activity

Point out the Share Your Faith activity and read aloud the directions.

- Have the children trace the letters to find out what the lion learned about being a friend.
- Invite the children to quietly think of someone who is a good friend to them and why they consider this person to be a good friend.
- Provide time for the children to share with a partner about their friend.

Quick Review
Good friends care for each other.

Discover

Objectives

- Identify Jesus as the Son of God who shows us the way to his Father
- Appreciate that God the Father loves us so much he sent his only Son to be with us
- Describe the Holy Trinity as God the Father, God the Son, and God the Holy Spirit, the one God in three Divine Persons

God Is Love

Ask: How does the Holy Trinity show love?

- Write the children's responses on the board or on chart paper.

Read aloud the first two paragraphs.

- Tell the children that they can know God's love by seeing how wonderfully they are made. Tell them they can recognize God's love in the things he created.
- Tell the children that there is another way to know God.
- Read the next paragraph.

Work with Words

Explain to the children that God the Father's Son is Jesus.

- Hold up an index card with the word *Jesus* on it.

Ask the children to raise their hands if they like to talk about their families. Tell them that Jesus liked to talk about God, his Father.

 God's Word

Proclaim "The Way to the Father."

- *Ask:* How does Jesus show you God the Father's love?

Discover

God Is Love

How does the Holy Trinity show love?

Catholic Faith Words

God the Father the First Divine Person of the Holy Trinity

Son of God a name for Jesus that tells you God is his Father. The Son of God is the Second Divine Person of the Holy Trinity.

God cares for you like a good friend does. He loves you like a loving parent or grandparent does. He loves you even more than you can imagine.

You call him **God the Father**. You see his love in creation. You learn about his love from Jesus, the **Son of God**.

God the Father sent his Son to Earth to show people his love.

God's Word

The Way to the Father
One of the Apostles said to Jesus, "Master, show us the Father." Jesus said to him, "...Whoever has seen me has seen the Father." Based on John 14:8–9

84 Chapter 4

Scripture Background

John 14:8–9

Because of Jesus, we know that our God is a God of love.

- Jesus' whole life—his words and his actions, what he said and didn't say—revealed the Father.
- Jesus' whole life was an expression of love for sinful humans. Since the Son became man in order to do his Father's will, the depth of the Father's love for us is unmistakably manifested in Jesus.

The Holy Trinity

God the Father, God the Son, and God the Holy Spirit are the **Holy Trinity**. The Holy Trinity is the one God in three Divine Persons.

- Sometimes we say God or Lord when we pray to God the Father, from whom all things come.

- Jesus showed God's love by teaching, healing, and loving others.

- God the Holy Spirit helps you know and love Jesus and his Father.

Catholic Faith Words

Holy Trinity the one God in three Divine Persons—God the Father, God the Son, and God the Holy Spirit

Connect Your Faith

Trace the Word Trace the word to find the name for the three Divine Persons in one God. Then color in the signs of the Trinity.

Trinity

Son

Holy Spirit

Father

The Holy Trinity **85**

Optional Activity

Activity Master 4: The Holy Trinity

Distribute copies of the activity found on catechist page 81E.

- Tell the children the illustration will help them remember the Holy Trinity.

- As an alternative, you may wish to send this activity home with the children.

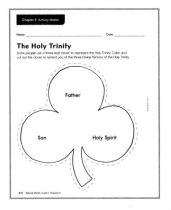

Chapter 4 Activity Master

Name _____ Date _____

The Holy Trinity
Some people use a three-leaf clover to represent the Holy Trinity. Color and cut out the clover to remind you of the three Divine Persons of the Holy Trinity.

Father

Son   Holy Spirit

81E *Alive in Christ,* Grade 1 Chapter 4

The Holy Trinity

Read aloud the text.

- Emphasize that the Holy Trinity is one God in the three Divine Persons—God the Father, God the Son, and God the Holy Spirit.

- Have the children sing the following words to the melody of "Mary Had a Little Lamb":

We believe in one God, in one God, in one God.
We believe in one God—Father, Son, and Spirit.
God the Father made us all, made us all, made us all.
God the Father made us all— the Earth and all that's in it.
God the Son is Jesus Christ, Jesus Christ, Jesus Christ.
God the Son is Jesus Christ— he came to show us love.
God the Spirit helps us grow, helps us grow, helps us grow.
God the Spirit helps us grow and learn the way of love.

Work with Words

Show the children an index card for *Holy Trinity* and review the definition.

Activity

Read aloud the directions and have the children complete the Connect Your Faith activity.

- Have the children trace the letters to complete the sentence.

Quick Review

The Holy Trinity is one God in three Divine Persons—God the Father, God the Son, and God the Holy Spirit.

Our Catholic Life

Ask: What do we know about God?

- Write the children's responses on the board or on chart paper.

Read the first paragraph.

Father, Son, and Holy Spirit

Invite the children to follow along as you read the bulleted text. Ask them to raise their hand every time you read the words love, loves, or loving.

⭐ Direct the children to find and circle the words *Father*, *Son*, and *Holy Spirit* in the bulleted text.

- Read aloud the rest of the page, using the words *plus* and *equals* when you read the equation.

- *Ask:* What is the most important thing to remember about God?
God loves us.

▶ Music Option: Sing with the students "Glory Be to the Father," downloaded from **aliveinchrist.osv.com**.

Refer to page 299 in the Our Catholic Tradition reference section of the Student Book for more on creeds. The creeds profess the Church's most important beliefs about the Holy Trinity and our Catholic faith.

Live

Our Catholic Life

What do we know about God?

Jesus taught some important things about God. The most important thing he taught is that God loves everyone.

Circle the words Father, Son, and Holy Spirit.

Father, Son, and Holy Spirit

- God made all things, and cares for creation as our loving (Father)
- God the Father sent his own (Son) Jesus, to save all people, because he loves us.
- God sent his (Holy Spirit) to be with us always, because he loves us.

God the Father, God the Son, and God the Holy Spirit are the Holy Trinity.

Here is a way to remember what you know about the Trinity.

Father + Son
+ Holy Spirit
= 1 God
= Love

86   Chapter 4

✓ Quick Tip

Recognizing God's Presence

Help the children understand that although they cannot see God, they experience his presence whenever they love and are loved.

- Ask the children to think about the ways in which they showed love or were shown love today.

- Remind the children that they can recognize his presence in these loving moments.

People of Faith

Saint Patrick, 387–493

Saint Patrick was kidnapped by pirates when he was just a boy. They took him to Ireland to be a slave. After six years, Patrick escaped and went back to his family. Years later, he returned to Ireland as a priest. He showed people a shamrock to explain the Holy Trinity; one God in three Divine Persons.

March 17

Discuss: How is the Sign of the Cross also the sign of the Holy Trinity?

 Learn more about Saint Patrick at **aliveinchrist.osv.com**

 © Our Sunday Visitor

Live Your Faith

Fill It In Fill in the blank with the name of the correct Person of the Holy Trinity.

1. My name is Jesus. I taught people about God, my Father.

   I am God the _Son_.

2. I am with you always to help you share God's love.

   I am God the _Holy Spirit_.

3. I made the whole world, and I love and care for all people.

   I am God the _Father_.

87

Catholic Social Teaching

Chapter Connections

To integrate Catholic Social Teaching into your lesson, choose one of the following features: Life and Dignity, pages 284–285; or Rights and Responsibilities, pages 288–289.

- Start the Live step of the process by talking about Saint Patrick on page 87. Then move directly to the Catholic Social Teaching feature.

- Or, to expand the lesson, complete both pages 86 and 87, then move to the Catholic Social Teaching feature.

- Return to Chapter 4 for the prayer on page 88.

People of Faith

Tell the children about Saint Patrick.

- Invite a volunteer to read aloud the People of Faith story.

- Explain that Saint Patrick is one of the world's most popular Saints.

- He was able to escape from Ireland after he had a dream. In the dream God told him to leave Ireland by way of the coast. He went to the coast, where sailors picked him up and brought him home.

- He returned to Ireland after another dream told him to go back.

- *Ask:* How is the Sign of the Cross also a sign of the Holy Trinity? The Sign of the Cross names the three Divine Persons of the Holy Trinity.

 Encourage the children to go to **aliveinchrist.osv.com** at home to learn more about Saint Patrick.

Activity

As a group, read aloud the directions and discuss the Live Your Faith activity.

- Allow time for the children to complete the activity.

- Invite volunteers to read aloud each statement.

Live

 Let Us Pray

Prayer of Praise

Tell the children they will pray a very old prayer of praise to the Holy Trinity.

- Explain that this is a very short prayer of praise to all three Divine Persons of the Holy Trinity—God the Father, God the Son, and God the Holy Spirit.

Prepare

Practice making the Sign of the Cross with the children.

 Rehearse "The Sign of the Cross," downloaded from **aliveinchrist.osv.com**.

Gather

Invite the children to process to the prayer space.

- Have the children prepare their minds and hearts for prayer.

Pray

 Begin the prayer by singing together, "The Sign of the Cross."

- Follow the order of prayer on the student page.

 Conclude by singing together "The Sign of the Cross."

 Let Us Pray

Prayer of Praise

Gather and begin with the Sign of the Cross.

 All: Sing "The Sign of the Cross"
In the name of the Father,
and of the Son,
and of the Holy Spirit,
Amen.

Leader: Glory be to the Father,

All: Glory be to the Father,

Leader: and to the Son,

All: and to the Son,

Leader: and to the Holy Spirit:

All: and to the Holy Spirit:

Leader: as it was in the beginning, is now,
and will be forever.

All: as it was in the beginning, is now,
and ever shall be,
world without end.
Amen.

88   Chapter 4

 Liturgy Link

Repeated Actions

Children will come to know and love the traditional prayers and hymns of the Catholic Church by praying or singing them over and over again.

- Six-year-old children love repetition. To have them repeat a prayer or song more than once can be both prayerful and enjoyable.

 Go to **aliveinchrist.osv.com** for Sunday readings, Scripture background, questions of the week, and seasonal resources.

FAMILY+FAITH
LIVING AND LEARNING TOGETHER

YOUR CHILD LEARNED >>>
This chapter introduces the Holy Trinity, the one God in three Divine Persons, and explains each Divine Person of God, what they do, and how they relate to one another.

God's Word
Read **Matthew 28:19–20** as a family. Talk about how each of you helps others learn about God.

Catholics Believe
- The Holy Trinity is God the Father, God the Son, and God the Holy Spirit.
- Jesus is the Son of God who came to show the Father's love and bring us closer to him.

To learn more, go to the *Catechism of the Catholic Church* #253–254 at **usccb.org**.

People of Faith
This week, your child met Saint Patrick. He used a common plant, the shamrock, to explain the profound mystery of the Holy Trinity.

CHILDREN AT THIS AGE >>>
How They Understand God as Trinity
The Holy Trinity is the most basic mystery of our faith, but it is still a mystery, even for us as adults. Many Catholic first graders have heard and said the words of the Sign of the Cross countless times. They are accustomed to hearing about God the Father, God the Son, and God the Holy Spirit. Still, your child may have particular difficulty understanding how God can be one and yet also three. This is a mystery that will continue to unfold as he or she grows in faith and in relationship with God.

CONSIDER THIS >>>
What did you discover about love when your child was first placed in your arms?

Did you feel indescribable love? That experience of love begins in the heart of God, for God is love. "When a family becomes a school of virtue and a community of love, it is an image of the loving communion of the Father, Son, and Holy Spirit. It is then an icon of the Trinity" (*USCCA, p. 377*).

LET'S TALK >>>
- Ask your child to name the three Divine Persons of the Holy Trinity.
- Show your child how we honor the Holy Trinity when we make the Sign of the Cross at the beginning and end of prayers.

LET'S PRAY >>>
Saint Patrick, help us teach others about God the Father, God the Son, and God the Holy Spirit in the Holy Trinity. Amen.

For a multimedia glossary of Catholic Faith Words, Sunday readings, seasonal and Saint resources, and chapter activities go to **aliveinchrist.osv.com**.

Family + Faith

Distribute the page to the children or parents/adult family members. Point out the chapter highlights, insights on how first graders understand concepts, the opportunity for the adults to reflect on their own experience and faith journey, and the family prayer.

Chapter 4 Review

A **Work with Words** Circle the correct answers.

1. Jesus is the ____ of God.

   (Son)   Father

2. Who are the three Divine Persons of the Holy Trinity?

   the Three Kings   (Father, Son, and Holy Spirit)

3. God is our ____ who loves and cares for us.

   cousin   (Father)

B **Check Understanding** Trace the letters to complete the sentence.

4. There are three Divine Persons in the

5. God the _____

   helps you know and love Jesus and the Father.

Go to **aliveinchrist.osv.com** for an interactive review.

Chapter Review

Use Catechist Quick Reviews to highlight lesson concepts.

A **Work with Words**
Have the children circle the correct answer.

B **Check Understanding**
Have the children trace the letters to complete each sentence.

Go to **aliveinchrist.osv.com** to prepare customized and downloadable assessments, send eAssessments, and assign interactive reviews.

The Holy Trinity   89–90

KEY CONCEPT

Jesus is both true God and true man. Jesus, Mary, and Joseph are the Holy Family.

DOCTRINAL CONTENT

- Signs of love are expressed in families. (CCC, 1656–1657)
- Jesus is the Son of God and a human being. (CCC, 423)
- The Holy Family is the name of the human family of Jesus, Mary, and Joseph. (CCC, 1655)
- Jesus grew up with Mary and Joseph in Nazareth, praying and learning. (CCC, 532–533)

TASKS OF CATECHESIS

Helping children grow in a faith that is "known, celebrated, lived, and expressed in prayer" (NDC, 20).

This chapter focuses on the following tasks of catechesis:

- Promoting Knowledge of the Faith
- Education for Community Life

Catechist Background

 He went and dwelt in a town called Nazareth, so that what had been spoken through the prophets might be fulfilled. "He shall be called a Nazorean." Matthew 2:23

➜ **Reflect** What do you think it was like for Jesus to grow up in Nazareth?

As he grew to adulthood in Nazareth, Jesus encountered many of the challenges that most children encounter. Like anyone else, Jesus had to learn how to bear his responsibilities as a member of a family, and how to make compromises that were assuredly necessary to preserve harmony even within a family as extraordinary as his. The *Catechism* suggests that Jesus' perfect obedience to his earthly parents can be seen as an image of his perfect obedience to his Father in Heaven. (*CCC*, 532)

Living in a family requires mutual respect, a willingness to work together, and self-sacrifice. In his Letter to the Colossians, Saint Paul told the early Christians, "Put on then . . . heartfelt compassion, kindness, humility, gentleness, and patience, bearing with one another and forgiving one another, if one has a grievance against another" (Colossians 3:12–13). Saint Paul's advice will never become outdated; these same principles must be followed today to produce a happy Christian family.

In his Letter, Saint Paul goes on to remind the Colossians of the Fourth Commandment: "Children, obey your parents in everything, for this is pleasing to the Lord" (Colossians 3:20). Loving your family sometimes takes effort. Most people would agree, however, that the effort is worth it. The rewards of belonging to a loving family are great.

➜ **Reflect** Who in your family has been a particular blessing for you recently?

Catechist's Prayer

Jesus, Mary, and Joseph, help me to make a family of the children in my care, united by the spirit of love that united you as a family. Amen.

Lesson Plan

Objectives	Process	Materials

⏱ Invite, 10 minutes

The Holy Family Page 91

- 💗 **Psalm 133:1** Pray the opening prayer.
- 📄 **Matthew 2:19–23** Reflect prayerfully on the Word.
- • Discuss What Do You Wonder questions.

🌐 **Optional Activity**
Chapter Poem: "My Family"

⏱ Discover, 35 minutes

Family Love Pages 92–93
- • Identify signs of love expressed in families

- • Explain that God loves all families.
- • Read "Tyler's Family," "Lainey's Family," and "David's Family."
- • **Share Your Faith Activity** Draw one way families show love.

☐ pencils
☐ crayons or markers

Jesus' Family Pages 94–95
- • Recognize Jesus as the Son of God and a human being
- • Define the Holy Family as the human family of Jesus, Mary, and Joseph
- • Appreciate that Jesus grew up with Mary and Joseph in Nazareth, praying and learning

- • **Catholic Faith Words** Mary, Holy Family
- • Explain that Jesus is the Son of God and human.
- 📄 **Luke 2:51–52** Proclaim "The Boy Jesus."
- ☆ Identify things the Holy Family did that you do with your family.
- • **Connect Your Faith Activity** Act out what families can do to show God's love.

☐ pencils
☐ index cards
☐ crayons or markers
- • **Optional Activity** Hand Puppets
☐ Activity Master 5 (Page 91E)

⏱ Live, 15 minutes

Our Catholic Life Pages 96–97

- • Explain Jesus grew up in a family much like any family.
- ☆ Match the pictures with the correct actions.
- • **People of Faith** Learn about Zechariah, Elizabeth, and John.
- • **Live Your Faith Activity** Draw a family picture.

☐ pencils
☐ crayons or markers

Pray with God's Word Page 98

- • Review the Mass response.
- ▶ Rehearse "Joseph was a Good Man."
- • Follow the order of prayer.

🌐 Download "Joseph was a Good Man."

Family + Faith Page 99
Point out that the Catholic Families page provides chapter highlights, information on how first graders understand faith concepts, and family prayer.

Chapter Review Page 100
🌐 **aliveinchrist.osv.com**
- • Customize and Download Assessments
- • Email Links to eAssessments
- • Interactive Student Reviews

ONLINE RESOURCES

 Go to **aliveinchrist.osv.com**

You will find:

- Interactive lesson planning with web specific content and additional activities
- Step by step lesson instruction from printed Catechist Edition for integrated lesson planning
- Custom-built assessments to download and eAssessment links
- Interactive reviews that provide scores and the option to review answers
- Sunday readings with background and questions of the week

 Go to **osvparish.com**

You will find:

- Ask the Experts Q and A
- General Catechist Helps
- Community Connections and Blogs

Sharing the Message with First Graders

The Holy Family When first graders hear that Jesus was once a child their age, it's natural for them to picture him in a family very much like their own. Just like they need someone to take care of them as they grow, so did Jesus. And it's important for them to realize that even Jesus had to listen to his mom and dad and follow their rules.

Teaching Tip: Be sensitive to children in the group who may have other family configurations. Many children live with grandparents, single parents and step parents. Focus on the connections that still exist between their families and the Holy Family. For example, that they have adults who take care of them the way Jesus did, they follow the rules like Jesus did, and so on.

How First Graders Understand

- First graders are eager to please you and other significant adults in their lives.
- Sometimes, first graders can be very emotional. Gentleness and humor work best to head off any outbursts.
- Remember that teaching young children is most successful when the catechist creates a family-like environment, one that expresses God's love.

"My family is important to me. I like to tell stories about what we do."

Chapter Connections

Chapter Poem
Invite

"My Family"

- Use this poem to expand the chapter introduction.
- The children will relate the poem to their own lives, reflecting on the gift of their own family.
- Connect learning about God to his gift of families.
- Have the children tell why family is important.

 Go to **aliveinchrist.osv.com** Lesson Planning section for this poem.

NCEA IFG: ACRE Edition
Discover

Knowledge of the Faith

- Objective: To know and understand the basic Catholic Teaching about the Incarnate Word Jesus Christ as the way, truth, and life

Communal Life

- Objective: To know the rights and responsibilities of the Christian faithful

Catholic Social Teaching
Live

 Use one of these features to introduce a principle and engage the children with an activity

- Life and Dignity, Pages 284–285
- Call to Community, Pages 286–287

Music Options

 Use one or more of the following songs to enhance catechetical learning or for prayer.

- "Joseph was a Good Man," Live Prayer, Page 98
- "Family of God," Discover, Page 94

LECTIONARY CONNECTION

Chapter 5 highlights Lectionary-connected themes such as Marriage, Fourth Commandment, family, and domestic church. If your parish aligns its curriculum to the liturgical year, you could use this chapter in connection with the following Sundays.

Year A

The Holy Family of Jesus, Mary, and Joseph—Fourth Commandment

The Baptism of the Lord—Baptism, mission

Third Sunday of Lent—faith, grace

Year B

The Holy Family of Jesus, Mary, and Joseph—Fourth Commandment, family

Twenty-seventh Sunday in Ordinary Time—Marriage

Year C

Third Sunday of Advent—Cardinal Virtues

The Holy Family of Jesus, Mary, and Joseph—family, domestic church

Go to **aliveinchrist.osv.com** for a complete correlation ordered by the Sundays of the year and suggestions for how to integrate the Scripture readings into chapter lessons.

Name _____ Date _____

Hand Puppets

Color the figures of the Holy Family.
Then cut the figures out. Fold back
the tabs and tape them together.
Now you have three hand puppets!
Tell stories about the Holy Family.

Jesus

Mary

Joseph

The Holy Family

Let Us Pray

Leader: Thank you, God, for our families.

How good and how pleasant it is,
when brothers dwell together as one!
Psalm 133:1

All: Help us to see your love and kindness in our families. Amen.

God's Word

Joseph was told in a dream to take Mary and Jesus to Galilee. They went to live there in the town of Nazareth. So God's promise came true…"He shall be called a Nazorean."
Based on Matthew 2:19–23

What Do You Wonder?

- What was it like to live in Nazareth?
- Did Jesus have to obey his parents?

91

Optional Activity

Chapter Poem: "My Family" *Verbal/Linguistic*

Use this poem after the opening prayer, before explaining that our families are a gift from God.

- Read the first six lines of the poem to the children.
- Ask them where they might go for help or comfort.
- Read the rest of the poem to the children.
- *Ask:* What is one way your family cheers you up?
- When finished, transition back to the lesson instruction.

 Go to **aliveinchrist.osv.com** for Chapter Poem.

Let Us Pray

Invite the children to gather in the prayer space and make the Sign of the Cross. Choose a child to be the leader. Read aloud the Psalm verse from a Bible. Prompt the children's response.

Have the children move out of the prayer space and back to their seats.

Explain that our families are a gift from God.

Say: Jesus had a family like we do and lived with his family in Nazareth. Let's listen to a reading from the Gospel of Matthew.

God's Word

Guide the children through the process of Scripture reflection.

- Invite them to close their eyes, be still and open their minds and hearts to what God is saying to them in this passage.
- Proclaim the Scripture.
- Maintain several moments of silence.
- *Ask:* What did you hear God say to you today?
- Invite volunteers to share.

What Do You Wonder?

Say: Our families are all different. We may have many brothers and sisters, others have none. Some live in a big city, others in the country on a farm.

Invite the children to respond to the questions. Ask what else they might wonder about Jesus' life as a child or his family.

Objective

• Identify signs of love expressed in families

Family Love

Ask: How can families show love?

• Write the children's responses on the board or on chart paper.

Talk to the children about families. Tell the children that some families are large and some are small. Tell them that some children live with their grandparents.

• Tell the children that God loves all families.

• Introduce the children to the families that live on Green Street.

• Read aloud the poems "Tyler's Family," "Lainey's Family," and "David's Family."

• Invite three children to each reread one poem each to the group.

Discover

Family Love

How can families show love?

God the Father loves all families. Meet the families who live on Green Street.

Tyler's Family

Tyler's Dad moved away, and Tyler is sad. Having an uncle to talk to makes Tyler feel glad.

Lainey's Family

"Let's read this email from your Gram," says Dad to Lainey.

"She says she is coming to visit soon."

92

🧍 Reaching All Learners

Including Everyone

Some children may never raise their hand to volunteer, even though they wish to take part.

• To include these children, ask them to role-play by representing the family members in the poems.

• As you read the poems, pretend to stop at each house where the children are sitting.

David's Family

There's David and Mama and Papa, too, on a picnic in the park.

"Fetch the tennis ball, Rocky," David says.

Rocky chases after the ball with a happy bark.

Share Your Faith

Think Draw one way your family shows love.

Share Tell one way your family shares God's love.

The Holy Family   93

Family Love, *continued*

- *Ask:* How are these families different? Tyler's dad doesn't live with him. Lainey's grandmother is coming to visit. David's family has a dog.
- *Ask:* How are the families alike? They are all showing love.
- *Ask:* How is each family showing love?
- Write all responses on the board or on chart paper.

Activity

Read aloud the directions for the Share Your Faith activity.

- *Ask:* How does your family show love?
- Give the children time to draw their families showing God's love.
- Walk around the room and give each child positive feedback about his or her family.

Quick Review

Family members care for one another and share God's love.

Objectives

- Recognize Jesus as the Son of God and a human being
- Define the Holy Family as the human family of Jesus, Mary, and Joseph
- Appreciate that Jesus grew up with Mary and Joseph in Nazareth, praying and learning

Jesus' Family

Ask: What was Jesus' family like?

- Write the children's responses on the board or on chart paper.

Tell the children that they are going learn about Jesus' family.

Read aloud the paragraph.

Work with Words

Tell the children that we call Jesus' family the Holy Family.

- Hold up index cards with *Mary* and *Holy Family* written on them.

Tell the children that Jesus' family shared God's love with each other just like their families do.

- *Ask:* What do you know about the Holy Family?

Read aloud the second paragraph.

- Explain to the children that Jesus was the Son of God, but he was also human like them.
- Emphasize that Jesus teaches us about God's love and how to live.

 Music Option: Have the children sing "Family of God," downloaded from **aliveinchrist.osv.com**.

Discover

© Our Sunday Visitor

Jesus' Family

What was Jesus' family like?

Long ago, Jesus was born into a family. Jesus lived with **Mary**, his mother, and his foster father, Joseph. They lived in a town called Nazareth. Jesus, Mary, and Joseph are called the **Holy Family**.

Jesus is the Son of God. Jesus is also human. He is like you in almost every way. Jesus shows you how to live. He teaches you about God's love.

Catholic Faith Words

Mary the Mother of Jesus, the Mother of God. She is also called "Our Lady" because she is our Mother and the Mother of the Church.

Holy Family the name for the human family of Jesus, Mary, and Joseph

94 Chapter 5

Optional Activity

Activity Master 5: Hand Puppets

Distribute copies of the activity found on catechist page 91E.

- Tell the children they can use the stories in the chapter for their puppet plays.
- As an alternative, you may wish to send this activity home with the children.

A Day in Nazareth

All families can share God's love. When Jesus was your age, he showed God's love in his family.

God's Word

The Boy Jesus

Jesus obeyed his family. He became wise and good. Jesus grew strong. God was pleased with him and so were the people.

Based on Luke 2:51–52

This is what could have happened when Jesus was young.

 Underline some things the Holy Family did that you do with your family.

- Following Jewish custom, the family begins the day with a prayer.

- Mary bakes bread for breakfast.

- Joseph makes a chair for his neighbors.

- Spending time together as a family.

Connect Your Faith

Act Out Family Life What are some things the Holy Family might have done together? With a partner, act out something families can do to show God's love.

95

Songs of Scripture

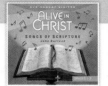

The Holy Family

As you teach the song, explain that putting God first and loving others helps our families be holy.

- Give each child a piece of construction paper in the shape of a heart.
- In the heart, have the children draw a picture of their family.
- Direct the children to draw arrows moving away from the heart to show how their family shares God's love with others.

▶ Use *Songs of Scripture*, Grades 1–3 CD, Track 6

A Day in Nazareth

Invite a volunteer to read aloud the introductory paragraph.

God's Word

Proclaim "The Boy Jesus."

- Ask the children to raise their hands every time they hear a word that describes, or tells about, Jesus. obeyed, wise, good, strong

- Explain to the children that Jesus passed through the same stages of growth as they are doing.

Have the children read what Jesus and his family did on an ordinary day at home.

- Write the following on the board or on chart paper to summarize each activity mentioned in the text: *pray*, *cook*, *work*, and *help*.

- Point to the words you have printed, and ask the children what they have learned about Jesus' family.

⭐ Have the children underline some things the Holy Family did that they do with their families.

Activity

Point out the Connect Your Faith activity and read aloud the directions.

- Provide time for the children to role-play family life situations that show God's love.

Quick Review

Catholics call Jesus' human family the Holy Family. The three members of the Holy Family are Jesus, Mary, and Joseph.

Our Catholic Life

Ask: What was it like for Jesus when he was growing up?

- Write the children's responses on the board or on chart paper.

Read aloud the first paragraph.

- Ask the children to name the members of Jesus' human family.

⭐ Draw attention to the matching activity and read the directions aloud. Invite volunteers to read aloud the actions on the left. Talk together about which pictures are the best match for each action.

Refer to page 302 in the Our Catholic Tradition reference section in the back of the Student Book to find out one way our Church honors Mary.

Our Catholic Life

What was it like for Jesus when he was growing up?

Jesus grew up in a human family. He and his family probably did many of the same things together that you and your family do.

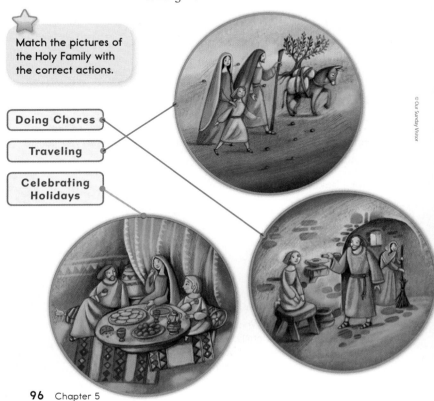

⭐ Match the pictures of the Holy Family with the correct actions.

Doing Chores

Traveling

Celebrating Holidays

✔ **Quick Tip**

Using Religious Imagination

Children use their religious imagination when they project themselves into the past to learn more about Jesus' life. Some ways to foster this skill include:

- asking the children to put themselves into the story when they hear or read Scripture.
- having the children draw their ideas about abstract religious concepts such as God and Heaven.

People of Faith

**Zechariah, Elizabeth, and John,
first century**

Elizabeth was Mary's cousin. She was
married to Zechariah. They did not have
children. One day an angel appeared
to Zechariah when he was praying. The
angel told him that he and Elizabeth would
have a son named John. Elizabeth and
Zechariah were very happy. When John
grew up, he was filled with the Holy Spirit.

November 5

Discuss: How are you filled with the
Holy Spirit?

 Learn more about Zechariah,
Elizabeth, and John at
aliveinchrist.osv.com

Live Your Faith

Draw Your Family
Draw a picture of your
family doing something
that the Holy Family
might have done
together.

MY FAMILY

The Holy Family **97**

 ## Catholic Social Teaching

Chapter Connections

To integrate Catholic Social Teaching into your lesson, choose one
of the following features: Life and Dignity, pages 284–285; or Call to
Community, pages 286–287.

- Start the Live step of the process by talking about Zechariah,
  Elizabeth, and John. Then move directly to the Catholic Social
  Teaching feature.
- Or, to expand the lesson, complete both pages 96 and 97, then
  move to the Catholic Social Teaching feature.
- Return to Chapter 5 for the prayer on page 98.

People of Faith

Tell the children about Zechariah,
Elizabeth, and John.

- Invite a volunteer to read aloud
  the People of Faith story.
- Explain that Zechariah, Elizabeth
  and John were a family that lived
  during Jesus' time.
- Mention that Zechariah and
  Elizabeth had been married for
  a long time and they had no
  children.
- Share that an angel appeared to
  Zechariah and told him that he
  and Elizabeth would have a son
  named John.
- *Ask:* How are you filled with the
  Holy Spirit?

 Encourage the children to go
to **aliveinchrist.osv.com**
at home to learn more about
Zechariah, Elizabeth and John.

Activity

Read aloud the directions for the
Live Your Faith activity.

- As a group, talk together about
  what the children might draw.
- Provide art materials and allow
  time for the children to work
  independently on their art work.
- Encourage the children to share
  their art work with a partner and
  with their families.

Let Us Pray

Pray with God's Word

Tell the children that they are going to listen to a Gospel story about Jesus and his family.

Prepare

Review the gestures and responses that Catholics make when the Gospel is read at Mass. (Refer to the Liturgy Link box below for more information.)

Have the children repeat several times the response, "Praise to you, Lord Jesus Christ."

 Rehearse "Joseph was a Good Man," downloaded from **aliveinchrist.osv.com**.

Gather

Invite the children to process to the prayer space. Have the children prepare their minds and hearts for prayer.

Pray

- Follow the order of prayer on the student page.
- Invite the children to stand while you proclaim the Gospel.

 Conclude by singing together "Joseph was a Good Man."

 Let Us Pray

Pray with God's Word

Gather and begin with the Sign of the Cross.

Leader: Today we learned about the Holy Family. Mary, Joseph, and Jesus help us to act with love in our families.

All: Thank you, Mary, for being the Mother of Jesus. Thank you, Joseph, for taking care of Jesus.

Leader: Let us listen to the Word of God. A reading from the holy Gospel according to Luke.

Read Luke 2:27–33.

All: Praise to you, Lord Jesus Christ.

Leader: Thank you, Jesus, for loving your family and thank you for our families. Help us to live with great love.

All: Amen.

 Sing "Joseph Was a Good Man"

 Liturgy Link

Crossing Forehead, Lips, and Heart

Review with the children the gestures we make after the priest or deacon at Mass announces which Gospel he is going to read.

- Show the children how to sign their forehead, lips, and heart with a small Sign of the Cross. Explain that they should say aloud "Glory to you, O Lord" as they do this.
- Explain that as we do this, we can say to ourselves, "May God be in my mind, on my lips, and in my heart."

 Go to **aliveinchrist.osv.com** for Sunday readings, Scripture background, questions of the week, and seasonal resources.

FAMILY + FAITH
LIVING AND LEARNING TOGETHER

YOUR CHILD LEARNED >>>

This chapter focuses on God's love for all families and the things the Holy Family did or could have done together.

God's Word

Read **Mark 10:13–16** to see how Jesus wants us to care for children and families.

Catholics Believe

- Jesus is both true God and true man.
- Jesus, Mary, and Joseph are the Holy Family.

To learn more, go to the *Catechism of the Catholic Church* #531–534 at **usccb.org**.

People of Faith

This week, your child met Zechariah, Elizabeth, and John. These relatives of Jesus trusted God to direct their lives.

CHILDREN AT THIS AGE >>>

How They Understand the Holy Family When first graders hear that Jesus was once a child their age, it's natural for them to picture him in a family very much like their own. Just like they need someone to take care of them as they grow, so did Jesus. And it's important for them to realize that even Jesus had to listen to his mom and dad and follow their rules. Make these important connections to show your child that Jesus was like them in all things except he did not sin.

CONSIDER THIS >>>

Who was the person who had the most influence in your life?

It is important to recognize the power of models in our lives. They help us to imagine what is possible. The Holy Family is the best model for us and our family life. "The Christian home is the place where the children receive the first proclamation of the faith. For this reason the family is rightly called "the domestic church," a community of grace and prayer, a school of human virtues and of Christian charity (CCC, 1666)" (*USCCA, p. 290*).

LET'S TALK >>>

- Have your child name the members of the Holy Family.
- Share a story about how you've honored Mary and/or Joseph.

LET'S PRAY >>>

 Dear Elizabeth, Zechariah, and John, pray for us that God will bless our family with happiness. Amen.

For a multimedia glossary of Catholic Faith Words, Sunday readings, seasonal and Saint resources, and chapter activities go to **aliveinchrist.osv.com**.

Alive in Christ, Grade 1 Chapter 5 **99**

Distribute the page to the children or parents/adult family members. Point out the chapter highlights, insights on how first graders understand concepts, the opportunity for the adults to reflect on their own experience and faith journey, and the family prayer.

Chapter 5 Review

A **Work with Words** Trace the words to complete the sentences.

1. is the mother of Jesus.

2. Jesus is the Son of God and he is also .

3. Mark an X next to the things Jesus might have done with his family.

 pray   talk   [X] visit

[X] eat   [X] play   [X] help

4. Jesus, Mary, and Joseph are called the

B **Check Understanding** Circle ways you can help your family.

5.

Go to **aliveinchrist.osv.com** for an interactive review.

100 Chapter 5 Review

Use Catechist Quick Reviews to highlight lesson concepts.

A **Work with Words**
Have the children trace the letters to complete each statement and identify with an *X* what Jesus might have done with his family.

B **Check Understanding**
Have the children circle the pictures that show ways to help their family.

 Go to **aliveinchrist.osv.com** to prepare customized and downloadable assessments, send eAssessments, and assign interactive reviews.

The Holy Family **99–100**

KEY CONCEPT

Jesus told short stories, or parables, to teach others something about God. The Bible is the Word of God written in human words.

DOCTRINAL CONTENT

- Jesus told stories like the Lost Sheep to show us how God watches over and guides us, always welcoming us back. (CCC, 605)

- A parable is a short story Jesus told about everyday life to teach something about God. (CCC, 546)

- The Bible is the Church's holy book. (CCC, 104, 138)

- The two parts of the Bible are the Old Testament and the New Testament. (CCC, 120)

TASKS OF CATECHESIS

Helping children grow in a faith that is "known, celebrated, lived, and expressed in prayer" (NDC, 20).

This chapter focuses on the following tasks of catechesis:

- Promoting Knowledge of the Faith

- Moral Formation

Catechist Background

 "I will open my mouth in parables, I will announce what has lain hidden from the foundation [of the world]."
Matthew 13:35

➜ **Reflect** What is your favorite parable? Why?

All the Gospels agree that much of Jesus' public teaching took the form of parables, brief stories about incidents of everyday life that contained a profound religious message. *Parable* comes from the Greek word *parabolé*, which conveys the idea of putting two things side by side in order to compare them. Jesus intended that his audience relate the parables to their own experiences as members of the community that worshipped the God of Israel. In the process, they were to discover surprising truths about God, his love, and the demands that he made of his People.

In the parable of the Lost Sheep, for example, Jesus compared God to a shepherd who temporarily abandons the rest of the flock to seek out the one sheep that has become lost. The message is that, to him, every member of his flock is precious, even those who have strayed farthest into sin. Jesus hoped his parables would lead his hearers to faith, to conversion of heart. No matter how many times we read the parables or hear them proclaimed, they are always new, because through them, the voice of God addresses each one of us directly.

➜ **Reflect** How can you share God's Word with others today?

Catechist's Prayer

Lord Jesus, you taught how to love God and neighbor through your parables. Though the stories are simple, they are not always easy to live by. Help me follow the example you have given me. Amen.

Lesson Plan

Objectives	Process	Materials

Invite, 10 minutes

About the Bible Page 101

- ♥ **Psalm 23:1** Pray the opening prayer.
- 📖 **Matthew 13:34–35** Reflect prayerfully on the Word.
- Discuss What Do You Wonder questions.

🔊 **Optional Activity**
Chapter Story: "A True Friend"

Discover, 35 minutes

We Learn from Stories
Pages 102–103
- Recognize that Jesus told stories like the Lost Sheep to show us how God watches over and guides us, always welcoming us back

- Explain that Jesus told stories about God's love.
- 📖 **Luke 15:3–6** Proclaim "The Parable of the Lost Sheep."
- ☆ Underline what went wrong in the story and what the shepherd did.
- Explain that God always wants us to come back to him.
- **Share Your Faith Activity** Identify the roles in the story.

☐ pencils
- **Optional Activity**
A Story About God
☐ Activity Master 6 (Page 101E)

Stories About God Pages 104–105
- Describe a parable as a short story that Jesus told about everyday life to teach something about God
- Identify the Bible as the Church's holy book
- Name two parts of the Bible as the Old Testament and the New Testament

- **Catholic Faith Words** parable, Old Testament, New Testament
- Explain that Jesus is like a shepherd
- 📖 **John 10:14–15** Proclaim "The Good Shepherd."
- ☆ Have the children underline the ways that Jesus is like a shepherd.
- Explain that the Bible is God's Word written down by humans.
- **Connect Your Faith Activity** Write the first books of the Old Testament and the New Testament.

☐ pencils
☐ Bible
- **Optional Activity**
The Good Shepherd

Live, 15 minutes

Our Catholic Life Pages 106–107
- Explain the two parts of the Bible.
- **People of Faith** Learn about Saint Paul of the Cross.
- **Live Your Faith Activity** Find the lost sheep.

☐ pencils
☐ crayons or markers

Prayer of Thanks Page 108
- Review the response with the children.
- ▶ Rehearse "The Good Shepherd."
- Follow the order of prayer.

🔊 Download "The Good Shepherd."

Family + Faith Page 109
Point out that the Catholic Families page provides chapter highlights, information on how first graders understand faith concepts, and family prayer.

Chapter Review Page 110
🔊 aliveinchrist.osv.com
- Customize and Download Assessments
- Email Links to eAssessments
- Interactive Student Reviews

ONLINE RESOURCES

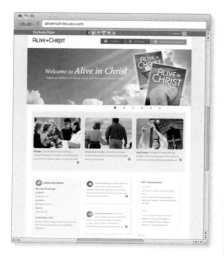

 Go to **aliveinchrist.osv.com**

You will find:

- Interactive lesson planning with web specific content and additional activities
- Step by step lesson instruction from printed Catechist Edition for integrated lesson planning
- Custom-built assessments to download and eAssessment links
- Interactive reviews that provide scores and the option to review answers
- Sunday readings with background and questions of the week

 Go to **osvparish.com**

You will find:

- Ask the Experts Q and A
- General Catechist Helps
- Community Connections and Blogs

Sharing the Message with First Graders

The Parables of Jesus First graders are very concrete thinkers. They learn through their senses and often take things literally. Because of this, they may not grasp the meaning of Jesus' parables, even with explanation. However, familiarity with these important stories Jesus told can lay the foundation for later, deeper understanding of Jesus' teaching. When they know Jesus' parables well, it will be easier to teach the great truths they convey when the children are ready to understand.

Teaching Tip: Many of Jesus' parables include objects such as, a coin or a mustard seed. When telling these stories, use props and pass them around to help make the stories more concrete for your young learners.

How First Graders Understand

- First graders learn through stories. Try to tell the story rather than read it.
- First graders learn the most from stories when they are able to hear them over and over again.
- First graders like to retell stories they have heard. Have the children use gestures or act out the story to help them remember.

"I really like to be read to."

Chapter Connections

Chapter Story

Invite

"A True Friend"

- Use this story to expand the chapter introduction.
- The children will relate the story to their own lives, reflecting on God's love for them.
- Connect how Jesus' stories teach us about God's love.

 Go to **aliveinchrist.osv.com** Lesson Planning section for this story.

NCEA IFG: ACRE Edition
Discover

Knowledge of the Faith

- Objective: To know and understand basic Catholic teaching about the Incarnate Word Jesus Christ as the way, truth, and life

Moral Formation

- Objective: To be aware of the importance of a well-formed conscience for decision making

Catholic Social Teaching
Live

 Use one of these features to introduce a principle and engage the children with an activity.

- Life and Dignity, Pages 284–285
- Option for the Poor, Pages 290–291

Music Options

 Use one or more of the following songs to enhance catechetical learning or for prayer.

- "The Good Shepherd," Live Prayer, Page 108
- "Jesus' Stories," Discover, Page 103

LECTIONARY CONNECTION

Chapter 6 highlights Lectionary-connected themes such as the Good Shepherd, redemption and God's love. If your parish aligns its curriculum to the liturgical year, you could use this chapter in connection with the following Sundays.

Year A

Fourth Sunday of Lent—Original Sin, social sin

Third Sunday of Easter—Paschal Mystery

Fourth Sunday of Easter—Good Shepherd

Year B

Twenty-fourth Sunday in Ordinary Time—faith, witness

Twenty-sixth Sunday in Ordinary Time—social justice, holiness

Twenty-ninth Sunday in Ordinary Time—redemption

Year C

Fourth Sunday of Easter—Trinity, divinity of Christ

Twenty-fourth Sunday in Ordinary Time—God's love

Thirtieth Sunday in Ordinary Time—humility, prayer

 Go to **aliveinchrist.osv.com** for a complete correlation ordered by the Sundays of the year and suggestions for how to integrate the Scripture readings into chapter lessons.

Name _____ Date _____

A Story About God

Color the pictures below. Then cut them out. Use the pictures
to tell the story of the Good Shepherd.

About the Bible

 Let Us Pray

Leader: Jesus called God the Father his shepherd. He watches over all of us.

"The LORD is my shepherd; there is nothing I lack." **Psalm 23:1**

All: Help us to trust in you, O God. Amen.

 God's Word

Jesus used stories when he spoke to the people. God's promise from long ago came true…"I will open my mouth in parables, I will announce what has lain hidden from the foundation of the world."

Based on Matthew 13:34–35

? What Do You Wonder?

- What are some of the stories that Jesus told?
- Where do you find the stories that Jesus tells us?

© Our Sunday Visitor

101

Optional Activity

Chapter Story: "A True Friend" *Verbal/Linguistic*

Use this story after the opening prayer, before explaining that Jesus told stories to teach about God's love.

- Read aloud the story while the children follow along.
- *Ask:* Why did Bug help Squirrel? Possible response: Bug didn't want anything bad to happen to Squirrel.
- *Say:* Bug was a good friend to Squirrel. Who is a good friend to you?
- When finished, transition back to the lesson instruction.

 Go to **aliveinchrist.osv.com** for Chapter Story.

 Let Us Pray

Invite the children to gather in the prayer space and make the Sign of the Cross. Choose a child to read aloud the Psalm verse from a Bible. Prompt the children's response.

Have the children move out of the prayer space and back to their seats.

Explain that Jesus told stories to teach about God's love.

Say: Jesus loved to tell stories about God the Father and his Kingdom. He used stories to teach us. Let's listen to the Gospel of Matthew to learn more about this.

 God's Word

Guide the children through the process of Scripture reflection.

- Invite them to close their eyes, be still and open their minds and hearts to what God is saying to them in this passage.
- Proclaim the Scripture.
- Maintain several moments of silence.
- *Ask:* What did you hear God say to you today?
- Invite volunteers to share.

What Do You Wonder?

Say: The stories of Jesus help us to learn how to follow him. Your life tells a story about another person who follows Jesus—You!

Invite the children to respond to the questions. Ask what else they might wonder about Jesus and the stories he told.

Objective

• Recognize that Jesus told stories like the Lost Sheep to show us how God watches over and guides us, always welcoming us back

We Learn from Stories

Ask: How is God like a shepherd?

• Write the children's responses on the board or on chart paper.

Read aloud the introductory paragraph.

• Tell the children that Jesus told stories about everyday life to teach lessons about God and his love for people.

Point out the illustration.

• Invite the children to describe what they see in the illustration.

God's Word

Proclaim "The Parable of the Lost Sheep."

⭐ Invite the children to underline what went wrong in the story. Then have the children circle what the shepherd did.

• *Ask:* Have you ever lost something? How did you feel when you found it?

We Learn from Stories

How is God like a shepherd?

Jesus was a wonderful storyteller. His stories tell about God's love. Jesus told this story about a shepherd.

1. Underline what went wrong in the story.

2. Circle what the shepherd did.

God's Word

The Parable of the Lost Sheep

There was a shepherd. He cared for 100 sheep. One sheep ran away. The shepherd was very worried. The shepherd left all his other sheep. He had to find the sheep that ran away.

The shepherd found the lost sheep. He was very happy. He told all his friends and neighbors that he had found his sheep.

Based on Luke 15:3–6

© Our Sunday Visitor

102 Chapter 6

Scripture Background

Luke 15:3–6

The work of a shepherd involves watchfulness, caring, and courage.

• In the Old Testament, the image of the shepherd defending his flock was used as a symbol both for God and for Israel's king.

• Jesus called himself the Good Shepherd, ready to lay down his life for his sheep.

• The Church refers to herself as God's flock.

Our Shepherd

In this story, the shepherd is like God. The sheep are like people. God does not want you to leave him. He will watch over you all the time, just like a shepherd.

When you make bad choices, you are like the lost sheep. Even when you don't choose what is right, God always wants you to come back to him. He wants you to love him and others. He wants you to know that he will always be there for you no matter what.

Share Your Faith

Think Draw lines to match the questions to the correct answers.

Who is the shepherd like? ●   ● Lost Sheep

Who are the sheep like? ●   ● God

What are you like when you make bad choices? ●   ● People

Share Discuss what God wants for us.

About the Bible **103**

Optional Activity

Activity Master 6: A Story About God

Distribute copies of the activity found on catechist page 101E.

- Read aloud the directions. Help the children cut out and order the pictures.
- As an alternative, you may wish to send this activity home with the children.

Our Shepherd

Ask the children what lesson Jesus is teaching about God's love in "The Parable of the Lost Sheep."

- If the children have difficulty answering, retell the story with God as the shepherd. Let the children interject when they catch on.

Read aloud the text.

- Tell the children that God's love is great and that he is happy when people come back to him.

Point out the photo.

- Invite the children to describe what they see in the photo.
- Ask the children to explain what the photo has in common with the parable of the Lost Sheep.
- Help the children to understand that God's love is like the love of a parent. A parent cares for us and guides us. A parent always loves us and welcomes us home.

 Music Option: Have the children sing, "Jesus' Stories," downloaded from **aliveinchrist.osv.com**.

Activity

Read aloud the directions for the Share Your Faith activity.

- Read through the activity and complete it together as a group.
- Discuss what God wants for us.

Quick Review

God is a shepherd because he watches over people and cares for them.

Objectives

- Describe a parable as a short story that Jesus told about everyday life to teach something about God
- Identify the Bible as the Church's holy book
- Name two parts of the Bible as the Old Testament and the New Testament

Stories About God

Ask: What can you find in the Bible?

- Write the children's responses on the board or on chart paper.

Read aloud both paragraphs.

- Tell the children what a parable is.
- Explain that the story that Jesus told about the lost sheep is an example of a parable.
- Ask the children to listen for how Jesus is like a shepherd.

 God's Word

Proclaim "The Good Shepherd."

- Explain that Jesus is the shepherd in the stained glass window.
- Direct the children to underline the ways that Jesus is like a shepherd.
- Explain that when Jesus says, "I will lay down my life for the sheep," he means he will do anything for them.

Stories about God

What can you find in the Bible?

A parable is a short story that teaches something important. The story you just read about the lost sheep is a parable. Jesus told parables to teach people about God.

Jesus is like a shepherd. He loves all God's people. He always cares for them. Read this parable that Jesus told.

> Underline the ways that Jesus is like a shepherd.

 God's Word

The Good Shepherd

"I am the good shepherd, and I know mine and mine know me, just as the Father knows me and I know the Father; and I will lay down my life for the sheep." John 10:14–15

104

Optional Activity

The Good Shepherd *Visual/Spatial*

Jesus as the Good Shepherd carrying one of his sheep was one of the most popular subjects of early Christian art.

- Have the children draw a picture of Jesus as the Good Shepherd with his sheep.
- When the children have finished their drawings, post them around the prayer space.

The Holy Book

The parable of the Good Shepherd is in the Bible. The Bible is the Word of God written in human words. The Bible is the Church's holy book.

There are two parts to the Bible. The first part is the **Old Testament**. It is about times before Jesus was born.

The second part is the **New Testament**. It tells about Jesus and his followers. The stories and parables that Jesus told are part of the New Testament.

Catholic Faith Words

Old Testament the first part of the Bible about God and his People before Jesus was born

New Testament the second part of the Bible about the life and teachings of Jesus, his followers, and the early Church

Connect Your Faith

Write about the Bible Use a Bible to find the answers to these questions.

1. Find the first book in the Old Testament. Trace the name of the book on the line below.

   Genesis

2. Find the first book of the New Testament. Trace the name of the book on the line below.

   Matthew

The Holy Book

Read aloud all three paragraphs.

- Show the children the Bible. Tell them that the Bible contains many smaller books.
- Point out the Old Testament and the New Testament.
- Explain that the Bible is different from every other book in the world. It is the Church's holy book.
- Tell the children that God speaks to us through the words in the Bible.
- Pass around the Bible so each child has a chance to see it and hold it.

Activity

Point out the Connect Your Faith activity and read aloud the directions.

- Show the children the Bible's table of contents.
- Help them find the titles of the first book of the Old Testament and the first book of the New Testament.
- Write *Genesis* and *Matthew* on the board or chart paper.
- Have the children trace the letters to write the titles of each book.

Quick Review

The Church's holy book is called the Bible. It is made up of the Old Testament and the New Testament.

✓ Quick Tip

Old Testament

The Old Testament used by Catholics contains forty-six books, written in various literary forms. They include stories, legends, poems, proverbs, law, and history.

New Testament

Twenty-seven books, written in the first century A.D., form the New Testament. The four Gospels recount the public life of Jesus. Acts describes the early development of the Church. The rest of the New Testament consists of Letters composed by early Church leaders and the Book of Revelation.

Our Catholic Life

Ask: What can you find in the Bible?

• Write the children's responses on the board or on chart paper.

Write the word *Bible* on the board or on chart paper. Show the children the Bible.

• Invite the children to listen carefully as you read the first two paragraphs.

• Emphasize that the stories in the Bible tell us about God's love for us and for all creation. The Bible also tells us how we can show our love for God.

• *Ask:* Where do you hear stories from the Bible?

The Two Parts of the Bible

• Direct attention to the chart, and have the children follow along as you read aloud the contents of the chart.

• *Ask:* What are some of your favorite Bible stories?

Refer to the Our Catholic Tradition reference section on student page 310. Explain that we hear stories, or readings from the Bible at Mass, during the Liturgy of the Word.

Live

Our Catholic Life

What can you find in the Bible?

The Bible is full of stories about God's love. The words of the Bible tell us how to show love for him and others.

You hear stories from the Bible at church, in school, and at home. You may have seen stories from the Bible made into books or videos.

The Two Parts of the Bible

The Old Testament	The New Testament
Here you will find stories about God and his People before Jesus was born. These stories are about holy men and women like Noah, Moses, Ruth, Jonah, and Daniel.	You will find the parables, or teaching stories, Jesus told here. The New Testament also tells about the coming of the Holy Spirit and the work of the first followers of Jesus.

© Our Sunday Visitor

106 Chapter 6

✓ Quick Tip

Applying the Bible Message

When sharing Bible stories with children, make a point of asking the following questions.

• What does this story mean to you?

• What can you learn from this story?

• How can you live the message of this story in your own life?

People of Faith

Saint Paul of the Cross, 1694–1775

Saint Paul of the Cross tried being a soldier, but decided that he wanted to be a priest instead. As a young man he spent a lot of time praying and reading the Bible to learn about Jesus. He read about Jesus' Death on the Cross. He wanted to always remember Jesus' sacrifice. That's why he added the words "of the Cross" to his name. Saint Paul helps us to remember that God is close to us and never forgets us.

October 19

Discuss: What story from the Bible helps you remember God's love?

 Learn more about Saint Paul at **aliveinchrist.osv.com**

© Our Sunday Visitor

Live Your Faith

Follow the Maze Use a pencil or crayon to find the right path through the maze so the shepherd can find his lost sheep.

About the Bible **107**

Catholic Social Teaching

Chapter Connections

To integrate Catholic Social Teaching into your lesson, choose one of the following features: Life and Dignity, pages 284–285; or Option for the Poor, pages 290–291.

- Start the Live step of the process by talking about Saint Paul of the Cross on page 107. Then move directly to the Catholic Social Teaching feature.
- Or, to expand the lesson, complete both pages 106 and 107, then move to the Catholic Social Teaching feature.
- Return to Chapter 6 for the prayer on page 108.

People of Faith

Tell the children about Saint Paul of the Cross.

- Invite a volunteer to read aloud the People of Faith story.
- Saint Paul of the Cross is known for his burning love for God.
- He traveled all over Italy, preaching about Jesus. He told people that Jesus' Death on the Cross was the greatest sign of God's love for us.
- As Saint Paul of the Cross traveled about doing good, all sorts of signs from Heaven happened around him. Everyone believed that these signs showed that God was with Saint Paul in an extraordinary way.
- *Ask:* What story from the Bible helps you remember God's love?

Encourage the children to go to **aliveinchrist.osv.com** at home to learn more about Saint Paul of the Cross.

Activity

Read aloud the directions for the Live Your Faith activity.

- Suggest that the children use their fingers to trace the maze paths before using a pencil or crayon.
- Allow time for the children to work independently on the activity.
- Ask the children to explain in their own words the meaning of the Parable of the Lost Sheep.

Let Us Pray

Prayer of Thanks

Tell the children that they will give thanks to Jesus, the Good Shepherd, for taking care of them.

Prepare

Teach the children the response, "Thank you, Jesus."

- Invite one person to be the leader.

 Rehearse "The Good Shepherd," downloaded from **aliveinchrist.osv.com**.

Gather

Invite the children to process to the prayer space.

Make sure that the children are seated comfortably. Have the children prepare their minds and hearts for prayer.

Have the leader stand near the prayer table.

Pray

Follow the order of prayer on the student page.

 Conclude by singing together "The Good Shepherd."

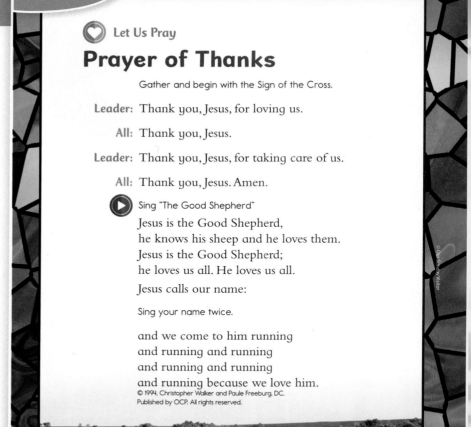

Live

Let Us Pray

Prayer of Thanks

Gather and begin with the Sign of the Cross.

Leader: Thank you, Jesus, for loving us.

All: Thank you, Jesus.

Leader: Thank you, Jesus, for taking care of us.

All: Thank you, Jesus. Amen.

Sing "The Good Shepherd"

Jesus is the Good Shepherd,
he knows his sheep and he loves them.
Jesus is the Good Shepherd;
he loves us all. He loves us all.
Jesus calls our name:

Sing your name twice.

and we come to him running
and running and running
and running and running
and running because we love him.

108 Chapter 6

 Liturgy Link

The Bible at Mass

Review the readings used at Mass.

- Explain to the children that the first of three readings at Mass is usually taken from the Old Testament, the second from the New Testament, and the third from one of the Gospels.

- Everyone stands when the Gospel is read, to honor the Lord Jesus.

Go to **aliveinchrist.osv.com** for Sunday readings, Scripture background, questions of the week, and seasonal resources.

FAMILY + FAITH
LIVING AND LEARNING TOGETHER

YOUR CHILD LEARNED >>>

This chapter teaches about the Bible, the holy book of the Church and its two parts—the Old Testament and the New Testament—that contain stories about God and his love for us.

God's Word

 Read **Matthew 13:10–15** to find out why Jesus used parables to teach.

Catholics Believe

- Jesus told short stories, or parables, to teach others something about God.
- The Bible is the Word of God written in human words.

To learn more, go to the *Catechism of the Catholic Church* #134–139 at **usccb.org**.

People of Faith

This week, your child met Blessed John XXIII. Known as "Good Pope John," he was both a student of the Bible and great storyteller.

CHILDREN AT THIS AGE >>>

How They Understand the Parables of Jesus First graders are very concrete thinkers. They learn through their senses and often take things literally. Because of this, they may not grasp the meaning of Jesus' parables, even with explanation. However, familiarity with these important stories Jesus told can lay the foundation for a later, deeper understanding of Jesus' teaching. When your child knows Jesus' parables, it will be easier to teach the great truths they convey when he or she is ready to understand.

CONSIDER THIS >>>

What is your favorite family story?

Stories of our personal history help us to discover that we are part of a bigger picture. Being a member of the Church helps us to be connected to the stories of salvation history. "The Holy Trinity brought the Church into being. The Father called the Church into existence. The Son established the Church. The Holy Spirit filled the Church with power and wisdom at Pentecost. The Holy Trinity abides with the Church always, creatively and providentially" (*USCCA, pp. 112–113*).

LET'S TALK >>>

- Have your child explain what the Bible is.
- Share one of your favorite stories from the Old or New Testaments.

LET'S PRAY >>>

Dear God, help our family always remember the good things you have done for us and to share those stories with others. Amen.

For a multimedia glossary of Catholic Faith Words, Sunday readings, seasonal and Saint resources, and chapter activities go to **aliveinchrist.osv.com**.

Alive in Christ, Grade 1 Chapter 6 **109**

Chapter 6 Review

A **Work with Words** Circle the correct answer.

1. The ____ is God's Word written in human words.

(Bible)   prayer

2. The ____ is about Jesus' life and teachings.

Old Testament   (New Testament)

3. A ____ is a short story that teaches something about God.

prayer   (parable)

4. The ____ is the first part of the Bible about God and his People before Jesus was born.

(Old Testament)   New Testament

B **Check Understanding** Draw a heart around the correct answer.

5. How is God like the Good Shepherd?

He is lost   ♡ He loves us

 Go to **aliveinchrist.osv.com** for an interactive review.

110 Chapter 6 Review

Family + Faith

Distribute the page to the children or parents/adult family members. Point out the chapter highlights, insights on how first graders understand concepts, the opportunity for the adults to reflect on their own experience and faith journey, and the family prayer.

Chapter Review

Use Catechist Quick Reviews to highlight lesson concepts.

A **Work with Words**
Have the children circle the correct answer.

B **Check Understanding**
Have the children draw a heart around the correct answer.

Go to **aliveinchrist.osv.com** to prepare customized and downloadable assessments, send eAssessments, and assign interactive reviews.

About the Bible **109–110**

Use Catechist Quick Reviews in each chapter to highlight lesson concepts for this unit and prepare for the Unit Review.

Have the children complete the Review pages. Then discuss the answers as a group. Review any concepts with which the children are having difficulty.

 Work with Words

Have the children trace the words to answer the questions.

Unit Review

A **Work with Words** Trace the words to answer the questions.

1. Who are the three Divine Persons in the Holy Trinity?

Father

Son

Holy Spirit

2. Who is the Son of God?

Jesus

3. What can you find in the Bible?

Stories about

God

Trinity **111**

Unit Review

B Check Understanding Circle the correct answer.

4. Jesus taught us to call God by what name?

John   Adam   (Father)

5. Who are Jesus, Mary, and Joseph?

The Trinity   The Church   (The Holy Family)

6. What stories did Jesus tell?

(Parables)   Prayer   Sheep

7. Who made all things?

The Shepherd   (God)   The Family

8. Who did God send to save his people?

(God the Son)   God the Father   Holy Family

9. What is the Church's holy book?

Old Testament   New Testament   (The Bible)

C Make Connections Draw one thing that we can learn about God from the Bible.

10.

B Check Understanding
Have the children circle the correct answer.

C Make Connections
Have the children draw one thing that we can learn about God from the Bible.

Go to **aliveinchrist.osv.com** to prepare customized and downloadable assessments, send eAssessments, and assign interactive reviews.

Jesus Christ

Our Catholic Tradition

- Jesus healed people. When he did this, he showed God's love for them. (CCC, 1509)

- Jesus showed his power when he healed others, and many people believed in him. (CCC, 548)

- Jesus showed us that the most important Commandment is to love God and to love others. (CCC, 2083)

- Jesus showed us how to pray when he taught his friends the Lord's Prayer. (CCC, 2759)

How does Jesus' command to love God with all your heart lead us to pray and care for others?

Unit 3 Overview

Chapter 7

The children will:

- identify Blessed Mother Teresa as an example of how we are to share God's love by caring for the sick
- recognize that Jesus' healings showed God the Father's power and love
- understand faith as the gift of believing and trusting in God so much that we do what he asks us to do

 Catholic Social Teaching: Live Your Faith

- Option for the Poor, Pages 290–291
- Human Solidarity, Pages 294–295

Chapter 8

The children will:

- identify words and actions that are signs of love
- understand that a Commandment is a law that God made for people to obey
- recognize that in the Great Commandment, Jesus taught to love God above all else and to love others the way you love yourself

 Songs of Scripture "LOVE God"

 Catholic Social Teaching: Live Your Faith

- Life and Dignity, Pages 284–285
- The Dignity of Work, Pages 292–293

Chapter 9

The children will:

- define prayer as talking and listening to God
- become more aware of the need to pray to get close to God
- learn that the Lord's Prayer is the prayer that Jesus taught his followers to pray to God the Father

 Catholic Social Teaching: Live Your Faith

- Life and Dignity, Pages 284–285
- Call to Community, Pages 286–287

Preview Unit Theme

Ask: What is the unit theme?

Summarize that the unit focuses on Jesus Christ.

Invite volunteers to read aloud each of the bullets in Our Catholic Tradition.

Explain to the children that they will learn about these things in the next three chapters.

Have the children study the photos and images. Invite volunteers to describe what they see. What do these images say about the unit theme?

Ask: How does Jesus' command to love God with all your heart lead us to pray and care for others?

After some discussion, explain to the children that they will be exploring this question in the next three chapters.

KEY CONCEPT

Jesus' healing actions show God's power and love. Faith is the gift of believing in God and doing as he asks.

DOCTRINAL CONTENT

- Blessed Mother Teresa is an example of how we are to share God's love by caring for the sick. (CCC, 2447)

- Jesus' healings showed God the Father's power and love. (CCC, 1503)

- Faith is the gift of believing and trusting in God so much that we do what he asks us to do. (CCC, 1814)

TASKS OF CATECHESIS

Helping children grow in a faith that is "known, celebrated, lived, and expressed in prayer" (NDC, 20).

This chapter focuses on the following tasks of catechesis.

- Promoting Knowledge of the Faith
- Education for Community Life

Catechist Background

Jesus went around to all the towns and villages, teaching in their synagogues, proclaiming the gospel of the kingdom, and curing every disease and illness. Matthew 9:35

➜ **Reflect** When have you felt God's healing love?

Anyone reading the Gospels for the first time must be struck by the amount of attention that is devoted to Jesus' acts of healing. Jesus healed many people—people with physical disabilities, people who were possessed by devils, and people suffering from leprosy and other debilitating diseases for which there was, at the time, no cure. Jesus lived amidst sickness, suffering, and early death in a society that believed that these things were punishments for sin. Jesus healed those who were sick to end their physical suffering, but also to convey a message about God's universal love and compassion.

Disciples who follow in Jesus' footsteps can become signs, as he is, of God's loving compassion. But in order to do this, Christians must learn to see Jesus in those who suffer. Blessed Mother Teresa of Calcutta became a sign of his presence for the people of Calcutta because she saw the face of Jesus in the faces of the city's poor. You, too, can be a sign of God for others.

➜ **Reflect** How are you a healing presence for others?

Catechist's Prayer

Jesus, Teacher and Healer, thank you for entrusting these children to me. Bless me with a generous heart that sees each child as your image. Amen.

Lesson Plan

Objectives	Process	Materials

Invite, 10 minutes

Jesus the Healer Page 115

- ♥ **Psalm 4:4** Pray the opening prayer.
- 📖 **Matthew 9:35** Reflect prayerfully on the Word.
- Discuss What Do You Wonder questions.

📶 **Optional Activity**
Chapter Story:
"How Are You?"

Discover, 35 minutes

Share God's Love Pages 116–117
- Identify Blessed Mother Teresa as an example of how we are to share God's love by caring for the sick

- Explain that Blessed Mother Teresa showed God's love when she cared for the poor and the sick.
- ☆ Circle what Blessed Mother Teresa did for those who were sick and dying.
- **Share Your Faith Activity** Identify how to help others who are sick.

☐ pencils

Jesus Heals Pages 118–119
- Recognize that Jesus' healings showed God the Father's power and love
- Understand faith as the gift of believing and trusting in God so much that we do what he asks us to do

- **Catholic Faith Words** faith
- Explain that Jesus healed people.
- 📖 **Luke 8:40–56** Proclaim "Have Faith."
- ☆ Underline what Jesus said to Jarius.
- **Connect Your Faith Activity** Draw part of the Scripture story.

☐ pencils
☐ crayons or markers
☐ index cards
- **Optional Activity**
Jesus' Life
☐ Activity Master 7
(Page 115E)

Live, 15 minutes

Our Catholic Life Pages 120–121

- Explain that like Jesus, people can care for those who are sick.
- ☆ Identify how to help someone feel better.
- **People of Faith** Learn about Saint Louise de Marillac.
- **Live Your Faith Activity** Thank someone who made you feel better when you were sick.

☐ pencils
☐ crayons or markers

Prayer for Healing Page 122

- Remind the children that prayer is a wonderful gift to give anyone who is sick.
- ▶ Rehearse "Heal Us, Lord."
- Follow the order of prayer.

📶 Download "Heal Us, Lord."

Family + Faith Page 123
Point out that the Catholic Families page provides chapter highlights, information on how first graders understand faith concepts, and family prayer.

Chapter Review Page 124
📶 **aliveinchrist.osv.com**
- Customize and Download Assessments
- Email Links to eAssessments
- Interactive Student Reviews

ONLINE RESOURCES

 Go to **aliveinchrist.osv.com**

You will find:

- Interactive lesson planning with web specific content and additional activities
- Step by step lesson instruction from printed Catechist Edition for integrated lesson planning
- Custom-built assessments to download and eAssessment links
- Interactive reviews that provide scores and the option to review answers
- Sunday readings with background and questions of the week

 Go to **osvparish.com**

You will find:

- Ask the Experts Q and A
- General Catechist Helps
- Community Connections and Blogs

Sharing the Message with First Graders

Jesus' Healings Illnesses and healing are still mysterious processes for many first grade children. We understand Jesus' healings as miraculous (and also as signs of his power and his spiritual healing), but children might sometimes see the healing and care that parents and doctors give as being quite similar. One difference we can point out is the immediacy of healing in Jesus' ministry. This shows that Jesus was able to heal in a way that no one else could.

Teaching Tip: As you talk about Jesus' healings with the children, focus especially on Jesus' compassion for others. He understood how people felt when they were suffering and wanted them to feel better.

How First Graders Understand

- Since first graders are so hands-on, they often pick-up germs. When they have a sore throat, or stomach ache, they like being cared for.
- First graders worry when they have to be separated from an ill family member who is in the hospital.
- Help first graders understand how God will take care of them and their families.

"When I am sick, my mom always makes me feel better."

Chapter Connections

Chapter Story

Invite

"How Are You?"

Use this story to expand the chapter introduction.

- The children will relate the story to their own lives, reflecting what makes them feel better when they are sick.
- Connect the children's experience of feeling better to being healed.

 Go to **aliveinchrist.osv.com** Lesson Planning section for this story.

NCEA IFG: ACRE Edition

Discover

Knowledge of the Faith

- Objective: To know and understand basic Catholic teaching about the Incarnate Word Jesus Christ as the way, truth, and life

Communal Life

- Objectives: To know the origin, mission, structure, and communal nature of the Church; to know the rights and responsibilities of the Christian faithful

Catholic Social Teaching

Live

 Use one of these features to introduce a principle and engage the children with an activity.

- Option for the Poor, Pages 290–291
- Human Solidarity, Pages 294–295

Music Options

 Use one or more of the following songs to enhance catechetical learning or for prayer.

- "Heal Us, Lord," Live Prayer, Page 122
- "Kindness," Discover, Page 117
- "Loving Others," Discover, Page 117
- "Jesus Wants to Help Us," Discover, Page 119

LECTIONARY CONNECTION

Chapter 7 highlights Lectionary-connected themes such as Divine Revelation, creation, faith, and love. If your parish aligns its curriculum to the liturgical year, you could use this chapter in connection with the following Sundays.

Year A
Twenty-ninth Sunday in Ordinary Time—faith, love of neighbor
Thirty-third Sunday in Ordinary Time—common good

Year B
Fourth Sunday of Easter—Trinity, Divine Revelation
Sixth Sunday of Easter—love, faith

Year C
Second Sunday of Easter—faith, love for God
Twentieth Sunday in Ordinary Time—creation

Go to **aliveinchrist.osv.com** for a complete correlation ordered by the Sundays of the year and suggestions for how to integrate the Scripture readings into chapter lessons.

Name _____ Date _____

Jesus' Life

Use words and pictures to tell about one part of Jesus' life.

Jesus the Healer

♡ Let Us Pray

Leader: Just as Jesus healed the sick and cared for his followers, the Apostles…

"Know that the LORD works wonders for his faithful one." **Psalm 4:4**

All: May we have the same faith and trust that Jesus can heal us. Amen.

✝ God's Word

Jesus went to every town and village. He taught in their meeting places and preached the Good News about God's Kingdom. Jesus also healed people with different kinds of disease and sickness. **Based on Matthew 9:35**

❓ What Do You Wonder?

- How does your faith in Jesus help you?
- When you are sick, what makes you better?

Jesus the Healer **115**

Optional Activity

Chapter Story: "How Are You?" *Verbal/Linguistic*

Use this story after the opening prayer, before explaining that when we are sick, we want to feel better.

- Read the story aloud as the children follow along.
- Ask the children why Jordan feels sick.
- *Ask:* What is one thing that makes you feel better when you are sick?
- After having the children tell what they learned about healing, transition back to the lesson instruction.

 Go to **aliveinchrist.osv.com** for Chapter Story.

🕐 Invite

♡ Let Us Pray

Invite the children to gather in the prayer space and make the Sign of the Cross. Read aloud the Psalm verse from a Bible. Prompt the children's response.

Have the children move out of the prayer space and back to their seats.

Explain that when we are sick, we want to feel better, or be healed.

Say: When people are sick and need to be healed, we look for doctors and medicines to help them get better. We also ask God for his help.

✝ God's Word

Guide the children through the process of Scripture reflection.

- Invite them to close their eyes, be still and open their minds and hearts to what God is saying to them in this passage.
- Proclaim the Scripture.
- Maintain several moments of silence.
- *Ask:* What did you hear God say to you today?
- Invite volunteers to share.

What Do You Wonder?

Say: Jesus helps people when they are sick. He cares and makes himself very close to those who are suffering. We are comforted when we have faith that Jesus is with us when we are sick.

Invite the children to respond to the questions. Ask what else they might wonder about their faith in Jesus and Jesus healing people.

Jesus the Healer **115**

Objective

- Identify Blessed Mother Teresa as an example of how we are to share God's love by caring for the sick

Share God's Love

Show the children the pictures of Blessed Mother Teresa.

- *Ask:* How did Mother Teresa love people?
- List the children's responses on the board or on chart paper.

Read aloud the first paragraph.

- Tell the children that the story about Mother Teresa takes place in Calcutta, India, where many poor people live in the streets.

Read aloud the introductory paragraph.

Blessed Mother Teresa

Read aloud "Blessed Mother Teresa."

- ⭐ Have the children circle Mother Teresa's loving actions. She smiled, held people's hands, prayed with them and for them.
- *Ask:* What prayer can you say for someone who is sick?

Share God's Love

How did Mother Teresa love people?

As a child, Mother Teresa loved to read stories about missionaries, especially those who spread Jesus, message and cared for people in India. When she became a religious sister she went to India to teach children about God's love.

Mother Teresa cared for the poor and sick in India. Read about how she showed God's love.

Blessed Mother Teresa

The streets of Calcutta, India, were very crowded with people. Many people were sick. They lived on the streets.

Mother Teresa saw a sick man. His clothes were dirty. He was covered with mud and very thin. The man was dying.

Before she became a religious sister, Mother Teresa's given name was Agnes.

© Our Sunday Visitor

116 Chapter 7

(i) Catechist Background

Blessed Mother Teresa of Calcutta

Agnes Gonxha Bojaxhiu (1910–1997) was only eighteen when she was sent by her community, the Sisters of Loretto in Ireland, to teach in Calcutta, India. In Calcutta, thousands of people are homeless, living on its streets.

- Mother Teresa, as she came to be known, left her religious order and founded a new one, the Missionaries of Charity.
- Mother Teresa was beatified by Pope Saint John Paul II in 2003.

Mother Teresa smiled at him. No one ever smiled at him. She and another nun took him to their hospital.

Mother Teresa had a hospital for the dying. There she and other women cared for people who were very sick. They held hands with dying people. They prayed with them and for them.

 Circle one thing that Blessed Mother Teresa did for those who were sick and dying.

God's Goodness

Blessed Mother Teresa knew that God's goodness is in all people. The people she helped could hear love in her voice. They could see love in her sweet smile. They could feel God's love in her touch.

Think Circle the things you would like to do to help others who are sick.

Share Choose one thing and talk about it with a partner.

Jesus the Healer **117**

God's Goodness

Read aloud the paragraph.

- Ask the children to recall some of the things Mother Teresa did for people. Possible responses: kind words, her smile, caring touch

- Tell the children that people experience God's love through the loving actions of other people.

- Explain that God the Father wants them to treat everyone as lovingly as they would treat his Son, Jesus.

 Music Option: Have the children sing, "Kindness" or "Loving Others," downloaded from **aliveinchrist.osv.com**.

Activity

Read aloud the directions for the Share Your Faith activity.

- Have the children work independently to circle their answers.

- After a short time, have them discuss with a partner.

Quick Review

Blessed Mother Teresa showed people God's love by caring for very poor people in India who were sick or dying.

✓ Quick Tip

A Sensitive Topic

When you talk about those who are sick and dying, remember that some children you teach may be grieving the death of someone close.

- Be ready to provide these children with assurance that death is not the end.

- Tell them that the Church encourages them to hope that loved ones are happy with God.

Discover

Objectives

- Recognize that Jesus' healings showed God the Father's power and love
- Understand faith as the gift of believing and trusting in God so much that we do what he asks us to do

Jesus Heals

Ask: Why did Jesus heal people?

- Write the children's responses on the board or on chart paper.

Read aloud the paragraph.

 ### God's Word

Tell the children that they will hear a Scripture story about Jesus' power to heal.

Proclaim "Have Faith."

- When you have read the first two paragraphs, pause and ask the children what they think Jesus will do next.
- Finish proclaiming the Scripture story.
- ⭐ Invite the children to underline what Jesus said to Jairus.
- Point out the illustration.
- Invite the children to describe what they see.

Work with Words

Hold up an index card with the word *faith* written on it.

- Ask the children why they think Jairus asked Jesus to heal his daughter.

Jesus Heals

Why did Jesus heal people?

When Jesus saw sick people, he felt sad for them. He did whatever he could to help people who needed him.

> ### Catholic Faith Words
>
> **faith** believing in God and all that he helps us understand about himself. Faith leads us to obey God.

⭐ Underline what Jesus said to Jarius.

 ### God's Word

Have Faith

One day a man named Jairus came to Jesus. Jairus said, "My daughter is very sick. I know you can help her."

Jesus agreed. On the way to Jairus' house, a servant came. "It is too late, he said to Jairus. Your daughter is dead."

Jesus told Jairus, "Do not be afraid; just have faith and she will be saved."

Then Jesus went into the house and took the daughter's hand. Jesus said, "Child, arise!" The girl's breath returned, and she got up. Her parents were full of joy.
Based on Luke 8:40–56

© Our Sunday Visitor

118

Scripture Background

Luke 8:40–56

Jairus was the father of the girl whom Jesus raised from the dead in Luke 8:40–56.

- He was an important man in the community.
- He was the ruler of a synagogue near Capernaum.

Jesus' Healing Actions

Jesus made people well. When Jesus healed people, it was a sign of God's power and love. His healing actions often changed their hearts, too. They saw God's love and power in Jesus. They came to believe in Jesus and have **faith** in him.

➜ What was Jesus' healing a sign of?

Connect Your Faith

Draw the Story Draw the part of the story about Jesus' healing that you like best.

Jesus the Healer **119**

Optional Activity

Activity Master 7: Jesus' Life

Distribute copies of the activity found on catechist page 115E.

• Tell the children that they will learn how to tell people about Jesus in a new way—without spoken words.

• As an alternative, you may wish to send this activity home with the children.

Jesus' Healing Actions

Read aloud the paragraph.

• Explain to the children how Jesus' acts of healing brought about bigger results than the simple restoration of bodily health.

• Tell the children that Jesus is God's Son, and when Jesus healed people, they felt God's power and love.

• Refer the children to page 305 in the Our Catholic Tradition reference section in the back of the Student Book to read how the Church brings God's healing to people through the Sacrament of Anointing of the Sick.

 Music Option: Have the children sing, "Jesus Wants to Help Us," downloaded from **aliveinchrist.osv.com**.

Activity

Point out the Connect Your Faith activity.

• Read aloud the directions.

• Provide art supplies and have the children work independently to draw their pictures.

• Invite the children to share their drawings with a partner.

Quick Review

Jesus was able to heal people because he is God. He healed them in order to show his Father's power and love.

Live

Our Catholic Life

Ask: How can you help people feel better?

- Lists the children's responses on the board or on chart paper.

Read aloud the first paragraph.

- Invite the children to give examples of how Jesus helped people who were sick, lonely, or sad.

Ways to Help Others

Introduce the chart and read it aloud.

 Invite the children to place a check mark next to the things they have done to help someone feel better.

Have the children act out ways to reach out to people who are sick, lonely or sad.

- Arrange the children into groups. Have them choose examples from the chart or from the list on the board or have them come up with their own ideas.
- Allow time for groups to act out their scenarios.

Our Catholic Life

How can you help people feel better?

Jesus helped people who were sick. He gave hope and friendship to people who were lonely. He did these things as signs of God's love. You can share signs of God's love, too.

Ways to Help Others

- Write a note or make a card that says you are thinking of the person
- Tell some jokes to cheer up the person.
- Do a chore to help the person.
- Pray for the person.
- Draw a colorful picture for the person.
- Record a song for the person.
- Help make a treat for the person to eat when he or she feels better.

 Place a check mark next to things you have done to help someone feel better.

© Our Sunday Visitor

120 Chapter 7

✓ Quick Tip

Practicing Empathy

Young children may not know the meaning of the word *empathy*, but they can use their imaginations to put themselves in another's place.

- Reinforce lessons on empathy by asking the children to ask themselves, "How would I feel if this were happening to me?"
- Remind the children of the Golden Rule: Treat others as you want them to treat you.

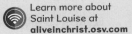

People of Faith

Saint Louise de Marillac, 1591–1660

Saint Louise lived in France. After her husband died, she was very sad. She met Saint Vincent de Paul and they started the Daughters of Charity, a group of nuns that worked in hospitals, homes, prisons, and during wars. Saint Louise wanted to share God's love by helping the poor and the sick. There are still over 25,000 Daughters of Charity who help the poor.

March 15

Discuss: How do you share God's love with others?

 Learn more about Saint Louise at **aliveinchrist.osv.com**

© Our Sunday Visitor

Live Your Faith

Thank Someone who has made you feel better when you were sick. Write their name and circle the thing that they gave you to help you feel better.

_____

Dear _____

Thank you for giving me:

Food

Love

Medicine

Jesus the Healer **121**

People of Faith

Tell the children about Saint Louise de Marillac.

- Invite a volunteer to read aloud the People of Faith story.
- Explain that Saint Vincent de Paul was overwhelmed with all the work that needed to be done to care for the poor and neglected children.
- As he got to know Saint Louise de Marillac, Saint Vincent de Paul realized that she was intelligent, humble, and very strong. In fact he found that she was the answer to his prayers. She and the Daughters of Charity were the helpers he needed.
- *Ask:* How do you share God's love with others? Possible answers: care for those who are sick, donate food

 Encourage the children to go to **aliveinchrist.osv.com** at home to learn more about Saint Louise de Marillac.

Activity

Read aloud the directions for the Live Your Faith activity.

- Direct the children to write the name of someone who made them feel better.
- Have the children circle what the person gave them to make them feel better.

Catholic Social Teaching

Chapter Connections

To integrate Catholic Social Teaching into your lesson, choose one of the following features: Option for the Poor, pages 290–291; or Human Solidarity, pages 294–295.

- Start the Live step of the process by talking about Saint Louise de Marillac on page 121. Then move directly to the Catholic Social Teaching feature.
- Or, to expand the lesson, complete both pages 120 and 121, then move to the Catholic Social Teaching feature.
- Return to Chapter 7 for the prayer on page 122.

Let Us Pray
Prayer for Healing

Tell the children that people who are sick need our prayers.

Prepare

Ask the children to name people they know who are sick, so that the group can pray for them.

- Teach the children their responses.

 Rehearse "Heal Us, Lord," downloaded from **aliveinchrist.osv.com**.

Gather

Invite the children to process to the prayer space. Have them bring their books and place them on their laps.

- Invite the children to quiet themselves for prayer.
- Ask them to think of people who are sick.

Pray

Follow the order of prayer on the student page.

 Conclude by singing "Heal Us, Lord."

Live

Let Us Pray
Prayer for Healing

Gather and begin with the Sign of the Cross.

Leader: Jesus, Son of God, we pray for those who are sick. For children who are sick, we pray.

All: Help them be strong and well again.

Leader: Jesus, Son of God, we pray for those who are sick. For children who are sick, we pray.

All: Help them be strong and well again.

Leader: For all people who are sick, we pray.

All: Help them be strong and well again.

Leader: Jesus, Son of God, we pray for those who take care of the sick. For all who care for others, we pray.

All: Give them grace and strength. Amen.

Sing "Heal Us, Lord"
Heal us, Lord.
We feel the power of your love.
Let your Spirit come unto us.
© 2001, John Burland. All rights reserved.

122   Chapter 7

Liturgy Link

Praying for Those Who Are Sick

Remind the children that prayer is a wonderful gift to give anyone who is sick.

- Prepare a big cardboard flower with a stiff stem and room for several construction paper petals.
- On each petal, have the children print the name of a person for whom they want to pray, and attach it to the flower.

 Go to **aliveinchrist.osv.com** for Sunday readings, Scripture background, questions of the week, and seasonal resources.

FAMILY+FAITH
LIVING AND LEARNING TOGETHER

YOUR CHILD LEARNED >>>

This chapter is about how Jesus healed people who were sick and cared for those who were lonely; he asks us to help others who are sick or sad.

God's Word

 Read **Matthew 9** to learn about Jesus' teachings and the many miracles that he worked.

Catholics Believe

• Jesus' healing actions show God's power and love.
• Faith is the gift of believing in God and doing as he asks.

To learn more, go to the *Catechism of the Catholic Church* #547–550 at **usccb.org**.

People of Faith

This week, your child met Saint Louise de Marillac, the founder of a religious order dedicated to the care of those who are poor and sick.

CHILDREN AT THIS AGE >>>

How They Understand Jesus' Healings Illnesses and healing are still mysterious processes for many first grade children. As adults, we understand Jesus' healings as being miraculous (a sign of his power and his spiritual strength), but your child might sometimes see the healing and care that parents and doctors give as being quite similar. One difference we can point out is the immediacy of healing in Jesus' ministry. This shows that Jesus was able to heal in a way that no one else could.

CONSIDER THIS >>>

What makes a relationship grow?

Relationships require a commitment of time and presence. Faith is a relationship with God that begins as a gift, but like all our relationships requires time and presence. "God never forces his truth and love upon us. He reveals himself to us as free human beings, and our faith response to him is made within the context of freedom" (*USCCA, p. 39*).

LET'S TALK >>>

• Ask your child how Jesus cared for those who were sick.
• Share a time when someone made you feel better physically, emotionally, or spiritually.

LET'S PRAY >>>

 Dear Saint Louise, pray for us so we can be patient when we are sick and help us be kind to those who are feeling sad. Amen.

For a multimedia glossary of Catholic Faith Words, Sunday readings, seasonal and Saint resources, and chapter activities go to **aliveinchrist.osv.com**.

Alive in Christ, Grade 1 Chapter 7 **123**

Chapter 7 Review

A **Check Understanding** Trace the words to answer the questions.

1. What did Blessed Teresa of Calcutta do to show God's love to sick people?

She cared.

2. What did Jesus do to show God's power and love?

He healed.

3. What is faith?

Believing in
God.

B **Make Connections** Circle the right answer.

4. How can you help a sick person?

play   fight   (pray)

5. How can you help a sad person?

swim   (visit them)   sleep

Go to **aliveinchrist.osv.com** for an interactive review.

124 Chapter 7 Review

Distribute the page to the children or parents/adult family members. Point out the chapter highlights, insights on how first graders understand concepts, the opportunity for the adults to reflect on their own experience and faith journey, and the family prayer.

Chapter Review

Use Catechist Quick Reviews to highlight lesson concepts.

A **Work with Words**
Have the children trace the words to answer each question.

B **Check Understanding**
Have the children circle the correct answer.

Go to **aliveinchrist.osv.com** to prepare customized and downloadable assessments, send eAssessments, and assign interactive reviews.

KEY CONCEPT

A Commandment is a law that God made for people to obey. The Great Commandment teaches that you are to love God above all else and love others as you love yourself.

DOCTRINAL CONTENT

- A Commandment is a law that God made for people to obey. (CCC, 2056)

- Jesus taught the Great Commandment to love God above all else and to love others the way you love yourself. (CCC, 2055)

TASKS OF CATECHESIS

Helping children grow in a faith that is "known, celebrated, lived, and expressed in prayer" (NDC, 20).

This chapter focuses on the following tasks of catechesis:

- Moral Formation
- Education for Community Life

Catechist Background

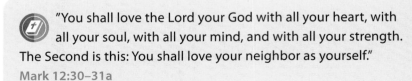

"You shall love the Lord your God with all your heart, with all your soul, with all your mind, and with all your strength. The Second is this: You shall love your neighbor as yourself."

Mark 12:30–31a

→ **Reflect** Why is it important to love your neighbor?

One of Jesus' followers, a scholar of the law, questioned him about inheriting eternal life. Instead of telling him, Jesus asked the scholar how he read the law, and the scholar responded with what is referred to as the Great Commandment. Jesus affirmed his answer. Love for God is the greatest commandment, and love for neighbor is like it.

Who is your neighbor? Jesus died for all people out of love. He died even for those who were his enemies. The Lord asks you to love as he does, loving even those who are the most difficult to love.

The crazy driver, the bad-mouthed child around the block, the ornery grandparent, the grumpy grocery store checker, the beggar on the street—on a daily basis there are many people with whom you may have a difficult time. The command to love them can be a great test of faith, yet that challenge comes from Jesus. Catholics are called to see those who are sick, poor, and disadvantaged as neighbors. Catholics are called to love the child who disrespects them, the parent who grieves them, and the co-worker who antagonizes them.

→ **Reflect** Who is your "neighbor"?

Catechist's Prayer

God of many blessings, I cherish the gifts you have given me. I promise to use these gifts to help the children know you. Amen.

Lesson Plan

Objectives	Process	Materials

⏱ Invite, 10 minutes

Jesus Teaches Love Page 125

- ♥ **Psalm 119:44** Pray the opening prayer.
- ✷ **Mark 12:28–31** Reflect prayerfully on the Word.
- Discuss What Do You Wonder questions.

🌐 **Optional Activity**
Chapter Poem:
"Favorite Gifts"

⏱ Discover, 35 minutes

Show Your Love Pages 126–127
- Identify words and actions that are signs of love

- Explain that gifts can be a way to show love.
- ☆ Underline what Brooke and her grandpa liked to do.
- Explain that there are many ways to show love.
- **Share Your Faith Activity** Identify how to show love for others.

☐ pencils
☐ crayons or markers

Love God and Others Pages 128–129
- Understand that a Commandment is a law that God made for people to obey
- Recognize that in the Great Commandment, Jesus taught to love God above all else and to love others the way you love yourself

- **Catholic Faith Words** Commandment, Great Commandment
- Explain that we should love God and others.
- ✷ **Luke 10:25–28** Proclaim "The Greatest Commandment."
- ☆ Circle what the law says about loving God and others.
- **Connect Your Faith Activity** Match the actions in the pictures to the words.

☐ pencils
☐ index cards
- **Optional Activity** Love God and Others
☐ Activity Master 8 (Page 125E)

⏱ Live, 15 minutes

Our Catholic Life Pages 130–131

- Explain that there are many ways to show love for God and others.
- ☆ Write one way to love God and one way to love others.
- **People of Faith** Learn about Saint Thomas of Villanova.
- **Live Your Faith Activity** Draw one way someone has shown God's love this week.

☐ pencils
☐ crayons or markers

Pray with God's Word Page 132

- Teach the children their responses.
- ▶ Rehearse "Loving God."
- Follow the order of prayer.

🌐 Download "Loving God."

Family + Faith Page 133

Point out that the Catholic Families page provides chapter highlights, information on how first graders understand faith concepts, and family prayer.

Chapter Review Page 134

🌐 aliveinchrist.osv.com

- Customize and Download Assessments
- Email Links to eAssessments
- Interactive Student Reviews

ONLINE RESOURCES

 Go to **aliveinchrist.osv.com**

You will find:

- Interactive lesson planning with web specific content and additional activities
- Step by step lesson instruction from printed Catechist Edition for integrated lesson planning
- Custom-built assessments to download and eAssessment links
- Interactive reviews that provide scores and the option to review answers
- Sunday readings with background and questions of the week

 Go to **osvparish.com**

You will find:

- Ask the Experts Q and A
- General Catechist Helps
- Community Connections and Blogs

Sharing the Message with First Graders

The Great Commandment The concrete way of thinking that is characteristic of most first graders may sometimes make it difficult for them to know how to love God, whom they cannot see, above all things. However, adults in their lives can make this practical for them by helping them understand that we show our love for God by talking with him and making the choices he would have us make. We also show love to God when we are kind and loving towards others.

Teaching Tip: Throughout the year, when talking about good things we should do as followers of Christ, refer both to how these actions are loving towards God and also how they are loving towards others.

How First Graders Understand

- First graders like to sing. Teach them new songs as well as sing songs they are already familiar with.
- First graders can solve problems. Give them some puzzles and situations that they can try to figure out.
- Repetition and recognition work well with first graders. Point out that their kindness, care, and forgiveness for others are signs of their love for God.

"I like to dance and move around. Use music, gestures, sign language and role-play during the lesson."

Chapter Poem

Invite

"Favorite Gifts"

Use this poem to expand the chapter introduction.

- The children will relate the poem to their own lives, reflecting on a special gift someone has given to them.
- Connect the children's experience to what makes a gift special.

 Go to **aliveinchrist.osv.com** Lesson Planning section for this poem.

NCEA IFG: ACRE Edition

Discover

Moral Formation

- Objectives: To be knowledgeable about the teachings of Jesus and the Church as the basis of Christian morality and to understand Catholic Social Teaching; to be aware of the importance of a well-formed conscience for decision making

Communal Life

- Objectives: To know the origin, mission, structure, and communal nature of the Church; to know the rights and responsibilities of the Christian faithful

Catholic Social Teaching

Live

 Use one of these features to introduce a principle and engage the children with an activity.

- Life and Dignity, Pages 284–285
- The Dignity of Work, Pages 292–293

Music Options

 Use the following song to enhance catechetical learning or for prayer.

- "Loving God," Live Prayer, Page 132

LECTIONARY CONNECTION

 Chapter 8 highlights Lectionary-connected themes such as compassion, love for God, and charity. If your parish aligns its curriculum to the liturgical year, you could use this chapter in connection with the following Sundays.

Year A

First Sunday of Advent—Holy Family, Fourth Commandment

Twenty-third Sunday in Ordinary Time—conversion

Thirtieth Sunday in Ordinary Time—Great Commandment

Year B

Fifth Sunday of Easter—mission

Sixth Sunday of Easter—charity

Twenty-third Sunday in Ordinary Time—compassion

Twenty-ninth Sunday in Ordinary Time—sacrifice

Year C

Third Sunday of Lent—God's mercy

Fourth Sunday of Lent—good works

Second Sunday of Easter—love for God

Twenty-sixth Sunday in Ordinary Time—compassion, social justice

Go to **aliveinchrist.osv.com** for a complete correlation ordered by the Sundays of the year and suggestions for how to integrate the Scripture readings into chapter lessons.

Name _____   Date _____

Love God and Others

Listen to each sentence. Draw a happy face next to some ways
to love God and others.

☐ **1.** Say "I'm sorry."

☐ **2.** Pick up your toys.

☐ **3.** Tell someone they can't play.

☐ **4.** Pray.

☐ **5.** Make your brother or sister cry.

☐ **6.** Help at home.

☐ **7.** Go to Mass.

☐ **8.** Help a classmate who is sad.

☐ **9.** Take something that does not belong to you.

☐ **10.** Push or shove someone.

Jesus Teaches Love

 Let Us Pray

Leader: God, we want to follow your teachings.

"I will keep your law always,
for all time and forever." Psalm 119:44

All: God, we want to follow your teachings.
Amen.

God's Word

One of the men asked Jesus: "Teacher, what is the most important commandment?" Jesus answered: "Love the Lord your God with all your heart, soul, and mind...and love others as much as you love yourself." Based on Mark 12:28–31

What Do You Wonder?

- Why is it important to love others?
- How do you show love?

125

© Our Sunday Visitor

Optional Activity

Chapter Poem: "Favorite Gifts" *Verbal/Linguistic*

Use this poem after the opening prayer, before explaining that God gave us laws to help us live together.

- Read aloud the poem.
- Ask the children what kinds of gifts they like to receive.
- *Ask:* What is a special gift someone has given to you?
- After having the children tell you what they learned about gifts, transition back to the lesson instruction.

 Go to **aliveinchrist.osv.com** for Chapter Poem.

❤ Let Us Pray

Invite the children to gather in the prayer space and make the Sign of the Cross. Choose a child to be the leader. Read aloud the Psalm verse from a Bible. Prompt the children's response.

Have the children move out of the prayer space and back to their seats.

Explain that God gave us laws to help us live together.

Say: Jesus came to show and teach us about God's love. Let's listen to a reading from the Gospel of Matthew to find out more.

✝ God's Word

Guide the children through the process of Scripture reflection.

- Invite them to close their eyes, be still and open their minds and hearts to what God is saying to them in this passage.
- Proclaim the Scripture.
- Maintain several moments of silence.
- *Ask:* What did you hear God say to you today?
- Invite volunteers to share.

What Do You Wonder?

Say: Love is very important in each of our lives. God loves us as we are and asks us to love others as much as we love ourselves.

Invite the children to respond to the questions. Ask what else they might wonder about God's love and how we share God's love with others.

Discover

Objective
- Identify words and actions that are signs of love

Show Your Love
Ask: What gift can you give?

- Write the children's responses on the board or on chart paper.

The Gift
Read aloud the first page of the story.

- Read the story a second time and involve the children in the story by asking one child to pretend to be Brooke and another to be Brooke's mom.
- Give the "actors" simplified lines of what is in the text on this page.
- As you read, give the children a cue, such as pointing a finger, for when to say their lines.
- ⭐ Direct the children to underline the things that Brooke and her grandpa like to do.
- *Ask:* What do you think Brooke will give her grandpa?

Show Your Love
What gift can you give?

The Gift

Brooke asked, "Mom, what can I do for Grandpa's birthday?"

Mom said, "Let's think. What do you and Grandpa like to do?"

<u>"We like to build sandcastles at the beach. He plays checkers with me, too,"</u> said Brooke.

Mom asked, "Is there anything else?"

"Yes!" Brooke said. "<u>He likes my drawings.</u> He always saves them. I've got it! Thanks, Mom!"

> ⭐ Underline the things that Brooke and her Grandpa like.

© Our Sunday Visitor

126 Chapter 8

🏃 Reaching All Learners

Critical Thinking
The question above asks the children to suggest what Brooke will give her grandpa. The children need to use the clues in the story to figure out a logical answer.

- Some children may give a general answer, such as "candy."
- These children need direction in thinking back to what they heard. If needed, reread those story sections.

On Grandpa's birthday, Brooke gave him a gift.

It was a drawing of Brooke and Grandpa playing checkers together. The picture said, "I love you, Grandpa."

"Thank you, Brooke," said Grandpa. "This is the best gift! I will hang it up for everyone to see."

"Great!" Brooke said happily. "Let's go play checkers!"

© Our Sunday Visitor

Share Your Faith

Think How did Brooke show love with her gift? Draw one way you can show love to someone else.

Share Share your work with a partner.

127

Finish reading the story.

- Ask the children to look at Brooke's drawing.
- Discuss with the children how Brooke showed her love for her grandpa.
- Ask the children to name other gifts that don't cost money and show love. Possible answers: a smile, a hug, some help, something you make

Activity

Read aloud the directions for the Share Your Faith activity.

- Discuss the answer to the first question together as a group.
- Invite the children to draw how they show love for someone else.
- Have the children share their drawing with a partner.

Quick Review

The best gift to give someone is love.

Optional Activity

Chores Can Be Gifts *Verbal/Linguistic*

Discuss with the children how family chores can be seen as gifts to the whole family.

- Have the children ask family members about some of the things they do to help the family.
- Explain that family members should do their chores out of love for one another.

Objectives

- Understand that a Commandment is a law that God made for people to obey
- Recognize that in the Great Commandment, Jesus taught to love God above all else and to love others the way you love yourself

Love God and Others

Ask: What did Jesus teach about love?

- Write the children's responses on the board or on chart paper.

Read aloud the paragraph.

- Explain that people have always argued about the best way to please God.
- Tell the children that one man asked Jesus whether his answer was correct.

 God's Word

Proclaim "The Greatest Commandment."

- Have the children say the question the man asked.
- Then have them say aloud the answer the man gave to Jesus' question.
- Have the children circle what the law says about loving God and others.
- *Ask:* How much should you love God and others? Love God above all else, and others as yourself.

Love God and Others

What did Jesus teach about love?

Brooke's drawing was a sign of her love for her Grandpa. Listen to one of Jesus' teachings on love.

> Circle what the law says about loving God and others.

 God's Word

The Greatest Commandment

One day a man said, "I want to be happy with God forever. What should I do?"

Jesus asked, "What is written in the law?"

The man replied, "You shall love the Lord, your God, with all your heart, with all your being, with all your strength, and with all your mind, and your neighbor as yourself."

Jesus said, "You have answered correctly." Based on Luke 10:25–28

 Songs of Scripture

LOVE God

Teach these hand motions for the chorus of "LOVE God."

- Have the children cross their arms over their chest when singing or spelling *love*.
- For *God*, have them extend both arms upward.
- For *praise*, have them place their hands around their mouths like a megaphone.

> ▶ Use *Songs of Scripture*, Grades 1–3 CD, Track 4

The Great Commandment

A **Commandment** is a law that God made for people to obey. Loving God and others is the most important Commandment. This law is called the Great Commandment.

The **Great Commandment** teaches you to love God more than anything. It also tells you to love others as you love yourself.

➜ **What are some ways parents show love to their children?**

Catholic Faith Words

Commandment a law that God made for people to obey

Great Commandment the law that tells you to love God above all else and to love others the way you love yourself

Connect Your Faith

Match the Picture Match the actions in the pictures to the different ways that someone in your family shows love for God and others.

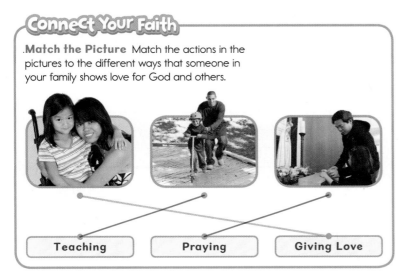

| Teaching | Praying | Giving Love |

Jesus Teaches Love **129**

Optional Activity

Activity Master 8: Love God and Others

Distribute copies of the activity on catechist page 125E.

- Tell the children that they will create a checklist of ways to show love.
- As an alternative, you may wish to send the activity home with the children.

The Great Commandment

Read aloud the paragraphs.

- Explain to the children that the main way you show your love for God is by obeying his command to love other people.

Work with Words

Hold up index cards with the words *Commandment* and *Great Commandment* written on them.

- Have the children say the words aloud.
- Read aloud the definitions.
- Refer the children to pages 314–315 in the Our Catholic Tradition reference section in the back of the Student Book for more about the Great Commandment and the Ten Commandments.

Ask: What are some ways parents show love to their children? Possible responses: care for them, make meals, help with school-work, pray with them

Activity

Point out the Connect Your Faith activity and read aloud the directions.

- Direct the children to match the actions in the pictures to the correct words below.
- Review the correct answers with the children.

Quick Review

The Great Commandment tells people to love God and love others.

Our Catholic Life

Ask the children to recall the Great Commandment.

Ask: How can you show love for God and for others?

- Write their answers on the board or on chart paper.

Read aloud the first sentence.

- Draw attention to the chart by reading the second sentence.

Love God and Others

- Read aloud the heading of the left column *Love God*.
- Invite the children to follow along as three volunteers take turns reading aloud the suggestions.
- Repeat this process for the other column headed *Love Others*.
- ⭐ Direct the children to write on the chart one way they can love God and one way they can love others.
- Invite volunteers to share their ideas.
- Encourage the children to do what they have written. Remind them that when they do these things, they are following Jesus and living the Great Commandment.

Our Catholic Life

How can you show love for God and for others?

There are many ways to keep the Great Commandment. Here are some ways that you can show love for God and for others.

Love God and Others

Love God	Love Others
Pray at meals and bedtime.	Do what parents and family members ask of you without grumbling.
Learn about God at home, at church, and in school.	Share what you have.
Get to know the stories in the Bible.	Be kind. Don't tease or fight.

 On the line above, write one way you can love God and love others.

© Our Sunday Visitor

✓ Quick Tip

Expressing Affection

People have different ways of expressing affection, often related to family history and cultural customs.

- Help the children see that love, affection, and friendship can be expressed in a variety of ways, from kind words to comforting gestures.
- Remind the children that expressions of affection may be appropriate or inappropriate depending on the people and the circumstances involved.

People of Faith

Saint Thomas of Villanova, 1486–1555

Saint Thomas was a teacher, a monk, and a bishop in Spain. He wanted to love people like Jesus did. He always tried to live the Great Commandment. Saint Thomas gave his money to people who had nothing. He tried to help them find work, too. He found homes for many orphaned children. He paid to free many slaves. Because of all the good things he did, Saint Thomas was called "Father of the Poor."

September 8

Discuss: When has your family given food to the poor?

 Learn more about Saint Thomas at **aliveinchrist.osv.com**

Live Your Faith

Draw a picture of a time when you shared with someone else.

131

Catholic Social Teaching

Chapter Connections

To integrate Catholic Social Teaching into your lesson, choose one of the following features: Life and Dignity, pages 284–285; or the Dignity of Work, pages 292–293.

- Start the Live step of the process by talking about Saint Thomas of Villanova on page 131. Then move directly to the Catholic Social Teaching feature.

- Or, to expand the lesson, complete both pages 130 and 131, then move to the Catholic Social Teaching feature.

- Return to Chapter 8 for the prayer on page 132.

People of Faith

Tell the children about Saint Thomas of Villanova.

- Invite a volunteer to read aloud the People of Faith story.

- Explain that Saint Thomas of Villanova lived in Spain.

- Each morning several hundred poor came to Thomas' door and received a meal, wine and money. Some people criticized him and said people took advantage of him. To that Saint Thomas replied, "If there are people who refuse to work, that is for the government and the police to deal with. My duty is to assist and relieve those who come to my door."

- He wore shabby mended clothes and was often called absent-minded. His fellow friars were often embarrassed by him.

- *Ask:* When has your family given food to the poor?

 Encourage the children to go to **aliveinchrist.osv.com** at home to learn more about Saint Thomas of Villanova.

Activity

Read aloud the directions and discuss the Live Your Faith activity as a group.

- Allow time for the children to draw and share their pictures.

Let Us Pray
Pray with God's Word

Prepare
Teach the children their responses.

 Rehearse "Loving God," downloaded from **aliveinchrist.osv.com**.

Gather
Invite the children to process to the prayer space.

- Make sure the children are seated comfortably.
- Prompt the children to quiet themselves for prayer.

Pray
Follow the order of prayer on the student page.

- Optional reading: Luke 8:16.

 Conclude by singing together "Loving God."

Live

Let Us Pray
Pray with God's Word

Gather and begin with the Sign of the Cross.

Leader: Blessed be God.

All: Blessed be God forever.

Leader: A reading from the holy Gospel according to Matthew.

Read Matthew 5:14–16.

The Gospel of the Lord.

All: Praise to you, Lord Jesus Christ.

 Sing "Loving God"

Love the Lord, your God,
with all your heart,
with all your soul,
with all your mind,
and with all your strength.
Love the Lord, your God,
with all your heart,
with all your soul,
with all your mind,
and with all your strength.

© 2010, Chet A. Chambers. Published by Our Sunday Visitor, Inc.

132 Chapter 8

Liturgy Link

Processions
Have groups of children recall times they have seen processions during Mass.

- Appoint children to pretend to be the cross-bearer, the servers, the reader, and the priest in an entrance procession.

 Go to **aliveinchrist.osv.com** for Sunday readings, Scripture background, questions of the week, and seasonal resources.

FAMILY+FAITH
LIVING AND LEARNING TOGETHER

YOUR CHILD LEARNED >>>

This chapter explains that a Commandment is a law God made for people to obey, and that we are called to love God and others.

God's Word
 Read **Mark 12:28–31** to learn more about how Jesus wants us to love God.

Catholics Believe
- A Commandment is a law that God made for people to obey.
- The Great Commandment teaches that you are to love God above all else and love others as you love yourself.

To learn more, go to the *Catechism of the Catholic Church* #2052–2055 at **usccb.org**.

People of Faith
This week, your child met Saint Thomas of Villanova, a Spanish bishop whose generosity to the poor gave him the name, "Father of the Poor."

CHILDREN AT THIS AGE >>>

How They Understand the Great Commandment The concrete way of thinking that is characteristic of most first graders may sometimes make it difficult for them to know how to love God, whom they cannot see, above all things. However, you can make this practical for your child by helping him or her understand that we show our love for God by talking with him and making the good choices he wants us to make. We also show love to God when we are kind and loving toward others.

CONSIDER THIS >>>

What is the greatest priority in your life?

Our first response would probably be family. Yet, Jesus said we must love God first then everything falls in order, including our relationships. "You shall love the Lord, your God, with all your heart, with all your soul, and with all your mind. This is the greatest and the first commandment. The second is like it: You shall love your neighbor as yourself (Mt 22:37–39)" (*USCCA, p. 309*).

LET'S TALK >>>
- Have your child name one way he/she shows love to God and one way he/she shows love to others.
- Talk about why God's laws are important.

LET'S PRAY >>>
 Saint Thomas, help us care for people who don't have enough money and people who are hungry. Amen.

For a multimedia glossary of Catholic Faith Words, Sunday readings, seasonal and Saint resources, and chapter activities go to **aliveinchrist.osv.com**.

Alive in Christ, Grade 1 Chapter 8 **133**

Chapter 8 Review

A **Work with Words** Circle the correct word to complete each sentence.

1. A Commandment is a ___ God made for people to obey.

    parable   (law)

2. ___ taught the Great Commandment.

    (Jesus)   Jarius

3. The Great Commandment begins with ___ God.

    (loving)   knowing

4. You can love God by ___.

    (praying)   pushing

B **Check Understanding** Draw a picture to show a way to love others.

5.

Go to **aliveinchrist.osv.com** for an interactive review.

134 Chapter 8 Review

Chapter Review

Use Catechist Quick Reviews to highlight lesson concepts.

A **Work with Words**
Have the children circle the correct word to complete each sentence.

B **Check Understanding**
Have the children draw a picture to show a way to love others.

 Go to **aliveinchrist.osv.com** to prepare customized and downloadable assessments, send eAssessments, and assign interactive reviews.

Jesus Teaches Love **133–134**

KEY CONCEPT

Prayer is talking and listening to God. Jesus taught his friends how to pray the Lord's Prayer.

DOCTRINAL CONTENT

- Prayer is talking and listening to God. (CCC, 2559)
- We need prayer to get close to God. (CCC, 2565)
- The Lord's Prayer is the prayer that Jesus taught his followers to pray to God the Father. (CCC, 2759)

TASKS OF CATECHESIS

Helping children grow in a faith that is "known, celebrated, lived, and expressed in prayer" (NDC, 20).

This chapter focuses on the following tasks of catechesis:

- Promoting Knowledge of the Faith
- Teaching to Pray

Catechist Background

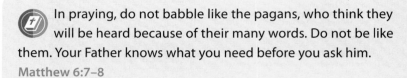

In praying, do not babble like the pagans, who think they will be heard because of their many words. Do not be like them. Your Father knows what you need before you ask him.
Matthew 6:7–8

➜ **Reflect** Why is prayer important?

Jesus was a man of prayer. He prayed alone on a mountaintop; he prayed as he was baptized; he prayed before choosing his Apostles; and he prayed during his agony in the garden before his arrest. Jesus prayed often, and eventually his disciples asked him to teach them how to pray. Jesus responded by teaching his disciples the Lord's Prayer.

Jesus not only prayed often, but he also prayed with confidence of being heard. His example is one of serenity and trust. Yet most people find it difficult to pray as Jesus prayed. A busy life, unfruitful liturgical experiences, or spiritual emptiness can be obstacles to prayer. The question may arise in the human heart, "What good does it do to pray?"

"Prayer is the raising of one's mind and heart to God" (CCC, 2559). In sadness, emptiness, and great need, find the humility to turn to the Father, who is always ready to meet you. Whatever your faults or grievances, "God tirelessly calls [you] to that mysterious encounter known as prayer" (CCC, 2567). So persevere in prayer. Go with your family or friends to worship together at Mass. Willingly surrender your struggles to God. The next time you take a moment to have a cup of tea or coffee, invite him along for a short visit.

➜ **Reflect** Is prayer a part of your daily life right now?

Catechist's Prayer

God the Father, I praise you. God the Son, I love you. God the Holy Spirit, I welcome you. Infuse my life with your presence. Amen.

Lesson Plan

Objectives	Process	Materials
Invite, 10 minutes		
Jesus Teaches Us to Pray Page 135	◯ Psalm 145:2 Pray the opening prayer. 📖 Matthew 6:6-8 Reflect prayerfully on the Word. • Discuss What Do You Wonder questions.	📶 **Optional Activity** Chapter Story: "Talk to God"
Discover, 35 minutes		
Stay Close to God Pages 136–137 • Define prayer as talking and listening to God • Become more aware of the need to pray to get close to God	• **Catholic Faith Words** prayer • Explain that prayer helps us stay close to God. ☆ Underline what it means to pray. • Explain that we can pray anywhere. • **Share Your Faith Activity** Draw one thing to thank God for.	☐ pencils ☐ index card ☐ crayons or markers • **Optional Activity** A Prayer Card ☐ Activity Master 9 (Page 135E)
Learn to Pray Pages 138–139 • Learn that the Lord's Prayer is the prayer that Jesus taught his followers to pray to God the Father	• **Catholic Faith Words** Lord's Prayer • Explain that there are many ways to pray. 📖 Ephesians 5:18–20 Proclaim "How to Pray." ☆ The students will circle some ways they can give thanks and to color the music notes. • **Connect Your Faith Activity** Write the name of someone you pray with.	☐ pencils ☐ index cards ☐ crayons or markers
Live, 15 minutes		
Our Catholic Life Pages 140–141	• Recall the Lord's Prayer. • **People of Faith** Learn about Saint Ephrem the Hymnist. • **Live Your Faith Activity** Trace the words of the prayer.	☐ pencils
Anytime Prayer Page 142	• Teach the children their responses. ▶ Rehearse "The Lord's Prayer." • Follow the order of prayer.	📶 Download "The Lord's Prayer."

Family + Faith Page 143

Point out that the Catholic Families page provides chapter highlights, information on how first graders understand faith concepts, and family prayer.

Chapter Review Page 144

📶 **aliveinchrist.osv.com**
- Customize and Download Assessments
- Email Links to eAssessments
- Interactive Student Reviews

ONLINE RESOURCES

 Go to **aliveinchrist.osv.com**

You will find:

- Interactive lesson planning with web specific content and additional activities
- Step by step lesson instruction from printed Catechist Edition for integrated lesson planning
- Custom-built assessments to download and eAssessment links
- Interactive reviews that provide scores and the option to review answers
- Sunday readings with background and questions of the week

 Go to **osvparish.com**

You will find:

- Ask the Experts Q and A
- General Catechist Helps
- Community Connections and Blogs

Sharing the Message with First Graders

Prayer Children who grow up in Catholic families, parishes, and schools have many opportunities to see people praying and to say prayers in groups. Children begin to respond to and relate to an unseen God when they see adults in their lives leading by example by talking to God. It's important for them to know that God is a friend they can talk to in their own words. It's also important to teach them that prayer is listening as well as speaking.

Teaching Tip: Use prayer in every session. Alternate styles of prayer between spontaneous and short traditional prayers. Use the various forms of prayer mentioned in the *Catechism*.

How First Graders Understand

- First graders are verbal and like to talk.
- To first graders, you are a model to be imitated. Let them hear you pray. Offer an example of joy and reverence in prayer.
- First graders may expect God to answer their prayers immediately.

"I think prayers are important. Give me quiet time to pray by myself and with others."

Chapter Story

Invite

"Talk to God"

Use this story to expand the chapter introduction.

- The children will relate the story to their own lives, reflecting on their own prayers.
- Connect the story to how and why we pray.

 Go to **aliveinchrist.osv.com** Lesson Planning section for this story.

NCEA IFG: ACRE Edition

Discover

Knowledge of the Faith

- Objective: To know and understand basic Catholic teaching about the Incarnate Word Jesus Christ as the way, truth, and life

Prayer

- Objective: To recognize and learn how to engage in Catholic forms of personal and communal prayer and ways of deepening one's spiritual life

Catholic Social Teaching

Live

 Use one of these features to introduce a principle and engage the children with an activity.

- Life and Dignity, Pages 284–285
- Call to Community, Pages 286–287

Music Options

 Use one or more of the following songs to enhance catechetical learning or for prayer.

- "The Lord's Prayer," Live Prayer, Page 142
- "Jesus, Please Hear Our Prayer," Discover, Page 139
- "Our Father," Discover, Page 139

LECTIONARY CONNECTION

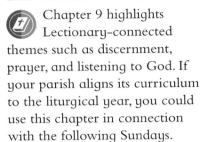 Chapter 9 highlights Lectionary-connected themes such as discernment, prayer, and listening to God. If your parish aligns its curriculum to the liturgical year, you could use this chapter in connection with the following Sundays.

Year A

First Sunday of Advent—Second Coming of Christ

Twenty-fourth Sunday in Ordinary Time—forgiveness, sacrifice

Twenty-seventh Sunday in Ordinary Time—salvation, justice, judgment

Our Lord Jesus Christ, King of the Universe—Kingdom of God, judgment

Year B

Third Sunday of Advent—discernment, listening to God

Second Sunday of Lent— trust God

Year C

Third Sunday of Easter—mission

Seventh Sunday of Easter—prayer

Twenty-fifth Sunday in Ordinary Time—social justice

Twenty-seventh Sunday in Ordinary Time—priesthood of all believers

Go to **aliveinchrist.osv.com** for a complete correlation ordered by the Sundays of the year and suggestions for how to integrate the Scripture readings into chapter lessons.

Name _____ Date _____

Thanks to God

In the box below draw a picture of something you are thankful for.

Trace the words of thanks to God.

Thank you God for everything.

Jesus Teaches Us to Pray

Let Us Pray

Leader: God, we praise you always.

"Every day I will bless you;
I will praise your name forever and
ever." Psalm 145:2

All: God, we praise you always. Amen.

✞ God's Word

When you pray, go into a room alone and close the door. Pray to God in private. God knows what you are doing and will reward you. When you pray, you don't have to talk on and on. God will listen to your short and long prayers. God knows what you need before you ask. Based on Matthew 6:6–8

? What Do You Wonder?

- Did Jesus pray?
- Why do we sometimes pray alone and sometimes together?

135

Optional Activity

Chapter Story: "Talk to God" *Verbal/Linguistic*

Use this story after the opening prayer, before explaining that God hears all our prayers.

- Read the story aloud as the children follow along.
- *Ask:* Why do you think Lamont's dad was praying? Possible responses: He loves Lamont. He's asking God to watch over Lamont.
- *Ask:* What do you think Lamont's family was celebrating?
- When finished, transition back to the lesson instruction.

 Go to **aliveinchrist.osv.com** for Chapter Story.

⏱ Invite

♥ Let Us Pray

Invite the children to gather in the prayer space and make the Sign of the Cross. Choose a child to be leader. Read aloud the Psalm verse from a Bible. Prompt the children's response.

Have the children move out of the prayer space and back to their seats.

Explain that God hears all our prayers.

Say: Sometimes we might think God does not hear us, because our prayer is not answered the way we would like it to be. But God does hear us. Let's listen to what Jesus says about praying.

✞ God's Word

Guide the children through the process of Scripture reflection.

- Invite them to close their eyes, be still and open their minds and hearts to what God is saying to them in this passage.
- Proclaim the Scripture.
- Maintain several moments of silence.
- *Ask:* What did you hear God say to you today?
- Invite volunteers to share.

What Do You Wonder?

Say: When we pray, we are talking with God about what we think we want or need, but sometimes God has a different answer for us.

Invite the children to respond to the questions. Ask what else they might wonder about God answering our prayers or the importance of prayer.

Objectives

- Define prayer as talking and listening to God
- Become more aware of the need to pray to get close to God

Stay Close to God

Ask: What are some ways to pray?

- Write the children's responses on the board or on chart paper.

Read aloud the text.

- Ask the children to think about how happy they are to talk to family and friends.
- Tell them that talking is a good way to stay close and that talking to God keeps you close to God.
- *Ask:* What are some things you can thank God for when you pray?

Point out the photograph.

- Ask the children to describe what they see.
- *Ask:* When do you pray with your family?

Work with Words

Explain that prayer is the way to have a friendship with God.

- Show the children the word *prayer* written on an index card.
- ⭐ Direct the children to underline what it means to pray.

Ask: When have you heard blessing prayers? Possible response: before or after meals, at the beginning of the day, before bed

---

Stay Close to God

What are some ways to pray?

Catholic Faith Words

prayer talking to and listening to God

 Underline what it means to pray.

Talking with family and friends helps you feel close to them. Talking to and listening to God is called **prayer**.

God wants us to be his friends. He asks us to pray to him. We feel close to God when we pray.

Blessing prayers thank God for the good things he gives you. They ask God to keep caring for you and others.

➔ What are some things you can thank God for when you pray?

136 Chapter 9

✓ Quick Tip

A Blessing

To help the children understand what a blessing is, teach them the words of this traditional blessing at meals: "Bless us O Lord, and these thy gifts which we are about to receive from thy bounty, through Christ our Lord. Amen."

- Explain that in this blessing we thank God for the food he has given us from his generous amount of gifts.

Pray Anywhere

You can pray wherever you are. You can talk to God at home or in church. You can pray in your classroom or on the playground.

Begin your prayer by thanking God the Father for all that he gives you.

Wherever you are, God will hear you. You can say your own prayer. You can say prayers of the Church. You can pray silently or out loud. Praying with your family before meals and at bedtime is a special way to stay close to God and one another.

Share Your Faith

Think Draw a picture of something you want to thank God for.

Share Share your picture with a friend.

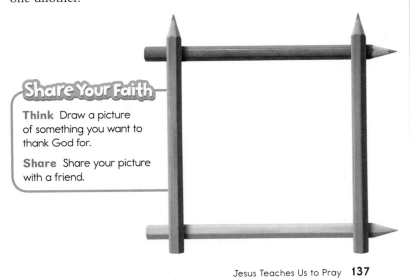

Jesus Teaches Us to Pray **137**

Optional Activity

Activity Master 9: Thanks to God

Distribute copies of the activity found on catechist page 135E.

- Tell the children they will be making a prayer card of their own.
- As an alternative, you may wish to send this activity home with the children.

Pray Anywhere

Ask the children about places they pray.

- Read aloud the text.
- Tell the children they can talk to God wherever they are.
- Have the children make an index card with a *Y* on one side and an *N* on the other side.
- Call out places, such as "in school," "in church," "in your bedroom," "on a bus," "on your bike," or "at a playground." Tell the children to hold the side of the card with the *Y* if the place is a place where you can pray, and the side with the *N* if it isn't.
- The *Y* should be held toward you each time. This reinforces the concept that prayer can take place anywhere.

Activity

Read aloud the directions for the Share Your Faith activity.

- Have the children discuss things they are thankful for.
- Allow the children time to complete their drawings.

Quick Review

You can talk to God anywhere about anything. He will always hear your prayers.

Objective

• Learn that the Lord's Prayer is the prayer that Jesus taught his followers to pray to God the Father

Learn to Pray

Ask: What special prayer did Jesus give his followers?

• Write the children's responses on the board or on chart paper.

Ask the children to discuss who taught them how to pray.

Read aloud the two paragraphs.

• Explain that every generation of Catholics learns certain prayers. Tell them that if they have Catholic parents and grandparents, they were taught to say these prayers too.

• Tell them that they will also learn the songs that are sung by the people in church on Sunday.

God's Word

Tell the children that this Scripture story tells us about different ways we should pray.

Proclaim "How to Pray."

• Ask the children to restate the message of this Scripture story in their own words.

 Invite the children to circle some ways they can give thanks and to color the music notes.

Learn to Pray

What special prayer did Jesus give his followers?

You can learn songs, words, and actions to talk with God. You can use them to pray any time you wish.

The Church family can learn to pray together from the Bible. We should always give thanks to God for all he has given us. Let's read what Paul tells us are some ways we can do that:

1. Circle ways that we can give thanks to God.
2. Color in the music notes below.

God's Word

How to Pray

Be filled with the Holy Spirit. Sing psalms, hymns, and spiritual songs—singing and playing to the Lord in your hearts, giving thanks always and for everything in the name of our Lord Jesus Christ to God the Father. *Based on Ephesians 5:18–20*

138   Chapter 9

Scripture Background

Ephesians 5:18–20

This part of the letter to the Ephesians instructs Christian converts on how to live as followers of Christ.

• The writer stresses that the converts' lives should be filled with prayer.

• They should pray together—and sing together—as a group, but they should also pray individually, in their hearts.

• Remind the children that Jesus called on God the Father, and asked us to do so, too.

The Lord's Prayer

At Mass and at other times, you pray a very important prayer called the **Lord's Prayer**. Jesus taught his friends to pray this way.

The Lord's Prayer

Our Father, who art in heaven,
hallowed be thy name;
thy kingdom come;
thy will be done
on earth as it is in heaven.
Give us this day our daily bread,
and forgive us our trespasses,
as we forgive those who
    trespass against us;
and lead us not into temptation,
but deliver us from evil. Amen.

Catholic Faith Words

Lord's Prayer the prayer Jesus taught his followers to pray to God the Father. This prayer is also called the Our Father.

Connect Your Faith

Pray Together Write the name of someone that you pray with.

_____

- -

_____

Jesus Teaches Us to Pray **139**

The Lord's Prayer

Read aloud the introductory paragraph. Ask the children to raise their hands if they have heard of the Lord's Prayer. Explain that the Lord Jesus taught the first Christians this prayer.

- Read aloud the first part of the Lord's Prayer (to "as it is in heaven"). Tell the children that since they are friends of Jesus, the Lord's Prayer is for them, too.

- Explain that at every Mass, the Church family stands and prays this prayer aloud.

- Help the children understand the words of the prayer by suggesting synonyms for any words they don't understand.

 Music Option: Have the children sing, "Jesus, Please Hear Our Prayer" or "Our Father," downloaded from **aliveinchrist.osv.com**.

Activity

Point out the Connect Your Faith activity and read aloud the directions.

- Ask the children to name who they pray with.

- Provide time for the children to write the names.

Quick Review

Jesus taught his friends how to pray to his Father. The prayer he taught them is called the Lord's Prayer. Christians still pray it today.

 Reaching All Learners

Understanding the Lord's Prayer

Explain to the children the difficult words in the first part of the prayer.

- *who art*—you who are (addressed to God)
- *hallowed*—called or treated as holy
- *thy kingdom*—God's rule on the Earth
- *thy will*—what God wants people to do

Our Catholic Life

Ask: What do we ask God for when we pray the Lord's Prayer?

- Write the children's responses on the board or on chart paper.

Invite the children to name some prayers they know by heart.

The Lord's Prayer

Introduce the chart by reading aloud the first paragraph.

- Ask the children to follow along as you read aloud the chart, pausing after each phrase of the prayer to read the simplified translation.

Have the children read aloud together the text of the Lord's Prayer from the first column of the chart.

- *Ask:* When do you pray the Lord's Prayer? Possible responses: at Mass, or at home.

Designate Side A and Side B. Have Side A read together the Words of the Prayer column again, pausing after each phrase for Side B to read together the What We Are Asking column.

Refer to pages 316–320 in the Our Catholic Tradition reference section in the back of the Student Book for more traditional prayers of the Church.

Our Catholic Life

What do we ask God when we pray the Lord's Prayer?

The chart below explains what we are asking God for when we pray the Lord's Prayer.

The Lord's Prayer

Words of the Prayer	What We Are Asking
Our Father, who art in heaven, hallowed be thy name;	God our Father, may we praise your holy name.
Thy kingdom come, thy will be done on earth as it is in heaven.	May we do what you ask here on Earth as the angels and Saints do in Heaven.
Give us this day our daily bread,	May we have the things we need today.
and forgive us our trespasses, as we forgive those who trespass against us;	Please forgive us for the things we do wrong, and help us forgive those who hurt us.
and lead us not into temptation, but deliver us from evil.	Keep us safe from anything that would harm us or lead us away from you.
Amen!	May it be so!

© Our Sunday Visitor

140 Chapter 9

 Quick Tip

How to Pray

Memorization, or learning by heart, is one of the first prayer skills children learn.

- Committing short traditional prayers and liturgical responses to memory helps children feel a part of the worshipping community, and gives them models for their own spontaneous or self-composed prayers.

- Children's comprehension of memorized prayers will mature as they do.

People of Faith

Saint Ephrem the Hymnist, 306–373

Saint Ephrem was a teacher and a poet, but he is best known for writing hymns. He wrote more than 400 hymns! He used the popular songs of his time, but changed the words to help people learn about Jesus and Mary and praise God. His hymns remind us how much God loves us and wants us to love him.

June 9

Discuss: How do you tell others how much God loves you?

 Learn more about Saint Ephrem at **aliveinchrist.osv.com**

Live Your Faith

Trace the Words Trace the words to complete the first lines of the Lord's Prayer.

Our _Father_

who art in _heaven_

hallowed be thy name.

People of Faith

Tell the children about Saint Ephrem the Hymnist.

- Invite a volunteer to read aloud the People of Faith story.
- Explain that although Saint Ephrem wrote hundreds of songs that inspired the Church, not much is known about his life. We do know that Saint Ephrem put religious words to music to make a point.
- During his lifetime, people were spreading untruths about religion. Saint Ephrem put the truth to music to counteract those who were against the Church.
- *Ask:* How do you tell others how much God loves you?

 Encourage the children to go to **aliveinchrist.osv.com** at home to learn more about Saint Ephrem the Hymnist.

Activity

Read aloud the directions to the Live Your Faith activity.

- Allow time for the children to work independently to trace the letters.
- Read aloud the prayer, inviting the children to supply the traced words.

 Catholic Social Teaching

Chapter Connections

To integrate Catholic Social Teaching into your lesson, choose one of the following features: Life and Dignity, pages 284–285; or Call to Community, pages 286–287.

- Start the Live step of the process by talking about Saint Ephrem the Hymnist on page 141. Then move directly to the Catholic Social Teaching feature.
- Or, to expand the lesson, complete both pages 140 and 141, then move to the Catholic Social Teaching feature.
- Return to Chapter 9 for the prayer on page 142.

Live

 Let Us Pray

Anytime Prayer

Say: When we pray, we are talking with God about what we think we want or need, but sometimes God has a different answer for us.

Prepare

Teach the children their responses.

 Rehearse "The Lord's Prayer," downloaded from **aliveinchrist.osv.com**.

Gather

Invite the children to process to the prayer space.

- Prompt the children to quiet themselves for prayer.

Pray

- Begin by leading the children in the Sign of the Cross.
- Follow the order of prayer on the student page.
- Invite the children to pray the Lord's Prayer either by turning back to page 139 or by joining in a sung version.

 Conclude by singing together "The Lord's Prayer."

 Let Us Pray

Anytime Prayer

Gather and begin with the Sign of the Cross.

Leader: We can pray in the morning, at the start of each day.

All: We can pray in the morning, at the start of each day.

Leader: And at every mealtime, we bow heads and pray.

All: And at every mealtime, we bow heads and pray.

Leader: We pray at our bedtime, at the end of our days.

All: We pray at our bedtime, at the end of our days.

Leader: For God is our Father, who listens always.

All: For God is our Father, who listens always.

Leader: Let us join in prayer to God our Father.

Pray the Lord's Prayer together.

 All: Sing "The Lord's Prayer"

 Liturgy Link

Gestures

Children will be familiar with clasping their hands together in prayer, but may not realize that other gestures may be used.

- Holding one's hands up toward the sky while praying is another method you may wish to describe to the children. This is known as the *orans* position or posture. Tell them to look at the priest for this prayer gesture during Mass.

 Go to **aliveinchrist.osv.com** for Sunday readings, Scripture background, questions of the week, and seasonal resources.

FAMILY+FAITH
LIVING AND LEARNING TOGETHER

YOUR CHILD LEARNED >>>

The chapter describes the ways and reasons we pray and introduces the words and meaning of the Lord's Prayer.

God's Word

Read **Matthew 6:6–8** to learn the ways that Jesus says we can pray.

Catholics Believe

• Prayer is talking and listening to God.

• Jesus taught his friends how to pray the Lord's Prayer.

To learn more, go to the *Catechism of the Catholic Church* #2607–2612 at **usccb.org**.

People of Faith

This week, your child met Saint Ephrem. He loved to sing and give praise to God. He personally wrote more than 400 hymns.

CHILDREN AT THIS AGE >>>

How They Understand Prayer Children who grow up in Catholic families, parishes, and schools have many opportunities to see people praying and to say prayers in groups. Children begin to respond to and relate to an unseen God when they see adults in their lives talking to God. It's important for your child to know that God is a friend he or she can talk to in his or her own words. It's also important to teach your child that prayer is listening as well as speaking.

CONSIDER THIS >>>

Who did you most depend on as a child?

Many people might answer a parent, or family member. It is necessary for a child's emotional well-being to know that there is someone he/she can depend upon, someone who is trustworthy. "A term that our Lord uses for Father is 'Abba! (Daddy) This implies that Jesus is saying that a relationship with God [the Father] should be like that of a child, very close, personal, and dependent" (*USCCA, p. 484*).

LET'S TALK >>>

• Talk with your child about the different ways your family prays together.

• Describe your favorite time or place to pray.

LET'S PRAY >>>

Dear God, help us to know how much you love us and let us always sing to you like Saint Ephrem did. Amen.

For a multimedia glossary of Catholic Faith Words, Sunday readings, seasonal and Saint resources, and chapter activities go to **aliveinchrist.osv.com**.

Alive in Christ, Grade 1 Chapter 9 **143**

Chapter 9 Review

A **Work with Words** Trace the words to complete the sentence.

1. You can pray by  .

2. One name to call God when you pray is
   Father .

3. Jesus taught his friends to pray the
   Lord's Prayer.

4. *Prayer* is talking and listening to God.

B **Check Understanding** Circle the correct answers.

5. What pictures show ways to pray?

Singing to God

Talking to God

Swimming

Go to **aliveinchrist.osv.com** for an interactive review.

144 Chapter 9 Review

Family + Faith

Distribute the page to the children or parents/adult family members. Point out the chapter highlights, insights on how first graders understand concepts, the opportunity for the adults to reflect on their own experience and faith journey, and the family prayer.

Chapter Review

Use Catechist Quick Reviews to highlight lesson concepts.

A **Work with Words**
Ask the children to trace the words to complete each sentence.

B **Check Understanding**
Have the children circle ways to pray.

Go to **aliveinchrist.osv.com** to prepare customized and downloadable assessments, send eAssessments, and assign interactive reviews.

Jesus Teaches Us to Pray **143–144**

Use Catechist Quick Reviews in each chapter to highlight lesson concepts for this unit and prepare for the Unit Review.

Have the children complete the Review pages. Then discuss the answers as a group. Review any concepts with which the children are having difficulty.

 Work with Words
Have the children circle the correct answer.

A Work with Words Circle the correct answer.

1. ____ is talking to and listening to God.

   Playing   (Prayer)

2. A ____ is a law God made for people to obey.

   (Commandment)   parable

3. ____ is the gift of believing in God and doing as he asks.

   Love   (Faith)

4. The Great Commandment is about ____ God above all else and your neighbor as yourself.

   knowing   (loving)

5. ____ teaches you to love God and others.

   (Jesus)   Jairus

© Our Sunday Visitor

Jesus Christ **145**

B Check Understanding Draw a line from the phrase in Column A to the correct word or words in Column B.

Column A   Column B

6. What Jesus did for some sick people

7. What God wants to be

8. A gift you can give

9. Where you can pray

10. God can hear your

love

healed

your friend

prayers

everywhere

Circle the words in the word search.

11–13.

Word Bank

Love

Pray

Laws

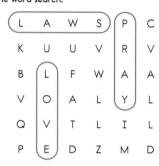

```
L  A  W  S  P  C
K  U  U  V  R  V
B  L  F  W  A  A
V  O  A  L  Y  L
Q  V  T  L  I  L
P  E  D  Z  M  D
```

© Our Sunday Visitor

C Make Connections Trace the words to answer the questions.

14. What prayer did Jesus teach?

The Lord's Prayer

15. How did Mother Teresa show God's love to others?

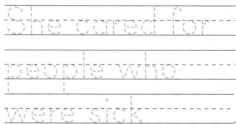

She cared for people who were sick.

© Our Sunday Visitor

B Check Understanding

6–10. Have the children draw a line from the phrases in Column A to the correct word or words in Column B.

11–13. Have the children circle the words in the word search.

C Make Connections Have the children trace the words to answer the questions.

Go to **aliveinchrist.osv.com** to prepare customized and downloadable assessments, send eAssessments, and assign interactive reviews.

Unit 3 Review   **146–147**

The Church

Our Catholic Tradition

- The Church is made up of the baptized people who believe in God and follow Jesus. (CCC, 751–752)

- We say "yes" to Jesus and as his Church share his message of God's Kingdom. (CCC, 763)

- God the Holy Spirit is at work with God the Father and God the Son in the whole world. (CCC, 686)

- The Holy Spirit guides people in the Church to live holy lives like the Saints. (CCC, 736)

How does the Holy Spirit help us to live as holy people?

Notre Dame Cathedral Paris, France

Unit 4 Overview

Chapter 10
Responding to God

The children will:

- connect that Noah said "yes" to God, and God promised to always keep him safe. The rainbow is a sign of that promise
- understand that Jesus invites everyone to God's Kingdom—the world of love, peace, and justice that God has in Heaven and is still being built on Earth
- appreciate that the Church shares Jesus' message about God's love
- identify the Church as a community of baptized people who believe in God and follow Jesus

 Catholic Social Teaching: Live Your Faith

- Call to Community, Pages 286–287
- Rights and Responsibilities, Pages 288–289

Chapter 11
The Church's Guide

The children will:

- learn that a guide helps us and shows us the way
- recognize the Holy Spirit as the Third Divine Person of the Holy Trinity
- discover Jesus' promise of the Holy Spirit to guide the Church
- appreciate that Saint Thérèse loved God very much and worked for him through her little jobs. She called this "The Little Way"

 Catholic Social Teaching: Live Your Faith

- Rights and Responsibilities, Pages 288–289
- The Dignity of Work, Pages 292–293

Chapter 12
Friends of God

The children will:

- recognize a Saint as someone who loved God very much, did his work on Earth, and is with him in Heaven
- define the word *holy* as unique and pure; set apart for God and his purposes
- appreciate that we are part of the family of Saints, connected to the Saints who lived before us and to those who believe in Jesus now

 Songs of Scripture
"You've Got to Love Them"

 Catholic Social Teaching: Live Your Faith

- Call to Community, Pages 286–287
- Rights and Responsibilities, Pages 288–289

Preview Unit Theme

Ask: What is the unit theme?

Summarize that the unit focuses on the Church.

Invite volunteers to read aloud each of the bullets in Our Catholic Tradition.

Explain to the children that they will learn about these things in the next three chapters.

Have the children study the photos and images. Invite volunteers to describe what they see. What do these images say about the unit theme?

Ask: How does the Holy Spirit help us to live as holy people?

After some discussion, explain to the children that they will be exploring this question in the next three chapters.

KEY CONCEPT

God invites everyone into his Kingdom. The Church is the community of all baptized people who believe in God and follow Jesus.

DOCTRINAL CONTENT

- Noah said "yes" to God, and God promised to always keep him safe. The rainbow is a sign of that promise. (CCC, 2569)

- Jesus invites everyone to God's Kingdom—the world of love, peace, and justice that is in Heaven and is still being built on Earth. (CCC, 543)

- The Church shares Jesus' message about God's love. (CCC, 737)

- The Church is a community of baptized people who believe in God and follow Jesus. (CCC, 782)

TASKS OF CATECHESIS

Helping children grow in a faith that is "known, celebrated, lived, and expressed in prayer" (NDC, 20).

This chapter focuses on the following tasks of catechesis:

- Promoting Knowledge of the Faith

- Education for Community Life

Catechist Background

 By faith Noah, warned about what was not yet seen, with reverence built an ark for the salvation of his household. [he]… inherited the righteousness that comes through faith.

Hebrews 11:7

➔ **Reflect** What does being faithful mean to you? How are you faithful?

Trust and loyalty are the crucial virtues of many great figures of Scripture. Despite being surrounded by great animosity and disbelief, Noah trusted the Lord and built an ark as he had been commanded. Abraham's fierce loyalty and faith in God led him to the point where he was about to sacrifice his son, because he had been told by an angel that God wanted him to. Despite his bodily weaknesses, Moses led the Israelites out of Egypt in response to God's call. Mary, the Mother of Jesus, said "yes" when God called on her. Jesus himself gave his life to reconcile all people with God.

Open up the newspaper and you may feel like burying your head in the sand. The world isn't exactly a picture of peace. When you stand alone, the society mirrored in the media is frightening. However, God does not ask you to wade through troubled times by yourself. Instead, he invites you to be a part of a community that says "yes"—yes to faith, yes to sharing his love with one another. With the support of the faith community, you can live in the peace of the Kingdom of God.

➔ **Reflect** How can you respond to God's invitation to participate more fully in your faith community?

Catechist's Prayer

 Yes, Lord, I welcome the opportunity to share your love with the children you have entrusted to me. Amen.

Lesson Plan

Objectives	Process	Materials

Invite, 10 minutes

Responding to God Page 159

- ♥ Psalm 57:10 Pray the opening prayer.
- Hebrews 11:7 Reflect prayerfully on the Word.
- Discuss What Do You Wonder questions.

🔊 **Optional Activity**
Chapter Poem:
"Saying 'Yes'"

Discover, 35 minutes

Trust in God Pages 150–151

- Connect that Noah said "yes" to God, and God promised to always keep him safe. The rainbow is a sign of that promise

- Explain that Noah says "yes" to God.
- Genesis 6:14–22, 7:1–10, 9:17 Proclaim "Noah Says 'Yes.'"
- ☆ Underline what God told Noah.
- **Share Your Faith Activity** Trace letters to tell how Noah felt.

☐ pencils

All Are Invited Pages 152–153

- Understand that Jesus invites everyone to God's Kingdom—the world of love, peace, and justice that God has in Heaven and is still being built on Earth
- Appreciate that the Church shares Jesus' message about God's love
- Identify the Church as the community of baptized people who believe in God and follow Jesus

- **Catholic Faith Words** Kingdom of God, Church
- Explain that everyone is invited into the Kingdom of God.
- Luke 14:16–23 Proclaim "The Parable of the Great Feast."
- ☆ Underline what the rich man said when no one showed up for the party.
- Explain that the Church works with God as he builds his Kingdom.
- **Connect Your Faith Activity** Find the hidden word.

☐ pencils
☐ crayons or markers
☐ index cards
- **Optional Activity** Kingdom of God
☐ Activity Master 10 (Page 149E)

Live, 15 minutes

Our Catholic Life Pages 154–155

- Explain that Mary said "yes" to God.
- Use the pictures to read "Mary's Story."
- **People of Faith** Learn about Blessed Mary Theresa.
- **Live Your Faith Activity** Draw a scene of Mary saying "yes" to God.

☐ pencils
☐ crayons or markers

"Yes" Prayer Page 156

- Choose four readers.
- ▶ Rehearse "Saying Yes."
- Follow the order of prayer.

🔊 Download "Saying Yes."

Family + Faith Page 157

Point out that the Catholic Families page provides chapter highlights, information on how first graders understand faith concepts, and family prayer.

Chapter Review Page 158

🔊 aliveinchrist.osv.com
- Customize and Download Assessments
- Email Links to eAssessments
- Interactive Student Reviews

ONLINE RESOURCES

 Go to **aliveinchrist.osv.com**

You will find:

- Interactive lesson planning with web specific content and additional activities

- Step by step lesson instruction from printed Catechist Edition for integrated lesson planning

- Custom-built assessments to download and eAssessment links

- Interactive reviews that provide scores and the option to review answers

- Sunday readings with background and questions of the week

 Go to **osvparish.com**

You will find:

- Ask the Experts Q and A
- General Catechist Helps
- Community Connections and Blogs

Sharing the Message with First Graders

Saying "Yes" to God God speaks to us in many ways when we learn to listen to his voice. Before first graders can understand what it means to say "yes" to God, they must understand how to discern the call of God. They do this as adults in their lives help them to hear God's Word in Scripture and to experience God's call in their talents and dreams and the opportunities of their daily lives. When children, even young children, become accustomed to looking for the ways in which God might be speaking to them, they can learn to hear this call of God. They become better and better at answering the question, "What might God be saying to you right now?"

Teaching Tip: Watch for opportunities to recognize children's talents, as the talents God gives us can be important clues about God's call in our lives.

How First Graders Understand

- First graders enjoy helping people. Show them how helping others is a way to follow Jesus.

- First graders like the word *yes* and want to hear it all the time. Help them understand that saying "yes" to God differs from mom saying, "Yes, you can have a cookie."

"I learn best when I am actively involved."

Chapter Connections

Chapter Poem
Invite

"Saying 'Yes'"

Use this poem to expand the chapter introduction.

- The children will relate the poem to their own lives, reflecting on their opportunities to say "yes" to others.
- Connect saying "yes" to others to saying "yes" to God.

 Go to **aliveinchrist.osv.com** Lesson Planning section for this poem.

NCEA IFG: ACRE Edition
Discover

Knowledge of the Faith

- Objective: To know and understand basic Catholic teaching about the Incarnate Word Jesus Christ as the way, truth, and life

Communal Life

- Objectives: To know the origin, mission, structure, and communal nature of the Church; to know the rights and responsibilities of the Christian faithful

Catholic Social Teaching
Live

 Use one of these features to introduce a principle and engage the children with an activity.

- Call to Community, Pages 286–287
- Rights and Responsibilities, Pages 288–289

Music Options

 Use one or more of the following songs to enhance catechetical learning or for prayer.

- "Saying Yes," Live Prayer, Page 156
- "Get On the Boat," Discover, Page 151
- "The Angel Came from Heaven," Live, Page 154

LECTIONARY CONNECTION

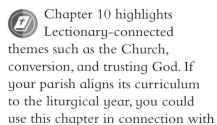 Chapter 10 highlights Lectionary-connected themes such as the Church, conversion, and trusting God. If your parish aligns its curriculum to the liturgical year, you could use this chapter in connection with the following Sundays.

Year A

Fourth Sunday of Advent—Virgin Birth

Second Sunday of Lent—God's grace, holiness

Thirty-first Sunday in Ordinary Time—the Church

Year B

First Sunday of Advent—conversion

Fourth Sunday of Advent—Mary

Second Sunday of Lent—trust God

Year C

Second Sunday of Advent—salvation

Fourth Sunday of Lent—good works, conversion

Thirty-second Sunday in Ordinary Time—Heaven

Go to **aliveinchrist.osv.com** for a complete correlation ordered by the Sundays of the year and suggestions for how to integrate the Scripture readings into chapter lessons.

Name _____ Date _____

Kingdom of God

You belong to the Catholic Church.

The Church invites people to God's Kingdom.

The Church shares God's love.

Draw a line from the person coming out of church to the picture of that same person sharing God's love.

Responding to God

♥ Let Us Pray

Leader: God, you are always faithful to us, help us to be faithful to you.

"I will praise you among the peoples, Lord;
I will chant your praise among the nations." Psalm 57:10

All: Dear God, help us to always say "yes" to you. Amen.

🔟 God's Word

"By faith Noah, warned about what was not yet seen, with reverence built an ark for the salvation of his household…he…[Noah] inherited the righteousness that comes through faith." Hebrews 11:7

? What Do You Wonder?
- What does faithful mean?
- How does God speak to us today?

149

Optional Activity

Chapter Poem: "Saying 'Yes'" *Verbal/Linguistic*

Use this poem after the opening prayer, before explaining that we are invited to say "yes" to God.

- Read the poem aloud as the children follow along.
- Ask the children for examples of other questions. Possible responses: Did you finish your homework? Would you like a cookie?
- *Ask:* When is it hard to say "yes"?
- Transition back to the lesson instruction.

 Go to **aliveinchrist.osv.com** for Chapter Poem.

⏱ Invite

♥ Let Us Pray

Invite the children to gather in the prayer space and make the Sign of the Cross. Invite a child to read aloud the Psalm verse from a Bible. Prompt the children's response.

Have the children move out of the prayer space and back to their seats.

Explain that we are invited to say "yes" to God.

Say: Each one of us is invited in faith to say "yes" to what God asks of us. Let's listen to a Bible story that says how Noah said "yes" to God.

🔟 God's Word

Guide the children through the process of Scripture reflection.

- Invite them to close their eyes, be still and open their minds and hearts to what God is saying to them in this passage.
- Proclaim the Scripture.
- Maintain several moments of silence.
- *Ask:* What did you hear God say to you today?
- Invite volunteers to share.

What Do You Wonder?

Say: Noah listened to God and said, "Yes." Each of us is invited by God to say "yes" at different times in our life.

Invite the children to respond to the questions. Ask what else they might wonder about faithfulness to God and how God speaks to us.

Discover

Objective

- Connect that Noah said "yes" to God, and God promised to always keep him safe. The rainbow is a sign of that promise

Trust in God

Ask: What did God promise Noah?

- Write the children's responses on the board or on chart paper.

Tell the children that God wants us to choose to say "yes" to him.

- Ask the children to gather and to listen for what God told Noah to do.

 God's Word

Proclaim "Noah Says 'Yes.'"

- Instruct the children to say "Yes, I will!" during the reading whenever you point to them.
- Read aloud with enthusiasm. Pause at the end of the third and fourth paragraphs and point to the children.

⭐ Have the children underline what God told Noah to do.

Invite the children to look at the illustration.

- Invite the children to share what they see in the illustration.

Trust in God

What did God promise Noah?

The story of Noah is in the Old Testament. Noah said "yes" when God asked him a very big question.

 God's Word

Noah Says "Yes"

Noah was a good man. God told Noah to build an ark, or very large boat.

God said it was going to rain for forty days and forty nights. There would be a flood. God wanted Noah to be safe.

⭐ Underline what God told Noah to do.

150 Chapter 10

✝ Scripture Background

Genesis 6:14–22, 7:1–23

The story of Noah is the story of God's first covenant with humans. In making a covenant, he binds himself by a promise to his People.

- After the great flood, God promises Noah and his family never again to destroy creation by a flood.
- God put a rainbow in the sky as a sign of his covenant.

Noah said "Yes, I will!" He built the ark even though he saw no rain anywhere.

God told Noah to take his family and two of each kind of animal into the ark. Noah said, "Yes!" and did as God said.

Then the rains came. The rivers swelled until they flooded all the Earth. Noah, his family, and all the animals stayed dry in the ark.

After forty days, the rain stopped. God promised that water would never flood the whole Earth again.

God gave Noah and his family a sign of his promise. God put a rainbow in the sky.

Based on Genesis 6:14–22, 7:1–10, 9:17

Share Your Faith

Think Trace the word that tells how Noah felt when he saw God's rainbow.

Happy

Share Talk with a partner about God's promise.

151

Optional Activity

Noah Lyrics *Musical*

Have the children devise lyrics about Noah to fit the familiar tune "Old MacDonald Had a Farm."

- You may want to begin with "God told Noah, 'Build an ark'…."
- Provide simple instruments to accompany the lyrics such as tambourines or triangles.
- If possible, have the children sing their song to other children in the program.

Noah Says "Yes,"

continued

Proclaim the rest of the Scripture story.

- *Ask:* Why were Noah, his family, and the animals safe? Possible responses: They were in the ark; God was taking care of them.

- Ask the children what they will think of the next time they see a rainbow in the sky.

 Music Option: Have the children sing, "Get On the Boat," downloaded from **aliveinchrist.osv.com**.

Activity

Read aloud the directions for the Share Your Faith activity.

- Have the children work independently to trace the letters.
- Provide time for the children to talk with a partner about God's promise.

Quick Review

God promised Noah he would never again destroy the Earth by a flood. The rainbow was a sign of that promise.

Objectives

- Understand that Jesus invites everyone to God's Kingdom—the world of love, peace, and justice that God has in Heaven and is still being built on Earth
- Appreciate that the Church shares Jesus' message about God's love
- Identify the Church as a community of baptized people who believe in God and follow Jesus

All Are Invited

Ask: How do you say "yes" to God?

- Write the children's responses on the board or on chart paper.

Read aloud the introductory paragraph.

Work with Words

Invite a child to read aloud the definition of *Kingdom of God*.

- Distribute index cards and have the children make vocabulary cards.

 God's Word

Proclaim "The Parable of the Great Feast."

⭐ Have the children underline what the rich man said.

- *Ask:* Who is the rich man in the story? God

- Explain that God invites everyone to join him and be happy with him forever.

All Are Invited

How do you say "yes" to God?

Jesus told a story about God's care for all people. In the story, everyone is invited into the **Kingdom of God**.

 God's Word

The Parable of the Great Feast

A rich man gave a big party. He invited many people. No one came.

The rich man spoke to his servants. "Go out and invite those who are poor, blind, and lame."

The servants did as the man asked. Soon the house was filled with happy people. There still was room for more people.

The rich man said, "Go and find people anywhere you can. Ask them to come to my party." Based on Luke 14:16–23

Underline what the rich man said when no one showed up for the party.

152

Optional Activity

Activity Master 10: Kingdom of God

Distribute copies of the activity on catechist page 149E.

- This activity helps the children understand how they are a part of God's Kingdom.
- As an alternative, you may wish to send this activity home with the children.

The Church

The **Church** shares Jesus' message about God's Kingdom.

You became a member of the Church when you were baptized. Your parents said "yes" to God for you. Now you can say "yes" to God for yourself.

You share love as a member of the Church. You work together with God as he builds his Kingdom.

You can invite others into God's Kingdom. You can ask them to say "yes" to God, too.

Catholic Faith Words

Kingdom of God the world of love, peace, and justice that is in Heaven and is still being built on Earth

Church the community of all baptized people who believe in God and follow Jesus

Connect Your Faith

Find the Hidden Word
Color the X's red and the O's blue, green, or yellow to find what you say when God calls you into his Kingdom.

Responding to God **153**

Quick Tip

Graphic Organizer

Say "Yes" to God

The Church

Tell the children that there were servants, or helpers, in the story Jesus told. Tell them the rich man asked the servants to go gather everyone in.

• Explain to the children that the members of the Church are like the servants in the story. Tell them God sends out the people who make up the Church to invite everyone to his Kingdom.

Read aloud the text.

Work with Words

Hold up an index card with the Catholic Faith Word *Church* on it. Explain the definition to the children.

Draw the graphic organizer from the Quick Tip box below on the board or on chart paper.

• Ask the children to name specific ways in which they can share God's love.

• Write the children's answers around the graphic organizer.

Activity

Point out the Connect Your Faith activity and read the directions aloud.

• Have the children work independently to complete the puzzle.

Quick Review

God invites everyone into his Kingdom. The job of the Church is to carry this invitation to all people.

Our Catholic Life

Ask: How did Mary answer God's question?

- List the children's responses on the board or on chart paper.

Read aloud the introductory paragraph.

Mary Says "Yes"

Help the children recall that Mary is the Mother of Jesus.

- Read aloud the first sentence, and help the children connect the picture of Mary with her name.
- Read aloud the picture story through to the next-to-last line, pausing at each picture to allow the children to supply the appropriate word.
- Read aloud the last line, inviting the children to read aloud the word *Yes.*
- *Ask:* How can you say "yes" to God?

 Music Option: Have the children sing, "The Angel Came from Heaven," downloaded from **aliveinchrist.osv.com**.

Our Catholic Life

How did Mary answer God's question?

God asked Mary to do something special, just as he had asked Noah. Here is Mary's story.

154   Chapter 10

 Scripture Background

Luke 1:26–38

The story on this page is based on the Annunciation.

- The Archangel Gabriel is mentioned in the Old Testament Book of Daniel, where he appears in a vision to announce the coming of the One who will bring the Kingdom.
- The Church celebrates the Feast of the Annunciation on March 25, nine months before Christmas.

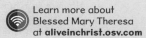

People of Faith

Blessed Mary Theresa of Jesus Gerhardinger, 1797–1879

May 9

Caroline Gerhardinger was born in Germany. She was a teacher, but she believed Jesus was asking her to be a nun. She always said "yes" to Jesus, so she started the School Sisters of Notre Dame. Caroline's new name was Mary Theresa of Jesus. She opened schools in Germany and the United States. She was happy to do what Jesus asked.

Discuss: Name one thing Jesus is asking you to do.

Learn more about Blessed Mary Theresa at **aliveinchrist.osv.com**

© Our Sunday Visitor

Live Your Faith

Draw a Scene from the story of Mary saying "yes" to God.

155

🌐 Catholic Social Teaching

Chapter Connections

To integrate Catholic Social Teaching into your lesson, choose one of the following features: Call to Community, pages 286–287; or Rights and Responsibilities, pages 288–289.

- Start the Live step of the process by talking about Blessed Mary Theresa on page 155. Then move directly to the Catholic Social Teaching feature.
- Or, to expand the lesson, complete both pages 154 and 155, then move to the Catholic Social Teaching feature.
- Return to Chapter 10 for the prayer on page 156.

People of Faith

Tell the children about Blessed Mary Theresa of Jesus Gerhardinger.

- Invite a volunteer to read aloud the People of Faith story.
- Explain that Blessed Mary Theresa, who was encouraged by her parish priest to become a teacher, believed that a child's needs for love, safety, and food were as important as a formal education. She said, "Let us never forget the love of Jesus for children, whom he took upon his lap and blessed." She was dedicated to helping women and children grow to their greatest potential.
- *Say:* Name one thing Jesus is asking you to do.
- Invite the children to silently think about their answer.

 Encourage the children to go to **aliveinchrist.osv.com** at home to learn more about Blessed Mary Theresa.

Activity

Read aloud the directions for the Live Your Faith activity.

- Allow time for the children to create their scenes.
- Invite volunteers to share their drawings.
- Refer to pages 301–303 in the Our Catholic Tradition reference section in the back of the Student Book for more about Mary.

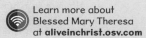

Responding to God   **155**

Live

Live

 Let Us Pray

"Yes" Prayer

Tell the children they will say "yes" to God in prayer.

Prepare

Choose four readers, one to say each of the lines labeled leader. Allow the children to practice.

- Teach the children their response.

 Rehearse "Saying Yes," downloaded from **aliveinchrist.osv.com**.

Gather

Invite the children to gather in the prayer space. Have everyone hold hands, except for the leaders, who will hold their books.

Pray

Follow the order of prayer on the student page.

- *Leader's prayer:* Heavenly Father, help us follow the examples of Noah and Mary, so that we may always say "yes" to you.

 Conclude by singing together "Saying Yes."

 Let Us Pray

"Yes" Prayer

Gather and begin with the Sign of the Cross.

Leader: Lord, you ask us to be kind to our families.

All: We say "yes!"

Leader: You ask us to share what we have.

All: We say "yes!"

Leader: You want us to ask everyone to play.

All: We say "yes!"

Leader: Let us pray.

Bow your heads as the leader prays.

All: Amen.

 Sing "Saying Yes"
Saying yes, saying yes to our God.
Jesus, you're my friend.
You are here with me.
I know you are always by my side.
© 1998, John Burland. All rights reserved.

156 Chapter 10

 Liturgy Link

Praying as One

It can be a powerful experience when a group prays with one voice.

- Have the children practice saying the response together.
- You may want to have the children beat tambourines after each response.

 Go to **aliveinchrist.osv.com** for Sunday readings, Scripture background, questions of the week, and seasonal resources.

FAMILY+FAITH
LIVING AND LEARNING TOGETHER

YOUR CHILD LEARNED >>>

This chapter examines the story of Noah and how Catholics say "yes" to God and describes the Kingdom of God as the world of love, peace, and justice that is in Heaven and is still being built on Earth.

God's Word

 Read **Hebrews 11:7** to learn why Noah was given the blessings that come to those who believe.

Catholics Believe

- God invites everyone into his Kingdom.
- The Church is the community of all baptized people who believe in God and follow Jesus.

To learn more, go to the *Catechism of the Catholic Church* #541–546 at usccb.org.

People of Faith

This week, your child met Blessed Mary Theresa of Jesus, the founder of the School Sisters of Notre Dame.

CHILDREN AT THIS AGE >>>

How They Understand Saying "Yes" to God God speaks to us in many ways. We simply need to learn to listen to his voice. Before first-graders can understand what it means to say "yes" to God, they must understand how to recognize the call of God. They can do this when adults in their lives help them to hear God's Word in Scripture. Children also experience God's call in their talents, dreams, and opportunities in their daily lives. As time goes on, your child will become better and better at answering the question, "What might God be saying to me right now?"

CONSIDER THIS >>>

When did you realize that your perspective was limited by your personal experience?

You may have realized this when you got married and your spouse's family did things differently, or when you went to a foreign country, or made a friend from another place in the world. As human beings we are limited. We need God's help to recognize what is truth. "...the Holy Spirit, dwelling in the Church, draws the body of the faithful to believe what truly belongs to the faith" (USCCA, 25).

LET'S TALK >>>

- Talk about the teacher who first taught you about God.
- Give an example of a time in your life when you've said "yes" to God.

LET'S PRAY >>>

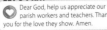 Dear God, help us appreciate our parish workers and teachers. Thank you for the love they show. Amen.

 For a multimedia glossary of Catholic Faith Words, Sunday readings, seasonal and Saint resources, and chapter activities go to aliveinchrist.osv.com.

Family + Faith

Distribute the page to the children or parents/adult family members. Point out the chapter highlights, insights on how first graders understand concepts, the opportunity for the adults to reflect on their own experience and faith journey, and the family prayer.

Chapter 10 Review

A **Work with Words** Circle the correct word to complete each sentence.

1. Mary said ____ to God's invitation.

("yes")　　　　"no"

2. God invites ____ people into his Kingdom.

(all)　　　　some

3. Being ____ is a way of saying "yes" to God.

(kind)　　　　unfair

4. The community of baptized people who believe in God and follow Jesus is called ____.

(the Church)　　　　the class

5. God put a ____ in the sky as a sign to Noah.

bird　　　　(rainbow)

B **Check Understanding** Mark an X in front of the ways to say "yes" to God.

6. [X] Pray with your family.

7. [X] Take care of a brother or sister.

8. [　] Argue with your parents.

 Go to **aliveinchrist.osv.com** for an interactive review.

Chapter Review

Use Catechist Quick Reviews to highlight lesson concepts.

A **Work with Words** Have the children circle the correct word to complete each sentence.

B **Check Understanding** Have the children mark an *X* in front of the ways to say "yes" to God.

 Go to **aliveinchrist.osv.com** to prepare customized and downloadable assessments, send eAssessments, and assign interactive reviews.

Responding to God **157–158**

KEY CONCEPT
God the Holy Spirit is the Third Divine Person of the Holy Trinity. The Holy Spirit fills people's hearts with love and guides the Church.

DOCTRINAL CONTENT
- A guide helps us and shows us the way. (CCC, 729)
- The Holy Spirit is the Third Divine Person of the Holy Trinity. (CCC, 243)
- Jesus promised us that the Holy Spirit would guide the Church. (CCC, 747)
- Saint Thérèse loved God very much and worked for him through her little jobs. She called this "The Little Way." (CCC, 1477)

TASKS OF CATECHESIS
Helping children grow in a faith that is "known, celebrated, lived, and expressed in prayer" (NDC, 20).

This chapter focuses on the following tasks of catechesis:
- Promoting Knowledge of the Faith
- Education for Community Life

Catechist Background

The fruit of the Spirit is love, joy, peace, patience, kindness, generosity, faithfulness, gentleness, self-control. If we live in the Spirit, let us also follow the Spirit. Galatians 5:22–23, 25

→ **Reflect** How does the Holy Spirit guide you?

In Catholic Tradition, the Holy Spirit is recognized as the Third Divine Person of the Holy Trinity. The Holy Spirit was given to Jesus' followers after his Ascension and has continued to be poured out to strengthen disciples on their journey of life. Today he remains with the Body of Christ, forever guiding the Church to God the Father.

In the depths of anxiety and worry, the Holy Spirit can guide you to the light. Think about a time you were in need of God's love and guidance. Dealing with a difficult child, facing a hostile person, or living with ambiguity can present challenges. The Holy Spirit was at work in the kind words, love, or loving actions of another that helped get you through this tough period.

Jesus breathed the Holy Spirit on his disciples on the day of Pentecost. He sent forth his disciples to share his message. The Holy Spirit strengthens his followers to do the same—leading them to the truth and encouraging them to bear witness to the Good News of Jesus. He is active in the Church. He continues to minister through you and others.

→ **Reflect** How has the Holy Spirit strengthened you this day?

Catechist's Prayer
Holy Spirit, come dwell in me. Shower me with your life so that I may carry out the work that Jesus began. Help me be a sign of your presence to others. Amen.

Lesson Plan

Objectives	Process	Materials
Invite, 10 minutes		
The Church's Guide Page 159	○ Psalm 143:10 Pray the opening prayer. ▣ Galatians 5:22–23, 25 Reflect prayerfully on the Word. • Discuss What Do You Wonder questions.	◉ **Optional Activity** Chapter Story: "Who Can Help?"
Discover, 35 minutes		
God the Holy Spirit Pages 160–161 • Learn that a guide helps us and shows us the way • Recognize the Holy Spirit as the Third Divine Person of the Holy Trinity • Discover Jesus' promise of the Holy Spirit to guide the Church	• **Catholic Faith Words** Holy Spirit ☆ Underline who is a guide that helps people stay close to God the Father. ▣ John 14:26 Proclaim "Jesus Promises the Holy Spirit." • Explain that the Holy Spirit guides the Church. • **Share Your Faith Activity** Complete the puzzle.	☐ pencils ☐ index card • **Optional Activity** A Sign of the Holy Spirit ☐ Activity Master 11 (Page 159E)
Ways to God Pages 162–163 • Appreciate that Saint Thérèse loved God very much and worked for him through her little jobs. She called this "The Little Way"	• Explain that other people can show us the way to God. ☆ Underline how Saint Thérèse showed her love for God. • Explain that Saint Thérèse guided people to God. • **Connect Your Faith Activity** Solve the puzzle.	☐ pencils
Live, 15 minutes		
Our Catholic Life Pages 164–165	• Talk about the gifts the Holy Spirit gave Jesus' friends. ☆ Identify a favorite gift of the Holy Spirit. • **People of Faith** Learn about Saint Rose of Lima. • **Live Your Faith Activity** Identify actions that show love for God.	☐ pencils ☐ crayons or markers
Asking Prayer Page 166	• Create a gesture to go with the words *Holy Spirit*. ▶ Rehearse "The Holy Spirit." • Follow the order of prayer.	◉ Download "The Holy Spirit."

Family + Faith Page 167

Point out that the Catholic Families page provides chapter highlights, information on how first graders understand faith concepts, and family prayer.

Chapter Review Page 168

◉ aliveinchrist.osv.com

• Customize and Download Assessments
• Email Links to eAssessments
• Interactive Student Reviews

Teaching This Grade

ONLINE RESOURCES

 Go to **aliveinchrist.osv.com**

You will find:

- Interactive lesson planning with web specific content and additional activities
- Step by step lesson instruction from printed Catechist Edition for integrated lesson planning
- Custom-built assessments to download and eAssessment links
- Interactive reviews that provide scores and the option to review answers
- Sunday readings with background and questions of the week

 Go to **osvparish.com**

You will find:

- Ask the Experts Q and A
- General Catechist Helps
- Community Connections and Blogs

Sharing the Message with First Graders

The Holy Spirit Even in the most general terms, "God" and "Trinity" are abstract concepts for first grade children, but the Holy Spirit tends to be the most elusive of all. It's difficult for children this age to grasp this Person of God who also dwells within the hearts of all Christians. Adults can help make this more concrete by referring to Gifts and Fruits of the Holy Spirit, as well as helping children understand that the Holy Spirit helps us to make good choices and prompts us to be loving towards others.

Teaching Tip: Gifts and Fruits of the Holy Spirit lend themselves to concrete props for lessons. Find some concrete elements for this lesson about what can be an abstract concept.

How First Graders Understand

- First graders do not like to make mistakes. Help them understand that they can learn from their mistakes.
- Young children do not hesitate to admit they need help. Lead them to see that the Holy Spirit gives them the spiritual help that they need.
- Children this age think of parents and teachers as helpers.

"I like doing things by myself. Help me learn that sometimes things get done better in a group."

Chapter Connections

Chapter Story

Invite

"Who Can Help?"

Use this story to enhance the chapter introduction.

- The children will relate the story to their own lives, reflecting on the people who guide them.
- Connect the people who guide us to the guidance of the Holy Spirit.

 Go to **aliveinchrist.osv.com** Lesson Planning section for this story.

NCEA IFG: ACRE Edition

Discover

Knowledge of the Faith

- Objective: To know and understand basic Catholic teaching about the Incarnate Word Jesus Christ as the way, truth, and life

Communal Life

- Objectives: To know the origin, mission, structure, and communal nature of the Church; to know the rights and responsibilities of the Christian faithful

Catholic Social Teaching

Live

 Use one of these features to introduce a principle and engage the children with an activity.

- Rights and Responsibilities, Pages 288–289
- The Dignity of Work, Pages 292–293

Music Options

 Use one or more of the following songs to enhance catechetical learning or for prayer.

- "The Holy Spirit," Live Prayer, Page 166
- "Come to Us, Holy Spirit," Discover, Page 161
- "Holy Spirit," Discover, Page 161
- "Spirit Be with Us," Discover, Page 163

LECTIONARY CONNECTION

 Chapter 11 highlights Lectionary-connected themes such as the Church, the Holy Spirit and the Holy Trinity. If your parish aligns its curriculum to the liturgical year, you could use this chapter in connection with the following Sundays.

Year A

Sixth Sunday of Easter—Holy Spirit

Seventh Sunday of Easter—Nicene Creed

Pentecost Sunday—Holy Spirit, Church

Year B

Second Sunday of Easter—peace

Fifth Sunday of Easter—the Church

Pentecost Sunday—Holy Spirit

The Most Holy Trinity—Holy Trinity

Year C

Sixth Sunday of Easter—peace

Pentecost Sunday—Holy Spirit

The Most Holy Trinity—Holy Trinity

Twenty-ninth Sunday in Ordinary Time—faith in prayer

Go to **aliveinchrist.osv.com** for a complete correlation ordered by the Sundays of the year and suggestions for how to integrate the Scripture readings into chapter lessons.

Name _____ Date _____

A Sign of the Holy Spirit

In the blank boxes, draw two ways the Holy Spirit helps you do good things.
Then, cut out the dove and the squares. Next, punch out the four holes.
Use string or yarn to hang the squares from the dove.

The Church's Guide

 Let Us Pray

Leader: Thank you, God, for your Holy Spirit.

"Teach me to do your will,
for you are my God.
May your kind spirit guide me
on ground that is level." Psalm 143:10

All: Holy Spirit guide and teach us. Amen.

God's Word

"…the fruit of the Spirit is love, joy, peace, patience, kindness, generosity, faithfulness, gentleness, self-control.…If we live in the Spirit, let us also follow the Spirit."
Galatians 5:22–23, 25

? What Do You Wonder?

- What helps you be patient and kind, to show love?
- How do you know that the Holy Spirit is with you?

The Church's Guide **159**

Optional Activity

Chapter Story: "Who Can Help?" *Verbal/Linguistic*

Use this story after the opening prayer, before explaining that the Holy Spirit guides us every day.

- Read aloud the story as the children follow along.
- Arrange the group into pairs. Have each pair act out one of the ways a guide helps lead and teach children.
- After asking the children to name someone who is a guide for them, transition back to the lesson instruction.

 Go to **aliveinchrist.osv.com** for Chapter Story.

⏱ **Invite**

♥ **Let Us Pray**

Invite the children to gather in the prayer space and make the Sign of the Cross. Invite a volunteer to read aloud the Psalm verse from a Bible. Prompt the children's response.

Have the children move out of the prayer space and back to their seats.

Explain that the Holy Spirit guides us every day.

Say: The Holy Spirit guides us on our daily journey. Let's listen to a reading from the Bible to learn more.

⊕ **God's Word**

Guide the children through the process of Scripture reflection.

- Invite them to close their eyes, be still and open their minds and hearts to what God is saying to them in this passage.
- Proclaim the Scripture.
- Maintain several moments of silence.
- *Ask:* What did you hear God say to you today?
- Invite volunteers to share.

What Do You Wonder?

Say: The Holy Spirit is given to us to guide us, and he lives within us.

Invite the children to respond to the questions. Ask what else they might wonder about the Holy Spirit and the Holy Spirit's action in their lives.

Objectives

- Learn that a guide helps us and shows us the way
- Recognize the Holy Spirit as the Third Divine Person of the Holy Trinity
- Discover Jesus' promise of the Holy Spirit to guide the Church

God the Holy Spirit

Ask: How does the Holy Spirit guide us?

- List the children's answers on the board or on chart paper.

Read aloud the first paragraph.

- Ask the children to share any experiences of guides. Emphasize that guides lead us and teach us.

Read aloud the second paragraph.

- *Ask:* Who is the guide that helps you stay close to God the Father?

Work with Words

Hold up an index card with the words *Holy Spirit*.

- Invite a volunteer to read aloud the definition.
- Remind the children that the Holy Trinity is God the Father, God the Son, and God the Holy Spirit.
- Refer to page 316 in the Our Catholic Tradition reference section in the back of the Student Book. Point out that the Glory Be is a prayer to the Holy Trinity.

Discover

Guides are there to help us on our journey.

© Our Sunday Visitor

Catholic Faith Words

Holy Spirit the Third Divine Person of the Holy Trinity

God the Holy Spirit

How does the Holy Spirit guide us?

We need guides to help lead us and teach us. A ranger guides people who visit a park. A tour guide helps people to find important places in a city that they are visiting. A guide in the children's museum can help children to learn about the interesting things that are there.

You need a guide to stay close to God the Father and to Jesus, who is also God the Son. God the **Holy Spirit** will help guide you.

160 Chapter 11

 Quick Tip

Helpers

The Holy Spirit is described in the text as a Helper and Teacher.

- Ask the children to name different types of helpers and teachers, such as firefighters, medical professionals, their teachers at school, and so on.
- Tell the children that the Holy Spirit inspires such people to help and teach others.

The Work of the Holy Spirit

Jesus would soon be going back to God the Father. He promised his followers that a helper would come.

 God's Word

Jesus Promises the Holy Spirit

Jesus said, "The holy Spirit that the Father will send in my name—he will teach you everything and remind you of all that [I] told you." John 14:26

The guide who came to them is <u>the Holy Spirit</u>. The Holy Spirit is with us today. He lives in the whole Church.

 Underline the guide that Jesus promised to send.

Share Your Faith

Think How is the Holy Spirit a guide to the whole Church? Connect the dots to find a symbol of the Holy Spirit.

Share Talk about how the Holy Spirit is a guide.

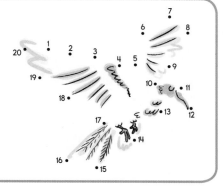

Optional Activity

Activity Master 11: A Sign of the Holy Spirit

Distribute copies of the activity found on catechist page 159E.

- Tell the children that they will cut out a dove to make a mobile, which represents the Holy Spirit.
- As an alternative, you may wish to send this activity home with the children.

The Work of the Holy Spirit

Read aloud the introductory paragraph.

 God's Word

Tell the children that Jesus knew he would leave his followers one day and return to God his Father. Tell them he promised his followers a Guide to be with them always.

Proclaim "Jesus Promises the Holy Spirit."

- Discuss with the children how Jesus' followers would have felt after hearing Jesus' words.

Read aloud the rest of the text.

- ⭐ Have the children underline the guide that Jesus promised to send.
- *Ask:* What does the Holy Spirit do?

▶ Music Option: Have the children sing, "Come to Us, Holy Spirit" or "Holy Spirit," downloaded from **aliveinchrist.osv.com**.

Activity

Read aloud the directions for the Share Your Faith activity.

- Have the children complete the activity.
- Discuss how the Holy Spirit is a Guide.

Quick Review

The Holy Spirit is the Third Divine Person of the Holy Trinity. Jesus promised to send the Holy Spirit to his followers to guide them.

Discover

Objective

- Appreciate that Saint Thérèse loved God very much and worked for him through her little jobs. She called this "The Little Way"

Ways to God

Ask: Who can show you the way to God?

- Write the children's responses on the board or on chart paper.

Tell the children that they are about to hear about a person who helped others find God.

Read aloud "Saint Thérèse of Lisieux."

- ⭐ Have the children underline how Saint Thérèse showed her love for God.

- Ask the children what Saint Thérèse's little way was.

- Ask the children to name examples of things they can do every day to follow the little way.

Ways to God

Who can show you the way to God?

Sometimes other people can show us the way to God. Saint Thérèse found a simple way to God.

Saint Thérèse of Lisieux

⭐ Underline how Saint Thérèse worked for God.

Thérèse was the youngest child in her family. She knew that God loved her. She loved God very much, too.

She felt that God had not called her to do some of the great big, brave things that some of the Saints had done. But <u>she knew she could still work for God through her little jobs.</u> This is called "the little way." She knew that God would see the love in her work.

Saint Thérèse of Lisieux

162 Chapter 11

Optional Activity

Sing and Learn *Musical*

After reading about Saint Thérèse's little way, invite the children to sing the words below to the tune of "Here We Go 'Round the Mulberry Bush."

Thérèse, Thérèse, your little way,

your little way, your little way.

Thérèse, Thérèse, your little way,

can guide us all to God.

- If possible, have the children sing this song to other children in the program.

After Thérèse grew up, she wrote about her little way in a book. Many people read the book and followed the little way. Thérèse helped many people find God. She is a special Saint.

→ **How does Thérèse's little way help people to do what God asks?**

A Guide for Everyone

Saint Thérèse led people to God's love. She did this because God the Holy Spirit guided her work. The Holy Spirit guides you, too. He will keep you close to God the Father and to God the Son.

Connect Your Faith

Use the Code Solve the code to learn who guides the Church. Write the letter that matches each number in the phrase below.

1 = H	2 = I	3 = L	4 = O	5 = P
6 = R	7 = S	8 = T	9 = Y	

God the H O L Y
           1 4 3 9

S P I R I T
7 5 2 6 2 8

(i) Catechist Background

Saint Thérèse of Lisieux 1873–1897

Saint Thérèse was part of a pious French family. Her parents, Louis and Zelie Martin, were beatified in 2008. Five of the Martin daughters became Carmelite nuns.

- Even as a child, Thérèse showed remarkable devotion to Jesus. She petitioned her local bishop as well as Pope Leo XIII to allow her to enter the Carmelite convent at an early age.
- Her autobiography, *The Story of a Soul*, was published after her death. It has been translated into 35 languages.
- Thérèse called herself "the little flower of Jesus."

Saint Thérèse of Lisieux,
continued

Ask the children the question at the end of the story.

- Emphasize that any person can use the little way to honor God.

Point out the photographs of the parents and children on pages 162 and 163.

- *Ask:* How are the people in the photos following the little way?

A Guide for Everyone

Read aloud the paragraph.

- Emphasize that both the Holy Spirit and the Saints or holy people can keep us close to God.

 Music Option: Have the children sing, "Spirit Be with Us," downloaded from **aliveinchrist.osv.com**.

Activity

Point out the Connect Your Faith activity and read aloud the directions.

- Have the children work in pairs to solve the puzzle.

Quick Review

The Holy Spirit guides you and helps you stay close to God the Father and to God the Son.

Our Catholic Life

Ask: How does the Holy Spirit help you?

- List the children's responses on the board or on chart paper.

Ask volunteers to review what they know about the Holy Spirit.

Invite the children to pay careful attention as you read aloud the first paragraph.

- *Ask:* How did the Holy Spirit help Jesus' friends? He gave them gifts like courage and understanding.

Gifts of the Holy Spirit

- Read aloud the words in the Gift column. Invite the children to join you in reading aloud the How it Helps column.

- ⭐ Have the children check off two Gifts of the Holy Spirit that they have seen in their family.

- *Ask:* When can you ask the Holy Spirit to help you?

Our Catholic Life

How does the Holy Spirit help you?

The Holy Spirit came to help Jesus' friends. He gave them gifts like courage and understanding. Here are the Gifts the Holy Spirit gives you.

Check off two Gifts of the Holy Spirit that you have seen in your family this week.

© Our Sunday Visitor

Gifts of the Holy Spirit

	Gift	How it Helps
☐	wisdom	helps you see yourself and others as God sees you
☐	understanding	helps you get along with others
☐	right judgment (counsel)	helps you make good choices
☐	courage (fortitude)	helps you act bravely
☐	knowledge	helps you know God better
☐	reverence (piety)	helps you pray every day
☐	wonder and awe (fear of the Lord)	helps you understand how great and powerful God is

164

✓ Quick Tip

Dealing with Anxiety

Young children sometimes experience anxiety or phobias such as fear of the dark. Remind the children that God is always with them.

- Help the children compose brief prayers asking the Holy Spirit's help in times of anxiety.

- Explain that he often helps us through other people, such as family members and teachers who help us overcome our fears.

People of Faith

Saint Rose of Lima, 1586 –1617

August 23

Saint Rose of Lima was named Isabel at birth. Her family said she was as pretty as a flower, so they called her "Rose." The Holy Spirit gave Rose the gift of piety. She prayed and fasted every day. She loved God's wonderful world. She used her gift to grow beautiful flowers that she sold to help support her family and care for the poor.

Discuss: What gifts has the Holy Spirit given you?

 Learn more about Saint Rose of Lima at **aliveinchrist.osv.com**

Live Your Faith

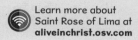

Follow the Holy Spirit If the action below shows love for God and others, color the dove of the Spirit. If the action does not show love, cross out the dove.

 Share your new toy with a friend.

 Call someone a bad name.

 Help fold the laundry.

 Pray.

 Throw trash on the playground.

The Church's Guide **165**

Catholic Social Teaching

Chapter Connections

To integrate Catholic Social Teaching into your lesson, choose one of the following features: Rights and Responsibilities, pages 288–289; or The Dignity of Work, pages 292–293.

- Start by talking about Saint Rose of Lima on page 165. Then move directly to the Catholic Social Teaching feature.
- Or, to expand the lesson, complete both pages 164 and 165, then move to the Catholic Social Teaching feature.
- Return to Chapter 11 for the prayer on page 166.

People of Faith

Tell the children about Saint Rose of Lima.

- Invite a volunteer to read aloud the People of Faith story.
- Explain that Saint Rose of Lima's love for Jesus was so strong at a young age that she never married, as her parents wanted her to do. In fact, her father forbade her to become a nun. Instead, she continued to live with her parents and care for the sick and the hungry. She would bring people into her room to care for them.
- In addition to growing flowers to sell, her exquisite lace and embroidery skills helped care for the poor and her family.
- Saint Rose is the patron Saint of Latin America and the Philippines.
- *Ask:* What gifts has the Holy Spirit given you?

 Encourage the children to go to **aliveinchrist.osv.com** at home to learn more about Saint Rose of Lima.

Activity

Read aloud the directions and discuss the Live Your Faith activity as a group.

- Allow time for the children to complete the activity.
- Invite volunteers to share their answers.

Live

 Let Us Pray
Asking Prayer

Prepare

Teach the children their response.

- Invite the children to create a gesture to go with the words *Holy Spirit*. Work together as a group and practice the gesture. Have the children use the gesture every time they sing the words *Holy Spirit* in the celebration song.

 Rehearse "The Holy Spirit," downloaded from **aliveinchrist.osv.com**.

Gather

Invite the children to process to the prayer space.

- Have the children sit in a circle and quiet themselves for prayer.

Pray

Follow the order of prayer on the student page.

 Conclude by singing together "The Holy Spirit."

- Encourage the children to teach their parents the gesture that was created for *Holy Spirit*.

Live

 Let Us Pray
Asking Prayer

Gather and begin with the Sign of the Cross.

Leader: When I ask others to play,

All: Come, Holy Spirit, guide me.

Leader: When I am afraid to do what is right,

All: Come, Holy Spirit, guide me.

Leader: When I need to help others,

All: Come, Holy Spirit, guide me.

 Sing "The Holy Spirit"

The Holy Spirit, sent from God above.
The Holy Spirit, bringing peace and love.
Receive the power of the Holy Spirit today!

The Holy Spirit, giving strength each day.
The Holy Spirit, showing us the way.
Receive the power of the Holy Spirit today!

 Liturgy Link

The *Orans* Position

You may wish to have the children pray the Asking Prayer in the *orans* position of prayer, an ancient Jewish and early Christian position of readiness.

- Tell the children to raise their arms extended out to the sides, elbows bent, with their palms open upward.

- When the prayer is finished, have the children lower their arms.

 Go to **aliveinchrist.osv.com** for Sunday readings, Scripture background, questions of the week, and seasonal resources.

FAMILY+FAITH
LIVING AND LEARNING TOGETHER

YOUR CHILD LEARNED >>>
This chapter explores Jesus' promise to send the Holy Spirit—the Third Divine Person of the Holy Trinity—to guide the Church.

God's Word
 Read **John 14:15–26** to learn how the Holy Spirit is always with us.

Catholics Believe
- God the Holy Spirit is the Third Person of the Holy Trinity.
- The Holy Spirit fills people's hearts with love and guides the Church.

To learn more, go to the *Catechism of the Catholic Church* #737–741 at **usccb.org**.

People of Faith
This week, your child met Saint Rose of Lima. Rose used the Gifts of the Holy Spirit to live a holy life in 17th century Peru.

CHILDREN AT THIS AGE >>>
How They Understand the Holy Spirit Even in the most general terms, "God" and "Trinity" are abstract concepts for first-grade children, but the Holy Spirit tends to be the most elusive of all. It's difficult for children this age to grasp this Person of God who also dwells within the hearts of all Christians. You can help make this more concrete by referring to Gifts and Fruits of the Holy Spirit. It will also help if your child understands that the Holy Spirit helps us to make good choices and prompts us to be loving toward others.

CONSIDER THIS >>>
Do you remember a time when you really needed a guide?

Maybe the journey was long, or the best of directions were still not clear. A good guide can lessen frustration, get you where you need to be, or in some cases give you information you didn't know. The Holy Spirit guides the Church. Whenever you need direction, or you seek to know God's will in your life, remember—"We do not work alone. The Holy Spirit is our teacher and guide" (*USCCA, p.16*).

LET'S TALK >>>
- Ask your child to share a time when he or she was guided or helped.
- Share about a time when the Holy Spirit guided you or helped you pray.

LET'S PRAY >>>
Saint Rose, pray for us that we may always use the Gifts of the Holy Spirit in our lives. Amen.

For a multimedia glossary of Catholic Faith Words, Sunday readings, seasonal and Saint resources, and chapter activities go to **aliveinchrist.osv.com**.

Alive in Christ. Grade 1 Chapter 11 **167**

Family + Faith

Distribute the page to the children or parents/adult family members. Point out the chapter highlights, insights on how first graders understand concepts, the opportunity for for the adults to reflect on their own experience and faith journey, and the family prayer.

Chapter 11 Review

(A) Work with Words Circle the correct answer to complete each sentence.

1. Jesus promised to send ____.

    the Church   (the Holy Spirit)

2. The Holy Spirit guides the ____.

    (Church)   animals

3. The Holy Spirit is the ____ Divine Person of the Trinity.

    First   (Third)

4. The Holy Spirit gives us ____ to guide us.

    (gifts)   time

(B) Check Understanding Trace the answers to the questions.

5. Who did Jesus send to guide us?

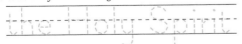

6. What is one way you can follow the Holy Spirit?

168 Chapter 11 Review

 Go to **aliveinchrist.osv.com** for an interactive review.

Chapter Review

Use Catechist Quick Reviews to highlight lesson concepts.

(A) Work with Words Have the children circle the correct answer to complete each sentence.

(B) Check Understanding Have the children trace the words to answer the questions.

 Go to **aliveinchrist.osv.com** to prepare customized and downloadable assessments, send eAssessments, and assign interactive reviews.

The Church's Guide **167–168**

KEY CONCEPT

Saints are heroes of the Church who can show us how to live. People in the Church are called to live holy lives, as Mary and all the Saints did.

DOCTRINAL CONTENT

- Saints are heroes of the Church who loved God very much, did his work on Earth, and are now with him in Heaven. (CCC, 823, 828)

- Holy means unique and pure, set apart for God and his purposes. (CCC, 825)

- We are part of the family of Saints, connected to the Saints who lived before us and to those who believe in Jesus now. (CCC, 946–948)

TASKS OF CATECHESIS

Helping children grow in a faith that is "known, celebrated, lived, and expressed in prayer" (NDC, 20).

This chapter focuses on the following tasks of catechesis:

- Promoting Knowledge of the Faith

- Missionary Initiation

Catechist Background

 "But I say to you, love your enemies, and pray for those who persecute you, that you may be children of your heavenly Father." Matthew 5:44–45

➡ **Reflect** Who are people you treat with kindness even when they are not always kind to you?

The Church has long held the practice of canonizing some of her members who have heroically lived faithful lives. These men and women serve as mentors and models of faith for the Church, whose members continue to strive to live as Jesus taught. By calling attention to the lives of the faithful of the past, the Church of today helps people act with faith and conviction.

Along your journey of life, certain people have been your guides, encouraging you. In the same way, the Saints of the Church inspire loving faith and perseverance. Their lives are a living testimony to the Gifts of the Holy Spirit. Reflect on how as a catechist, teacher, parent, or friend, you are a living testimony and an inspiration of faith to others.

As a baptized Catholic, you are a part of a holy People, the Communion of Saints. As a member of the Body of Christ, you are called to nourish and sustain faith—your own and that of others. The Saints in Heaven are intercessors for you, bringing your needs to God.

➡ **Reflect** Of the many canonized Saints, whom might you choose to be your intercessor or model?

Catechist's Prayer

Saints of God, you have given me wonderful examples of holiness. Pray that I have the strength and courage to love God and others as you did. Amen.

Lesson Plan

Objectives	Process	Materials

Invite, 10 minutes

Friends of God Page 169

- Psalm 40:5 Pray the opening prayer.
- Matthew 5:44–45 Reflect prayerfully on the Word.
- Discuss What Do You Wonder questions.

Note: In this chapter, the Chapter Poem is in the Discover step of the lesson process.

Discover, 35 minutes

Holy People Pages 170–171
- Recognize a Saint as someone who loved God very much, did his work on Earth, and is with him in Heaven
- Define the word *holy* as unique, and pure; set apart for God and his purposes

- **Catholic Faith Words** Saint, angel, holy
- Explain that Saints showed their love for God.
- ☆ Underline what Saints did more than anything.
- Luke 10:38–42 Proclaim "Martha and Mary."
- Explain that the children are part of the family of Saints.
- **Share Your Faith Activity** Name someone who serves God.

- 🌐 **Optional Activity** Chapter Poem: "Friends"
- ☐ pencils
- ☐ index cards
- **Optional Activity** Make a Halo
- ☐ Activity Master 12 (Page 169E)

All Kinds of Saints Pages 172–173
- Appreciate that we are part of the family of Saints, connected to the Saints who lived before us and to those who believe in Jesus now

- Explain that the Saints lived a good life and loved God and others.
- Read about Mary, Saint Juan Diego, Saint King Louis IX, and Saint Kateri Tekakwitha.
- **Connect Your Faith Activity** Match the descriptions to the holy person.

- ☐ pencils

Live, 15 minutes

Our Catholic Life Pages 174–175

- Explain that God wants everyone to be a Saint.
- ☆ Identify ways to be a friend of God.
- **People of Faith** Learn about Saint Dominic.
- **Live Your Faith Activity** Find the hidden message.

- ☐ pencils
- ☐ crayons, markers, or colored pencils

Litany of the Saints Page 176

- Explain what a litany is.
- ▶ Rehearse "Oh, When the Saints."
- Follow the order of prayer.

- 🌐 Download "Oh, When the Saints."

Family + Faith Page 177
Point out that the Catholic Families page provides chapter highlights, information on how first graders understand faith concepts, and family prayer.

Chapter Review Page 178
🌐 aliveinchrist.osv.com
- Customize and Download Assessments
- Email Links to eAssessments
- Interactive Student Reviews

ONLINE RESOURCES

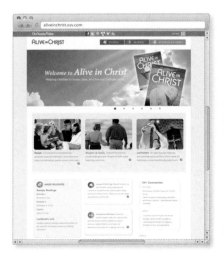

 Go to **aliveinchrist.osv.com**

You will find:

- Interactive lesson planning with web specific content and additional activities
- Step by step lesson instruction from printed Catechist Edition for integrated lesson planning
- Custom-built assessments to download and eAssessment links
- Interactive reviews that provide scores and the option to review answers
- Sunday readings with background and questions of the week

 Go to **osvparish.com**

You will find:

- Ask the Experts Q and A
- General Catechist Helps
- Community Connections and Blogs

Sharing the Message with First Graders

Holy People Every child has heroes. Some "heroes" are better examples than others. "Heroes" can also differ in their longevity. A child who is enamored with preschool-friendly characters will just a few years later find those former "heroes" laughable. The Saints, on the other hand, are great examples, and they have staying power. Children can relate to Saints because they are real people who lived the Christian life in their own time and situation. In order to fully take advantage of the great examples Saints can be, it's important that kids have an opportunity to learn not only of their extraordinary virtue, but also the ways in which the Saints' daily lives were ordinary. This helps us to relate and connect with the Saints as real human beings.

Teaching Tip: Consider helping the children begin a collection of holy cards by buying them in bulk and passing them out throughout the year. You might even wish to provide children with a tool to keep their collection together, such as a trading card album page.

How First Graders Understand

- First graders like to be praised for good work and good behavior. Catch them being good.
- First graders like to help. Give them some jobs to do.
- First graders have heard the word *holy*. Broaden their understanding of holiness to include people who are filled with the Holy Spirit.

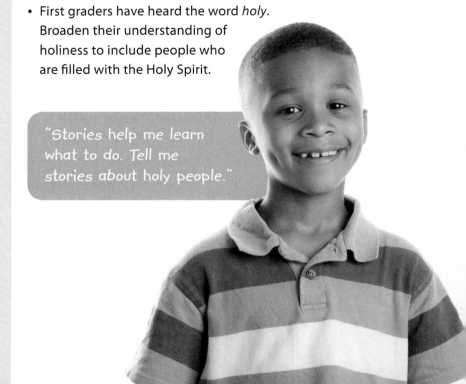

"Stories help me learn what to do. Tell me stories about holy people."

Chapter Connections

Chapter Poem

Invite

"Friends"

Use this poem to expand the chapter introduction.

- The children will relate the poem to their own lives, reflecting on their experience of friendship.
- Connect friendship to a relationship with God.

 Go to **aliveinchrist.osv.com** Lesson Planning section for this poem.

NCEA IFG: ACRE Edition

Discover

Knowledge of the Faith

- Objective: To know and understand basic Catholic teaching about the Incarnate Word Jesus Christ as the way, truth, and life

Missionary Spirit

- Objectives: To recognize the centrality of evangelization as the Church's mission and identity embodied in vocation and service; to be aware of how cultures are transformed by the Gospel

Catholic Social Teaching

Live

 Use one of these features to introduce a principle and engage the children with an activity.

- Call to Community, Pages 286–287
- Rights and Responsibilities, Pages 288–289

Music Options

 Use one or more of the following songs to enhance catechetical learning or for prayer.

- "Oh, When the Saints," Live Prayer, Page 176
- "Sing a Song to the Saints," Discover, Page 171
- "Litany of Saints," Discover, Page 173
- "We Gather Around Your Throne," Live, Page 174

LECTIONARY CONNECTION

 Chapter 12 highlights Lectionary-connected themes such as loving others, service, and the Kingdom of God. If your parish aligns its curriculum to the liturgical year, you could use this chapter in connection with the following Sundays.

Year A

Twenty-fifth Sunday in Ordinary Time—law of love

Thirty-first Sunday in Ordinary Time—the Church, Holy Spirit

Year B

Fourth Sunday of Advent—Mary

Twenty-fifth Sunday in Ordinary Time—call to service

Thirty-third Sunday in Ordinary Time—Kingdom of God

Year C

The Holy Family of Jesus, Mary, and Joseph—domestic church

Fifth Sunday of Easter—new commandment

Twenty-third Sunday in Ordinary Time—Kingdom of God

Go to **aliveinchrist.osv.com** for a complete correlation ordered by the Sundays of the year and suggestions for how to integrate the Scripture readings into chapter lessons.

Friends of God **169D**

Name _____   Date _____

Make a Halo

Color the halo and decorate it, too. Then, cut out the halo.
Let the halo remind you to live as a friend of God.

Friends of God

 Let Us Pray

Leader: We trust in you always, O Lord.

"Blessed the man who sets
his security in the LORD." Psalm 40:5

All: We trust in you always, O Lord. Amen.

 **God's Word**

"But I say to you, love your enemies, and pray for those who persecute you, that you may be children of your heavenly Father."
Matthew 5:44–45

© Our Sunday Visitor

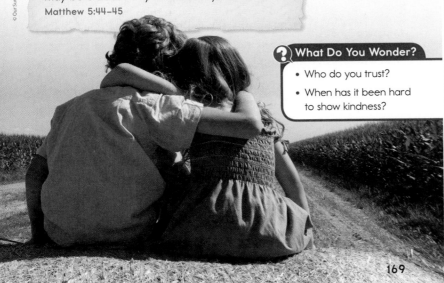

? What Do You Wonder?

- Who do you trust?
- When has it been hard to show kindness?

169

 Songs of Scripture

You've Got to Love Them

A handshake can be a sign of reconciliation. It takes a real choice and a generous spirit to extend your hand to another after a conflict.

- Teach the song and each time the children sing the phrase *You've got to love them*, have them turn to a designated partner and shake hands.

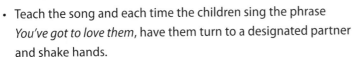

▶ Use *Songs of Scripture*, Grades 1–3 CD, Track 7

 Let Us Pray

Invite the children to gather in the prayer space and make the Sign of the Cross. Invite a child to be the leader while you read aloud the Psalm verse from a Bible. Prompt the children's response.

Have the children move out of the prayer space and back to their seats.

Explain that holy people trust God.

Say: Holy people have always trusted in God. Let's listen to a reading from the Gospel of Matthew to find out what Jesus says about how we should treat others.

 God's Word

Guide the children through the process of Scripture reflection.

- Invite them to close their eyes, be still and open their minds and hearts to what God is saying to them in this passage.
- Proclaim the Scripture.
- Maintain several moments of silence.
- *Ask:* What did you hear God say to you today?
- Invite volunteers to share.

What Do You Wonder?

Say: To live as holy people, we need to trust in God and love everyone.

Invite the children to respond to the questions. Ask what else they might wonder about trusting God and loving others.

Discover

Objectives

- Recognize a Saint as someone who loved God very much, did his work on Earth, and is with him in Heaven
- Define the word *holy* as unique, and pure; set apart for God and his purposes

Holy People

Ask: What does Jesus ask you to do?

- Write the children's answers on the board or on chart paper.

Read aloud the first paragraph.

 Have the children underline what the Saints did more than anything.

Work with Words

Hold up index cards with the words *Saint* and *angel* on them.

- Read aloud the definitions for both words.
- Emphasize that everyone is called to be a Saint by loving God and loving others.

God's Word

Explain to the children that they will listen to a story from the Gospel according to Luke about Jesus and his friends.

- Proclaim "Martha and Mary."
- Tell the children to listen for things people can do to show that they are God's friends.

Discover

Jesus visits the home of two sisters named Martha and Mary.

 Underline what Saints did more than anything.

Holy People

What does Jesus ask you to do?

Saints are God's friends. Saints said and did good things when they lived on Earth. They showed their love for God more than anything. They now live with God and the **angels** forever in Heaven.

You can learn from the Bible how to be God's friend.

© Our Sunday Visitor

God's Word

Martha and Mary

Jesus visited two sisters named Martha and Mary. Mary sat next to Jesus and listened to everything he said. Martha did all the cooking and cleaning. She was doing all the work! Martha started to get angry with her sister.

Optional Activity

Chapter Poem: "Friends" *Verbal/Linguistic*

Use this poem before beginning the lesson instruction on this page.

- Read the poem aloud as the children follow along.
- Ask the children what this poem is about. friends
- *Ask:* What are two words that describe a good friend?
- After having the children tell why it is good to have friends, transition back to the lesson instruction.

 Go to **aliveinchrist.osv.com** for Chapter Poem.

Martha said to Jesus, "Mary is making me do all the work. Please tell her to help me!" Jesus replied, "Martha, you worry about so many things. Mary is doing what is most important. She is listening to me. Nobody can take that away from her." **Based on** Luke 10:38–42

Family of Saints

Saints are **holy** people. They are filled with the Holy Spirit. Holy people serve God with love.

Catholics celebrate many Saints. You are part of the Catholic Church and her family of Saints! You are connected to the Saints who lived before you. You are also connected to holy people who live now.

Catholic Faith Words

Saint a hero of the Church who loved God very much, led a holy life, and is now with God in Heaven.

angel a type of spiritual being that does God's work, such as delivering messages from God or helping to keep people safe from harm

holy unique and pure; set apart for God and his purposes

Share Your Faith

Think Write the name of someone you know who serves God.

_____

– – – – – – – – – – – – – – – – –

_____

Share Tell a partner about this person. Talk about ways you can serve God.

Saint Anthony

Friends of God **171**

Family of Saints

Read aloud the first paragraph of Family of Saints.

Work with Words

Hold up an index card with the word *holy* and explain to the children what it means.

- Explain to the children that Catholic artists often indicate which of the figures in their pictures are Saints by painting halos above their heads.

- Point out the halos in the mosaic of Saint Anthony and Jesus.

Read aloud the second paragraph and tell the children that they are all part of the family of Saints.

 Music Option: Have the children sing, "Sing a Song to the Saints," downloaded from **aliveinchrist.osv.com**.

Activity

Read aloud the directions for the Share Your Faith activity.

- Have the children work independently to write a name. After a short time, have them discuss this person with a partner.

Optional Activity

Activity Master 12: Make a Halo

Distribute copies of the activity found on catechist page 169E.

- Tell the children that they will cut out a halo and decorate it.

- As an alternative, you may wish to send this activity home with the children.

Quick Review

Saints are holy people who are friends of God and live with him forever.

Objective

- Appreciate that we are part of the family of Saints, connected to the Saints who lived before us and to those who believe in Jesus now

All Kinds of Saints

Ask: How do Saints show their love?

- Write the children's answers on the board or on chart paper.

Read aloud the first two paragraphs.

- Emphasize that Mary, the Mother of Jesus, is the first and greatest Saint. Point out that Mary is our Mother too, because she loves and cares for us.

Tell the children that stories about the Saints can help them learn how to be holy.

Ask the children to put their finger next to each Saint as you read aloud "All Kinds of Saints."

- Have the children circle a word or words that tell how the Saint showed love for God. For example, *Saint Juan Diego went to Mass; Saint Louis cared for the sick and less fortunate; Saint Kateri devoted her life to prayer.*

All Kinds of Saints

How do Saints show their love?

Stories about the Saints help you learn how to be holy. Saints are heroes of the Church. They loved God very much and led holy lives. Mary, the Mother of Jesus, is the first and greatest of the Saints.

Mary is the Mother of God, and our Mother, too. She loves and cares for us just as she did for Jesus.

➜ **How can we thank Mary for her love?**

© Our Sunday Visitor

A Simple Man

Saint Juan Diego was visited by Our Lady of Guadalupe on his way to Mass. He spent the rest of his life sharing his story with others.

172 Chapter 12

✓ Quick Tip

Ordinary People

Saints were real people who did ordinary things.

- Point out to the children that the Saints in these stories were real people.
- Remind them that Saints were like us and did things such as parenting, going to Mass, praying and caring for the sick, with great love for God and others.

A King   1

Saint Louis IX of France was a powerful man. He used his position as king to help care for the sick and less fortunate. He served meals near his palace to people in need.

The Daughter of a Warrior   3

Saint Kateri Tekakwitha is the first Native American to become a Saint. She devoted her life to prayer, penance, and those who were sick or old.

Connect Your Faith

Matching Read the descriptions below. Match each description with a holy person on these pages. Write the number in the box next to the person's picture.

1. Used his position to help feed and take care of others.

2. Shared his vision with others.

3. Devoted herself to a life of prayer and penance.

Friends of God   **173**

✓ Quick Tip

Saints Around the World

The children in your group may come from a variety of cultural backgrounds.

- Use the study of Saints to develop their appreciation for cultural diversity.
- Find pictures of the patron Saints of a variety of countries and show them to the children.

All Kinds of Saints,

continued

- *Ask:* Which of these people would you want to be like?
- *Ask:* How can you be a holy person?

Explain to the children that the Church prays with the Saints. Refer to page 320 in the Our Catholic Tradition reference section in the back of the Student Book for more about praying with the Saints.

 Music Option: Have the children sing, "Litany of Saints," downloaded from **aliveinchrist.osv.com**.

Activity

Read aloud the directions for the Connect Your Faith activity.

- Ask the children to locate the boxes found near each Saint's picture.
- Tell the children that they are going to write a number in each box.
- Read each numbered phrase with the children.
- Allow time for them to identify which Saint the phrase describes.
- Ask volunteers to share their answers.

Quick Review

The Saints showed their love for God and for other people in many different ways.

Our Catholic Life

Ask: How can you be a Saint?

- Write the children's answers on the board or on chart paper.

Invite the children to listen carefully as your read aloud the first paragraph.

Ways to Be God's Friend

Draw attention to the list by reading the introductory sentence.

- Invite seven children to take turns reading aloud the list.
- ⭐ Have the children place an *X* next to what they already do to be God's friend.

Point out the picture. Ask the children to tell what they see.

- *Ask:* How is the boy in the picture showing that he is God's friend?
- *Ask:* What is one way that you can show that you are trying to be a Saint today?

 Music Option: Have the children sing, "We Gather Around Your Throne," downloaded from **aliveinchrist.osv.com**.

Our Catholic Life

How can you be a Saint?

Saints are not just people who lived a long time ago. God wants you to be a Saint, too! You are God's friend. Jesus shows you how to be holy, and the Holy Spirit helps you live a holy life every day.

Here are some ways you can show that you are God's friend.

⭐ Place an X next to the things you do already.

Ways to Be God's Friend

- ☐ Think about other people, not just yourself.
- ☐ Treat everyone with kindness.
- ☐ Help when someone needs you.
- ☐ Pray every day.
- ☐ Learn more about God.
- ☐ Try your best to do what is right.
- ☐ Love others as Jesus did.

© Our Sunday Visitor

174 Chapter 12

✓ Quick Tip

Choosing Good Friends

Remind the children that being a good friend as well as choosing good friends can help them grow in their friendship with God.

- Ask the children to think about what makes a good friend.
- Help the children see that their choice of companions can contribute to or distract from their ability to show love for God and others.

People of Faith

Saint Dominic, 1170–1221

Saint Dominic was a very good speaker. He told people about Jesus. When he talked about God, people came from all over to listen. They wanted to be holy like Dominic. He said that hearing about God wasn't enough. He said that if you want to be holy, you need to praise God and bless other people. He also said that it is more important to be good and do the right thing than to talk all the time.

August 8

Discuss: What good thing have you done today?

Learn more about Saint Dominic at **aliveinchrist.osv.com**

© Our Sunday Visitor

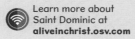

Being a Saint Color the X's red and the O's another color to find the hidden message.

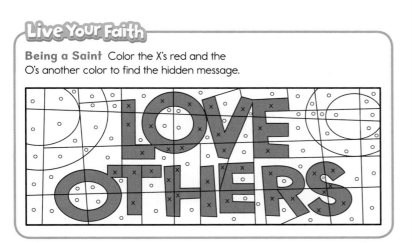

Friends of God **175**

🌐 Catholic Social Teaching

Chapter Connections

To integrate Catholic Social Teaching into your lesson, choose one of the following features: Call to Community, pages 286–287; or Rights and Responsibilities, pages 288-289.

- Start by talking about Saint Dominic on page 175. Then move directly to the Catholic Social Teaching feature.
- Or, to expand the lesson, complete both pages 174 and 175, then move to the Catholic Social Teaching feature.
- Return to Chapter 12 for the prayer on page 176.

People of Faith

Tell the children about Saint Dominic.

- Invite a volunteer to read aloud the People of Faith story.
- Explain that Saint Dominic saw the need for a new religious order to address the spiritual needs of the growing population of that era. He combined dedication with systematic education, but maintained a more organizational flexibility than other monastic orders or the clergy.
- Explain that the spread of the Rosary and Marian devotion is attributed to the preaching of Saint Dominic. The Rosary has been at the heart of the Dominican order for centuries.
- *Ask:* What good thing have you done today?
- If there is time, invite the children to join you in praying a decade of the Rosary.

> Encourage the children to go to **aliveinchrist.osv.com** at home to learn more about Saint Dominic.

Activity

Read aloud the directions to the Live Your Faith activity.

- Supply the children with markers, crayons or colored pencils. Each child should have a red and a variety of other colors.
- Allow time for the children to solve the puzzle.
- Invite volunteers to share the hidden message.

Live

Live

 Let Us Pray

Litany of the Saints

Explain to the children what a litany is. Refer to the Liturgy Link box below for more information.

Prepare

Tell the children that they will walk in procession to the prayer space as they say the litany.

- Explain that they will ask for the prayers of the Saints they just read about.

 Rehearse "Oh, When the Saints," downloaded from **aliveinchrist.osv.com**.

Gather

Line up the children on the opposite side of the room from the usual prayer space. Stand at the head of the line.

Pray

Follow the order of prayer on the student page.

- Process to the prayer space with the children while praying the litany.

 Conclude by singing together "Oh, When the Saints."

 Let Us Pray

Litany of the Saints

Gather and begin with the Sign of the Cross.

Leader: When we pray with the Saints, we ask them to pray with us and for us. Holy Mary,

All: pray for us.

Leader: Saint Juan Diego,

All: pray for us.

Leader: Saint Louis IX,

All: pray for us.

Leader: Saint Kateri,

All: pray for us.

 Sing "Oh, When the Saints"

Oh, when the saints go marching in;
Oh, when the saints go marching in;
Oh, Lord, I want to be
in that number,
when the saints go
marching in.

 Liturgy Link

A Litany

A litany is any prayer in which certain short phrases are said over and over again.

- Litanies are often prayed as people are walking in processions in church.
- The litany most commonly heard is the Litany of the Saints, used at the Easter Vigil. The litany on this page is based on it.

Go to **aliveinchrist.osv.com** for Sunday readings, Scripture background, questions of the week, and seasonal resources.

FAMILY+FAITH
LIVING AND LEARNING TOGETHER

YOUR CHILD LEARNED >>>

This chapter explains how Saints are people who loved God very much, did his work on Earth, and are with him in Heaven.

God's Word

Read **Matthew 5:44–45** to learn how God wants us to love those who mistreat us.

Catholics Believe

- Saints are heroes of the Church who can show us how to live.
- People in the Church are called to live holy lives, as Mary and all the Saints did.

To learn more, go to the *Catechism of the Catholic Church* #956–958 at **usccb.org.**

People of Faith

This week, your child met Saint Dominic, the founder of the Order of Preachers, called the Dominicans, whose special gifts help them spread the Gospel.

CHILDREN AT THIS AGE >>>

How They Understand Holy People Every child has heroes. Some "heroes" are better examples than others. "Heroes" can also differ in their longevity. The Saints, on the other hand, are great examples, and they have staying power. Children can relate to Saints because they are real people who lived the Catholic life in their own time and situation. In order to fully take advantage of the great examples Saints can be, it's important that kids have an opportunity to learn not only of their extraordinary virtue, but also the ways in which the Saints' daily lives were ordinary. This helps us to relate and connect with the Saints as real human beings.

CONSIDER THIS >>>

How does your child feel when he or she is chosen to do something special?

When a teacher or coach gives your child an opportunity to let his/her gifts or talents shine, it is a real moment of joy. How different our lives would be if we were more conscious that God has called each of us to use the gifts and talents he has given us to transform the world. "God calls all the members of the Church to fidelity to the union with him begun at Baptism and continued in the other Sacraments" (*USCCA, p. 146*). We are indeed chosen and it should give us joy.

LET'S TALK >>>

- Talk about your favorite Saints. Who were they and what did they do?
- Ask your child to think of some ways he or she can live a holy life.

LET'S PRAY >>>

Saint Dominic, pray for us that we may be good listeners when people tell us about God. Amen.

For a multimedia glossary of Catholic Faith Words, Sunday readings, seasonal and Saint resources, and chapter activities go to **aliveinchrist.osv.com.**

Family + Faith

Distribute the page to the children or parents/adult family members. Point out the chapter highlights, insights on how first graders understand concepts, the opportunity for the adults to reflect on their own experience and faith journey, and the family prayer.

Chapter 12 Review

A **Work with Words** Circle the correct answer.

1. The greatest Saint is ____.

   Saint Louis IX   **(Mary)**

2. To be holy means to be set apart for ____.

   (God)   Mary

3. You are ____.

   God's Father   **(God's friend)**

B **Check Understanding** Trace the words to answer the questions.

4. What do we call heroes of the Church who loved God, lived holy lives, and are now with God in Heaven?

   Saints

5. What do we call the spiritual beings that do God's work?

   angels

Go to **aliveinchrist.osv.com** for an interactive review.

Chapter Review

Use Catechist Quick Reviews to highlight lesson concepts.

A **Work with Words**
Have the children circle the correct answer.

B **Check Understanding**
Have the children trace the words to answer the questions.

Go to **aliveinchrist.osv.com** to prepare customized and downloadable assessments, send eAssessments, and assign interactive reviews.

Friends of God   **177–178**

Use Catechist Quick Reviews in each chapter to highlight lesson concepts for this unit and prepare for the Unit Review.

Have the children complete the Review pages. Then discuss the answers as a group. Review any concepts with which the children are having difficulty.

A **Work with Words**

Have the children trace the words to complete each sentence.

4–6. Have the children draw a line to the best ending for the sentence.

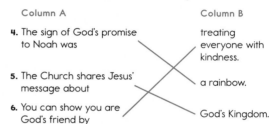

Unit Review

A **Work with Words** Trace the words to answer the questions.

1. The ⟨Kingdom⟩ of God is the world of love, peace, and justice that is in Heaven and is still being built on Earth.

2. The ⟨Holy Spirit⟩ guides the Church.

3. ⟨Saints⟩ are people who loved God very much, led holy lives, and are now with God in Heaven.

Draw a line from Column A to the best ending in Column B.

Column A	Column B
4. The sign of God's promise to Noah was	treating everyone with kindness.
5. The Church shares Jesus' message about	a rainbow.
6. You can show you are God's friend by	God's Kingdom.

B Check Understanding Trace the words to answer the questions.

7. What did Jesus promise his followers?

He would send
the Holy Spirit.

8. How did Noah say "yes" to God?

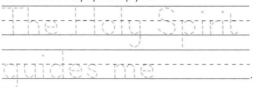

He built the ark.

9. How does the Holy Spirit help you?

The Holy Spirit
guides me.

10. Why are Saints called holy?

They serve God
with love.

C Make Connections Draw one way to show a welcoming heart.

11.

B **Check Understanding**
Have the children trace the words to answer the questions.

C **Make Connections**
Have the children draw one way to show a welcoming heart.

 Go to **aliveinchrist.osv.com** to prepare customized and downloadable assessments, send eAssessments, and assign interactive reviews.

Morality

Our Catholic Tradition

- Jesus' words and actions teach us that we are to love and serve God and others. (CCC, 1721)

- The Ten Commandments are laws from God that tell us how to love God and others. (CCC, 2067)

- Sometimes we sin, but God always offers forgiveness when we are truly sorry. (CCC, 605, 982)

- God wants us to forgive others and forgive ourselves. (CCC, 1968)

Why does God give us Commandments?

Unit 5 Overview

Chapter 13

Disciples Serve

The children will:

- understand that Jesus washed his disciples' feet to show us how to serve and love one another
- recognize that Jesus asks us to have a kind, giving heart when we serve and help others
- identify a disciple as a follower of Jesus who believes in him and lives by his teaching
- connect serving others with serving God

 Catholic Social Teaching: Live Your Faith

- Option for the Poor, Pages 290–291
- The Dignity of Work, Pages 292–293

Chapter 14

Making Choices

The children will:

- recognize the Ten Commandments as God's laws that tell us how to love God and others
- appreciate that God created us with free will because he wants us to make good choices
- define free will as the ability to choose whether to obey God or disobey God
- examine consequences as a significant part of a decision-making process

 Songs of Scripture "His Laws Make Us Free"

 Catholic Social Teaching: Live Your Faith

- Call to Community, Pages 286–287
- Rights and Responsibilities, Pages 288–289

Chapter 15

Showing Sorrow

The children will:

- define sin as the choice to disobey God on purpose and do what you know is wrong. It is not an accident or a mistake
- describe the consequences of sin as hurting our friendship with God and others
- understand that Jesus wants us to be sorry for our sins and turn to God our forgiving Father.
- realize that God wants us to be close to him and will always forgive us when we say we are sorry

 Catholic Social Teaching: Live Your Faith

- Rights and Responsibilities, Pages 288–289
- Option for the Poor, Pages 290–291

Preview Unit Theme

Ask: What is the unit theme?

Summarize that the unit focuses on morality.

Invite volunteers to read aloud each of the bullets in Our Catholic Tradition.

Explain to the children that they will learn about these things in the next three chapters.

Have the children study the photos and images. Invite volunteers to describe what they see. What do these images say about the unit theme?

Ask: Why does God give us Commandments?

After some discussion, explain to the children that they will be exploring this question in the next three chapters.

KEY CONCEPT

Jesus' words and actions teach us how to love and serve God. When you serve others, you are serving God.

DOCTRINAL CONTENT

- Jesus washed his disciples' feet to show us how to serve and love one another. (CCC, 1337)
- Jesus asks us to have a kind, giving heart when we serve and help others. (CCC, 1823)
- A disciple is a follower of Jesus who believes in him and lives by his teachings. (CCC, 618)
- Serving others is a way to serve God. (CCC, 1816)

TASKS OF CATECHESIS

Helping children grow in a faith that is "known, celebrated, lived, and expressed in prayer" (NDC, 20).

This chapter focuses on the following tasks of catechesis:

- Education for Community Life
- Missionary Initiation

Catechist Background

 The greatest among you must be your servant. Whoever exalts himself will be humbled; but whoever humbles himself will be exalted. Matthew 23:11–12

➜ **Reflect** What do you do to serve others and your community?

During the Passover celebration with his disciples, Jesus—teacher, master, and honored guest—washed the feet of his disciples. Having astonished his followers with his humble service, he then turned and commissioned them to go and do the same. This command still challenges even the most fervent Christians.

Think for a moment about a person you have helped or served—a child, a parent, your spouse, or your boss. Now, imagine the roles being reversed, and the person serving you. This can be a humbling experience. Christ's love is similar. When Jesus washed his disciples' feet, it foreshadowed his greatest act of service—an act that would come only hours after the Last Supper. Jesus gave his life for all people, and all were undeserving. Jesus humbled himself for you out of love. You are called to do the same for others.

Think about those who are sometimes considered the lowliest in society—those who are poor, ill, or in prison. Imagine what it would be like to wash their feet. Find in Jesus' message the challenge to do the unthinkable. Serve those who are marginalized in your neighborhood and your parish, honoring their God-given dignity.

➜ **Reflect** Whom does the Lord call you to serve?

Catechist's Prayer

 Lord Jesus, help me to recognize moments of grace and help the children do the same. Amen.

Lesson Plan

Objectives	Process	Materials
Invite, 10 minutes		
Disciples Serve Page 183	○ **Psalm 101:1** Pray the opening prayer. ◉ **Matthew 23:11–12** Reflect prayerfully on the Word. • Discuss What Do You Wonder questions.	◉ **Optional Activity** Chapter Poem: "At Your Service"
Discover, 35 minutes		
Jesus the Servant Pages 184–185 • Understand that Jesus washed his disciples' feet to show us how to serve and love one another • Recognize that Jesus asks us to have a kind, giving heart when we serve and help others	• **Catholic Faith Words** serve • Explain that Jesus taught people to serve. ◉ **John 13:2–17** Proclaim "The Washing of the Disciples' Feet." ☆ Underline what Jesus did to teach his followers. • Explain that good helpers serve with love in their hearts. • **Share Your Faith Activity** Draw how to help or serve people.	☐ pencils ☐ index cards ☐ crayons or markers • **Optional Activity** Watch Me Serve! ☐ Activity Master 13 (Page 183E)
Disciples of Jesus Pages 186–187 • Identify a disciple as a follower of Jesus who believes in him and lives by his teaching • Connect serving others with serving God	• **Catholic Faith Words** disciple • Explain that Jesus used both words and actions to teach. ☆ Draw one way someone has helped them. • Explain that when we serve others, we serve God. • **Connect Your Faith Activity** Solve the word search.	☐ pencils ☐ crayons or markers ☐ index cards
Live, 15 minutes		
Our Catholic Life Pages 188–189	• Explain there are many ways to follow Jesus. ☆ Identify ways they would like to help. • **People of Faith** Learn about Venerable Father Solanus Casey. • **Live Your Faith Activity** Match the actions to the pictures.	☐ pencils
A Promise Prayer Page 190	• Select one or more children to read the leader parts. ▶ Rehearse "Jesus in the Morning." • Follow the order of prayer.	◉ Download "Jesus in the Morning."

Family + Faith Page 191

Point out that the Catholic Families page provides chapter highlights, information on how first graders understand faith concepts, and family prayer.

Chapter Review Page 192

◉ aliveinchrist.osv.com
• Customize and Download Assessments
• Email Links to eAssessments
• Interactive Student Reviews

ONLINE RESOURCES

 Go to **aliveinchrist.osv.com**

You will find:

- Interactive lesson planning with web specific content and additional activities
- Step by step lesson instruction from printed Catechist Edition for integrated lesson planning
- Custom-built assessments to download and eAssessment links
- Interactive reviews that provide scores and the option to review answers
- Sunday readings with background and questions of the week

 Go to **osvparish.com**

You will find:

- Ask the Experts Q and A
- General Catechist Helps
- Community Connections and Blogs

Sharing the Message with First Graders

Serving Others Because they are naturally more focused on their own needs than on the needs of others, first graders might sometimes fail to notice the ways in which they might be helpful to another person. They have a hard time getting into the mindset of someone else and often miss opportunities to serve not because they are selfish, but because they failed to notice someone else's need.

Teaching Tip: Point out times when someone needs help or encouragement and encourage the children to think of some ways to be of service. It might also help to offer a few suggestions if the children are unable to come up with ideas on their own.

How First Graders Understand

- First graders enjoy caring for and playing with younger children. Provide them with the opportunity to do this.
- First graders want to be followers of Jesus. Share with them some ways that they can do that, such as sharing a smile with someone.
- Give first graders the opportunity to serve through helping. Establish routines, such as setting up the room or passing out supplies.

"I like helping others when I know how to do it. Give me some jobs to do."

Chapter Connections

Chapter Poem

Invite

"At Your Service"

Use this poem to enhance the chapter introduction.

- The children will relate the poem to their own lives, reflecting on a time that they were a good helper.
- Connect being a good helper with serving others.

 Go to **aliveinchrist.osv.com** Lesson Planning section for this poem.

NCEA IFG: ACRE Edition

Discover

Communal Life

- Objectives: To know the origin, mission, structure, and communal nature of the Church; to know the rights and responsibilities of the Christian faithful

Missionary Spirit

- Objectives: To recognize the centrality of evangelization as the Church's mission and identity embodied in vocation and service; to be aware of how cultures are transformed by the Gospel

Catholic Social Teaching

Live

 Use one of these features to introduce a principle and engage the children with an activity.

- Option for the Poor, Pages 290–291
- The Dignity of Work, Pages 292–293

Music Options

 Use one or more of the following songs to enhance catechetical learning or for prayer.

- "Jesus In the Morning," Live Prayer, Page 190
- "Jesu, Jesu," Discover, Page 185

LECTIONARY CONNECTION

 Chapter 13 highlights Lectionary-connected themes such as sin and Jesus our Redeemer. If your parish aligns its curriculum to the liturgical year, you could use this chapter in connection with the following Sundays.

Year A

First Sunday of Lent—Original Sin

Twelfth Sunday in Ordinary Time—Original Sin

Year B

Third Sunday of Easter—Jesus the Redeemer

Tenth Sunday in Ordinary Time—Adam in the garden

Year C

Fifth Sunday of Lent—woman caught in adultery

Eighth Sunday in Ordinary Time—judging others

 Go to **aliveinchrist.osv.com** for a complete correlation ordered by the Sundays of the year and suggestions for how to integrate the Scripture readings into chapter lessons.

Name _____ Date _____

Watch Me Serve!

Think of three people you can serve. Print one of the names on each coupon. Then cut out the coupons. Give the coupons to the three people. Be sure to find loving ways to serve them!

Service Coupon

I want to serve _____

like Jesus served others.

Service Coupon

I want to serve _____

like Jesus served others.

Service Coupon

I want to serve _____

like Jesus served others.

Disciples Serve

 Let Us Pray

Leader: O Lord, teach me how to help others.

"I sing of mercy and justice;
to you, LORD, I sing praise." *Psalm 101:1*

All: O Lord, teach me how to help others.
Amen.

 God's Word

The greatest among you must be your servant. Whoever thinks they are more important than someone else is wrong. Whoever thinks everyone is important is right. *Based on Matthew 23:11–12*

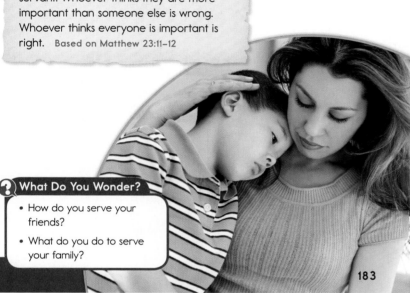

? What Do You Wonder?

- How do you serve your friends?
- What do you do to serve your family?

183

Optional Activity

Chapter Poem: "At Your Service" *Verbal/Linguistic*

Use this poem after the opening prayer, before explaining that we should love and serve all God's people.

- Read the poem aloud as the children follow along.
- *Ask:* Why did Rosa help Felipe? Possible response: because he is too little to tie his shoes, because she is older and wants to help
- After inviting volunteers to tell about a time when they were a good helper, transition back to the lesson instruction.

 Go to **aliveinchrist.osv.com** for Chapter Poem.

Let Us Pray

Invite the children to gather in the prayer space and make the Sign of the Cross. Choose a child as leader. Read aloud the Psalm verse from a Bible. Prompt the children's response.

Have the children move out of the prayer space and back to their seats.

Say: Because God made each of us, we should love and serve all God's People. Listen now to the Gospel according to Matthew to hear what Jesus said about this.

God's Word

Guide the children through the process of Scripture reflection.

- Invite them to close their eyes, be still and open their minds and hearts to what God is saying to them in this passage.
- Proclaim the Scripture.
- Maintain several moments of silence.
- *Ask:* What did you hear God say to you today?
- Invite volunteers to share.

What Do You Wonder?

Say: Jesus asks us to do something that sometimes might feel hard to do—treat each other with respect.

Invite the children to respond to the questions. Ask what else they might wonder about what it means to serve.

Objectives

- Understand that Jesus washed his disciples' feet to show us how to serve and love one another
- Recognize that Jesus asks us to have a kind, giving heart when we serve and help others

Jesus the Servant

Ask: What does it mean to serve others?

- List the children's responses on the board or on chart paper.

Tell the children that God sent his Son, Jesus, to show people how to love.

Work with Words

Hold up an index card with the word *serve* on it. Invite a volunteer to read aloud the definition.

God's Word

Gather the children around you.

- Tell the children to imagine that they are people in the Bible story along with Jesus. Ask them to imagine what their feet would look like after a very long journey.
- Proclaim "The Washing of the Disciples' Feet."
- ⭐ Have the children underline what Jesus did to teach his followers.

Point out the illustration.

- Invite the children to describe what they see happening in the illustration.

Jesus the Servant

What does it mean to serve others?

Jesus taught people to **serve**. We learn from this Bible story that sometimes this surprised them.

Catholic Faith Words

serve to help or give others what they need in a loving way

⭐ Underline what Jesus did to teach his followers.

God's Word

The Washing of the Disciples Feet

One night Jesus shared a special meal with his followers. During supper, Jesus got up and tied a towel around his waist. He poured water into a basin. Jesus washed and dried his disciples' feet. His followers were surprised to see their teacher do the work of a servant.

© Our Sunday Visitor

184   Chapter 13

🔲 Scripture Background

John 13:2–17

In biblical times, hosts provided towels with water for their guests to wash the dust from their feet, or had a slave wash their feet.

- In the Scripture story, Jesus himself washed the feet of his followers to demonstrate in a dramatic way that they must be prepared to serve each other.

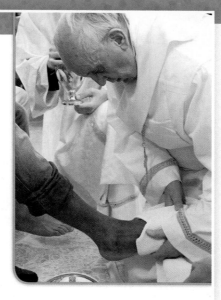

"Yes, I am your teacher," Jesus said. "If I wash your feet, you should do the same. Serve others." Based on John 13:2–17

Serve Like Jesus

Jesus served his followers. He taught them to serve others. Good helpers serve with love in their hearts. You can serve others in many ways.

Share Your Faith

Think Draw a picture of something you can do to help, or serve, people in your neighborhood.

Share Share your idea with a partner.

Serve Like Jesus

Tell the children that good helpers serve others.

Read aloud the paragraph.

- Point out that good helpers serve with love in their hearts.
- *Ask:* Why is it important to serve with love in your hearts? Possible responses: that is what Jesus taught us to do, serving others is showing God's love to others
- Have the children discuss some ways that people their age can serve others.

Point out the photo.

- Invite the children to tell what they see happening in the photo.

▶ Music Option: Have the children sing, "Jesu, Jesu," downloaded from **aliveinchrist.osv.com**.

Activity

Read aloud the directions for the Share Your Faith activity.

- Have the children work independently to draw their pictures.
- Have the children share their drawings with a partner.

Quick Review

Good servers give people what they need. By washing their feet, Jesus taught his followers to take the role of servant.

Optional Activity

Activity Master 13: Watch Me Serve!

Distribute copies of the activity found on catechist page 183E.

- Tell the children that they will show God's love by serving. Refer to the Quick Tip box on page 186 for examples.
- As an alternative, you may wish to send this activity home with the children.

Discover

Objectives

- Identify a disciple as a follower of Jesus who believes in him and lives by his teaching
- Connect serving others with serving God

Disciples of Jesus

Ask: How can you be a follower of Jesus?

- Write the children's responses on the board or on chart paper.

Read aloud both paragraphs.

Work with Words

Hold up an index card with the word *disciple* on it.

- Have the children say *disciple*.
- Read aloud the definition.

Draw a gift box on the board or on chart paper.

- Tell the children that serving others is like giving someone a gift.
- Invite volunteers to suggest "gifts" that they can give by serving.
- Write their suggestions in the box.

 Have the children draw one way someone has helped them.

Disciples of Jesus

How can you be a follower of Jesus?

Catholic Faith Words

disciple a follower of Jesus who believes in him and lives by his teachings

Jesus used more than words to teach about God's love and how to serve others. He used actions, too. He showed people how to trust in his Father and help others.

You are a **disciple** of Jesus. This means you believe in him and follow his example. Jesus helped others.

➤ How can you be a helper to those around you?

© Our Sunday Visitor

Draw one way someone else has helped you.

✓ Quick Tip

Helpful Hints

Children may run out of ideas on how they can serve others.

- They should be able to list concrete actions, such as making their beds at home or helping a teacher pass out papers at school, but may miss more subtle ways.
- Help them by letting them know that they also serve through such actions as listening attentively at school or in church and being cooperative at home.

Serve God and Others

Serving others made Jesus happy. Jesus served others with a kind heart. You can serve by letting others choose first or go ahead of you in line. You can serve by listening when someone needs a friend. When you serve, you can show God's love.

God asks you to serve with a kind, happy heart. By serving others, you serve him. He wants you to be the best you can be. By developing good habits, your actions can make others happy.

Connect Your Faith

Word Search Use the Word List to find the words in the Word Search. Circle each word when you find it.

T	G	O	D	T	O	A	A
S	M	I	L	E	C	G	W
E	G	R	S	E	R	V	E
T	F	L	O	V	E	Y	O
V	A	F	K	H	E	L	P
U	R	U	T	K	R	D	B

Word List

help
smile
love
serve
God

Disciples Serve **187**

Serve God and Others

Tell the children to make a grumpy face, and then ask them if that is the way to help others.

Read aloud both paragraphs.

- Ask the children to show what their faces might look like when they serve others in a loving way.
- Ask the children to tell you when it might be hard to serve others with a smile.

Point out the photo.

- *Ask:* How are the children serving others?
- *Ask:* Do you respond with a happy heart when you are asked to set the table?

Activity

Read aloud the directions for the Connect Your Faith activity.

- Read the words in the Word List that the children are to search for.
- Give them time to find the words. Note that some children may find the activity difficult to do and may work better with a partner.

Quick Review

To be a follower of Jesus means to serve others joyfully as Jesus did.

✓ Quick Tip

Word Searches

To help them with the activity, show the children the quickest way to do a word search.

- Read the list of words that you are to find.
- Read each line from left to right. Circle each word that you find.
- After you find a word, cross it off the list.

Our Catholic Life

Ask: How can you follow Jesus and serve others?

- Write the children's responses on the board or on chart paper.
- Invite volunteers to retell the story of Jesus washing the feet of his friends.

Refer the children to page 313 in the Our Catholic Tradition reference section of the Student Book.

- Explain that on Holy Thursday we remember that Jesus washed the disciples' feet.

Have the children listen as you read aloud the first two paragraphs.

- Emphasize that Jesus asks us to do what he did.
- Explain that doing what Jesus did is not just about washing feet, it means that we follow Jesus by serving others.

Follow Jesus and Serve Others

- Point out the list of ways to follow Jesus and serve others.
- ⭐ Have the children place a check mark next to the things they would like to do to serve others.
- Remind the children that when they do these things, they are following Jesus.

Live

Our Catholic Life

How can you follow Jesus and serve others?

Jesus gave his friends an example of how to serve others. He said, "Follow me. Do what I do."

Following Jesus doesn't just mean washing people's feet. There are many ways to follow Jesus and serve others with love. Here are some ideas.

Place a check mark next to the things you would like to do.

Follow Jesus and Serve Others

- ☐ Hug someone who is lonely.
- ☐ Share food with someone who is hungry.
- ☐ Give a coat to someone who is cold.
- ☐ Cheer up someone who is sad.
- ☐ Help someone up who has fallen down.

© Our Sunday Visitor

188   Chapter 13

 Quick Tip

Offering Solidarity

One of the ways children can learn to serve others is by practicing solidarity, the ability to stand with others in a time of trouble.

- Remind the children to share one another's good times and bad times.
- Ask the children to treat one another as they would want to be treated.

People of Faith

Venerable Father Solanus Casey, 1870–1957

Solanus Casey wanted to be a priest, but he couldn't be a regular priest because he didn't get good grades in school. He asked God to show him how he could best serve others. Father Solanus listened to people and helped them with their problems. Many people were cured of sickness when Father Solanus prayed for them.

Discuss: What can you do to help one of your friends today?

 Learn more about Father Solanus Casey at **aliveinchrist.osv.com**

Live Your Faith

Match the Actions Match one way that you could help the people in the pictures.

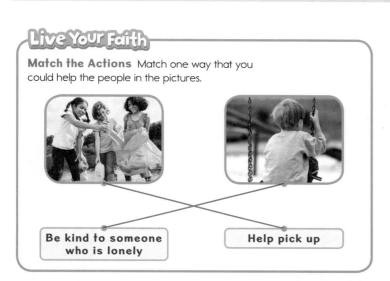

Be kind to someone who is lonely

Help pick up

© Our Sunday Visitor

Catholic Social Teaching

Chapter Connections

To integrate Catholic Social Teaching into your lesson, choose one of the following features: Option for the Poor, pages 290–291; or The Dignity of Work, pages 292–293.

- Start the Live step of the process by talking about Venerable Father Solanus Casey on page 189. Then move directly to the Catholic Social Teaching feature.

- Or, to expand the lesson, complete both pages 188 and 189, then move to the Catholic Social Teaching feature.

- Return to Chapter 13 for the prayer on page 190.

People of Faith

Tell the children about Venerable Father Solanus Casey.

- Invite a volunteer to read aloud the People of Faith story.

- Explain that Venerable Father Solanus Casey was born on a farm in Oak Grove, Wisconsin. He had nine brothers and six sisters. After being ordained a priest in 1904, he spent twenty years in New York City, Harlem, NY, and Yonkers, NY.

- In 1924, he was assigned to St. Bonaventure Monastery in Detroit where he worked for twenty years. At the Monastery door he met thousands of people of every age and from every walk of life. He earned recognition as "The Door Keeper." He was always ready to listen to anyone at any time, day or night.

- *Ask:* What can you do to help one of your friends today?

 Encourage the children to go to **aliveinchrist.osv.com** at home to learn more about Venerable Father Solanus Casey.

Activity

Read aloud the directions and discuss the Live Your Faith activity as a group.

- Allow time for the children to match the actions to the pictures.

Let Us Pray
A Promise Prayer

Prepare

If you have good readers in your group, consider having those children take one or more of the leader parts of the prayer.

- Teach the children their response.

 Rehearse "Jesus in the Morning," downloaded from **aliveinchrist.osv.com**.

Gather

Gather the children in the prayer space. Have them stand in a large circle.

- Prompt the children to quiet themselves for prayer.

Pray

Follow the order of prayer on the student page.

- Begin by leading the children in the Sign of the Cross.

- Read each of the four invocations. Have the children respond to each with prayer and movement: After the children pray, "I will follow Jesus and serve," invite them to "follow" by taking two or three steps toward the center of the circle. Gradually, the circle will tighten, and the children will form a closer group.

 Conclude by singing together "Jesus in the Morning."

Live

Let Us Pray
A Promise Prayer

Gather and begin with the Sign of the Cross.

Leader: Jesus said, "I am among you as the one who serves." Luke 22:27

Follow in Jesus' footsteps. Pray to be one who serves.

Leader: When someone needs a friend,

All: I will follow Jesus and serve.

Leader: When a job at home needs doing,

All: I will follow Jesus and serve.

Leader: When someone needs cheering up,

All: I will follow Jesus and serve.

Leader: When anyone needs help,

All: I will follow Jesus and serve.

 All: Sing "Jesus in the Morning"
Jesus, Jesus,
Jesus in the morning,
Jesus at the noontime;
Jesus, Jesus, Jesus when
the sun goes down!

190 Chapter 13

 ## Liturgy Link

Praying with Gestures

Young children are physical. When we engage their bodies in prayer, their minds and hearts will follow.

- Use two simple gestures for their response: Have the children point to themselves with their thumbs (I will follow Jesus). Then have them extend their hands out to others (and serve).

- Make up a few gestures for the song, or invite the children to help you.

 Go to **aliveinchrist.osv.com** for Sunday readings, Scripture background, questions of the week, and seasonal resources.

FAMILY+FAITH
LIVING AND LEARNING TOGETHER

YOUR CHILD LEARNED >>>
This chapter identifies a disciple as a follower of Jesus who believes in him, lives by his teaching, and connects serving others with serving God.

God's Word
 Read **Matthew 23:11–12** to learn who is truly greatest in God's eyes, the one seated at the table or the one who serves.

Catholics Believe
• Jesus' words and actions teach us how to love and serve God.
• When you serve others, you are serving God.
To learn more, go to the *Catechism of the Catholic Church* #1822–1827 at **usccb.org**.

People of Faith
This week, your child met Venerable Father Solanus Casey. He spent his life serving others in the humble job of doorkeeper.

CHILDREN AT THIS AGE >>>
How They Understand Serving Others Because they are naturally more focused on their own needs than on the needs of others, first-graders might sometimes fail to notice the ways in which they might be of help to another person. You can help your child with this by pointing out times when someone needs help or support and encouraging your child to think of some ways to be of service. It might also help to offer a few suggestions if he or she is unable to come up with ideas on his or her own.

CONSIDER THIS >>>
What motivates you to help others?

We all have different reasons for acting with charity. As Christians, however, we are united by the understanding that we are of service to one another because we have been united to Christ in Baptism and we act in his name. "In this communion of the Church, the members are called to love God, others, and self, and so to be a communal witness of the love by which Christ saved the world. By divine love we are joined to the communion of the Father, Son, and Holy Spirit" (*USCCA, p. 119*).

LET'S TALK >>>
• Talk about how Jesus washed his friends' feet and how they might have felt to have received his kindness.
• Ask your child to think of someone in your neighborhood who could use help. What kinds of things can you and your family do to help this person?

LET'S PRAY >>>
 Dear God, help us do our chores without complaining. Amen.

For a multimedia glossary of Catholic Faith Words, Sunday readings, seasonal and Saint resources, and chapter activities go to **aliveinchrist.osv.com**.

Alive in Christ, Grade 1 Chapter 13 **191**

Family + Faith

Distribute the page to the children or parents/adult family members. Point out the chapter highlights, insights on how first graders understand concepts, the opportunity for the adults to reflect on their own experience and faith journey, and the family prayer.

Chapter 13 Review

A **Work with Words** Draw a heart next to each sentence that tells about a person who is serving.

1. ☐ Elena sees her teacher carrying a big stack of books. Elena walks away.
2. ♡ A child is hurt on the playground. Trevor leads the crying child to a teacher.
3. ♡ Alison sets the table for supper.

B **Check Understanding** Circle the best answer.

4. Jesus washed his friends' feet as a sign of ____.

   (serving)   playing

5. When you serve others, you show your ____ for God.

   hope   (love)

6. God wants you to be a ____ of Jesus.

   leader   (disciple)

7. Name one way to serve God and others.

   _____
   _____
   _____
   _____
   _____

Go to **aliveinchrist.osv.com** for an interactive review.

192 Chapter 13 Review

Chapter Review

Use Catechist Quick Reviews to highlight lesson concepts.

A **Work with Words** Have the children draw a heart next to each sentence that tells about a person who is serving.

B **Check Understanding** Have the children circle the best answer and name one way to serve God and others.

Go to **aliveinchrist.osv.com** to prepare customized and downloadable assessments, send eAssessments, and assign interactive reviews.

Disciples Serve **191–192**

KEY CONCEPT

The Ten Commandments are God's laws to help people love him and others. God gives people the freedom to choose.

DOCTRINAL CONTENT

- The Ten Commandments are God's laws that tell people how to love him and others. (CCC, 2067)
- Free will is the ability to choose whether to obey God or disobey God. (CCC, 1731)
- God created us with free will because he wants us to make good choices. (CCC, 1743)
- All choices have consequences, or results, that can show love and respect or hurt others. (CCC, 1739)

TASKS OF CATECHESIS

Helping children grow in a faith that is "known, celebrated, lived, and expressed in prayer" (NDC, 20).

This chapter focuses on the following tasks of catechesis:

- Promoting Knowledge of the Faith
- Moral Formation

Catechist Background

"You shall love the Lord, your God, with all your heart, with all your being, with all your strength, and with all your mind, and your neighbor as yourself." Luke 10:27

➜ **Reflect** What helps you to make good choices?

God the Creator gave each person the gift of free will to make choices regarding good and evil, right and wrong. God also gave his People another gift. Through Moses, he provided a norm for human choices: the Ten Commandments. The Commandments reveal essential truths and guide us toward eternal life. Jesus summed them up by telling his disciples to love God with all their hearts and to love others as themselves (Luke 10:27). God's law calls people to love even when it is most difficult—the neighbor who doesn't stop talking, children who visit an elderly parent only when they need money, or the sibling who has emotional problems.

Along life's journey, people make wrong turns. The Israelites who followed Moses were weary travelers who took to worshipping idols in the desert, complaining about the scarcity of food and water, and failing to trust in God. Sometimes it is a challenge for us to trust God and follow the commandment of love. However, God calls his People to responsibility. When you fail to show love, you must be willing to seek forgiveness.

➜ **Reflect** Who in your life is in need of forgiveness? What can you do for him or her?

Catechist's Prayer

Lord, help me be more faithful to you. Give me the strength to follow your Commandments when I am most tempted to do only what pleases me. Amen.

Lesson Plan

Objectives	Process	Materials

Invite, 10 minutes

Making Choices Page 193

- 💗 Psalm 119:17 Pray the opening prayer.
- 📖 Luke 10:25–28 Reflect prayerfully on the Word.
- Discuss What Do You Wonder questions.

📡 **Optional Activity**
Chapter Poem:
"Let Me See"

Discover, 35 minutes

Types of Choices Pages 194–195
- Recognize the Ten Commandments as God's laws that tell us how to love God and others

- **Catholic Faith Words** Ten Commandments
- Explain that some choices are easy and some are difficult.
- ☆ Circle how your choices can affect others.
- 📖 Deuteronomy 10:12–13 Proclaim "God's Commandments."
- **Share Your Faith Activity** Name some of God's teachings.

☐ pencils
☐ index cards
☐ Gift bag or wrapped box
- **Optional Activity**
  Hard Choices

Good Choices Pages 196–197
- Define free will as the ability to choose whether to obey God or disobey God
- Appreciate that God created us with free will because he wants us to make good choices
- Examine consequences as a significant part of a decision-making process

- **Catholic Faith Words** obey, free will
- Explain that The Ten Commandments can help us make loving choices.
- Explain that all choices have consequences.
- **Connect Your Faith Activity** Circle the good choice.

☐ pencils
☐ index cards
- **Optional Activity**
  Make Good Choices
☐ Activity Master 14
  (Page 193E)

Live, 15 minutes

Our Catholic Life Pages 198–199

- Explain that the Ten Commandments help us show love for God and others.
- ☆ Identify some ways to keep the Commandments.
- **People of Faith** Learn about Saint Frances Cabrini.
- **Live Your Faith Activity** Draw a picture of how to follow a Commandment.

☐ pencils

A Helping Prayer Page 200

- Select six readers.
- ▶ Rehearse "C-H-O-I-C-E-S."
- Follow the order of prayer.

📡 Download
"C-H-O-I-C-E-S."

Family + Faith Page 201

Point out that the Catholic Families page provides chapter highlights, information on how first graders understand faith concepts, and family prayer.

Chapter Review Page 202

📡 aliveinchrist.osv.com
- Customize and Download Assessments
- Email Links to eAssessments
- Interactive Student Reviews

Teaching This Grade

ONLINE RESOURCES

 Go to **aliveinchrist.osv.com**

You will find:

- Interactive lesson planning with web specific content and additional activities
- Step by step lesson instruction from printed Catechist Edition for integrated lesson planning
- Custom-built assessments to download and eAssessment links
- Interactive reviews that provide scores and the option to review answers
- Sunday readings with background and questions of the week

 Go to **osvparish.com**

You will find:

- Ask the Experts Q and A
- General Catechist Helps
- Community Connections and Blogs

Sharing the Message with First Graders

Making Choices Rules are very important to children in first grade. They are just beginning to understand cause and effect, the idea that the world works according to certain rules, so they tend to form their ideas about various places and situations based on what the rules are. They also become distressed when someone else is not following the rules, even when it does not directly impact them.

Teaching Tip: Help children this age make good choices by providing them with clear, developmentally appropriate, and consistent guidelines for behavior.

How First Graders Understand

- Making choices can be difficult for first graders. Explain to them how they can make better choices.
- First graders are beginning to see consequences for their behavior.
- Witness to children by example. Keep in mind that your actions and the way you treat others will be remembered longer than your words.

"I generally see things as right or wrong, with very little middle ground."

Chapter Connections

Chapter Poem
Invite

"Let Me See"

Use this poem to enhance the chapter introduction.

- The children will relate the poem to their own lives, reflecting on who the loving people are in their lives.
- Connect being loving to making good choices.

 Go to **aliveinchrist.osv.com** Lesson Planning section for this poem.

NCEA IFG: ACRE Edition
Discover

Knowledge of the Faith

- Objective: To know and understand basic Catholic teaching about the Incarnate Word Jesus Christ as the way, truth, and life

Moral Formation

- Objectives: To be knowledgeable about the teachings of Jesus and the Church as the basis of Christian morality and to understand Catholic Social Teaching; to be aware of the importance of a well-formed conscience for decision making

Catholic Social Teaching
Live

 Use one of these features to introduce a principle and engage the children with an activity.

- Call to Community, Pages 286–287
- Rights and Responsibilities, Pages 288–289

Music Options

 Use one or more of the following songs to enhance catechetical learning or for prayer.

- "C-H-O-I-C-E-S," Live Prayer, Page 200
- "Choices," Discover, Page 194
- "God's Good Rules," Discover, Page 195
- "My Ten Commandments," Discover, Page 195
- "Come to Us, Holy Spirit," Discover, Page 196

LECTIONARY CONNECTION

Chapter 14 highlights Lectionary-connected themes such as choices, consequences, and Catholic Social Teaching. If your parish aligns its curriculum to the liturgical year, you could use this chapter in connection with the following Sundays.

Year A

First Sunday of Lent—dignity of the human person

Twenty-sixth Sunday in Ordinary Time—choices, conscience

Year B

Third Sunday of Lent—Ten Commandments

Twenty-sixth Sunday in Ordinary Time—Catholic Social Teaching

Year C

Fifth Sunday of Lent—God's love, sin

The Ascension of the Lord—Holy Spirit

Go to **aliveinchrist.osv.com** for a complete correlation ordered by the Sundays of the year and suggestions for how to integrate the Scripture readings into chapter lessons.

Name _____   Date _____

Make Good Choices

Look carefully at the pictures below. They tell
a story. Help the children in the story make
a good choice. In the empty box, draw
a picture of the good choice they make.

Making Choices

 Let Us Pray

Leader: God, please help us make good choices.

"Be kind to your servant that I may live,
that I may keep your word."
Psalm 119:17

All: God, help us make good choices. Amen.

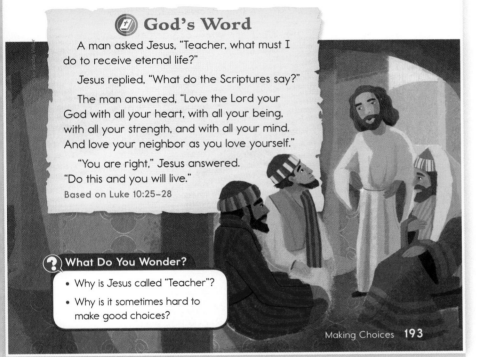

 God's Word

A man asked Jesus, "Teacher, what must I do to receive eternal life?"

Jesus replied, "What do the Scriptures say?"

The man answered, "Love the Lord your God with all your heart, with all your being, with all your strength, and with all your mind. And love your neighbor as you love yourself."

"You are right," Jesus answered. "Do this and you will live."
Based on Luke 10:25–28

? What Do You Wonder?

- Why is Jesus called "Teacher"?
- Why is it sometimes hard to make good choices?

Making Choices **193**

Optional Activity

Chapter Poem: "Let Me See" *Verbal/Linguistic*

Use this poem after the opening prayer, before explaining that Jesus teaches us to make good choices.

- Read the poem aloud as the children follow along.
- Ask the children what they think good choices are. Possible responses: to be helpful or friendly
- *Ask:* Who is a loving person in your life? How do they show love?
- After the discussion, transition back to the lesson instruction.

 Go to **aliveinchrist.osv.com** for Chapter Poem.

Invite

Let Us Pray

Invite the children to gather in the prayer space and make the Sign of the Cross. Invite a child to be the leader. Read aloud the Psalm verse from a Bible. Prompt the children's response.

Have the children move out of the prayer space and back to their seats.

Explain that Jesus teaches us to make good choices.

Say: Jesus teaches us how to make good choices. Let's listen to a reading from the Gospel of Luke. In this reading, Jesus tells us how we can make good and loving choices.

God's Word

Guide the children through the process of Scripture reflection.

- Invite them to close their eyes, be still and open their minds and hearts to what God is saying to them in this passage.
- Proclaim the Scripture.
- Maintain several moments of silence.
- *Ask:* What did you hear God say to you today?
- Invite volunteers to share.

What Do You Wonder?

Say: Jesus gives us the answer of how to make good choices: love God, my neighbor, and myself.

Invite the children to respond to the questions. Ask what else they might wonder about Jesus the teacher and making good choices.

Objective

- Recognize the Ten Commandments as God's laws that tell us how to love God and others

Types of Choices

Ask: How does God help us make choices?

- List the children's responses on the board or on chart paper.

Read aloud both paragraphs. Tell the children that some choices are easy to make because they don't require you to do something that you don't want to.

⭐ Have the children circle how certain choices can affect others.

- *Ask:* What are some choices children your age make?
- Have the children make some choices that are easy. Present them with a choice between two kinds of pizza, and ask children to choose which pizza they prefer.
- Invite volunteers to think of other choices, such as which of two games to play or which of two television shows to watch.
- Remind the children that choices between right and wrong are often harder to make.

 Music Option: Have the children sing, "Choices," downloaded from **aliveinchrist.osv.com**.

Types of Choices

How does God help us make choices?

Some choices are easy to make. If you are choosing between two kinds of healthful foods, both choices are good ones. Making this kind of choice will not hurt you or anyone else.

Other choices are hard to make. Sometimes it can be difficult to choose between right and wrong. The choices you make can help others or hurt them.

> Circle how your choices can affect others.

➔ What are some choices children your age make?

© Our Sunday Visitor

194 Chapter 14

Optional Activity

Hard Choices *Interpersonal*

Tell the children to imagine that they borrowed a bike from an older brother or sister without asking. The bike was too big, so it got scratched when you fell.

- Invite the children to discuss possible courses of action, and whether those choices are easy or hard.

A Gift from God

Long ago, God wanted to help his People know how to live. He gave the **Ten Commandments** to a special man named Moses. Moses helped the people understand God's laws. These laws still help us make good choices. The Ten Commandments are listed on page 314 of your book.

© Our Sunday Visitor

Catholic Faith Words

Ten Commandments God's laws that tell people how to love him and others

 God's Word

God's Commandments

Moses said, "What does the Lord, your God, ask of you? God wants you to respect him and to follow him. The Lord your God wants you to love and serve him with all your heart and all your soul. God wants you to obey his commandments and teachings."

Based on Deuteronomy 10:12–13

Share Your Faith

Think What are some of God's teachings?

Share In groups, talk about what God asks us to do.

 Songs of Scripture

His Laws Make Us Free

Tell the children that they are going to play "Thumbs Up, Thumbs Down."

- Explain that you will say a rule. If the rule is one of God's rules, they are to show thumbs up. "Tell the truth" is an example.

- If the rule is not one of God's rules, they are to show thumbs down. For example, "Be selfish," is not one of God's rules.

- After a number of statements, teach "His Laws Make Us Free."

 Use *Songs of Scripture*, Grades 1–3 CD, Track 8

A Gift from God

Read aloud the first paragraph.

- Ask the children to share a rule they have at home.

Work with Words

Present a wrapped box or gift bag (containing an index card with *Ten Commandments* written on it). Tell the children that a gift from God is inside.

- Have the children open the gift and discover an index card with *Ten Commandments* written on it.

- Explain that the Ten Commandments are a gift from God that help people make good choices.

 God's Word

Tell the children that the Ten Commandments were given to a leader named Moses.

- Proclaim "God's Commandments."

> Music Option: Have the children sing, "God's Good Rules" or "My Ten Commandments," downloaded from **aliveinchrist.osv.com**.

Activity

Read aloud the directions.

- Discuss the Think portion of the activity.

- Provide time for small groups to discuss what God asks us to do.

Quick Review

The Ten Commandments are God's laws. They help people know how to show love for God and others.

Objectives

- Define free will as the ability to choose whether to obey God or disobey God
- Appreciate that God created us with free will because he wants us to make good choices
- Examine consequences as a significant part of a decision making process

Good Choices

Ask: How do your choices affect you and others?

- Write the children's responses on the board or on chart paper.

Read aloud all three paragraphs.

Work with Words

Show index cards to the children with the words *obey* and *free will* on them. Read aloud and explain the definitions.

Draw the graphic organizer on the board or on chart paper.

- Use it to introduce the concept of choices and their consequences.
- Give the children examples. Ask them what they would do if they were at a bake sale with their favorite cookies sitting out and no one watching. Or ask them what they would do if someone left money on a desk and left the room.
- Have the children respond with what they think the right choice would be.
- Ask them what the consequences would be of the wrong choice.
- Discuss the steps for making a good choice.

Good Choices

How do your choices affect you and others?

God created you to be free. You can choose to **obey** God. When you do what God asks, you choose what is good and you grow closer to God. Bad choices make you turn away from God.

Being able to choose whether to obey God or disobey God is called **free will**. God created us with free will because he wants us to choose good.

The Ten Commandments can help you use your free will to make loving choices.

Catholic Faith Words

obey to do things or act in certain ways that are requested by those in authority

free will being able to choose whether to obey God or disobey God. God created us with free will because he wants us to make good choices.

196 Chapter 14

Steps to Good Choices

1. Think about whether your choice shows love for God and others.

2. Ask yourself and others if your choice follows the Ten Commandments and things Jesus would do.

3. Pray to the Holy Spirit to guide you.

✓ Quick Tip

Graphic Organizer

We choose.

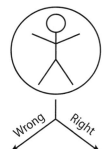

Wrong   Right

Result   Result

Consequences

All choices have consequences, or results. Bad choices have consequences that can hurt you or others. Good choices have good consequences. They help you show love and respect for yourself, others, and God.

Good choices have good results for you and others.

Connect Your Faith

Good or Bad? Circle the picture that shows the good choice.

Making Choices **197**

Consequences

Read aloud the paragraph.

- Explain that the word *consequence* means the results of a choice.

Point out the photo and read aloud the caption.

- Ask the children to describe what they see in the picture.
- Discuss what kinds of choices this child probably made that led to the consequences they see in the picture.

 Music Option: Have the children sing, "Come to Us, Holy Spirit," downloaded from **aliveinchrist.osv.com**.

Activity

Point out the Connect Your Faith activity and read aloud the directions.

- Have the children circle the picture that shows the good choice.

Quick Review

Because you are created free, you are able to choose. Three steps can help guide you to make good moral choices: (1) Decide whether the choice shows love. (2) Ask if the choice follows the Ten Commandments. (3) Pray for the Holy Spirit's guidance.

Optional Activity

Activity Master 14: Make Good Choices

Distribute copies of the activity found on catechist page 193E.

- Tell the children that they will draw a good choice to complete a story.
- As an alternative, you may wish to send this activity home with the children.

Our Catholic Life

Ask: How can you keep the Ten Commandments?

• Write the children's responses on the board or on chart paper.

Remind the children where the Ten Commandments came from.

Living the Ten Commandments

Draw attention to the chart and read aloud the introductory paragraph.

• Have the children listen as you read aloud ways to live each of the Ten Commandments.

☆ Have the children circle the Commandments that focus on God and underline the ones that focus on loving others and yourself.

Refer the children to page 314 in the Our Catholic Tradition reference section of the Student Book for more information about the Ten Commandments and what they mean.

Our Catholic Life

How can you keep the Ten Commandments?

The Ten Commandments help you know how to show love for God and for others. Here are some ways you can keep the Commandments.

Living The Ten Commandments

1. Love God more than anyone or anything.
2. Use God's name with respect.
3. Take time to pray. Go to Mass with your family on Sundays, or Saturday evenings.
4. Love your family. Treat everyone in your family kindly. Obey the rules.
5. Stay away from fighting. Find peaceful ways to solve problems.
6. Respect your body and the bodies of others. Think about the way you speak and act.
7. Care for other people's things. Take care of what you have.
8. Be honest. Say only good things about people.
9. Be true to family members and friends.
10. Be thankful for what you have.

1. Circle the Commandments that focus on loving God.
2. Underline the ones that focus on loving others and yourself.

© Our Sunday Visitor

198 Chapter 14

✓ Quick Tip

Choices

Children may not realize how many choices they make every day. While some choices, such as what to eat, might be guided by a parent, children still make choices while on the playground, in the classroom, and at home.

• Lead a short discussion on these types of choices, and how children can rely on the Ten Commandments and the Great Commandment to make the right ones.

People of Faith

People of Faith

Saint Frances Cabrini, 1850–1917

Saint Frances Cabrini lived in Italy. She wanted to go to China to teach the people there about God. Pope Leo XIII asked her to go the United States instead. Mother Frances had a choice. She decided to obey the Pope. She left Italy and went to the United States where she built schools, orphanages, and hospitals.

November 13

Discuss: Talk about a hard choice you had to make.

 Learn more about Saint Frances at **aliveinchrist.osv.com**

© Our Sunday Visitor

Live Your Faith

Choose Read the Ten Commandments on page 314. Pick one and draw a picture of one way you can follow that Commandment this week.

Catholic Social Teaching

Chapter Connections

To integrate Catholic Social Teaching into your lesson, choose one of the following features: Call to Community, pages 286–287; or Rights and Responsibilities, pages 288–289.

- Start the Live step of the process by talking about Saint Frances Cabrini on page 199. Then move directly to the Catholic Social Teaching feature.
- Or, to expand the lesson, complete both pages 198 and 199, then move to the Catholic Social Teaching feature.
- Return to Chapter 14 for the prayer on page 200.

People of Faith

Tell the children about Saint Frances Cabrini.

- Invite a volunteer to read aloud the People of Faith story.
- Explain that Saint Frances Cabrini was the first American citizen to be named a Saint.
- At the request of Pope Leo XIII, she came to the United States in 1889 to help Italian immigrants.
- Both her deep trust in God and her innate administrative ability helped her in her mission.
- She soon opened schools, hospitals, and orphanages that successfully supported the Italian immigrants.
- Because of her work, she is the patron Saint of immigrants.
- Invite the children to talk about a hard choice they had to make.

 Encourage the children to go to **aliveinchrist.osv.com** at home to learn more about Saint Frances Cabrini.

Activity

Read aloud and discuss the directions for the Live Your Faith activity together as a group.

- Allow time for the children to draw their pictures.

Live

 Let Us Pray
A Helping Prayer

Prepare

Choose six readers and allow them to practice reading their parts.

- Teach the children their response.

 Rehearse "C-H-O-I-C-E-S," downloaded from **aliveinchrist.osv.com**.

Gather

Invite the children to process to the prayer space.

- Have the children sit in a circle.
- Prompt the children to quiet themselves for prayer.

Pray

Being by leading the children in the Sign of the Cross.

- Follow the order of prayer on the student page.

 Conclude by singing together "C-H-O-I-C-E-S."

Live

 Let Us Pray
A Helping Prayer

Gather and begin with the Sign of the Cross.

Leader: Ask the Holy Spirit for help to make wise and loving choices.

Reader 1: When I forget to put God first,

All: Holy Spirit, help me choose to love.

Reader 2: When I am lazy and do not want to pray,

All: Holy Spirit, help me choose to love.

Reader 3: When I don't feel like listening to my parents,

All: Holy Spirit, help me choose to love.

Reader 4: When I am angry and want to say or do something hurtful,

All: Holy Spirit, help me choose to love.

Reader 5: When I want to take something that doesn't belong to me,

All: Holy Spirit, help me choose to love.

Reader 6: When I think about telling a lie,

All: Holy Spirit, help me choose to love.

 Sing "C-H-O-I-C-E-S"

 Liturgy Link

The Sign of the Cross

Remind the children that the Sign of the Cross is the way Catholics often begin prayers.

- The Sign of the Cross is a reminder that God is one God in three Divine Persons.
- It also reminds Catholics that they were baptized in the name of the Father, and of the Son, and of the Holy Spirit.

 Go to **aliveinchrist.osv.com** for Sunday readings, Scripture background, questions of the week, and seasonal resources.

FAMILY+FAITH
LIVING AND LEARNING TOGETHER

YOUR CHILD LEARNED >>>

This chapter explains free will as a gift from God and the Ten Commandments as God's Laws that tell us how to love God and others.

God's Word

Read **Luke 10:25–28** to find out what Jesus said is the most important Commandment.

Catholics Believe

- The Ten Commandments are God's Laws to help people love him and others.
- God gives people the freedom to choose.

To learn more, go to the *Catechism of the Catholic Church* #2056–2060 at **usccb.org**.

People of Faith

This week, your child met Saint Frances Cabrini, the first American citizen to be canonized. Saint Frances wanted to be a missionary to China, but came to the U.S. instead.

CHILDREN AT THIS AGE >>>

How They Understand Making Choices Rules are very important to children in first grade. They are just beginning to understand cause and effect, the idea that the world works according to certain rules, so they tend to form their ideas about various places and situations based on what the rules are. They also become distressed when someone else is not following the rules, even when it does not directly impact them. You can help your child make good choices by providing him or her with clear, developmentally appropriate, and consistent guidelines for behavior.

CONSIDER THIS >>>

What moves you to do the right thing, to choose what is good?

Sometimes we know the right thing to do, but we aren't brave enough or motivated enough to do so. Living in right relationship with God helps us to live in right relationship with others. The Holy Spirit will give you the grace to do God's will. "The moral life requires grace...the grace that comes to us from Christ in the Spirit is as essential as love and rules and, in fact, makes love and keeping the rules possible" (*USCCA, p. 318*).

LET'S TALK >>>

- Ask your child to talk about some choices he or she has made recently.
- Talk about doing something you didn't want to do at first, but that later turned out to be the right thing to do.

LET'S PRAY >>>

Saint Frances Cabrini, pray for us that we may make the right choices and always obey our mothers and fathers. Amen.

 For a multimedia glossary of Catholic Faith Words, Sunday readings, seasonal and Saint resources, and chapter activities go to **aliveinchrist.osv.com**.

Family + Faith

Distribute the page to the children or parents/adult family members. Point out the chapter highlights, insights on how first graders understand concepts, the opportunity for the adults to reflect on their own experience and faith journey, and the family prayer.

Chapter 14 Review

A **Work with Words** Circle the correct word to complete each sentence.

1. The Ten Commandments are God's ___.

(laws)   stories

2. God gave ___ the Ten Commandments.

Jesus   (Moses)

3. I show love for God when I choose what is ___.

easy   (good)

4. A bad choice can ___ us and others.

(hurt)   help

5. ___ choices have consequences.

Some   (All)

6. We ___ God when we do what he asks.

(obey)   disobey

B **Check Understanding** Write your answer on the space below.

7. What is being able to choose whether to obey or disobey God called?

free will

 Go to **aliveinchrist.osv.com** for an interactive review.

Chapter Review

Use Catechist Quick Reviews to highlight lesson concepts.

A **Work with Words**
Have the children circle the correct word to complete each sentence.

B **Check Understanding**
Have the children write their answer in the space provided.

Go to **aliveinchrist.osv.com** to prepare customized and downloadable assessments, send eAssessments, and assign interactive reviews.

KEY CONCEPT

God always forgives those who are truly sorry and ask his forgiveness. God asks that we forgive others and ourselves.

DOCTRINAL CONTENT

- Sin is the choice to disobey God on purpose and do what you know is wrong. It is not an accident or a mistake. (CCC, 1850)

- The consequences of sin are hurting your friendship with God and others. (CCC, 1849)

- God wants us to be close to him and will always forgive us when we say we are sorry. (CCC, 1431–1432)

- Jesus wants us to be sorry for our sins and turn to God our forgiving Father. (CCC, 1427)

TASKS OF CATECHESIS

Helping children grow in a faith that is "known, celebrated, lived, and expressed in prayer" (NDC, 20).

This chapter focuses on the following tasks of catechesis:

- Promoting Knowledge of the Faith

- Moral Formation

Catechist Background

"If my brother sins against me, how often must I forgive him? As many as seven times?" Jesus answered, "I say to you, not seven times but seventy-seven times." Matthew 18:21–22

→ **Reflect** What helps you to forgive others?

Sin can cause harm and alienate one from God and others. Jesus knew the human condition. Jesus himself faced the temptation to sin, but he chose not to give in. Jesus reached out to those who had sinned. He forgave them and called them to change their ways. Through his own life, Death, Resurrection, and Ascension, Jesus overcame the power of sin.

Christians are called to be signs of Christ's forgiveness and compassion. Jesus forgave sins and then welcomed sinners to sit at his table. Christians are called to follow the example of Jesus—a challenge, indeed.

Think about someone whom you have a difficult time forgiving. Put aside your own hurt and walk in that person's shoes for a moment. What is the experience of that person? What is his or her loneliness and pain? Occasionally, a hurt is so deep that forgiving the offender doesn't seem to be an option. Yet your own anger can cause a deeper wound if it is allowed to fester. Lighten your burden. God's love is abundant. Pray for the strength to forgive and the grace to be forgiven.

→ **Reflect** Whom do you need to forgive?

Catechist's Prayer

 Heavenly Father, help me instill in the children the willingness to ask forgiveness and the desire to forgive others freely. Amen.

Lesson Plan

Objectives	Process	Materials

Invite, 10 minutes

Showing Sorrow Page 203

- Psalm 5:12 Pray the opening prayer.
- Matthew 18:21–22 Reflect prayerfully on the Word.
- Discuss What Do You Wonder questions.

Optional Activity
Chapter Story: "Forgiveness"

Discover, 35 minutes

Obeying God Pages 204–205

- Define sin as the choice to disobey God on purpose and do what you know is wrong. It is not an accident or a mistake
- Describe the consequences of sin as hurting our friendship with God and others
- Understand that Jesus wants us to be sorry for our sins and turn to God our forgiving Father

- **Catholic Faith Words** sin
- ☆ Underline what helps our friendship with God.
- Explain that God wants us to be sorry when we sin.
- Luke 15:11–32 Proclaim "The Forgiving Father."
- **Share Your Faith Activity** Share an example of selfishness.

☐ pencils
☐ index card

Ask for Forgiveness Pages 206–207

- Realize that God wants us to be close to him and will always forgive us when we say we are sorry

- ☆ Have the children underline what God wants them to do.
- Explain that God wants us to forgive others.
- Explain that God will always forgive us.
- **Connect Your Faith Activity** Draw how to make things better after hurting a friend's feelings.

☐ pencils
☐ crayons or markers
- **Optional Activity** Show Love
☐ Activity Master 15 (Page 203E)

Live, 15 minutes

Our Catholic Life Pages 208–209

- Explain that the Holy Spirit can help us make up for doing something wrong.
- Examine steps for making better choices.
- **People of Faith** Learn about Saint Dismas.
- **Live Your Faith Activity** Identify words or actions that show forgiveness.

☐ pencils
☐ crayons or markers

Prayer for Forgiveness Page 210

- Rehearse "Children of God."
- Follow the order of prayer.

Download "Children of God."

Family + Faith Page 211

Point out that the Catholic Families page provides chapter highlights, information on how first graders understand faith concepts, and family prayer.

Chapter Review Page 212

aliveinchrist.osv.com
- Customize and Download Assessments
- Email Links to eAssessments
- Interactive Student Reviews

ONLINE RESOURCES

 Go to **aliveinchrist.osv.com**

You will find:

- Interactive lesson planning with web specific content and additional activities
- Step by step lesson instruction from printed Catechist Edition for integrated lesson planning
- Custom-built assessments to download and eAssessment links
- Interactive reviews that provide scores and the option to review answers
- Sunday readings with background and questions of the week

 Go to **osvparish.com**

You will find:

- Ask the Experts Q and A
- General Catechist Helps
- Community Connections and Blogs

Sharing the Message with First Graders

Saying "I'm Sorry" Many young children are forced to apologize when they have done something wrong even though they may not fully realize the impact their behavior had on the other person. This type of apology is often insincere and may lead to a child using "I'm sorry" as an automatic response when he or she gets into trouble.

Teaching Tip: Help children make amends sincerely by helping them understand what the behavior felt like for the other person. Sometimes it helps to hear from the other person how they felt. Also, a concrete action to help make up for the wrong is often better than words alone.

How First Graders Understand

- When young children act inappropriately, correct the behavior but tell them you still care about them.
- Teach first graders the words and actions that help them ask for forgiveness.
- Teach young children why they should be sorry.

"Teaching forgiveness is teaching me how to love others as God loves us."

Chapter Story

"Forgiveness"

Use this story to enhance the chapter introduction.

- The children will relate the story to their own lives, reflecting on how they show they are sorry.
- Connect being sorry with forgiveness.

 Go to **aliveinchrist.osv.com** Lesson Planning section for this story.

NCEA IFG: ACRE Edition

Knowledge of the Faith

- Objective: To know and understand basic Catholic teaching about the Incarnate Word Jesus Christ as the way, truth, and life

Moral Formation

- Objectives: To be knowledgeable about the teachings of Jesus and the Church as the basis of Christian morality and to understand Catholic Social Teaching; to be aware of the importance of a well-formed conscience for decision making

Catholic Social Teaching

 Use one of these features to introduce a principle and engage the children with an activity.

- Rights and Responsibilities, Pages 288–289
- Option for the Poor, Pages 290–291

Music Options

 Use one or more of the following songs to enhance catechetical learning or for prayer.

- "Children of God," Live Prayer, Page 210
- "I'm Sorry," Discover, Page 207

LECTIONARY CONNECTION

 Chapter 15 highlights Lectionary-connected themes such as forgiveness, reconciliation and justification. If your parish aligns its curriculum to the liturgical year, you could use this chapter in connection with the following Sundays.

Year A

Second Sunday of Advent—justice, peace

Twenty-fourth Sunday in Ordinary Time—forgiveness

Year B

Second Sunday of Advent—repent

First Sunday of Lent—Baptism

Twenty-sixth Sunday in Ordinary Time—social justice

Year C

Second Sunday of Advent—salvation

Fifth Sunday of Lent—reconciliation

Thirty-first Sunday in Ordinary Time—justification

 Go to **aliveinchrist.osv.com** for a complete correlation ordered by the Sundays of the year and suggestions for how to integrate the Scripture readings into chapter lessons.

Name _____   Date _____

God's Love

Cut out the puzzle pieces. Then put the pieces together to discover what God says when we are sorry.

Showing Sorrow

Let Us Pray

Leader: May we learn that God forgives us always and forever. Amen.

Create a clean heart for me, O God; renew in me a strong spirit.
Based on Psalm 51:12

All: Thank you God for teaching us how to forgive.

God's Word

Peter went up to Jesus and asked, "How many times should I forgive someone who does something wrong to me? Is seven times enough?" Jesus answered: "Not just seven times, but seventy-seven times!" Based on Matthew 18:21–22

What Do You Wonder?
- Who do you forgive?
- When do you say "I'm sorry"?

203

Optional Activity

Chapter Story: "Forgiveness" *Verbal/Linguistic*

Use this story after the opening prayer, before explaining that Jesus teaches us to forgive and to ask for forgiveness.

- Read aloud the story as the children follow along.
- Ask the children for some other examples of what they shouldn't do.
- Ask: How do you show you are sorry?
- After the discussion, transition back to the lesson instruction.

 Go to **aliveinchrist.osv.com** for Chapter Story.

Invite

Let Us Pray

Invite the children to gather in the prayer space and make the Sign of the Cross. Have a child read aloud the Psalm verse from a Bible. Prompt the children's response.

Have the children move out of the prayer space and back to their seats.

Explain that Jesus teaches us to forgive and to ask for forgiveness.

Say: Jesus teaches us how important it is to forgive and to say "I'm sorry." Listen to how many times Jesus says we need to forgive someone.

God's Word

Guide the children through the process of Scripture reflection.

- Invite them to close their eyes, be still and open their minds and hearts to what God is saying to them in this passage.
- Proclaim the Scripture.
- Maintain several moments of silence.
- *Ask:* What did you hear God say to you today?
- Invite volunteers to share.

What Do You Wonder?

Say: For Jesus, forgiveness is what we need to do all the time and not count how often we do it.

Invite the children to respond to the questions. Ask what else they might wonder about asking for forgiveness and forgiving others.

Objectives

- Define sin as the choice to disobey God on purpose and do what you know is wrong. It is not an accident or a mistake

- Describe the consequences of sin as hurting your friendship with God and others

- Understand that Jesus wants us to be sorry for our sins and turn to God our forgiving Father

Obeying God

Ask: How can you help your friendship with God stay strong?

- Write the children's responses on the board or on chart paper.

Read aloud the first paragraph.

Work with Words

Hold up an index card with the word *sin* on it. Read the definition to the children.

- Tell the children that every time you sin, you disobey God.

Read aloud the last two paragraphs.

 Have the children underline what helps their friendship with God grow stronger.

- *Ask:* When can it feel hard to obey God?

- *Ask:* How can you make right choices?

- Reassure the children that God forgives us when we are sorry, ask for forgiveness, and promise to do better.

Discover

It is important to take time to think about our choices.

Obeying God

How can you help your friendship with God stay strong?

 Underline what helps your friendship with God grow stronger.

When you choose to do something you know is wrong, you disobey God. When you disobey God, you commit a **sin**. Accidents or mistakes are not sins. We do not do them on purpose.

When you sin, it hurts your friendship with God. You also hurt yourself and others when you do not choose to do good.

God wants you to obey him. He asks you <u>to love him and others with your whole heart</u>. When you do this, your friendship with God grows stronger.

204 Chapter 15

(i) Catechist Background

Forgiveness

Remind the children about the words of the Lord's Prayer.

- Have them pay close attention to the phrase "forgive us our trespasses as we forgive those who trespass against us."

- Tell them that God wants us to forgive others as well as ask forgiveness for what we have done.

Being Sorry

Jesus told a story about how God wants you to act when you are sorry.

God's Word

The Forgiving Father

Once a father had two sons. The younger son wanted half of his father's money so he could leave home. The father sadly gave the younger son the money.

The son left and wasted all his money. He got a job feeding pigs. He was sad and cold and all alone. The son started to walk home. He hoped that his father would give him a better job.

When the son returned, he cried, "I am sorry I have sinned. I am not good enough to be your son." The father hugged his son and threw a big party.

The older son was angry that his father forgave him. But the father said, "He has come home. We must welcome him."

Based on Luke 15:11–32

© Our Sunday Visitor

Catholic Faith Words

sin a person's choice to disobey God on purpose and do what he or she knows is wrong. Accidents and mistakes are not sins.

Think Think about some times when people are selfish.

Share Share one example with your partner.

205

Scripture Background

Luke 15:11–32

The younger son in this story offended his father by asking for his inheritance so that he could squander it on foolish, harmful, things.

- He also offended his family by forsaking Israel, the land in which God had settled his Chosen People.
- Jesus knew that this story would powerfully show that God his Father is always willing to forgive sinners.

Being Sorry

Invite the children to listen to a story Jesus told. Ask them to listen carefully to how God wants us to act when we are sorry.

God's Word

Proclaim "The Forgiving Father."

- Ask the children to retell the story in their own words by asking them what happened in the beginning, middle, and end of the story.
- *Ask:* Who asks for forgiveness in the story? the younger brother
- *Ask:* How does the father react? Possible responses: he forgives his son, he throws a party for his son, he hugs his son
- Explain that when we sin, God wants us to ask for forgiveness like the younger son. When we are sorry and ask for forgiveness, God will always forgive us, just like the father in the story.

Activity

Read aloud the directions for the Share Your Faith activity.

- Discuss the first part of the activity together.
- Provide time for the children to share an example with a partner.

Quick Review

Sin is the choice to disobey God. God always forgives people who sin if they are truly sorry.

Objective

- Realize that God wants us to be close to him and will always forgive us when we say we are sorry

Ask for Forgiveness

Ask: How does God know if you are sorry for not obeying him?

- Write the children's responses on the board or on chart paper.

Read aloud the text.

⭐ Have the children underline what God wants them to do.

Explain to the children that to forgive someone is to let go of our anger about what someone has done.

- *Ask:* How does it feel when you say, "I'm sorry," and are forgiven?
- Tell the children that saying "I'm sorry" and "I forgive you" go together like two pieces to a puzzle—they mend a friendship, whether the friendship is between two people or between a person and God.
- *Ask:* How does God know if you are sorry for not obeying him?

Point out the picture.

- Ask the children to tell what they see in the picture.
- Discuss what might be happening in the picture.

Discover

Ask for Forgiveness

How does God know if you are sorry for not obeying him?

Jesus taught that his Father forgives sinners. God forgives us when we are truly sorry and ask his forgiveness through the Church.

<u>God wants you to forgive, too.</u> God wants all people to be friends.

When people forgive, they show love for God and others. When you ask someone to forgive you, you hope the person will say "Yes!"

It's not always easy to forgive someone that has hurt you or made you mad. God wants you to give that person another chance to make things better.

⭐ Underline what God wants you to do.

206 Chapter 15

Optional Activity

Activity Master 15: God's Love

Distribute copies of the activity found on catechist page 203E.

- This activity helps the children understand that God forgives us when we are sorry.
- As an alternative, you may wish to send this activity home with the children.

Make Things Better

God wants you to be close to him. When you sin, you can say "I'm sorry. Please forgive me. I will try to make better choices."

God will always say "I forgive you!" God is always ready to forgive you. God's love for you never ends.

➜ **When have you felt God's love?**

Connect Your Faith

Draw an Ending Work with a partner. Imagine that you have hurt someone's feelings. Draw a way to make things better.

207

Make Things Better

Read aloud the first paragraph.

- Read aloud the second paragraph. Read the first sentence and omit the word *always*. Ask the children how often they can try harder to make good choices and lead them to the word *always*.

- Do the same with the second sentence; omit the word *always* and make it a game for them to guess how often God forgives.

- Read the final sentence, and then ask each child to turn to someone who sits nearby and share the statement.

- *Ask:* When have you felt God's love?

 Music Option: Have the children sing "I'm Sorry," downloaded from **aliveinchrist.osv.com**.

Activity

Read aloud the directions for the Connect Your Faith activity.

- Have the children work with a partner to complete the activity.

- Invite volunteers to share their drawings.

Quick Review

God is always ready to forgive.

 ## Reaching All Learners

Early Readers

Children with reading proficiency may benefit from a more challenging activity.

- Invite these children to write words on their drawings.

- Ask volunteers to read their words or sentences to the group.

Our Catholic Life

Ask: How can you make up for doing something wrong?

- Write the children's responses on the board or on chart paper.

Read aloud the introductory paragraph.

- Emphasize that when it may seem hard to make things better, the Holy Spirit will help them.

Making Things Better

- Draw attention to the numbered steps and the pictures.
- Ask four children to read aloud the numbered steps.
- *Ask:* Why should you ask for the Holy Spirit's help when you do something wrong?
- Practice the steps with the children by talking through a scenario, such as borrowing and breaking something that belongs to an older sibling, or ignoring a parent when they ask you to set the table.

Teach the children the first few lines of the Prayer to the Holy Spirit:

Come, Holy Spirit, fill the hearts of your faithful.

And kindle in them the fire of your love.

- Encourage the children to pray this prayer when they face a difficult choice.

Live

Our Catholic Life

How can you make up for doing something wrong?

When you make a bad choice, you hurt others and yourself. It might seem hard to make things better. The Holy Spirit will help you. Here are some steps to follow.

Making Things Better

© Our Sunday Visitor

1 Think about what you have done. Tell God you are sorry.

2 Tell the person you hurt that you are sorry and ask for forgiveness.

3 Do whatever you can to make up for what you did wrong.

4 Ask the Holy Spirit to help you do better in the future.

208 Chapter 15

✓ Quick Tip

Reconciling

Help the children see that forgiveness is an important part of bringing peace, not only to relationships with family and friends, but also to the world.

- Remind the children to look for peaceful, nonviolent resolutions to conflicts.
- Ask the children to serve as mediators when their friends or siblings quarrel.

People of Faith

Saint Dismas, first century

Saint Dismas was crucified at the same time as Jesus. He knew that he had done bad things. He asked forgiveness for all the things he stole. Then he asked Jesus to remember him in Heaven. Jesus told Saint Dismas that he would be with God in Paradise. Saint Dismas discovered that when we are sorry for our sins, God will always forgive us.

March 25

Discuss: What is the best way to let someone know you are sorry?

 Learn more about Saint Dismas at **aliveinchrist.osv.com**

Live Your Faith

Thumbs Up or Down Circle the thumbs up if the words or actions show forgiveness. Circle the thumbs down if they do not.

  Saying you are sorry.

  Saying "no" when someone asks you for forgiveness.

  Asking the person you've hurt for forgiveness.

  Asking the Holy Spirit to help you do better in the future.

Showing Sorrow **209**

🌐 Catholic Social Teaching

To integrate Catholic Social Teaching into your lesson, choose one of the following features: Rights and Responsibilities, pages 288–289; or Option for the Poor, pages 290–291.

- Start the Live step of the process by talking about Saint Dismas on page 209. Then move directly to the Catholic Social Teaching feature.
- Or, to expand the lesson, complete both pages 208 and 209, then move to the Catholic Social Teaching feature.
- Return to Chapter 15 for the prayer on page 210.

People of Faith

Tell the children about Saint Dismas.

- Invite a volunteer to read aloud the People of Faith story.
- Explain that all we know about Saint Dismas is that he is remembered as the Good Thief who was crucified with Jesus. The other thief is known as Gestas. Saint Dismas is remembered as good because he asked for forgiveness. His feast day is March 25.
- We hear the story of Saint Dismas on Palm Sunday of the Lord's Passion Year C. He says to Jesus, "Jesus, remember me when you come into your kingdom." Jesus replies, "Today you will be with me in paradise." (See Luke 23:42-43.)
- *Ask:* What is the best way to let someone know you are sorry?

 Encourage the children to go to **aliveinchrist.osv.com** at home to learn more about Saint Dismas.

Activity

Read aloud the directions for the Live Your Faith activity.

- Complete and discuss the activity together.

Live

 Let Us Pray

Prayer for Forgiveness

This prayer is based on the Act of Contrition. If there is time, refer the children to page 318 in the Our Catholic Tradition reference section of the Student Book to also teach them an Act of Faith, Hope, and Love.

Prepare

Explain to the children that they will echo the lines of the prayer after you say them.

 Rehearse "Children of God," downloaded from **aliveinchrist.osv.com**.

Gather

Invite the children to process to the prayer space.

- Have the children sit in a circle.
- Prompt the children to quiet themselves for prayer.

Pray

Follow the order of prayer on the student page.

- Begin with the Sign of the Cross.

 Conclude by singing together "Children of God."

 Let Us Pray

Prayer for Forgiveness

Gather and begin with the Sign of the Cross.

Leader: Together, let us tell God we are sorry and we will try to do better.
Repeat after me: My God, I am sorry for my sins with all my heart.

All: (Echo)

Leader: In choosing to do wrong and failing to do good,

All: (Echo)

Leader: I have sinned against you.

All: (Echo)

Leader: I do not want to sin because I love you.

All: (Echo)

Leader: I promise that with your help

All: (Echo)

Leader: I will try to do better. Amen.

All: (Echo)

 Sing "Children of God"

210 Chapter 15

 Liturgy Link

Rite of Penance

Explain to the children that the Act of Contrition is from the Sacrament of Penance and Reconciliation, which they will celebrate for the first time next year.

- Through the absolution of a priest, God forgives people for their sins.

 Go to **aliveinchrist.osv.com** for Sunday readings, Scripture background, questions of the week, and seasonal resources.

YOUR CHILD LEARNED >>>

This chapter explains the consequences of sin and our need for God's forgiveness.

God's Word

 Read **Matthew 18:21–22** to find out how many times Jesus tells us we need to forgive someone.

Catholics Believe

• God always forgives those who are truly sorry and ask his forgiveness.

• God asks that we forgive others and ourselves.

To learn more, go to the *Catechism of the Catholic Church* #1846–1850 at **usccb.org.**

People of Faith

This week, your child met Saint Dismas, the name given to the good thief who was crucified with Jesus.

CHILDREN AT THIS AGE >>>

How They Understand Saying "I'm Sorry" Many young children are forced to apologize when they have done something wrong even though they may not fully realize the impact their behavior had on the other person. You can help your child make amends sincerely by helping him or her understand what the behavior felt like for the other person. Sometimes it helps to hear from the other person how they felt. Also, a concrete action to help make up for the wrong is often better than words alone.

CONSIDER THIS >>>

Do you find it hard to admit that you've done something wrong?

For many people admitting they are wrong is a serious challenge. They may feel diminished or they may confuse what they did with who they are. As adults, however, we recognize that it is necessary to be honest about our failings or we will never be able to grow. "Confession liberates us from sins that trouble our hearts and makes it possible to be reconciled to God and others. We are asked to look into our souls and, with an honest and unblinking gaze, identify our sins. This opens our minds and hearts to God, moves us toward communion with the Church, and offers us a new future" (*USCCA, p. 238*).

LET'S TALK >>>

• Talk about times when it's been hard to obey God.

• Ask your child to talk about the steps to follow if they make a wrong choice.

LET'S PRAY >>>

Dear God, help us to always be sorry when we disobey you. Amen.

For a multimedia glossary of Catholic Faith Words, Sunday readings, seasonal and Saint resources, and chapter activities go to **aliveinchrist.osv.com.**

Alive in Christ, Grade 1 Chapter 15 **211**

Family + Faith

Distribute the page to the children or parents/adult family members. Point out the chapter highlights, insights on how first graders understand concepts, the opportunity for the adults to reflect on their own experience and faith journey, and the family prayer.

Chapter 15 Review

A **Work with Words** Write the letter of the word from the Word Bank that completes each sentence.

Word Bank
- a. love
- b. sin
- c. friendship
- d. sorry
- e. forgive

1. Disobeying God's law is called **b** .

2. When you **a** God, you show your love.

3. You can start over with God by saying I'm **d** .

4. When you sin, you hurt your **c** with God.

5. God will always **e** you.

B **Check Understanding** Number the steps to make things better.

6. **4** Ask the Holy Spirit to help you do better in the future.

1 Think about what you have done.

2 Ask the person you hurt to forgive you.

3 Do something to make up for it.

 Go to **aliveinchrist.osv.com** for an interactive review.

Chapter Review

Use Catechist Quick Reviews to highlight lesson concepts.

A **Work with Words**
Have the children write the letter of a word from the Word Bank to complete each sentence.

B **Check Understanding**
Have the children number the steps to make things better.

Go to **aliveinchrist.osv.com** to prepare customized and downloadable assessments, send eAssessments, and assign interactive reviews.

Showing Sorrow **211–212**

UNIT 5

Unit Review

Use Catechist Quick Reviews in each chapter to highlight lesson concepts for this unit and prepare for the Unit Review.

Have the children complete the Review pages. Then discuss the answers as a group. Review any concepts with which the children are having difficulty.

A Work with Words
Have the children circle the correct word to complete each sentence.

Unit Review

UNIT 5

A Work with Words Circle the correct word to complete each sentence.

1. Jesus taught his followers to ____ others.

   (serve) have fun with

2. The ____ Commandments tell how to love God and others.

   Five (Ten)

3. ____ choices help you show love and respect for God and others.

   Bad (Good)

4. When you ____ God, you sin.

   (disobey) obey

5. Jesus taught that God ____.

   forgets (forgives)

Unit Review

B Check Understanding Write your answers on the spaces below.

6. Name one way to serve others.

<u>Responses will vary.</u>

7. Tell about one Commandment.

<u>Responses will vary.</u>

8. Who forgives you when you say, "I'm sorry"?

<u>Responses will vary.</u>

C Make Connections Circle the pictures that show how to follow Jesus.

9.

10. Draw one way you can follow Jesus.

B Check Understanding
Have the children write their answers on the spaces provided.

C Make Connections
Have the children circle the pictures that show how to follow Jesus for problem 9.

For problem 10, have them draw one way they can follow Jesus.

 Go to **aliveinchrist.osv.com** to prepare customized and downloadable assessments, send eAssessments, and assign interactive reviews.

Sacraments

Our Catholic Tradition

- In the Bible, God tells us about his great love for us. (CCC, 231)

- The Seven Sacraments are special signs and celebrations that Jesus gave his Church. The Sacraments allow us to share in the life and work of God. (CCC, 1131)

- The Church celebrates the Seven Sacraments as signs of God's love and life. (CCC, 1116)

- Grace means sharing in God's help and life so that we may grow as his children. (CCC, 1996)

How does the grace we receive from the Seven Sacraments help us to grow closer to Jesus?

Unit 6 Overview

Chapter 16

Jesus the Savior

The children will:

- recognize Adam and Eve's choice to bring sin into the world
- reflect on God's love for people, even when they sin
- describe Jesus as our Savior, whom God sent to bring us back to him
- explain that Jesus died for all people to save them, giving his life so that people could have new life with God

 Catholic Social Teaching: Live Your Faith

- Option for the Poor, Pages 290–291
- Human Solidarity, Pages 294–295

Chapter 17

Holy Signs

The children will:

- identify the Seven Sacraments as special signs and celebrations that Jesus gave his Church
- appreciate that the Sacraments celebrate that Jesus is still with us, sharing his life and love
- recognize that every Sacrament has words and actions we do and things God does that we can't see that bring us life

 Catholic Social Teaching: Live Your Faith

- Human Solidarity, Pages 294–295
- Care for Creation, Pages 296–297

Chapter 18

We Are Welcomed

The children will:

- identify Baptism as the Sacrament that brings new life in God and makes the person a member of the Church
- name grace as God's gift of sharing his life and help
- examine the signs and symbols of Baptism

 Songs of Scripture
"Have You Ever Seen a Mustard Seed?"

 Catholic Social Teaching: Live Your Faith

- Rights and Responsibilities, Pages 288–289
- Human Solidarity, Pages 294–295

Preview Unit Theme

Ask: What is the unit theme?

Summarize that the unit focuses on the Sacraments.

Invite volunteers to read aloud each of the bullets in Our Catholic Tradition.

Explain to the children that they will learn about these things in the next three chapters.

Have the children study the photos and images. Invite volunteers to describe what they see. What do these images say about the unit theme?

Ask: How does the grace we receive from the Seven Sacraments help us to grow closer to Jesus?

After some discussion, explain to the children that they will be exploring this question in the next three chapters.

KEY CONCEPT

Even though humans sinned, God continued to love us and sent his Son to save us. Jesus died and rose to new life bringing us back to his Father.

DOCTRINAL CONTENT

- Adam and Eve chose to bring sin into the world. Their disobedience is called Original Sin. (CCC, 402–404)
- God did not stop loving people because of their sin. (CCC, 410)
- God sent his Son, Jesus, to be our Savior and bring people back to him. (CCC, 457)
- Jesus died for all people to save them, giving his life so that people could have new life with God. (CCC, 613)

TASKS OF CATECHESIS

Helping children grow in a faith that is "known, celebrated, lived, and expressed in prayer" (NDC, 20).

This chapter focuses on the following tasks of catechesis:

- Promoting Knowledge of the Faith
- Moral Formation

Catechist Background

The angel said to the women in reply. "Do not be afraid! I know that you are seeking Jesus the crucified. He is not here, for he has been raised just as he said." Matthew 28:5–6

→ **Reflect** When do you talk with Jesus?

Do not be afraid. Do not let your hearts be troubled. Do not fear. God the Father continually assures his People that there is no reason to fear, because he is with them. Yet it is human nature to be afraid—of the unknown or a new situation, of being alone, of what is to come. The shepherds who stood watch in the fields of Bethlehem were afraid. The women at the empty tomb were afraid. The Apostles were afraid when the resurrected Jesus first appeared to them and again as they huddled in an upstairs room awaiting the Holy Spirit.

Recall a time when you felt real fear. It might have been a fear about a physical or emotional pain, a family member being ill, or a relationship that ended. Think about your reaction. Did you ask anyone for help? Did you turn to God in prayer?

Throughout his ministry, Jesus listened and heard his followers' cries for help. Those who believe in him have no reason to fear. Jesus is the Savior whose loving gift of himself saved people. God knows all there is to know about you, even the number of hairs on your head, and loves you unconditionally. There is nothing to fear (see Matthew 10:26, 30).

→ **Reflect** From what fear has God rescued you?

Catechist's Prayer

Jesus, in all you said and did, you showed how to love. Help me live by your example. When I feel in need of comfort, may I trust in your everlasting love. Amen.

Lesson Plan

Objectives	Process	Materials

🕐 Invite, 10 minutes

Jesus the Savior Page 217

- 💜 Psalm 141:1 Pray the opening prayer.
- 📖 Matthew 28:5–6 Reflect prayerfully on the Word.
- Discuss What Do You Wonder questions.

📶 **Optional Activity**
Chapter Story: "The Rescue"

🕐 Discover, 35 minutes

Adam and Eve Pages 218–219

- Recognize Adam and Eve's choice to bring sin into the world
- Reflect on God's love for people, even when they sin

- **Catholic Faith Words** Original Sin
- Explain that Adam and Eve brought sin into the world when they chose to disobey God.
- ☆ Underline what God wanted Adam and Eve to do.
- Explain that God promised to send a Savior.
- **Share Your Faith Activity** Name how Jesus brings us closer to God.

☐ pencils
☐ index cards

New Life with God Pages 220–221

- Describe Jesus as our Savior, whom God sent to bring us back to him
- Explain that Jesus died for all people to save them, giving his life so that people could have new life with God

- **Catholic Faith Words** Resurrection
- Explain that Jesus saved people from their sins.
- 📖 Luke 23–24 Proclaim "Jesus Lives."
- ☆ Underline what the two angels said.
- Explain that the Church celebrates the Resurrection in a special way on Easter.
- **Connect Your Faith Activity** Find the hidden word.

☐ pencils
☐ index cards
☐ crayons or markers
- **Optional Activity** Jesus the Savior
☐ Activity Master 16 (Page 217E)

🕐 Live, 15 minutes

Our Catholic Life Pages 222–223

- Explain that after the Resurrection, Jesus sent all his friends to share the Good News of God's love.
- ☆ Identify how they will try to share the Good News this week.
- **People of Faith** Learn about Saint Josephine Bakhita.
- **Live Your Faith Activity** Make an Easter card.

☐ pencils
☐ crayons or markers

Prayer of Praise Page 224

- Create gestures.
- ▶ Rehearse "Savior of the World."
- Follow the order of prayer.

📶 Download "Savior of the World."

Family + Faith Page 225
Point out that the Catholic Families page provides chapter highlights, information on how first graders understand faith concepts, and family prayer.

Chapter Review Page 226
📶 **aliveinchrist.osv.com**
- Customize and Download Assessments
- Email Links to eAssessments
- Interactive Student Reviews

ONLINE RESOURCES

 Go to **aliveinchrist.osv.com**

You will find:

- Interactive lesson planning with web specific content and additional activities
- Step by step lesson instruction from printed Catechist Edition for integrated lesson planning
- Custom-built assessments to download and eAssessment links
- Interactive reviews that provide scores and the option to review answers
- Sunday readings with background and questions of the week

 Go to **osvparish.com**

You will find:

- Ask the Experts Q and A
- General Catechist Helps
- Community Connections and Blogs

Sharing the Message with First Graders

Jesus as Savior Children in first grade will have difficulty understanding the idea that Jesus gave his life as a sacrifice for us. However, they can understand that Jesus loved us so much that he wanted to show us how to live even though it meant he would die. First graders are just beginning to grasp the permanence of death, making them particularly open to the Gospel message, which says that death could not hold Jesus, and he is risen.

Teaching Tip: As you talk about Jesus' suffering and Death, provide hints that God is about to do something good. This type of foreshadowing helps them to be more engaged in the story and keeps them from getting overwhelmed with details of Jesus' Passion that can be difficult for young children to cope with.

How First Graders Understand

- Most children enjoy spring and summer best. Talk about all the signs of new life they see.
- Sometimes first graders can be afraid. Help them to know that God will keep them safe.
- Children, through personal experiences or through public events, know about acts of saving. Help connect the children's experience with God's salvation.

"Tell me how Christmas and Easter connect with Jesus' life."

Chapter Connections

Chapter Story

Invite

"The Rescue"

Use this story to expand the chapter introduction.

- The children will relate the story to their own lives, reflecting on their experiences of being saved.
- Connect the children's experience of being saved to Jesus coming to teach and save us.

 Go to **aliveinchrist.osv.com** Lesson Planning section for this story.

NCEA IFG: ACRE Edition

Discover

Knowledge of the Faith

- Objective: To know and understand basic Catholic teaching about the Incarnate Word Jesus Christ as the way, truth, and life

Moral Formation

- Objectives: To be knowledgeable about the teachings of Jesus and the Church as the basis of Christian morality and to understand Catholic Social Teaching; to be aware of the importance of a well-formed conscience for decision making

Catholic Social Teaching

Live

 Use one of these features to introduce a principle and engage the children with an activity.

- Option for the Poor, Pages 290–291
- Human Solidarity, Pages 294–295

Music Options

 Use one or more of the following songs to enhance catechetical learning or for prayer.

- "Savior of the World," Live Prayer, Page 224
- "Alleluia," Discover, Page 219
- "Gospel Acclamation," Discover, Page 219

LECTIONARY CONNECTION

 Chapter 16 highlights Lectionary-connected themes such as Baptism, faithfulness, and being saved by Christ. If your parish aligns its curriculum to the liturgical year, you could use this chapter in connection with the following Sundays.

Year A

Eleventh Sunday in Ordinary Time—sinners saved by Christ

Twenty Eighth Sunday in Ordinary Time—a feast for all peoples

Year B

Most Holy Body and Blood of Christ—"take and eat"

Eighth Sunday in Ordinary Time—God is forever faithful

Year C

Second Sunday of Easter—Baptism

Twenty-first Sunday in Ordinary Time—gather the nations

 Go to **aliveinchrist.osv.com** for a complete correlation ordered by the Sundays of the year and suggestions for how to integrate the Scripture readings into chapter lessons.

Name _____   Date _____

Jesus the Savior

Color the figure of Jesus and cut it out. Cut the picture strips, too. Put Jesus in every picture. Tell the story of Jesus, from the Last Supper to his Resurrection, to a family member.

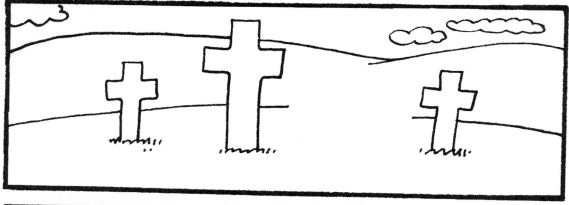

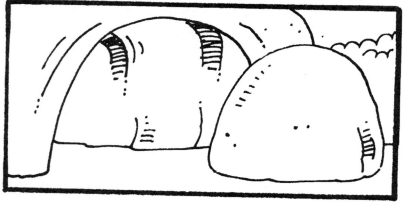

Jesus the Savior

Let Us Pray

Leader: Thank you for saving us, Jesus.

"LORD, I call to you; hasten to me;
listen to my plea when I call." Psalm 141:1

All: Thank you for saving us, Jesus. Amen.

God's Word

"Then the angel said to the women in reply, 'Do not be afraid! I know that you are seeking Jesus the crucified. He is not here, for he has been raised just as he said. Come and see the place where he lay.'" Matthew 28:5–6

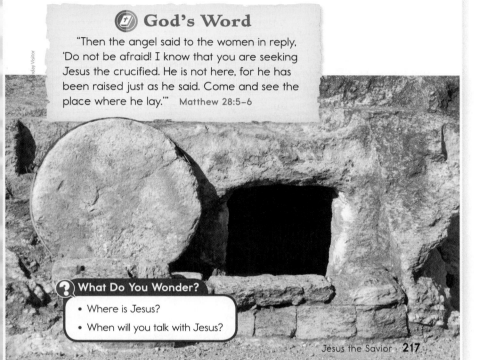

? What Do You Wonder?
- Where is Jesus?
- When will you talk with Jesus?

Jesus the Savior **217**

Optional Activity

Chapter Story: "The Rescue" *Verbal/Linguistic*

Use this story after the opening prayer, before explaining that Jesus came to teach and save us.

- Read the story aloud as the children follow along. Explain that Tanya did something that put her in need of being saved.
- *Ask:* Who saved Tanya?
- Ask the children to think of a story about someone who is saved from danger. Invite sharing, then transition back to the lesson instruction.

 Go to **aliveinchrist.osv.com** for Chapter Story.

Invite

Let Us Pray

Invite the children to gather in the prayer space and make the Sign of the Cross. Invite a child to be the leader. Read aloud the Psalm verse from a Bible. Prompt the children's response.

Have the children move out of the prayer space and back to their seats.

Explain that Jesus came to teach and save us.

Say: Jesus came to teach and save us. He shows us the way. Let's listen now to a reading from the Gospel of Matthew.

God's Word

Guide the children through the process of Scripture reflection.

- Invite them to close their eyes, be still and open their minds and hearts to what God is saying to them in this passage.
- Proclaim the Scripture.
- Maintain several moments of silence.
- *Ask:* What did you hear God say to you today?
- Invite volunteers to share.

What Do You Wonder?

Say: Because Jesus' friends saw him after he was raised from the dead, we know he lives. Jesus is with us too, even though we cannot see him like they did.

Invite the children to respond to the questions. Ask what else they might wonder about talking with Jesus.

Objectives

• Recognize Adam and Eve's choice to bring sin into the world

• Reflect on God's love for people, even when they sin

Adam and Eve

Ask: Why did God's people need to be saved?

• Write the children's responses on the board or on chart paper.

Read aloud the paragraph.

• Ask the children to retell the story in just a few words.

• On the board or on chart paper, write "First, Adam and Eve sinned."

Work with Words

Hold up an index card with the term *Original Sin* on it. Have everyone read it.

• Read the definition aloud.

God Loves

Read aloud the paragraph.

• Ask the children how God reacted to Adam and Eve's sin. He continued to love them.

 Have the children underline what God wanted Adam and Eve to do.

• *Ask:* How do you show love for God?

Adam and Eve

Why did God's people need to be saved?

God created the first people to be like him. He made them happy and gave them a garden to care for. Then Adam and Eve made a bad choice. They disobeyed God and brought sin into the world. This is called **Original Sin**.

Catholic
Faith Words

Original Sin the first sin committed by Adam and Eve and passed down to everyone

> Underline what God wanted Adam and Eve to do.

God Loves

Adam and Eve were no longer the kind of people God wanted them to be.

They broke their friendship with him. They suffered, and they missed God.

But God did not stop loving them. <u>He wanted them to love him.</u>

218 Chapter 16

(i) Catechist Background

Original Sin

The sin of Adam and Eve destroyed their descendants' friendship with God as well as their own.

• The doctrine of Original Sin is a difficult idea for first graders to understand. Explain that once sin came into the world, it became hard for people to be God's friends and to avoid sin.

God's Promise

God said, "I love you always. I will show you how much I love you. I will send a Savior to bring you back to me." God kept this promise. He sent his Son, Jesus, to us. Jesus' saves all people from sin. He is our Savior.

Share Your Faith

Think Trace the name of the Savior that God the Father sent to us.

_____

Jesus

_____

Share Talk with a partner about why God sent a Savior.

Jesus the Savior **219**

✓ Quick Tip

Savior

Have the children pronounce the word *Savior*. Ask them to say aloud what little word they hear at the beginning of the word *Savior—save*.

- *Say:* A Savior saves people. Jesus is the Savior who saved people from the sin that broke their friendship with God the Father. Jesus brought people back to him.

God's Promise

Have a volunteer read aloud the sentence you wrote on the board or chart paper: "First, Adam and Eve sinned."

- Explain that God was unhappy that our first parents had broken their friendship with him. Tell the children that God wanted the children and grandchildren of Adam and Eve to be his friends again.

- Read aloud the paragraph.

- On the board or on chart paper, write in big letters, "Then God sent a Savior." Explain that this is what he did to rescue people.

- Tell the children that we praise God for sending Jesus.

- Introduce the word *Alleluia* as meaning, "Praise God!"

 Music Option: Have the children sing, "Alleluia," (anytime except Lent) or "Gospel Acclamation," (during Lent) downloaded from **aliveinchrist.osv.com**.

Activity

Read aloud the directions for the Share Your Faith activity.

- Have the children work independently to trace the letters.

- After a short time, have them discuss with a partner.

Quick Review

After humans sinned, God promised to send a Savior, his own Son, to rescue them from their sin.

Discover

Objectives

- Describe Jesus as our Savior, whom God sent to bring us back to him
- Explain that Jesus died for all people to save them, giving his life so that people could have new life with God

New Life with God

Ask: How did Jesus save us from sin?

- Write the children's responses on the board or on chart paper.

Hold up an index card showing the word *Savior* as you read the introductory paragraph.

 ## God's Word

Gather the children to hear the Scripture story, "Jesus Lives."

- Proclaim the first paragraph of the Scripture story. Point to a crucifix and show the children how Jesus died.
- Ask the children to listen to what happened after Jesus died.
- Point to the art on the page after you proclaim the second paragraph of the Scripture story.
- ⭐ Have the children underline what the two angels said.
- *Ask:* What would you have thought about the empty cave if you had been there with the women?

New Life with God

How did Jesus save us from sin?

Jesus saved people from the power of sin. He also brought them back to God. Jesus is the Savior.

Underline what the two angels said.

⊕ God's Word

Jesus Lives

Some people did not believe that Jesus was God's Son. He was arrested and nailed to a Cross, where he died. His friends laid his body in a cave and blocked it with a large stone.

Some holy women went to visit the cave where Jesus was laid. The large stone was rolled away. The cave was empty. Two angels said, "Jesus is not here. He is risen from the dead!"

Then Jesus appeared to his followers.
Based on Luke 23–24

220 Chapter 16

⊕ Scripture Background

Resurrection

The word *resurrection* means "the act of rising from the dead."

- In the Gospel according to Matthew, an angel said to the women looking for Jesus after his Death, "Do not be afraid! I know that you are seeking Jesus the crucified. He is not there, for he has been raised just as he said" (Matthew 28:5–6).
- Jesus' Resurrection shows that all who love God will have new life in Heaven with him.

Jesus Saves

Jesus' name means, "God saves." He died for all people to save them from their sins. Jesus gave his life so that people could have new life with God.

Jesus being raised from the dead to new life is called the **Resurrection**. He was raised to new life by God the Father through the power of the Holy Spirit.

Jesus being raised to new life is a holy mystery. The Church celebrates the Resurrection in a special way on Easter.

➔ **How do you celebrate Easter?**

Catholic Faith Words

Resurrection the event of Jesus being raised from Death to new life by God the Father through the power of the Holy Spirit

Connect Your Faith

Make Stained Glass Color the letters blue and the surrounding shapes different colors to find who died to save us from our sins.

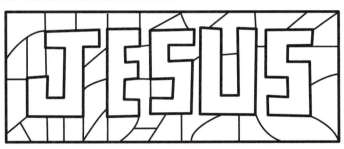

221

© Our Sunday Visitor

Jesus Saves

Read aloud both paragraphs. Have the children listen to learn the word we use for Jesus being raised from the dead.

Work with Words

Hold up an index card with the word *Resurrection*. Review the definition with the children.

On the board or on chart paper draw a graphic organizer: a cross with a heart drawn over the intersection of the cross.

- Inside the cross write, "Jesus the Savior."
- Use the graphic organizer to help summarize the Resurrection story.

Refer the children to page 299 in the Our Catholic Tradition reference section of the Student Book. Point out that when we pray the Apostles' Creed, we profess what we believe about Jesus' Death and Resurrection.

Activity

Point out the Connect Your Faith activity and read the directions aloud.

- Provide the children with crayons or markers.

Quick Review

Jesus is called the Savior because he saved people from their sins and brought them back to God. Jesus' being raised from the dead is called the Resurrection.

Our Catholic Life

Ask: How can you share the Good News of God's love?

- Write the children's responses on the board or on chart paper.

Read aloud the first paragraph.

- Emphasize that just like Jesus sent his own friends, he wants all of us to share the Good News of God's love.
- Point out that we can share the Good News by what we say and how we act.

Share the Good News

Draw attention to the list of ways to share Good News.

- Invite volunteers to read aloud the suggestions.
- ⭐ Invite the children to add a *T* next to the ones they will try to do this week.

Draw the children's attention to the picture.

- *Ask:* How might the girl be sharing the Good News?
- *Ask:* What are some other ways you can share the Good News?

Live

Our Catholic Life

How can you share the Good News of God's love?

After Jesus rose from the dead, he sent his friends to tell everyone the Good News of God's love.

Jesus wants you to share the Good News, too. You can share the Good News by what you say and how you act.

Here are some ways you can share Good News.

⭐ Add a "T" next to the things you will try to do this week.

Share the Good News

- ☐ Tell someone about Jesus.
- ☐ Invite a friend to come to Mass or a church event with you.
- ☐ Write a note or draw a picture to cheer up someone who is sad.
- ☐ Treat all people with kindness.
- ☐ Help someone make a good choice.
- ☐ Forgive someone who is sorry for hurting you.

222 Chapter 16

 Quick Tip

Confronting

Sharing Good News means speaking the truth, even when it is difficult.

- Help the children see that it is possible to stand up to negative peer pressure.
- Remind the children that speaking the truth does not mean being rude. Confronting people with the truth and suggesting better choices should always be done with respect and kindness.

People of Faith

Saint Josephine Bakhita, 1869–1947

February 8

Josephine (Giuseppina) Bakhita was born in Africa. At twelve, she was kidnapped and made a slave. She was a slave for many years. When she grew up, she stayed in a convent in Italy. She learned about Jesus there. She discovered that God loves us so much he died for us and wanted to help other people learn about Jesus, too. She became a religious sister and helped prepare missionaries to go to Africa.

Discuss: How can you let someone know more about Jesus?

 Learn more about Saint Josephine Bakhita at **aliveinchrist.osv.com**

Live Your Faith

Tell the Good News Trace the words that tell the Good News.

Jesus
is risen!

Jesus the Savior **223**

© Our Sunday Visitor

🌐 Catholic Social Teaching

Chapter Connections

To integrate Catholic Social Teaching into your lesson, choose one of the following features: Option for the Poor, pages 290–291; or Human Solidarity, pages 294–295.

- Start the Live step of the process by talking about Saint Josephine Bakhita on page 223. Then move directly to the Catholic Social Teaching feature.
- Or, to expand the lesson, complete both pages 222 and 223, then move to the Catholic Social Teaching feature.
- Return to Chapter 16 for the prayer on page 224.

People of Faith

Tell the children about Saint Josephine Bakhita.

- Invite a volunteer to read aloud the People of Faith story.
- Explain that Saint Josephine Bakhita was baptized as a young woman. After she was baptized, she was often seen kissing the baptismal font saying, "Here, I became a daughter of God!"
- Saint Josephine Bakhita was a humble and simple woman with a sweet nature, always smiling and showing kindness to everyone.
- She became known to all as "Mother Moretta," our Black Mother.
- *Ask:* How can you let someone know more about Jesus?

 Encourage the children to go to **aliveinchrist.osv.com** at home to learn more about Saint Josephine Bakhita.

Activity

Point out the Live Your Faith activity and read aloud the directions.

- Have the children trace the message in the activity box.
- Walk around the room as the children write, commenting on their work.

Let Us Pray
Prayer of Praise

Tell the children that in the prayer, they will be celebrating Jesus as the Savior. Explain that Savior is another name for Jesus.

Prepare

Write the words *Jesus*, *Savior*, and *Alleluia* on the board or on chart paper.

- Have the children come up with a gesture for each word.
- Practice all three gestures with the children. Explain that they will use them in their prayer together.
- Teach the children their response.

 Rehearse "Savior of the World," downloaded from **aliveinchrist.osv.com**.

Gather

Invite the children to process to the prayer space.

- Have the children remain standing for the prayer.

Pray

Follow the order of prayer on the student page.

- Begin by inviting the children to pray the sign of our salvation, the Sign of the Cross.

 Conclude by singing together "Savior of the World."

 Let Us Pray
Prayer of Praise

Gather and begin with the Sign of the Cross.

All: Jesus is Savior. Alleluia!

Leader: Save us, Savior of the world,
for by your Cross
and Resurrection,
you have set us free.
Mystery of Faith

All: Jesus is Savior. Alleluia!

Sing and sign a favorite Alleluia.

All: Jesus is Savior. Our hearts are filled with thanks.

 Sing "Savior of the World"
Save us, Lord, for you are the savior of the world.

Liturgy Link

Alleluia

The word *Alleluia*, a word of praise that has been used in Hebrew, Greek, and Latin languages, is used throughout the Psalms and in prayers at Mass.

- If your parish uses a particular musical version of this acclamation, teach the children the melody so that when they hear it at Mass, they will be able to join in saying, "Praise God."

 Go to **aliveinchrist.osv.com** for Sunday readings, Scripture background, questions of the week, and seasonal resources.

FAMILY+FAITH
LIVING AND LEARNING TOGETHER

YOUR CHILD LEARNED >>>

This chapter explains Original Sin and the need for a Savior. It covers Jesus' Death and Resurrection and explains Jesus' sacrifice as a gift of love.

God's Word

 Read **Matthew 28:5–6** to find out what the angel said to those looking for Jesus.

Catholics Believe

- Even though humans sinned, God continued to love us and sent his Son to save us.
- Jesus died and rose to new life bringing us back to his Father.

To learn more, go to the *Catechism of the Catholic Church* #639–642 at **usccb.org**.

People of Faith

This week, your child met Saint Josephine Bakhita, a former slave from Africa who became a religious sister in Italy.

CHILDREN AT THIS AGE >>>

How They Understand Jesus as Savior Children in first grade will have difficulty understanding the idea that Jesus gave his life as a sacrifice for us. However, they can understand that Jesus loved us so much that he wanted to show us how to live even though it meant he would die. First-graders are just beginning to grasp the permanence of death, making them particularly open to the Gospel message, which says that death could not hold Jesus, and he is risen.

CONSIDER THIS >>>

Have you ever thought about how the way you live your daily life is connected to Jesus' sacrifice?

It can be hard to grasp the importance of what Christ did for us, even for adults. It may seem impossible to live your life in a way that lives up to Jesus' sacrifice. Through our lives, our sufferings, our prayer and work, we are united with Christ. The important sacrifices that we make for each other and for God in our individual lives remind us of the importance of his sacrifice. "In a self-centered culture where people are taught to extend themselves only for something in return, the sacrifices each of us make, following the example of Jesus, who freely sacrificed his life in love for all, point to the reality and power of God's love for us" (*USCCA, p. 221*).

LET'S TALK >>>

- Talk about the ways we celebrate Jesus' Resurrection.
- Ask your child what he or she thinks about Jesus' sacrifice for us.

LET'S PRAY >>>

Dear God, help us to share your love with everyone we meet, like Saint Josephine did. Amen.

For a multimedia glossary of Catholic Faith Words, Sunday readings, seasonal and Saint resources, and chapter activities go to **aliveinchrist.osv.com**.

Distribute the page to the children or parents/adult family members. Point out the chapter highlights, insights on how first graders understand concepts, the opportunity for the adults to reflect on their own experience and faith journey, and the family prayer.

Chapter 16 Review

A **Work with Words** Complete each sentence with the letter of the correct word or words from the Word Bank.

Word Bank
a. loves
b. Savior
c. disobeyed
d. happy
e. Resurrection

1. Adam and Eve [c] God.

2. God always [a] his People.

3. The [e] is the name for Jesus' being raised from Death to new life.

4. Jesus is the [b].

5. God made people to be [d] with him.

B **Check Understanding** Circle the correct answers.

6. Adam and Eve disobeyed God and committed ____.

   a kind act   (Original Sin)

7. Jesus wants you to share ____.

   (the Good News)   sin

8. Jesus saves people from ____.

   work   (the power of sin)

Go to **aliveinchrist.osv.com** for an interactive review.

226 Chapter 16 Review

Use Catechist Quick Reviews to highlight lesson concepts.

A **Work with Words**
Have the children complete each sentence with the letter of the correct word or words from the Word Bank.

B **Check Understanding**
Have the children circle the correct answer.

Go to **aliveinchrist.osv.com** to prepare customized and downloadable assessments, send eAssessments, and assign interactive reviews.

KEY CONCEPT

The Church has Seven Sacraments. They are signs and celebrations that Jesus gave his Church. The Sacraments allow us to share in the life and work of God

DOCTRINAL CONTENT

- The Seven Sacraments are special signs and celebrations that Jesus gave his Church. (CCC, 1084)

- The Sacraments celebrate that Jesus is still with us, sharing his life and love. (CCC, 1131)

- Every Sacrament has words and actions we do and things God does that we can't see that bring us life. (CCC, 1123)

TASKS OF CATECHESIS

Helping children grow in a faith that is "known, celebrated, lived, and expressed in prayer" (NDC, 20).

This chapter focuses on the following tasks of catechesis:

- Promoting Knowledge of the Faith
- Liturgical Education

Catechist Background

 "You will realize that I am in my Father and you are in me and I in you." John 14:20

➜ **Reflect** How do you stay close to Jesus?

Jesus' words and actions lay the foundations for the Seven Sacraments of the Church. Jesus commissioned his disciples to baptize in the name of the Holy Trinity. He forgave people's sins and healed those who were sick and sent his Apostles forth to do the same. He performed his first miracle at the wedding in Cana. He instituted the Eucharist at the Last Supper. After the Resurrection, Jesus sent the Holy Spirit to the Apostles. That Spirit sustains the Church, both in the life of each member and through the ordained ministry.

In order to speak to the whole human person, the Seven Sacraments engage the senses. God uses words, actions, and material elements from the created world to celebrate the mystery of salvation and convey his grace. The celebration of the Sacraments gives glory to God. The Seven Sacraments are also for the sanctification of people. They make people holy. Sacraments are not magic. The people who receive the Sacraments must have the proper inner attitude in order for the Sacraments to be fruitful. Yet in the end all is gift. All is grace.

➜ **Reflect** How has your understanding of the Sacraments changed over time?

Catechist's Prayer

 Lord, may my words and actions be signs of the love and grace you give me. Amen.

Lesson Plan

Objectives	Process	Materials
Invite, 10 minutes		
Holy Signs Page 227	○ **Psalm 67:6** Pray the opening prayer. ○ **John 14:20** Reflect prayerfully on the Word. • Discuss What Do You Wonder questions.	◉ **Optional Activity** Chapter Story: "Many Signs"
Discover, 35 minutes		
Signs of Love Pages 228–229 • Identify the Seven Sacraments as special signs and celebrations that Jesus gave his Church	• **Catholic Faith Words** Seven Sacraments • Explain that both the Bible and Jesus tell us about God's love. ○ **John 14:18–19** Proclaim "The Advocate." ☆ Circle what Jesus said to his followers. • Explain that Jesus gave his Church the Seven Sacraments. • **Share Your Faith Activity** Name reminders of God.	☐ pencils ☐ index card
Signs and Celebrations Pages 230–231 • Appreciate that the Sacraments celebrate that Jesus is still with us, sharing his life and love • Recognize that every Sacrament has words and actions we do and things God does that we can't see that bring us life	• Explain that holy things are signs that tell us that God is here with us. • Give an overview of the Seven Sacraments. • **Connect Your Faith Activity** The children will draw a Sacrament they have seen.	☐ pencils ☐ crayons or markers • **Optional Activity** Holy Things ☐ Activity Master 17 (Page 227E)
Live, 15 minutes		
Our Catholic Life Pages 232–233	• Explain that the Church uses signs to celebrate the Seven Sacraments. ☆ Identify the signs and Sacraments seen. • **People of Faith** Learn about Mary. • **Live Your Faith Activity** Match the Sacraments with the correct symbol.	☐ pencils
Prayer of Thanks Page 234	• Select four children to carry the holy water and pictures of holy oil, a chalice, and a Host. ▶ Rehearse "The Seven Sacraments." • Follow the order of prayer.	◉ Download "The Seven Sacraments." ☐ holy water ☐ pictures of holy oil, a chalice, and a Host

Family + Faith Page 235

Point out that the Catholic Families page provides chapter highlights, information on how first graders understand faith concepts, and family prayer.

Chapter Review Page 236

◉ aliveinchrist.osv.com
• Customize and Download Assessments
• Email Links to eAssessments
• Interactive Student Reviews

ONLINE RESOURCES

 Go to **aliveinchrist.osv.com**

You will find:

- Interactive lesson planning with web specific content and additional activities
- Step by step lesson instruction from printed Catechist Edition for integrated lesson planning
- Custom-built assessments to download and eAssessment links
- Interactive reviews that provide scores and the option to review answers
- Sunday readings with background and questions of the week

 Go to **osvparish.com**

You will find:

- Ask the Experts Q and A
- General Catechist Helps
- Community Connections and Blogs

Sharing the Message with First Graders

The Seven Sacraments As visible signs of invisible, spiritual realities, the Seven Sacraments are difficult for children in first grade to understand. Still, they are such a vital part of the life of the Church that we want children to be exposed to learning about the Seven Sacraments very early. As time goes by, they will understand more fully.

Teaching Tip: Explain that a Sacrament is "something we can see that helps us understand what is happening that we cannot see." Also point out that in the Sacraments, people work together with God, with the people performing the visible sign, and God making present the invisible, spiritual reality.

How First Graders Understand

- First graders like to celebrate. Explain to them how the Seven Sacraments are celebrations.
- When teaching young children about signs and symbols be sure to use concrete examples.
- Words, actions, and holy things will be seen by young children as signs, or clues, of God's loving presence.

"Explain to me how objects and words are used as signs and symbols."

Chapter Connections

Chapter Story Invite

"Many Signs"

Use this story to enhance the chapter introduction.

- The children will relate the story to their own lives, reflecting on the signs of the current season.
- Help the children connect the signs of the seasons to understanding that a sign represents something else.

 Go to **aliveinchrist.osv.com** Lesson Planning section for this story.

NCEA IFG: ACRE Edition Discover

Knowledge of the Faith

- Objective: To know and understand basic Catholic teaching about the Incarnate Word Jesus Christ as the way, truth, and life

Liturgical Life

- Objective: To know the Paschal Mystery of Jesus: in the Church's liturgical life—feasts, seasons, symbols, and practices—and in the Sacraments as signs and instruments of grace

Catholic Social Teaching Live

 Use one of these features to introduce a principle and engage the children with an activity.

- Human Solidarity, Pages 294–295
- Care for Creation, Pages 296–297

Music Options

 Use the following song to enhance catechetical learning or for prayer.

- "The Seven Sacraments," Live Prayer, Page 234

LECTIONARY CONNECTION

 Chapter 17 highlights Lectionary-connected themes such as prayer, the Seven Sacraments, and God's love. If your parish aligns its curriculum to the liturgical year, you could use this chapter in connection with the following Sundays.

Year A

Palm Sunday of the Passion of the Lord—Paschal Mystery

Seventh Sunday of Easter—unity, holiness, Nicene Creed

Thirty-second Sunday in Ordinary Time—perseverance in prayer

Year B

Easter Sunday—Resurrection, Risen Lord

Third Sunday of Easter—Good News, Jesus Christ

Most Holy Body and Blood of Christ—Real Presence

Twenty-seventh Sunday in Ordinary Time—Matrimony

Year C

The Baptism of the Lord— forgiveness of sins

Easter Sunday—Resurrection, God's love

Twenty-eighth Sunday in Ordinary Time—prayer, thanksgiving

Go to **aliveinchrist.osv.com** for a complete correlation ordered by the Sundays of the year and suggestions for how to integrate the Scripture readings into chapter lessons.

Name _____ Date _____

Holy Things

Holy things are used in the celebration of the Seven Sacraments.
The holy things are signs that God is there.

Use the chart to color the shapes and show two holy things.

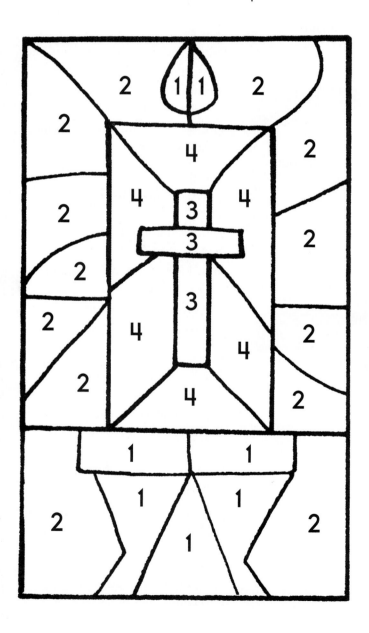

1 = yellow

2 = blue

3 = black

4 = white

Holy Signs

♡ Let Us Pray

Leader: God, we thank you for the gift of love.

"May the peoples praise you, God;
may all the peoples praise you!"
Psalm 67:6

All: God, we thank you for the gift of love.
Amen.

God's Word

"You will realize that I am in my Father and you are in me and I in you." John 14:20

© Our Sunday Visitor

? What Do You Wonder?

- How can you stay close to Jesus?
- Does Jesus know what is in your heart and in your mind?

Holy Signs **227**

Optional Activity

Chapter Story: "Many Signs" *Verbal/Linguistic*

Use this story after the opening prayer, before explaining that Jesus wants us to be close to him.

- Read the story aloud as the children follow along.
- Explain that a sign is something that represents another thing or gives clues about an event or object (as snow points to winter).
- *Ask:* What are some signs of the season you are in now?
- When finished, transition back to the lesson instruction.

 Go to **aliveinchrist.osv.com** for Chapter Story.

♡ Let Us Pray

Invite the children to gather in the prayer space and make the Sign of the Cross. Choose a child to be the leader. Read aloud the Psalm verse from a Bible. Prompt the children's response.

Have the children move out of the prayer space and back to their seats.

Explain that Jesus wants us to be closer to him.

Say: Jesus wants us to be close to him. Listen to what he tells us.

ⓔ God's Word

Guide the children through the process of Scripture reflection.

- Invite them to close their eyes, be still and open their minds and hearts to what God is saying to them in this passage.
- Proclaim the Scripture.
- Maintain several moments of silence.
- *Ask:* What did you hear God say to you today?
- Invite volunteers to share.

What Do You Wonder?

Say: Jesus loves us so much he wants our hearts to be one with his. Jesus gives us signs that we are one with him.

Invite the children to respond to the questions. Ask what else they might wonder about being close to Jesus.

Discover

Objective

• Identify the Seven Sacraments as special signs and celebrations that Jesus gave his Church

Signs of Love

Ask: How does the Church show and celebrate God's love?

• Write the children's responses on the board or on chart paper.

Read aloud the paragraph.

• Emphasize God's love for the children.

🔖 God's Word

Proclaim "The Advocate." Tell the children to listen for the promise Jesus made to his followers.

⭐ Invite the children to circle what Jesus said to his followers. Invite volunteers to share what they circled.

Point out the illustration.

• Ask the children to explain what the picture shows. a family bringing up the gifts at Mass

• Tell the children that Jesus is with us in a special way at Mass.

Signs of Love

How does the Church show and celebrate God's love?

You read about God's love in the Bible. You learn about God's love from Jesus. Jesus healed people as a sign of his Father's love.

🔖 God's Word

The Advocate

Jesus wanted to remain with his followers even when he returned to God the Father. This is what he said to them:

> "I will not leave you orphans; I will come to you. In a little while the world will no longer see me, but you will see me, because I live and you will live." *John 14:18–19*

 Circle what Jesus said to his followers.

228 Chapter 17

🔖 Scripture Background

John 14:18–19

Signs of God's love are found throughout the Bible.

• Noah saw a rainbow in the sky after the great flood as a sign of God's love (Genesis 6:11–8:22).

• God sent Jesus to show his love (Luke 2:1–20).

• The Holy Spirit came to the Apostles to guide them (Acts 2:1–12).

The Sacraments

God's love is something to celebrate. Jesus teaches that God is always with you!

The Holy Spirit fills you with God's love. When you show God's love to other people, the Holy Spirit is in you.

Jesus gave the Church special signs to help people celebrate that he is still here. These signs are called the **Seven Sacraments**.

Catholic Faith Words

Seven Sacraments special signs and celebrations that Jesus gave his Church. The Sacraments allow us to share in the life and work of God.

Share Your Faith

Think What are some pictures or items that remind you of God?

Share Share your answer with a partner.

Holy Signs **229**

(i) Catechist Background

Eucharist

In most dioceses, the Sacraments of Reconciliation and Penance and Eucharist are celebrated during a child's second grade year.

- Point out the photograph at the top of the page.
- Invite volunteers to explain what they see in the picture.
- Remind the children that the word *Eucharist* means "Thanksgiving."

The Sacraments

Read aloud all three paragraphs.

- Tell the children that Jesus is with us in special signs called the Seven Sacraments.

Work with Words

Hold up an index card with the term *Seven Sacraments* and read aloud the definition.

- Ask the children if they can name any of the Seven Sacraments. Prompt them to name especially the Sacraments of Baptism and Eucharist.
- Tell the children that they will be learning the names of the other Sacraments.

Refer to pages 304–305 in the Our Catholic Tradition reference section in the back of the Student Book for more about the Seven Sacraments.

Activity

Read aloud the directions for the Share Your Faith activity.

- Provide time for the children to talk with a partner. Afterward, invite sharing with the group.

Quick Review

Jesus gave his Church special signs and celebrations called the Seven Sacraments. The Seven Sacraments allow us to share in the life and work of God.

Objectives

- Appreciate that the Sacraments celebrate that Jesus is still with us, sharing his life and love
- Recognize that every Sacrament has words and actions we do and things God does that we can't see that bring us life

Signs and Celebrations

Ask: How is Jesus with us today?

- Write the children's responses on the board or on chart paper.

Explain that things that you can see, hear, touch, smell, and taste are used to celebrate the Sacraments.

- Share that these holy things are signs that tell us that God—the Father, the Son, and the Holy Spirit—is there with us.
- Point out that the Church has Seven Sacraments.
- Emphasize that Jesus gave us the Sacraments so that we can always know his love and care.

Signs and Celebrations

How is Jesus with us today?

Jesus gives us Sacraments so that we can always know his love and care.

The Sacraments are special signs and celebrations. Every Sacrament has words and actions we do and things God does that we can't see. When we celebrate the Seven Sacraments, Jesus is with us. The Holy Spirit makes him present to us.

© Our Sunday Visitor

230 Chapter 17

Optional Activity

Activity Master 17: Holy Things

Distribute copies of the activity found on catechist page 227E.

- Read the directions aloud. Explain how to color by number.
- As an alternative, you may wish to send this activity home with the children.

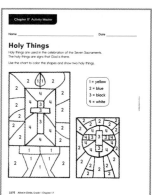

Sacraments of Initiation

- Baptism
- Confirmation
- Eucharist

Sacraments of Healing

- Penance and Reconciliation
- Anointing of the Sick

Sacraments at the Service of Communion

- Matrimony
- Holy Orders

Connect Your Faith

Draw a Sacrament Draw a Sacrament you have taken part in or have seen.

231

Catechist Background

The Seven Sacraments

The Catholic Church has Seven Sacraments: Baptism, Confirmation, Eucharist, Reconciliation and Penance, Anointing of the Sick, Matrimony, and Holy Orders.

- Each of the Seven Sacraments includes words, actions, and material elements.
- If received with the proper disposition, each of the Sacraments imparts God's grace to the recipient.

Signs and Celebrations,

continued

Point out the three boxes.

- Explain that each of the Seven Sacraments falls into one of three categories.
- The Sacraments of Initiation are Baptism, Confirmation, and Eucharist. These three Sacraments celebrate membership into the Catholic Church.
- The Sacraments of Healing are Reconciliation and Penance, and Anointing of the Sick. These Sacraments celebrate God's forgiveness and healing.
- The Sacraments at the Service of Communion celebrate people's commitment to serve God and the community.
- Have the children circle the Sacraments that they have seen.

Point out the Connect Your Faith Activity and read aloud the directions.

- Remind the children that they have circled the Sacraments they have seen above.
- Have them choose one that they have circled and draw it.
- Invite volunteers to share their drawings.

Quick Review

The Catholic Church has Seven Sacraments. The Sacraments help us celebrate that Jesus is with us.

Our Catholic Life

Ask: What signs are used to celebrate the Seven Sacraments?

- Write the children's responses on the board or on chart paper.

Invite the children to name the Sacraments with which they are familiar.

Draw attention to the chart, and read aloud the introduction.

- Invite the children to follow along as you read through the chart.
- Read aloud the names of the Sacraments, and invite the children to respond by reading aloud the names of the signs and what they stand for.

☆ Have the children place a check mark next to the Sacraments and signs they have seen.

- If time permits, invite the children to tell about their experiences.

Live

Our Catholic Life

What signs are used to celebrate the Seven Sacraments?

The Church celebrates Seven Sacraments. Each Sacrament uses words and signs that show God's love.

Place a check mark next to the Sacraments and signs you have seen.

Sacraments		Signs	
☐ Baptism		Water	God gives new life in Jesus.
☐ Confirmation		Holy Oil (Chrism)	The gifts of the Holy Spirit are given.
☐ Eucharist		Bread and Wine	The Body and Blood of Christ are present.
☐ Penance and Reconciliation		Outstretched Hand	God forgives those who are sorry.
☐ Anointing of the Sick		Holy Oil of the Sick	God helps heal our bodies and spirits.
☐ Matrimony		Wedding Rings	God blesses the love of a man and woman.
☐ Holy Orders		Holy Oil (Chrism)	God calls men to lead and serve the Church.

© Our Sunday Visitor

232 Chapter 17

✓ Quick Tip

Visit the Church

If possible, have the group visit the parish church to examine signs of the Sacraments.

- Arrange for a priest, deacon, or sacristan to show the children examples of the vessels used for the Sacraments.
- Tour the baptistery and Reconciliation room.

People of Faith

Mary, first century

Mary is the Mother of Jesus. She is the greatest of all Saints. One day an angel gave Mary a message: "You will have a son named Jesus." Mary was confused. She asked, "How can this be done?" The angel said, "The Holy Spirit will come upon you. Your son will be the Son of God." The Holy Spirit was with Mary. The Spirit is with us, too, in the Sacraments.

January 1

Discuss: What Sacraments have you received?

 Learn more about Mary at **aliveinchrist.osv.com**

Live Your Faith

Match the Signs Match the Sacraments on the left with the correct symbols on the right.

Baptism

Eucharist

Penance and Reconciliation

Matrimony

Catholic Social Teaching

Chapter Connections

To integrate Catholic Social Teaching into your lesson, choose one of the following features: Human Solidarity, pages 294–295; or Care for Creation, pages 296–297.

- Start the Live step of the process by talking about Mary on page 233. Then move directly to the Catholic Social Teaching feature.

- Or, to expand the lesson, complete both pages 232 and 233, then move to the Catholic Social Teaching feature.

- Return to Chapter 17 for the prayer on page 234.

People of Faith

Tell the children about Mary.

- Invite a volunteer to read aloud the People of Faith story.

- Explain that Mary, the Mother of Jesus, has a special place in the life of the Church.

- The Church honors her through special prayers, such as the Rosary, and through images, titles and feast days, and other prayers.

- Mary is honored because she is the Mother of Jesus and the perfect model of holiness.

- *Ask:* What Sacraments have you received?

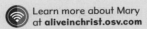 Encourage the children to go to **aliveinchrist.osv.com** at home to learn more about Mary.

Activity

Read aloud the directions for the Live Your Faith activity.

- If necessary review the pictures with the group so they understand what each one is.

- Allow time for the children to work independently on the matching activity.

- Review responses by arranging the group into two smaller groups. Have one group read aloud the names of the Sacraments, and have the other group respond by describing the appropriate signs.

Let Us Pray

Prayer of Thanks

Tell the children that in today's prayer, they will give thanks to Jesus for the Sacraments.

Prepare

Show the children the holy water, and pictures of holy oil, a chalice, and Host.

- Choose four children to carry the holy water and the pictures.
- Teach the children their response.

 Rehearse "The Seven Sacraments," downloaded from **aliveinchrist.osv.com**.

Gather

Arrange the children in a line at the opposite side of the room from the prayer space.

- Place the four children carrying the items in front of the line. Have all the children process to the prayer space.
- Invite the children to be seated and settle themselves for prayer.

Pray

Follow the order of prayer on the student page.

- Hold up each item as you say it in the prayer.

 Conclude by singing together "The Seven Sacraments."

 Let Us Pray

Prayer of Thanks

Gather and begin with the Sign of the Cross.

Leader: For Baptism's life-giving water,

All: Thank you, Jesus.

Leader: For holy oil that blesses,

All: Thank you, Jesus.

Leader: For the gift of your life in the Eucharist,

All: Thank you, Jesus.

 Sing "The Seven Sacraments"

The Sacraments,
the Seven Sacraments.
Signs that come from Jesus
and give us grace.
The Sacraments,
the Seven Sacraments.
Signs that God is with us
in a special way.
© 2008, John Burland. All rights reserved.

234 Chapter 17

 Liturgy Link

Holy Objects

Contact the parish to obtain holy water. Obtain pictures of holy oil, a chalice, and a Host.

- Teach the children to handle the objects respectfully.
- Explain that the water has been blessed, and is called holy water.
- Show the children each picture and share with them the names of each item.

Go to **aliveinchrist.osv.com** for Sunday readings, Scripture background, questions of the week, and seasonal resources.

FAMILY+FAITH
LIVING AND LEARNING TOGETHER

YOUR CHILD LEARNED >>>

This chapter identifies the Seven Sacraments as special signs and celebrations that Jesus gave his Church.

God's Word

 Read **John 14:20** to learn what Jesus says about being one with him and God the Father.

Catholics Believe

- The Church has Seven Sacraments. They are signs and celebrations that Jesus gave his Church.
- The Sacraments allow us to share in the life and work of God.

To learn more, go to the *Catechism of the Catholic Church* #1131–1134 at **usccb.org**.

People of Faith

This week, your child met Mary and learned a little about the Annunciation. Mary trusted the Holy Spirit, even when she didn't fully understand.

CHILDREN AT THIS AGE >>>

How They Understand the Sacraments As visible signs of invisible, spiritual realities, the Seven Sacraments are difficult for children in first grade to understand. Still, they are such a vital part of the life of the Church that we want children to be exposed to learning about the Sacraments very early. As time goes by, your child will understand more fully. In the meantime, you can explain that a Sacrament is something we can see that helps us understand something that we can't see. The people performing the visible sign and the community gathered work together with God making present the invisible, spiritual reality.

CONSIDER THIS >>>

What are some signs you recognize when your child is sick?

Is it flushed ears, or watery eyes? Or perhaps it is when he or she just wants to be held? We see these signs as indicators of something more. In the Seven Sacraments, we see signs that indicate something more—God's love and presence. "As we come to understand the Sacraments, it is important to recognize that the Sacraments have a visible and invisible reality, a reality open to all the human senses but grasped in its God-given depths with the eyes of faith" (USCCA, p.168).

LET'S TALK >>>

- At Mass, ask your child to point out some objects or actions that help people celebrate the Sacraments.
- Get out pictures from family Baptisms, First Communions, or weddings. Talk about the Sacraments that were celebrated on those days.

LET'S PRAY >>>

Holy Mary, Mother of God, pray for us now and always. Amen.

For a multimedia glossary of Catholic Faith Words; Sunday readings, seasonal and Saint resources, and chapter activities go to **aliveinchrist.osv.com**.

Alive in Christ, Grade 1 Chapter 17 **235**

© Our Sunday Visitor

Chapter 17 Review

A **Work with Words** Complete each sentence with the letter of the correct word or words from the Word Bank.

Word Bank
a. water
b. Seven
c. love

1. A sign of Baptism is **a** .

2. Sacraments are signs of God's **c** .

3. The Catholic Church has **b** Sacraments.

B **Check Understanding** Fill in the circle beside the correct answer.

4. What special signs and actions did Jesus give us?

○ Commandments   ● Sacraments

5. What do all Sacraments have?

○ bread   ● words and actions

6. What did Jesus do for people?

○ hurt them   ● healed them

7. What are the Sacraments?

● celebrations   ○ stories

8. What Sacrament has the Body and Blood of Christ?

● Eucharist   ○ Baptism

© Our Sunday Visitor

 Go to **aliveinchrist.osv.com** for an interactive review.

236 Chapter 17 Review

Family + Faith

Distribute the page to the children or parents/adult family members. Point out the chapter highlights, insights on how first graders understand concepts, the opportunity for the adults to reflect on their own experience and faith journey, and the family prayer.

Chapter Review

Use Catechist Quick Reviews to highlight lesson concepts.

A **Work with Words**
Have the children complete each sentence with the letter of the word from the Word Bank.

B **Check Understanding**
Have the children fill in the circle beside the correct answer.

 Go to **aliveinchrist.osv.com** to prepare customized and downloadable assessments, send eAssessments, and assign interactive reviews.

Holy Signs   **235–236**

KEY CONCEPT

Grace is God's gift of a share in his life and help. Baptism is the Sacrament in which a person is immersed in water or has water poured on him or her. Baptism brings new life in God and makes the person a member of the Church.

DOCTRINAL CONTENT

- Baptism is the Sacrament that brings new life in God and makes the person a member of the Church. (CCC, 1213)

- Grace is God's gift of sharing in his life and help. (CCC, 1996)

- In Baptism, a person is immersed, or has water poured over him or her in the name of the Father, Son, and Holy Spirit. (CCC, 1239)

- The baptized person is anointed, receives a white garment and is given the light of Christ. (CCC, 1241)

TASKS OF CATECHESIS

Helping children grow in a faith that is "known, celebrated, lived, and expressed in prayer" (NDC, 20).

This chapter focuses on the following tasks of catechesis:

- Promoting Knowledge of the Faith

- Liturgical Education

Catechist Background

 "Go into the whole world and proclaim the gospel to every creature. Whoever believes and is baptized will be saved."
Mark 16:15–16

→ **Reflect** How has being baptized made a difference in your life?

Recall and reflect upon the birth of a new member of the family. How did your family prepare for the arrival of this wonderful gift from God? What did you do to share that good news?

Like a family, the Church welcomes new members with open arms and hearts. You became a member of the Church through the Sacrament of Baptism. Baptism is more than a rite that confers membership. Through Baptism, a person is incorporated into Christ's Death and burial, and is born into a new life by the power of Christ's Resurrection. Through Baptism, a person is freed from sin and given entry into the new life of grace which Christ opened up for his followers.

You have probably faced difficult events in your personal existence such as the unexpected death of a loved one or the loss of a job. Such events can be devastating. These opportunities also hold out new opportunities for spiritual growth. At these times, you can find comfort in God's love and in the support of the Church community.

→ **Reflect** When have you most appreciated your faith community?

Catechist's Prayer

 Loving God, help me create a close, generous relationship with these children. Bless me with abundant energy. Amen.

Lesson Plan

Objectives	Process	Materials

Invite, 10 minutes

We Are Welcomed Page 237

- ♥ Psalm 104:10 Pray the opening prayer.
- Mark 16:15–16 Reflect prayerfully on the Word.
- Discuss What Do You Wonder questions.

Optional Activity
Chapter Poem:
"The Growing Table"

Discover, 35 minutes

Welcome! Pages 238–239

- Identify Baptism as the Sacrament that brings new life in God and makes the person a member of the Church
- Name grace as God's gift of sharing in his life and help

- **Catholic Faith Words** Baptism, grace
- Explain that Baptism makes a person a member of the Church.
- Acts 8:4–12 Proclaim "People Everywhere Believe."
- Share how Baptism helps people to do Jesus' work.
- **Share Your Faith Activity** Name one way to tell others about Jesus.

☐ pencils
☐ index cards
☐ pitcher of water
☐ bowl

Becoming Church Members
Pages 240–241

- Examine the signs and symbols of Baptism

- **Catholic Faith Words** godparents
- Explain what happens in Baptism.
- Explain that godparents are a sign of God's love.
- **Connect Your Faith Activity** Match the words with the pictures.

☐ pencils
☐ index cards
• **Optional Activity**
God Is There
☐ Activity Master 17 (Page 237E)

Live, 15 minutes

Our Catholic Life Pages 242–243

- Explain that with Baptism comes a call from God to be a sign of his life and love.
- ✩ Identify how to be a sign of God's life and love.
- **People of Faith** Learn about Saint Moses the Black.
- **Live Your Faith Activity** Create a frame for a picture of Baptism.

☐ pencils
☐ crayons or markers
☐ tape or glue
☐ art supplies

Blessing Prayer Page 244

- Introduce the practice of bowing.
- ▶ Rehearse "Yes, Lord, I Believe."
- Follow the order of prayer.

Download "Yes, Lord, I Believe."

Family + Faith Page 245

Point out that the Catholic Families page provides chapter highlights, information on how first graders understand faith concepts, and family prayer.

Chapter Review Page 246
aliveinchrist.osv.com
- Customize and Download Assessments
- Email Links to eAssessments
- Interactive Student Reviews

ONLINE RESOURCES

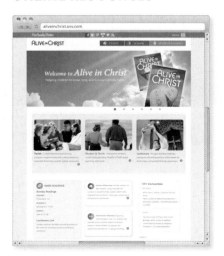

 Go to **aliveinchrist.osv.com**

You will find:

- Interactive lesson planning with web specific content and additional activities
- Step by step lesson instruction from printed Catechist Edition for integrated lesson planning
- Custom-built assessments to download and eAssessment links
- Interactive reviews that provide scores and the option to review answers
- Sunday readings with background and questions of the week

 Go to **osvparish.com**

You will find:

- Ask the Experts Q and A
- General Catechist Helps
- Community Connections and Blogs

Sharing the Message with First Graders

The Sacrament of Baptism First grade children are very curious about baptisms. There is always excitement when children this age are permitted to come near the baptismal font as someone is being baptized. They are intrigued by the pouring of the water, but are also able to understand, through the ritual actions and words of the rite, that something deeper is occurring, even if they are not yet quite ready to understand the sacramental meaning of Baptism.

Teaching Tip: Help children understand that blessing ourselves with holy water is a form of renewing our baptismal vows. Stop by the font to do this each time you enter the church with the children.

How First Graders Understand

- First graders like being part of a group. Explain to them what it means to be part of the Church.
- Young children learn by example. Show them what it means to be a good Catholic.
- Make the lesson about Baptism visual. Ask someone from the parish staff to help you show the children holy water, Sacred Chrism, the Oil of Catechumens, a baptismal candle, and a white baptismal garment—the signs used at a Baptism.

"Help me find a way to thank my family for bringing me to Baptism."

Chapter Connections

Chapter Poem

Invite

"The Growing Table"

Use this poem to expand the chapter introduction.

- The children will relate the poem to their own lives, reflecting on the how their family welcomes visitors.
- Connect welcoming visitors to the virtue of welcoming others.

 Go to **aliveinchrist.osv.com** Lesson Planning section for this poem.

NCEA IFG: ACRE Edition

Discover

Knowledge of the Faith

- Objective: To know and understand basic Catholic teaching about the Incarnate Word Jesus Christ as the way, truth, and life

Liturgical Life

- Objective: To know the Paschal Mystery of Jesus: in the Church's liturgical life—feasts, seasons, symbols, and practices—and in the Sacraments as signs and instruments of grace

Catholic Social Teaching

Live

 Use one of these features to introduce a principle and engage the children with an activity.

- Rights and Responsibilities, Pages 288–289
- Human Solidarity, Pages 294–295

Music Options

 Use one or more of the following songs to enhance catechetical learning or for prayer.

- "Yes, Lord, I Believe," Live Prayer, Page 244
- "Belonging Through Baptism," Discover, Page 238
- "We Welcome You into Our Church," Discover, Page 238
- "Share the Light," Live, Page 240
- "Gloria," Live Prayer, Page 244
- "Glory Be to the Father," Live Prayer, Page 244

LECTIONARY CONNECTION

 Chapter 18 highlights Lectionary-connected themes such as grace, Sacraments, and Baptism. If your parish aligns its curriculum to the liturgical year, you could use this chapter in connection with the following readings.

Year A

The Baptism of the Lord—Baptism and mission

Easter Sunday—Risen Lord, new life

Year B

Fourth Sunday of Lent—grace

Fifth Sunday of Lent—prayer

The Ascension of the Lord—Holy Spirit, Sacraments

Our Lord Jesus Christ, King of the Universe—Kingdom of God

Year C

Third Sunday of Advent—Cardinal Virtues

The Baptism of the Lord—Baptism, forgiveness of sins

Go to **aliveinchrist.osv.com** for a complete correlation ordered by the Sundays of the year and suggestions for how to integrate the Scripture readings into chapter lessons.

Name _____ Date _____

God Is There

Write the sentence number under the picture it tells about.

1. Your family brings you to church to be baptized.

2. The priest pours holy water on your head three times.

3. After the Baptism, the priest or deacon makes the Sign of the Cross on your head with holy oil.

4. You are given a white garment.

5. A candle is lit.

We Are Welcomed

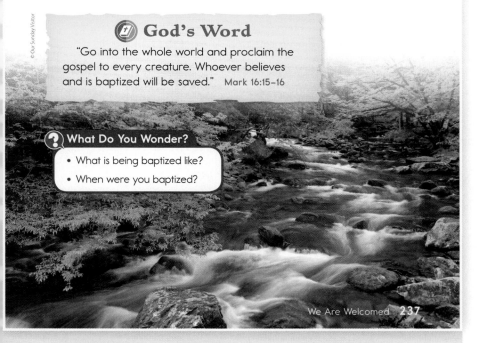

♡ Let Us Pray

Leader: God, You have given us water to refresh us.

You made springs flow in valleys that wind among the mountains.
Based on Psalm 104:10

All: Thank you, God, for living water that gives us life. Amen.

God's Word

"Go into the whole world and proclaim the gospel to every creature. Whoever believes and is baptized will be saved." Mark 16:15–16

❓ What Do You Wonder?

• What is being baptized like?
• When were you baptized?

We Are Welcomed **237**

Optional Activity

Chapter Poem: "The Growing Table" *Verbal/Linguistic*

Use this poem after the opening prayer, before explaining that water is an important sign of life.

• Read the poem aloud as the children follow along.
• *Ask:* How could the Ming family welcome the people?
• *Ask:* How does your family welcome visitors?
• After telling the children that welcoming others is important, transition back to the lesson instruction.

 Go to **aliveinchrist.osv.com** for Chapter Poem.

♡ Let Us Pray

Invite the children to gather in the prayer space and make the Sign of the Cross. Choose a child to be the leader. Read aloud the Psalm verse from a Bible. Prompt the children's response.

Have the children move out of the prayer space and back to their seats.

Explain that water is an important sign of life.

Say: Everything needs water to live. Baptism uses water as a sign of our new life. Listen to a reading from the Gospel of Mark that tells us more about Baptism.

God's Word

Guide the children through the process of Scripture reflection.

• Invite them to close their eyes, be still and open their minds and hearts to what God is saying to them in this passage.
• Proclaim the Scripture.
• Maintain several moments of silence.
• *Ask:* What did you hear God say to you today?
• Invite volunteers to share.

What Do You Wonder?

Say: Baptism is the Sacrament that gives us new life in Christ.

Invite the children to respond to the questions. Ask what else they might wonder about Baptism or their own Baptism.

© Our Sunday Visitor

Objectives

- Identify Baptism as the Sacrament that brings new life in God and makes the person a member of the Church
- Name grace as God's gift of sharing in his life and help

Welcome!

Ask: What Sacrament welcomes you into the Church?

- Write the children's responses on the board or on chart paper.

Work with Words

Use index cards to introduce the words *Baptism* and *grace.*

Tell the children that at Baptism holy water is poured on a person's head.

- Ask a child to pour a small amount of water from a pitcher into a bowl. Explain that Baptism is a welcoming celebration.
- Have a second child pour more water. Tell the children that through Baptism a person becomes a member of God's family, the Church.
- Have a third child pour more water. Explain that in Baptism we become children of God.
- *Ask:* How do you welcome people into your home or classroom?

 Music Option: Have the children sing, "Belonging Through Baptism" or "We Welcome You Into Our Church," downloaded from **aliveinchrist.osv.com**.

Discover

Welcome!

What Sacrament welcomes you into the Church?

Baptism makes you a child of God and member of the Church. It is your welcome into the Church. God chooses you to be in the Church family.

With Baptism, the Holy Spirit comes. God makes you his own child. You receive a share in his life. God's life and love in you is called **grace**.

After Jesus went back to his Father in Heaven, the followers of Jesus welcomed everyone to be part of the Church.

238 Chapter 18

Reaching All Learners

Up-Close Learning

Some children may never have seen a celebration of the Sacrament of Baptism.

- In order to give them a better understanding of what happens at a Baptism, make arrangements to teach the entire lesson in church, near the baptismal font.
- Bring in pictures or show a video of a family member's Baptism. Share with the children stories about the special day.

God's Word

People Everywhere Believe

Philip traveled to different towns to tell others the Good News about Jesus. He shared Jesus' message and his love. In the name of Jesus, he even healed people who were sick. Many people began to believe in Jesus and were baptized.   Based on Acts 8:4–12

People who are baptized and who follow Jesus are called Christians. Baptism helps you do Jesus' work.

You can be kind to others and obey your parents. You can tell others about Jesus and his love. You can show others you care by sharing.

➡ **What are other ways children can do Jesus' work?**

 ## Catholic Faith Words

Baptism the Sacrament in which a person is immersed in water or has water poured on him or her. Baptism takes away Original Sin and all personal sin, and makes a person a child of God and member of the Church.

grace God's gift of a share in his life and help

Share Your Faith

Think Write one way you can tell others about Jesus.

I, promise to

_____

– –

_____ .

Share As a group, make a list of different ways to tell others about Jesus.

We Are Welcomed   **239**

 ## Songs of Scripture

Have You Ever Seen a Mustard Seed?

This song teaches that God's Kingdom grows through our hearts and through our hands. Draw a large heart on chart paper.

- Ask each child to name a way to help our love for God to grow, such as praying or going to Mass. As they name one thing have them write their names in the heart.

- Teach "Have You Ever Seen a Mustard Seed?"

 Use *Songs of Scripture*, Grades 1–3 CD, Track 9

Welcome!, *continued*

Tell the children that they are going to hear a Bible story about Baptism.

 ## God's Word

Proclaim "People Everywhere Believe."

- Explain that after Jesus died, he sent his Apostles out into the world to share the Good News and baptize people.

Read aloud the two paragraphs.

- Point out the word *Christians* and explain that Christians are followers of Jesus.

Invite a volunteer to pour the remaining water from the pitcher into the bowl. Tell the children that the Holy Spirit comes to the person at Baptism and gives him or her the strength to do Jesus' work.

Activity

Read aloud the directions.

- Have the children work independently to write their ideas.

- After a short time, work with the group to compile a list of ideas.

Quick Review

In Baptism a person is cleansed of Original Sin and any personal sin, welcomed into the Church, becomes God's child, and receives grace to lead a holy life. God's life and love, communicated to people, is called grace.

Objective

- Examine the signs and symbols of Baptism

Becoming Church Members

Ask: What happens in Baptism?

- Write the children's responses on the board or on chart paper.

Invite the children to look at the pictures on this page as you read the captions.

- Ask the children which person is the one receiving Baptism. the baby

- Ask them to tell who else is shown in the photos. the baby's parents, godparents, and a priest

- Ask the children what objects are used in celebrating Baptism. holy water, a candle, a white garment, Sacred Chrism, the Oil of Catechumens

- Explain that the container of water in which people are baptized is called a font.

Tell the children that you will show the actions and say the words that are most important in Baptism.

- Refill the pitcher of water. Using the bowl, pour the water three times, once for each mention of the Holy Trinity.

- Have the children say the words with you as you pour the water.

Becoming Church Members

What happens in Baptism?

1 Holy Water is poured over you three times while these words are prayed: "[Your name], I baptize you in the name of the Father, and of the Son, and of the Holy Spirit" (**Rite of Baptism**).

2 The priest then says that you will remain a member of Christ forever and uses Sacred Chrism to make a cross on your head. This gesture is a sign that you are chosen by God to be a member of the Church.

© Our Sunday Visitor

3 You receive a white garment. It is a sign of your new life in Christ and your membership in the Church.

4 Your parents or godparents are given a lit candle. Light is a sign of Jesus. Jesus asks you to be like a light and show his love to others.

240 Chapter 18

 Catechist Background

Light of the World

From Genesis 1:3, when God said, "Let there be light," to Revelation 22:5, which states, "Night shall be no more, nor will they need light from lamp or sun, for the Lord God shall give them light," the Bible contains hundreds of references to light. In addition:

- Jesus is called the Light of the World.

- We are light for others when we bring Jesus' message to those in need.

Your parents and **godparents** are also signs of God's love. They promise that they will help you live as a child of God. The whole community will help you follow Jesus. They will be examples to you and will help you learn about the Church.

© Our Sunday Visitor

Catholic Faith Words

godparents two people chosen by your parents to help you follow Jesus. They are usually present at your Baptism.

Connect Your Faith

Match Game Draw lines to match the words and the pictures.

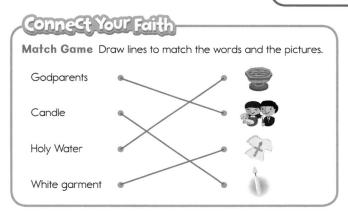

Godparents

Candle

Holy Water

White garment

We Are Welcomed **241**

Becoming Church Members, *continued*

Read aloud the paragraph.

- Emphasize that both our parents and our godparents promise to help us live as children of God.
- Explain that the entire parish promises to help us live as followers of Jesus.

Work with Words

Hold up an index card with the word *godparents* to introduce the new word.

- Suggest that when they go home, the children ask their families to tell them about their godparents.

Activity

Point out the Connect Your Faith activity and read aloud the directions for the matching game.

- Answer any questions the children may have.
- Give them time to complete the activity.

Optional Activity

Activity Master 18: God Is There

Distribute copies of the activity found on catechist page 237E.

- Tell the children to number the pictures to check their understanding of Baptism.
- As an alternative, you may wish to send this activity home with the children.

Quick Review

A priest or deacon baptizes a person by pouring holy water on his or her head while saying: "I baptize you in the name of the Father, and of the Son, and of the Holy Spirit." A candle, a white garment, the Oil of Catechumens, and Sacred Chrism are also used in the Sacrament of Baptism.

Our Catholic Life

Ask: How does your Baptism help you follow Jesus?

- Write the children's responses on the board or on chart paper.

Ask the children to listen carefully as you read aloud the first sentence.

- Read the next sentence and draw attention to the chart.

Ways to Answer God's Call

Have the children follow along as you read aloud each item.

- Explain that the boxes list ways to answer the call of Baptism.
- Organize the children into four groups, and have each group read aloud one of the boxes.
- ☆ Have the children check the things they can do this week to be a sign of God's life and love.
- *Ask:* What are some other ways you can be a sign of God's life and love?

Live

Our Catholic Life

How does your Baptism help you follow Jesus?

With Baptism, God called you to be a sign of his life and love. Here are some things God calls you to do.

Check off the things you can do this week to be a sign of God's life and love.

Ways to Answer God's Call

Show You Believe

Show that you believe in God the Father, God the Son, and God the Holy Spirit.

☐ Pray every day.

☐ Make the Sign of the Cross.

Be Like a Light

Be a light and share your goodness.

☐ Welcome everyone.

☐ Be a good example for younger children.

Live a New Life

Live a new life in the Church.

☐ Go to church with your family.

☐ Give up bad habits that lead to sin.

Love and Serve

Love and serve God.

☐ Do your chores cheerfully.

☐ Share what you have.

© Our Sunday Visitor

242 Chapter 18

Optional Activity

Renew Baptismal Promises

Have the children bless themselves by making the Sign of the Cross with holy water as a reminder of their baptismal commitment.

- Use a bowl of holy water on the prayer table, or gather the children around the holy water container or baptismal font in the parish church.
- Review and pray the Sign of the Cross.

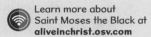

People of Faith

Saint Moses the Black, fourth century

Saint Moses was a robber when he was a young man. Many people were frightened of him because he was very tall and very mean and he became unhappy with his life. A monk told Moses about God and God's love for him. Moses was baptized and learned to love Jesus. Later he became a priest. He taught others about God's love and encouraged them to be baptized.

August 28

Discuss: Have you been at a Baptism? What did you see?

Learn more about Saint Moses the Black at **aliveinchrist.osv.com**

Live Your Faith

Baptism Memories Color the frame and the words. In the frame, draw or glue a picture of your Baptism.

I AM A CHILD OF GOD

We Are Welcomed **243**

🌐 Catholic Social Teaching

Chapter Connections

To integrate Catholic Social Teaching into your lesson, choose one of the following features: Rights and Responsibilities, pages 288–289; or Human Solidarity, pages 294–295.

- Start the Live step of the process by talking about Saint Moses the Black on page 243. Then move directly to the Catholic Social Teaching feature.
- Or, to expand the lesson, complete both pages 242 and 243, then move to the Catholic Social Teaching feature.
- Return to Chapter 18 for the prayer on page 244.

People of Faith

Tell the children about Saint Moses the Black.

- Invite a volunteer to read aloud the People of Faith story.
- Sometimes Saint Moses the Black's way of seeing things seemed odd to his fellow monks. One time when the abbot ordered the brothers to fast, some of the brothers came to Saint Moses before the fast was over. He prepared a meal for them. Instead of being punished for breaking the fast, the monks agreed that Moses had kept the commandment of hospitality instead.
- *Ask:* Have you been at a Baptism? What did you see?

 Encourage the children to go to **aliveinchrist.osv.com** at home to learn more about Saint Moses the Black.

Activity

Read aloud the directions for the Live Your Faith activity.

- Provide art materials, and have the children decorate their frames.
- Allow time for the children to draw pictures of their Baptism.
- The children may also take their empty frames home and invite family members' help in inserting baptismal photos.

Let Us Pray

Blessing Prayer

Introduce bowing as a prayerful action.

Prepare

Practice the prayer, bowing at the word *Glory* and remaining bowed through the words *the Holy Spirit*.

- Teach the children their response.
- Show the children the Glory Be prayer on page 316 in the Our Catholic Tradition reference section in the back of the Student Book.

 Rehearse "Yes, Lord, I Believe," downloaded from **aliveinchrist.osv.com**.

Gather

Invite the children to process to the prayer space.

- Have the children remain standing with enough space between them to allow them to bow.

Pray

Follow the order of prayer on the student page.

 Conclude by singing together "Yes, Lord, I Believe."

Alternate Music Options: "Gloria" or "Glory Be to the Father"

 Let Us Pray

Blessing Prayer

Gather and begin with the Sign of the Cross.

Leader: Glory be to the Father, and to the Son, and to the Holy Spirit:

All: as it was in the beginning, is now, and ever shall be, world without end. Amen.

Leader: Today we celebrate the gift of our Baptism. And so we remember that day by saying what we believe:

All: Sing "Yes, Lord, I Believe"

I believe in God the Father,
I believe in God the Son,
I believe in the Holy Spirit,
And the strength that makes us one.
I believe that Mother Mary
Is the Mother of God's Son.
I believe, I do believe.

© 2009, John Burland. All rights reserved.

 Liturgy Link

Bowing

Bowing is an act of respect that many religions use in their worship.

- You can bow with the head (a reverent nod) or with the whole body (from the waist).
- Catholics often bow to show reverence when they say the "Glory Be" doxology used in Mass and when they pass in front of the altar in church.

Go to **aliveinchrist.osv.com** for Sunday readings, Scripture background, questions of the week, and seasonal resources.

FAMILY+FAITH
LIVING AND LEARNING TOGETHER

YOUR CHILD LEARNED >>>
This chapter examines the signs and symbols of Baptism and explains that baptized people are children of God and members of the Church.

God's Word
Read **Mark 16:15–16** to learn about who is saved by Jesus Christ.

Catholics Believe
- Grace is God's gift of a share in his life and help.
- Baptism is the Sacrament in which a person is immersed in water or has water poured on him or her. Baptism brings new life in God and makes the person a member of the Church.

To learn more, go to the *Catechism of the Catholic Church* #1277–1282 at **usccb.org**.

People of Faith
This week, your child met Saint Moses the Black, a former robber in what is now Egypt, who became a dedicated monk and priest.

CHILDREN AT THIS AGE >>>
How They Understand Baptism First-grade children are very curious about Baptisms. There is always excitement when children this age are permitted to come near the baptismal font as someone is being baptized. They are intrigued by the pouring of the water. They are also able to understand that through the ritual actions and words of the rite, something deeper is occurring. Talk about your memories of your child's Baptism, and show him or her photos from that special day.

CONSIDER THIS >>>
How true is it for you that when you married your spouse you married his/her family?

One of the great joys and challenges of the first year of marriage is realizing that you are part of an entire "other" family. You married one person, but got a whole family. In Baptism, when we enter into divine life, by becoming one with Christ, we also got a whole family—the Church. "A person is initiated into God's people not by physical birth, but by a spiritual birth through faith in Christ and Baptism" (USCCA, p. 116).

LET'S TALK >>>
- Ask your child to name some ways he or she welcomes people at home.
- Talk about some ways God has called you and name some things you've done to answer God's call.

LET'S PRAY >>>
Dear Jesus, thank you for making us a part of your family through Baptism. Amen.

For a multimedia glossary of Catholic Faith Words, Sunday readings, seasonal and Saint resources, and chapter activities go to **aliveinchrist.osv.com**.

Family + Faith

Distribute the page to the children or parents/adult family members. Point out the chapter highlights, insights on how first graders understand concepts, the opportunity for the adults to reflect on their own experience and faith journey, and the family prayer.

Chapter 18 Review

A Work with Words Circle the correct answer.

1. ____ makes a person a child of God and member of the Church.

Working   (**Baptism**)

2. People who follow Jesus are called ____.

(**Christians**)   family

3. Sharing in God's life and help is called ____.

creation   (**grace**)

B Check Understanding Number the steps of Baptism in order from 1–4.

4. **4** You receive a lit candle.

2 Your head is marked with Sacred Chrism.

1 Water is poured over you three times.

3 You are given a white garment.

Go to **aliveinchrist.osv.com** for an interactive review.

Chapter Review

Use Catechist Quick Reviews to highlight lesson concepts.

A Work with Words Have the children circle the correct answer.

B Check Understanding Have the children number the steps of Baptism in order from 1–4.

Go to **aliveinchrist.osv.com** to prepare customized and downloadable assessments, send eAssessments, and assign interactive reviews.

We Are Welcomed **245–246**

Use Catechist Quick Reviews in each
chapter to highlight lesson concepts
for this unit and prepare for the
Unit Review.

Have the children complete the
Review pages. Then discuss the
answers as a group. Review any
concepts with which the children
are having difficulty.

A **Work with Words**

Have the children complete
each sentence with the
letter of the correct word or
words from the Word Bank.

A **Work with Words** Complete each sentence
with the letter of the correct word or words
from the Word Bank.

Word Bank

a. Grace

b. Savior

c. Jesus

d. Baptism

e. Sacraments

1. The Resurrection is the name for

c being raised from death to

new life.

2. Jesus is the b .

3. e are special signs and celebrations

that Jesus gave his Church.

4. d takes away sin and makes you a member

of the Church.

5. a is a sharing in God's life and help.

© Our Sunday Visitor

Sacraments **247**

B **Check Understanding** Circle the word or words that answers the question.

6. Who did God send to save people?

Mary   Mass   (Jesus)

7. Why does Jesus give us Sacraments?

(To show love)   To tell stories   To buy things

8. What does Baptism call you to be?

Good at sports   Tall   (A sign of love)

C **Make Connections** Trace the words that mean a sign of God's love.

9.

Draw a sign for the Sacraments listed below.

10. Baptism

11. Eucharist

12. Matrimony

B **Check Understanding**
Have the children circle the word or words that answer the question.

C **Make Connections**
Have the children trace the letters to name a sign of God's love.

10–12. Have the children draw the sign for each Sacrament listed.

Go to **aliveinchrist.osv.com** to prepare customized and downloadable assessments, send eAssessments, and assign interactive reviews.

Kingdom of God

Our Catholic Tradition

- Jesus is always with us in the Eucharist. (CCC, 1377)

- God wants us to be happy with him forever, in this world and in Heaven. (CCC, 1023)

- All people who follow Jesus and obey God's laws will eventually be with God in Heaven forever. (CCC, 1053, 1054)

- We have an important job on Earth to be a sign of God's Kingdom to others. (CCC, 546)

How do we know God's love— every day, at Mass, and in Heaven?

Unit 7 Overview

Preview Unit Theme

Ask: What is the unit theme?

Summarize that the unit focuses on the Kingdom of God.

Invite volunteers to read aloud each of the bullets in Our Catholic Tradition.

Explain to the children that they will learn about these things in the next three chapters.

Have the children study the photos and images. Invite volunteers to describe what they see. What do these images say about the unit theme?

Ask: How do we know God's love—every day, at Mass, and in Heaven?

After some discussion, explain to the children that they will be exploring this question in the next three chapters.

KEY CONCEPT

At Mass, we gather to worship God by reading from the Bible, giving thanks, and receiving Holy Communion. Jesus shares his Body and Blood with us in the Eucharist.

DOCTRINAL CONTENT

- The Last Supper is the meal Jesus shared with his disciples the night before he died. (CCC, 610)

- The Eucharist is the Sacrament in which Jesus gives himself, and the bread and wine become his Body and Blood. (CCC, 1333)

- The Mass is the gathering of Catholics to worship God and celebrate the Eucharist. (CCC, 1329–1330)

- In the Mass we hear God's Word, give thanks for his gifts, and receive Jesus in Holy Communion. (CCC, 1346–1347)

TASKS OF CATECHESIS

Helping children grow in a faith that is "known, celebrated, lived, and expressed in prayer" (NDC, 20).

This chapter focuses on the following tasks of catechesis:

- Promoting Knowledge of the Faith
- Liturgical Education

Catechist Background

 "Drink from it, all of you, for this is my blood of the covenant, which shall be shed on behalf of many for the forgiveness of sins." Matthew 26:28

➜ **Reflect** Why is eating a meal with people we love so important?

The word *Eucharist* comes from a Greek word that means "to give thanks." Jesus, knowing that the hour of his Death was approaching, changed bread and wine into his own Body and Blood. The Eucharist celebrates Jesus' great gift of himself poured out so that all could be saved. In praise and thanksgiving, the Mass celebrates this tremendous gift.

Reflect on your Sunday experience—is it a day you look forward to with joy because you are going to Mass? Preparation for this great act of thanksgiving can begin at home. Every Sunday, Catholics gather together in public worship to listen to God's Word, to recall the Paschal Mystery (Jesus' suffering, Death, and Resurrection), and to be fed with the Body and Blood of Christ. Being kind and charitable to family members or those you meet on the way to Mass can enhance your celebration of the Eucharist.

The Mass is a wonderful gift. It brings the people who are the Body of Christ together in unity and worship, and sends them out in mission. As a participant in the Eucharist, you provide spiritual support for other members of the Body of Christ. You model faith for the youth of the Church. Your expression of faith becomes a gift for others. So give praise and thanksgiving for God's loving gift, his Son Jesus! Fervently sing a hymn of praise, listen intently, pray from the heart, and extend Christ's peace.

➜ **Reflect** How does going to Mass help you to be a better disciple?

Catechist's Prayer

 Dear Jesus, I want to follow you. Bless me with a prayerful disposition and a reflective heart. Amen.

Lesson Plan

Objectives	Process	Materials

🕐 Invite, 10 minutes

We Give Thanks Page 251

- ♥ **Psalm 95:2** Pray the opening prayer.
- 📖 **Matthew 26:26–28** Reflect prayerfully on the Word.
- Discuss What Do You Wonder questions.

🔊 **Optional Activity**
Chapter Story:
"A Traditional Meal"

🕐 Discover, 35 minutes

The Eucharist Pages 252–253

- Recognize the Last Supper as the meal Jesus shared with his disciples the night before he died
- Define the Eucharist as the Sacrament in which Jesus gives himself, and the bread and wine become his Body and Blood

- **Catholic Faith Words** Last Supper, Eucharist
- 📖 **1 Corinthians 11:23–25** Proclaim "The Last Supper."
- ☆ Underline what Jesus said at the Last Supper.
- Explain that we celebrate the Sacrament of the Eucharist at Mass.
- **Share Your Faith Activity** Talk about what is happening in the photo.

☐ pencils
☐ index cards
- **Optional Activity** I Can Celebrate
☐ Activity Master 19 (Page 251E)

During Mass Pages 254–255

- Describe the Mass as the gathering of Catholics to worship God and celebrate the Eucharist
- Understand that in the Mass we hear God's Word, give thanks for his gifts, and receive Jesus in Holy Communion

- **Catholic Faith Words** Mass, Holy Communion
- Explain that Mass includes readings from the Bible and the celebration of Holy Communion.
- Name key words from each caption.
- Explain that the bread and wine become the Body and Blood of Jesus Christ.
- **Connect Your Faith Activity** Unscramble the words.

☐ pencils
☐ index cards

🕐 Live, 15 minutes

Our Catholic Life Pages 256–257

- Discuss what we see and do at Mass.
- ☆ Identify the things they see and do at Mass.
- **People of Faith** Learn about Pope Saint John XXIII.
- **Live Your Faith Activity** Have the children draw themselves at Mass.

☐ pencils
☐ crayons or markers

Reflection Prayer Page 258

- Review the guided reflection.
- Follow the order of prayer.

🔊 Download instrumental music.

Family + Faith Page 259
Point out that the Catholic Families page provides chapter highlights, information on how first graders understand faith concepts, and family prayer.

Chapter Review Page 260
🔊 aliveinchrist.osv.com
- Customize and Download Assessments
- Email Links to eAssessments
- Interactive Student Reviews

ONLINE RESOURCES

 Go to **aliveinchrist.osv.com**

You will find:

- Interactive lesson planning with web specific content and additional activities
- Step by step lesson instruction from printed Catechist Edition for integrated lesson planning
- Custom–built assessments to download and eAssessment links
- Interactive reviews that provide scores and the option to review answers
- Sunday readings with background and questions of the week

 Go to **osvparish.com**

You will find:

- Ask the Experts Q and A
- General Catechist Helps
- Community Connections and Blogs

Sharing the Message with First Graders

The Mass Some children in first grade have difficulty engaging in the Mass, perhaps because the language of the Mass, hymns, and homily often feel very much directed towards the adults in the parish. Helping children become familiar with what happens at Mass, the words that are said and their meanings helps them to begin to decode what may otherwise feel like a very adult event. At the same time, it's important and fitting that children (and adults) still view the Mass with a certain sense of awe and mystery.

Teaching Tip: To the extent possible, teach about the Mass in the church, where the Mass happens. This will help children remember the lessons better when they are actually in Mass.

How First Graders Understand

- First graders like parties. Help them understand how parties connect with Church celebrations.
- Help first graders understand that Mass is a celebration, a joy-filled experience of Jesus' love and presence. Teach them how to participate in Mass.
- First graders may not understand the word *mystery*, but they can sense God's presence. They can also sense that Mass is more than an ordinary gathering.

"I like being with those who love me. Show me how belonging to the Church is like being part of a loving family."

Chapter Story

"A Traditional Meal"

Use this story to expand the chapter introduction.

- The children will relate the story to their own lives, reflecting on their family celebrations.

 Go to **aliveinchrist.osv.com** Lesson Planning section for this story.

NCEA IFG: ACRE Edition

Knowledge of the Faith

- Objective: To know and understand basic Catholic teaching about the Incarnate Word Jesus Christ as the way, truth, and life

Liturgical Life

- Objective: To know the Paschal Mystery of Jesus in the Church's liturgical life—feasts, seasons, symbols, and practices and in the Sacraments as signs and instruments of grace

Catholic Social Teaching

 Use one of these features to introduce a principle and engage the children with an activity.

- Call to Community, Pages 286–287
- Human Solidarity, Pages 294–295

Music Options

 Use one or more of the following songs to enhance catechetical learning or for prayer.

- Instrumental music, Live Prayer, Page 258
- "Come Share this Meal," Discover, Page 253
- "Come to the Table," Discover, Page 253
- "Supper of the Lamb," Discover, Page 255

LECTIONARY CONNECTION

 Chapter 19 highlights Lectionary-connected themes such as Real Presence, Eucharist, and Resurrection. If your parish aligns its curriculum to the liturgical year, you could use this chapter in connection with the following Sundays.

Year A

Easter Sunday—Resurrection, Risen Lord

Pentecost Sunday—Holy Spirit, Church

Most Holy Body and Blood of Christ—Eucharist, Real Presence

Year B

Easter Sunday—Resurrection, Risen Lord

Most Holy Body and Blood of Christ—Eucharist, Real Presence

Year C

Easter Sunday—Resurrection, Risen Lord

Most Holy Body and Blood of Christ—Eucharist, Real Presence

Twenty-ninth Sunday in Ordinary Time—petition and intercession

Go to **aliveinchrist.osv.com** for a complete correlation ordered by the Sundays of the year and suggestions for how to integrate the Scripture readings into chapter lessons.

Name _____ Date _____

I Can Celebrate

Jesus is at Mass. I can give Jesus my love. At Mass people bring gifts to God. Some gifts are promises to do good. I give a gift.

Draw a picture of your gift to God.

We Give Thanks

 Let Us Pray

Leader: God, we worship you with joy.

"Let us come before him with a song
of praise,
joyfully sing out our psalms."
Psalm 95:2

All: God, we worship you with joy. Amen.

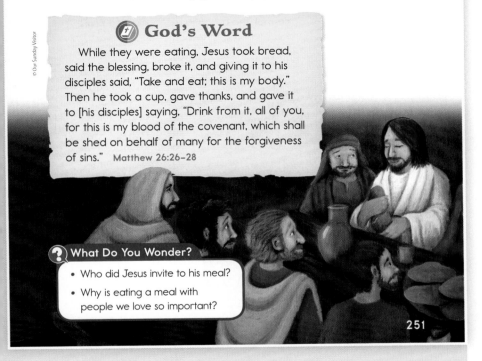

 God's Word

While they were eating, Jesus took bread, said the blessing, broke it, and giving it to his disciples said, "Take and eat; this is my body." Then he took a cup, gave thanks, and gave it to [his disciples] saying, "Drink from it, all of you, for this is my blood of the covenant, which shall be shed on behalf of many for the forgiveness of sins." Matthew 26:26–28

? What Do You Wonder?

- Who did Jesus invite to his meal?
- Why is eating a meal with people we love so important?

251

© Our Sunday Visitor

Optional Activity

Chapter Story: "A Traditional Meal" *Verbal/Linguistic*

Use this story after the opening prayer, before explaining that Jesus gave his life for us.

- Read the story aloud as the children follow along.
- Have the children discuss Thanksgiving and all the festivities associated with that special celebration—food, family members, prayer, decorations.
- When finished, transition back to the lesson instruction.

 Go to **aliveinchrist.osv.com** for Chapter Story.

🕐 **Let Us Pray**

Invite the children to gather in the prayer space and make the Sign of the Cross. Choose a child to read aloud the Psalm verse from a Bible. Prompt the children's response.

Have the children move out of the prayer space and back to their seats.

Explain that Jesus gave his life for us.

Say: Jesus gave his life for us and shares that life with us every day. Let's listen to a reading from the Gospel of Matthew to hear how.

God's Word

Guide the children through the process of Scripture reflection.

- Invite them to close their eyes, be still and open their minds and hearts to what God is saying to them in this passage.
- Proclaim the Scripture.
- Maintain several moments of silence.
- *Ask:* What did you hear God say to you today?
- Invite volunteers to share.

What Do You Wonder?

Say: Jesus shared a meal with his friends. He told them that he was giving them a special gift. He gave them himself in Holy Communion.

Invite the children to respond to the questions. Ask what else they might wonder about this meal with Jesus and the disciples or sharing a meal with others.

Objectives

- Recognize the Last Supper as the meal Jesus shared with his disciples the night before he died
- Define the Eucharist as the Sacrament in which Jesus gives himself, and the bread and wine become his Body and Blood

The Eucharist

Ask: Who is present in the Eucharist?

- Write the children's responses on the board or on chart paper.

Read aloud the first paragraph.

- Explain to the children that an important part of the Mass recalls Jesus' last meal with his friends before his Death. Tell them this meal is known as the Last Supper.

- Hold up an index card with the term *Last Supper* on it. Have everyone read it.

 God's Word

Proclaim "The Last Supper."

⭐ Invite the children to underline what Jesus said during the Last Supper.

- *Ask:* When do you hear these words at Mass?

- Explain that the priest says these words when God changes the bread and wine into the Body and Blood of Christ.

- Tell the children that Jesus promised that he would always be with his friends. Explain that Jesus is present in every Sacrament.

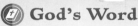
The Eucharist

Who is present in the Eucharist?

At Mass, the Church remembers an important night with Jesus. He shared a special meal with his followers. This meal is called the **Last Supper**.

 Underline what Jesus said during the Last Supper.

 God's Word

The Last Supper

On the night before he died, Jesus shared a special meal with his friends.

He took the bread, gave thanks and broke it, and said, "This is my body that is for you. Do this in remembrance of me."

Jesus took the cup and said, "This cup is the new covenant in my blood. Do this, as often as you drink it, in remembrance of me."
Based on 1 Corinthians 11:23–25

© Our Sunday Visitor

→ When do you hear these words?

(t) **Scripture Background**

1 Corinthians 11:23–25

One purpose of Saint Paul's first Letter to the Corinthians was to denounce the way that some Christians in Corinth were behaving at their worship services.

- In Chapter 11, Saint Paul recalls the words and actions of Jesus at the Last Supper to remind the Corinthians how he had taught them to celebrate the Eucharist.

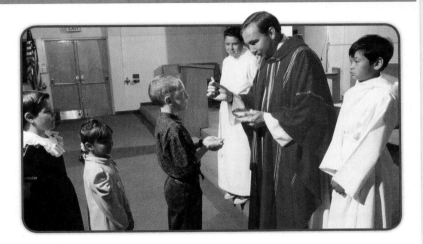

© Our Sunday Visitor

Giving Thanks

At Mass, we celebrate the Sacrament of the **Eucharist**. The word Eucharist means thanksgiving. Catholics are thankful for all God the Father's gifts, most especially his Son. We are thankful that Jesus is truly present in the Eucharist. Mass is celebrated in our parish church and in Catholic churches all over the world!

Catholic Faith Words

Last Supper the meal Jesus shared with his disciples the night before he died. At the Last Supper, Jesus gave himself in the Eucharist.

Eucharist the Sacrament in which Jesus shares himself, and the bread and wine become his Body and Blood

Share Your Faith

Think Look at the picture on this page.

Share Talk about what is happening in the picture.

We Give Thanks **253**

Giving Thanks

Read aloud the paragraph.

Work with Words

Hold up an index card to introduce the word *Eucharist*. Have the children practice pronouncing the word.

• Tell the children that the Eucharist has words and actions that show that Jesus is present.

• Ask the children if they recall the words of Jesus the priest says. Tell the children that the priest and people at Mass do what Jesus told the disciples to do at the Last Supper.

• Explain that they share his Body and Blood under the appearances of bread and wine. Say, "It still looks like bread and wine, but it is really Jesus himself."

• Refer to pages 310–311 in the Our Catholic Tradition reference section in the back of the Student Book for a list of the parts of the Mass.

 Music Option: Have the children sing, "Come Share this Meal," downloaded from **aliveinchrist.osv.com**.

Activity

Read aloud the directions for the Share Your Faith Activity.

• Have the children share their ideas of what is happening in the picture.

Quick Review

The word *Eucharist* means thanksgiving. Jesus gives himself under the appearances of bread and wine in the Eucharist.

Discover

Objectives

- Describe the Mass as the gathering of Catholics to worship God and celebrate the Eucharist
- Understand that in the Mass we hear God's Word, give thanks for his gifts, and receive Jesus in Holy Communion

During Mass

Ask: How do we celebrate at Mass?

- Write the children's responses on the board or on chart paper.

Read aloud the two paragraphs.

- Ask the children what words describe things that happen at celebrations. List these on the board or on chart paper. stories, songs, gifts, food

Work with Words

Hold up index cards with the terms *Mass* and *Holy Communion*.

- Introduce the terms to the children.

Point out the pictures to the children.

- *Ask:* What things do Catholics do at Mass?
- Have the children name key words from each caption.
- Print the children's answers on the board or on chart paper. Possible responses: gather, sing, pray, listen to stories, receive Jesus in Holy Communion

---

Discover

During Mass

What do we celebrate at Mass?

Many families celebrate their love for God with stories, songs, gifts, and food.

At **Mass**, the Church gathers to worship God. The Mass includes readings from the Bible, remembering that Jesus gave his life for us, and receiving **Holy Communion**.

➤ **What do you know about the Mass?**

Catholic Faith Words

Mass the gathering of Catholics to worship God. It includes readings from the Bible and the celebration of Holy Communion.

Holy Communion receiving Jesus' Body and Blood in the celebration of the Eucharist

1 You gather to sing and pray.

2 You listen to readings from the Bible.

(i) Catechist Background

Mass

Mass is a celebration. The Church family gathers as a community on Sundays to honor and praise God.

- Jesus is present at Mass in the assembly itself, in the priest who presides, and in the words of Scripture that are read.
- He is uniquely and truly present in the Eucharist.

Connect Your Faith

Word Scramble Unscramble the letters to find words that tell what the Church does during Mass. Trace the words.

ngsi

sing

tecelebra

celebrate

ksthan

thanks

3 The bread and the wine become the Body and Blood of Jesus.

4 Those who are old enough receive Jesus in Holy Communion.

We Give Thanks **255**

During Mass, *continued*

- Tell the children that family celebrations and Mass have similarities. Tell them Mass is very special because the bread and wine become Jesus himself.

- If applicable, explain to the children that next year they will prepare to receive Jesus in Holy Communion.

 Music Option: Have the children sing, "Come to the Table" or "Supper of the Lamb," downloaded from **aliveinchrist.osv.com**.

Activity

Read aloud the directions for the Connect Your Faith activity.

- Have the children work in pairs to unscramble the words that tell about the Mass.

Quick Review

At Mass the Church family gathers to celebrate God's love. Mass is the Church's greatest celebration of praise and thanks to God.

Optional Activity

Amen *Visual/Spatial*

Remind the children that the word *Amen* is a Hebrew word that means "I believe it" or "So be it."

- *Amen* is almost always said at the end of prayers.
- Have children write the word *Amen* on a separate sheet of paper and decorate the page.

Live

Our Catholic Life

Ask: What do you see and do at Mass?

- Write the children's responses on the board or on chart paper.
- Read aloud the introduction.

At Mass

Have the children follow along in their books as you read aloud the lists.

- Pause to describe people, items, and actions as necessary, referring to the pictures where appropriate.

⭐ Have the children circle the people and the things they have seen or done at Mass. Allow time for the children to check the lists.

- Read through the lists a second time. Have the children raise their hands each time you read something that they have circled.
- *Ask:* What else have you seen or done at Mass?

Our Catholic Life

What do you see and do at Mass?

When you go to Mass, you see many people and things. You do many things, too.

➜ **What else have you seen or done at Mass?**

 Circle the people and things you have seen or the things you have done at Mass.

At Mass

People You Might See	Things You Might See	Things You Might Do
• Priest	• Altar	• Make the Sign of the Cross.
• Altar server	• Candles	• Sing and pray.
• Song leader	• Book of Gospels	• Share a sign of peace.
• Reader	• Chalice	• Receive Holy Communion.
• Extraordinary Minister of Holy Communion	• Crucifix	

© Our Sunday Visitor

256 Chapter 19

Quick Tip

Family Involvement

Remember that a first grader's attendance at Mass is dependent upon family involvement in the parish.

- Help children understand that participation in the Sunday Mass is required.
- Do not put children on the spot about their individual Mass attendance; instead, be general and inclusive when discussing participation.

People of Faith

Blessed Pope John XXIII
(Angelo Roncalli), 1881–1963

Pope John XXIII was known for his kindness and generosity. He was named Pope when he was much older. He hadn't expected it. Many were surprised when he called together a special council of Bishops to talk about important things, like how Catholics worship at Mass and live in the world. Many people called him "Good Pope John."

October 11

Discuss: What can you tell others about the Mass?

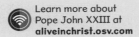 Learn more about Pope John XXIII at **aliveinchrist.osv.com**

Live Your Faith

Draw Yourself at Mass Draw a picture of yourself and your family at Mass.

Catholic Social Teaching

Chapter Connections

To integrate Catholic Social Teaching into your lesson, choose one of the following features: Call to Community, pages 286–287; or Human Solidarity, pages 294–295.

- Start the Live step of the process by talking about Pope Saint John XXIII on page 257. Then move directly to the Catholic Social Teaching feature.

- Or, to expand the lesson, complete both pages 256 and 257, then move to the Catholic Social Teaching feature.

- Return to Chapter 19 for the prayer on page 258.

People of Faith

Tell the children about Pope Saint John XXIII.

- Invite a volunteer to read aloud the People of Faith story.

- Pope Saint John XXIII is one of the best loved Popes of our time. He was a generous and humble man whose lived example taught people a great deal about following Christ. Even when he was dying of cancer, he worked tirelessly for world peace. He was even involved behind the scenes to help resolve an international crisis.

- Pope Saint John XXIII is most well known for calling the Second Vatican Council. Although he died before the council ended, he initiated an ecumenical council that breathed new life into the Church. He was canonized by Pope Francis in 2014.

- *Ask:* What can you tell others about the Mass?

 Encourage the children to go to **aliveinchrist.osv.com** at home to learn more about Pope Saint John XXIII.

Activity

Read aloud the directions for the Live Your Faith activity.

- Allow time for the children to draw their pictures.

- Invite volunteers to share their drawings.

Let Us Pray
Reflection Prayer

Prepare

Go through the reflection below to make it more personal and meaningful. Practice what you will say.

- Consider subdued lighting to facilitate the reflective experience.
- If you wish, have one of the children proclaim the reading from 1 Corinthians.

Gather

Lead the children in procession to the prayer space and invite them to be comfortably seated.

 Play quiet instrumental music downloaded from **aliveinchrist.osv.com**.

Pray

Follow the order of prayer on the student page and lead the children through the following guided reflection.

- Close your eyes. Wiggle your fingers. Take a deep breath. Let it out slowly. Now, relax.
- Imagine that you are with Jesus and his other friends at the special meal the night before he died.
- Where are you sitting? Is Jesus close to you? Is he looking at you? How do you feel?
- Look at the food on the table. What do you see? Do you see bread? Do you see wine?

Conclude by inviting the children to quietly return to their seats.

Live

 Let Us Pray
Reflection Prayer

Gather and begin with the Sign of the Cross.

Leader: Jesus, we ask you to open our hearts as we remember once again the gift of your life and love in Holy Communion.

Leader: A reading about the Last Supper from the Bible.

Read the adaptation of 1 Corinthians 11:23–25. (See page 252.)

The Word of the Lord.

All: Thanks be to God.

Leader: Lead the reflection prayer.

All: Pray the Glory Be together. (See page 316.)

Liturgy Link

Keeping the Lord's Day

Remind the children that participating in Mass is only part of fulfilling the Commandment to keep the Lord's Day.

- Encourage the children to think of ways they can help older family members have time to rest on Sunday.
- Brainstorm ways that family members can relax, pray, and help others on Sunday.

Go to **aliveinchrist.osv.com** for Sunday readings, Scripture background, questions of the week, and seasonal resources.

FAMILY + FAITH
LIVING AND LEARNING TOGETHER

YOUR CHILD LEARNED >>>
This chapter identifies the Mass as the Sacrament of the Eucharist, the Church's great celebration of praise and thanksgiving.

God's Word
Read **Matthew 26:26–28** to learn how Jesus shared a meal with his friends.

Catholics Believe
- At Mass, we gather to worship God by reading from the Bible, giving thanks, and receiving Holy Communion.
- Jesus shares his Body and Blood with us in the Eucharist.

To learn more, go to the *Catechism of the Catholic Church* #1322–1327 at **usccb.org**.

People of Faith
This week, your child met Blessed John XXIII. He helped to change the way that Catholics all over the world celebrate the Mass.

CHILDREN AT THIS AGE >>>
How They Understand the Mass Some children in first grade have difficulty engaging in the Mass, perhaps because the language of the Mass, hymns, and homily often feel very much directed toward the adults in the parish. Helping your child become familiar with what happens at Mass, the words that are said and their meanings can help him or her to begin to decode what may otherwise feel like a very adult event. At the same time, we need to retain our sense of awe and mystery at the miracle of God's love unfolding before us.

CONSIDER THIS >>>
Why is it so important to gather together for meals?

Eating together helps us grow and gain a greater sense of belonging and a true sense of ourselves. Those same human longings guide us to Mass. Here we are strengthened in our identity as members of the Body of Christ and grow in deeper communion with one another. "Holy Communion increases our union with Christ. Just as bodily food sustains our physical life, so Holy Communion nourishes our spiritual life. This Communion moves us away from sin, strengthening our moral resolve to avoid evil and turn ever more powerfully toward God" (*USCCA, p. 223*).

LET'S TALK >>>
- Ask your child to recall some things that he or she does during Mass.
- Talk about your favorite part of the Mass and how you first became familiar with what happens at Mass.

LET'S PRAY >>>
Dear God, help our family always give thanks for the good things you have done for us and to share those stories with others. Amen.

For a multimedia glossary of Catholic Faith Words, Sunday readings, seasonal and Saint resources, and chapter activities go to **aliveinchrist.osv.com**.

Alive in Christ, Grade 1 Chapter 19 **259**

Family + Faith

Distribute the page to the children or parents/adult family members. Point out the chapter highlights, insights on how first graders understand concepts, the opportunity for the adults to reflect on their own experience and faith journey, and the family prayer.

Chapter 19 Review

A **Work with Words** Fill in the blank with the letter of the correct word or words from the Word Bank.

Word Bank
a. Eucharist
b. Last Supper
c. Bible
d. bread and wine
e. Mass

1. Jesus shared the **b** with his disciples the night before he died.

2. The **d** become the Body and Blood of Christ.

3. The **e** is the gathering of Catholics to worship God.

4. Jesus shares himself in the Sacrament of the **a** .

5. You hear readings from the **c** at Mass.

B **Check Understanding** Circle the correct answer.

6. The word Eucharist means ____.

(thanksgiving)   Bible

7. The Mass includes the celebration of ____.

birthdays   (Holy Communion)

Go to **aliveinchrist.osv.com** for an interactive review.

Chapter Review

Use Catechist Quick Reviews to highlight lesson concepts.

A **Work with Words**
Have the children fill in the blank with the correct letter of the word or words from the Word Bank.

B **Check Understanding**
Have the children circle the correct answer.

Go to **aliveinchrist.osv.com** to prepare customized and downloadable assessments, send eAssessments, and assign interactive reviews.

We Give Thanks **259–260**

KEY CONCEPT

Jesus said those who die can have new life with him in Heaven. God invites all people to Heaven. All who follow Jesus and obey God's laws will go to Heaven.

DOCTRINAL CONTENT

- Heaven is living and being happy with God forever. (CCC, 1024)
- God desires for everyone to be happy with him forever. (CCC, 1045)
- Following Jesus and obeying God's laws are how we live in love now and forever. (CCC, 1693)

TASKS OF CATECHESIS

Helping children grow in a faith that is "known, celebrated, lived, and expressed in prayer" (NDC, 20).

This chapter focuses on the following tasks of catechesis:

- Moral Formation
- Teaching to Pray

Catechist Background

 Jesus said in reply, "The coming of the kingdom of God cannot be observed, and no one will announce, 'Look, here it is,' or, 'There it is.' For behold, the kingdom of God is among you." Luke 17:20–21

→ **Reflect** What does God's Kingdom look like?

The mystery of Christ's Death and Resurrection is an experience that plays out over and over again in daily life. How one interprets that experience is the key to following Jesus through death to resurrected glory.

Ponder for a moment some of the illnesses or sufferings you endure— physical, social, emotional, or spiritual ailments. Often the road to recovery is long and difficult, leading many to question: When will it ever end? Yet when recovery is complete, there is a sense of newness.

This is an experience of the Paschal Mystery. Dying to your old self in the pain and suffering of illnesses and hardships, you are raised to a new life and a new way of being. These experiences can lead you to appreciate the meaning of Christ's Death and Resurrection. By sharing this appreciation with others, you can help to build the Body of Christ.

Eternal happiness is a gift Jesus won for all people. Death is not the end. Jesus assured his Apostles that there is life after death and that there is a heavenly dwelling place. It is a gift that has been offered to you.

→ **Reflect** How does hope of eternal life change your expectations regarding death?

Catechist's Prayer

 Lord, sometimes I feel lost and alone. Help me quiet myself to feel your presence, to know your love within me. Amen.

Lesson Plan

Objectives	Process	Materials
Invite, 10 minutes		
Forever with God Page 261	● Psalm 27:11 Pray the opening prayer. 📖 Luke 17:20–21 Reflect prayerfully on the Word. • Discuss What Do You Wonder questions.	📶 **Optional Activity** Chapter Story: "Life Cycles"
Discover, 35 minutes		
Life Forever with God Pages 262–263 • Describe Heaven as living and being happy with God forever	• **Catholic Faith Words** Heaven • Explain that Jesus made a promise about life after death. 📖 John 14:1–3 Proclaim "Together Always." • Explain that after death, Jesus' followers can have new life with God. • **Share Your Faith Activity** Draw things that make them happy.	☐ pencils ☐ index cards ☐ crayons or markers
Happy Forever Pages 264–265 • Identify God's desire for everyone to be happy with him forever • Recognize that following Jesus and obeying God's laws are how we live in love now and forever	• Explain that all holy people who have died are living in love and happiness with the Holy Trinity. • Explain that everyone is invited to Heaven. ☆ Draw someone who has helped them learn about following Jesus. • **Connect Your Faith Activity** Write one action that Jesus wants us to do.	☐ pencils ☐ crayons or markers • **Optional Activity** The Way to Heaven ☐ Activity Master 20 (Page 261E)
Live, 15 minutes		
Our Catholic Life Pages 266–267	• Discuss what we do when someone dies. ☆ Identify what they or someone in their family has done after someone died. • **People of Faith** Learn about Saint Emily de Vialar. • **Live Your Faith Activity** Say a prayer for someone who has died.	☐ pencils
Prayer for the Dead Page 268	• Designate Side 1 and Side 2. ▶ Rehearse "Around Your Throne." • Follow the order of prayer.	📶 Download "Around Your Throne."

Family + Faith Page 269
Point out that the Catholic Families page provides chapter highlights, information on how first graders understand faith concepts, and family prayer.

Chapter Review Page 270
📶 **aliveinchrist.osv.com**
• Customize and Download Assessments
• Email Links to eAssessments
• Interactive Student Reviews

ONLINE RESOURCES

 Go to **aliveinchrist.osv.com**

You will find:

- Interactive lesson planning with web specific content and additional activities
- Step by step lesson instruction from printed Catechist Edition for integrated lesson planning
- Custom-built assessments to download and eAssessment links
- Interactive reviews that provide scores and the option to review answers
- Sunday readings with background and questions of the week

 Go to **osvparish.com**

You will find:

- Ask the Experts Q and A
- General Catechist Helps
- Community Connections and Blogs

Sharing the Message with First Graders

Life with God First graders are still forming a concept of Heaven as they struggle with the idea that death is a permanent change and is different from sleeping. If they have had a grandparent or another family member who died, they might have been told that the person "went to Heaven." They tend to think of Heaven as a place somewhere way up in the sky. Eternal life, a difficult concept even for us as adults, is fairly incomprehensible for young children, though sometimes the wait for something they are excited about can feel like an eternity!

Teaching Tip: Encourage the children to speculate about what Heaven may look or be like. Explain that in reality, it will be better than anything we could imagine.

How First Graders Understand

- First graders like to be imaginative. Lead them to think about what life forever with Jesus will be like.
- Most first graders do not like thinking about death. Help them understand that all living beings eventually die.
- Most first grade children have at least heard of the word *Heaven*, and may have preconceived notions. Your goal is to lead them to a Christian understanding.

"I like to discover and explore new things. Tell me more about Heaven."

Chapter Connections

Chapter Story

Invite

"Life Cycles"

Use this story to expand the chapter introduction.

- The children will relate the story to their own lives, reflecting on the life cycles they see in nature.

 Go to **aliveinchrist.osv.com** Lesson Planning section for this story.

NCEA IFG: ACRE Edition

Discover

Moral Formation

- Objective: To be knowledgeable about the teachings of Jesus and the Church as the basis of Christian morality and to understand Catholic Social Teaching

Prayer

- Objective: To recognize and learn how to engage in Catholic forms of personal and communal prayer and ways of deepening one's spiritual life

Catholic Social Teaching

Live

 Use one of these features to introduce a principle and engage the children with an activity.

- Option for the Poor, Pages 290–291
- Human Solidarity, Pages 294–295

Music Options

 Use one or more of the following songs to enhance catechetical learning or for prayer.

- "Around Your Throne," Live Prayer, Page 268
- "Now Thank We All Our God," Discover, Page 263
- "Do This In Memory of Me," Discover, Page 265

LECTIONARY CONNECTION

 Chapter 20 highlights Lectionary-connected themes such as the Paschal Mystery, prayer, and the Kingdom of God. If your parish aligns its curriculum to the liturgical year, you could use this chapter in connection with the following Sundays.

Year A

Fifth Sunday of Lent—Paschal Mystery

Third Sunday of Easter—Paschal Mystery

Thirty-second Sunday in Ordinary Time—prayer

Year B

Fifth Sunday of Lent—prayer

Twenty-fifth Sunday in Ordinary Time—call to service

Thirty-third Sunday in Ordinary Time—Kingdom of God

Year C

Thirtieth Sunday in Ordinary Time—humility, prayer

Our Lord Jesus Christ, King of the Universe—Kingdom of God, Kingship of Christ

 Go to **aliveinchrist.osv.com** for a complete correlation ordered by the Sundays of the year and suggestions for how to integrate the Scripture readings into chapter lessons.

Name _____   Date _____

The Way to Heaven

Jesus tells how to love. Showing love is the way to Heaven.
Write the word from the Word Bank to fill in the blanks.

Word Bank
· · · · · · · · · · · ·
share

help

forgive

pray

kind

1. I show love when I
_____

– – – – – – – – – – – – – – – – – – – at home.
_____

2. I show love when I
_____

– – – – – – – – – – – – – – – – with those who are poor.
_____

3. I show love when I
_____
– – – – – – – – – – – – – – –
_____.

4. I show love when I am
_____
– – – – – – – – – – – – – –
_____

and not mean.

5. I show love when I
_____
– – – – – – – – – – – – – –
_____

others and make up.

Forever with God

♥ Let Us Pray

Leader: God, guide us and love us every day.

> "LORD, show me your way;
> lead me on a level path
> because of my enemies."
> Psalm 27:11

All: God, guide us and love us every day. Amen.

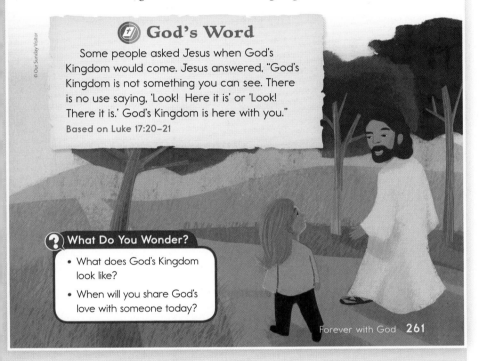

① God's Word

Some people asked Jesus when God's Kingdom would come. Jesus answered, "God's Kingdom is not something you can see. There is no use saying, 'Look! Here it is' or 'Look! There it is.' God's Kingdom is here with you."

Based on Luke 17:20–21

？ What Do You Wonder?

- What does God's Kingdom look like?
- When will you share God's love with someone today?

Forever with God **261**

Optional Activity

Chapter Story: "Life Cycles" *Verbal/Linguistic*

Use this story after the opening prayer, before explaining that Jesus teaches us to be happy.

- Read the story aloud as the children follow along.
- Explain that a caterpillar goes through its life in four stages: egg, caterpillar, chrysalis, and butterfly.
- *Ask:* What happens to a plant at the end of its life?
- When finished, transition back to the lesson instruction.

Go to **aliveinchrist.osv.com** for Chapter Story.

⏱ Invite

♥ Let Us Pray

Invite the children to gather in the prayer space and make the Sign of the Cross. Choose a child to be the leader. Read aloud the Psalm verse from a Bible. Prompt the children's response.

Have the children move out of the prayer space and back to their seats.

Explain that Jesus teaches us how to be happy.

Say: Jesus teaches us how to be happy and live each day of our lives. Listen to understand how Jesus told his friends about this.

① God's Word

Guide the children through the process of Scripture reflection.

- Invite them to close their eyes, be still and open their minds and hearts to what God is saying to them in this passage.
- Proclaim the Scripture.
- Maintain several moments of silence.
- *Ask:* What did you hear God say to you today?
- Invite volunteers to share.

What Do You Wonder?

Say: Jesus is telling us that if we live with God every day we will be happy. When we love God and do what he asks we are helping him to build his Kingdom here on Earth.

Invite the children to respond to the questions. Ask what else they might wonder about the Kingdom of God.

Objective

• Describe Heaven as living and being happy with God forever

Life Forever with God

Ask: What is Heaven?

• Write the children's responses on the board or on chart paper.

Read aloud the first paragraph.

• Lead the children through a simple enactment of a flower's life cycle.

• Ask the children to curl up in a ball. Tell them that plants start out as seeds.

• Have the children stand, and tell them that plants grow.

• Ask them to stand on their toes with arms stretched up. Tell them that flowers bloom.

• Ask the children to drop to the floor, and tell them that the flower dies.

• Remind them that Jesus promised his followers life after death.

God's Word

Proclaim "Together Always."

• Ask the children to listen for Jesus' promise.

• *Ask:* What do you think it is like with God the Father?

Discover

Life Forever with God

What is Heaven?

Like plants and animals, people have life cycles. People are born, they live, and then they die. Listen to the promise Jesus made about life after death.

© Our Sunday Visitor

Catholic Faith Words

Heaven the full joy of living with God forever

God's Word

Together Always

Jesus told his followers, "Don't worry. Have faith in God, and have faith in me. There are many rooms in my Father's house. I am going ahead of you to get a place ready for you. I will come back. When it is time, I will take each of you home to my Father's house. We will be together always."

Based on John 14:1–3

➔ What do you think it is like with God the Father?

262 Chapter 20

Scripture Background

John 14:1–3

Like an earlier reading, this Scripture story is based on Jesus' farewell discourse to his disciples at the Last Supper, as reported by the Gospel according to John.

• In this passage, Jesus explains that the disciples should be happy he is going away because he is returning to his Father's house to prepare a place for them. Because of Jesus, Christians can hope to be united with God forever in the joy of Heaven.

Happiness Forever

Jesus said that he will come back to bring his followers to his Father's house. Jesus said they will have joy that will never end. After death, Jesus' followers can have new life with God. They can be full of happiness. **Heaven** is the full joy of living with God forever.

Share Your Faith

Think Draw some things that make you happy here on Earth.

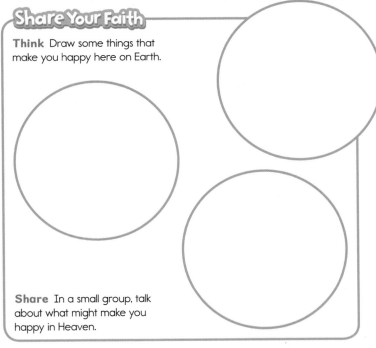

Share In a small group, talk about what might make you happy in Heaven.

© Our Sunday Visitor

Forever with God **263**

Reaching All Learners

The Subject of Death

The emphasis of the chapter is on everlasting happiness. In some children, however, particularly those who have recently experienced a death in the family, the text may prompt sad or scary feelings.

- Be alert to the possibility that children may have such a reaction. Be accepting and comforting to them.
- Alert parents or guardians of any child that showed such a reaction.

Happiness Forever

Read aloud the paragraph.

Work with Words

Hold up an index card with the word *Heaven*. Explain to the children that Heaven is the full joy of living with God and the Saints forever.

- Help the children understand that the phrase Jesus uses in the Scripture story—"my Father's house"—is a metaphor for Heaven.
- Ask the children why they think *house* is a good word to describe Heaven. Lead the children to focus on the house as a setting for family happiness.
- Tell the children that holy people have new life with God forever.

 Music Option: Have the children sing, "Now Thank We All Our God," downloaded from **aliveinchrist.osv.com**.

Activity

Read aloud the directions for the Share Your Faith activity.

- Have the children work independently to draw their ideas.
- Provide time for the children to talk in a small group about what might make them happy in Heaven.

Quick Review

Life and happiness with God and the Saints forever is called Heaven.

Forever with God **263**

Objectives

- Identify God's desire for everyone to be happy with him forever
- Recognize that following Jesus and obeying God's laws are how we live in love now and forever

Happy Forever

Ask: What do you need to do to be happy with God forever?

- Write the children's responses on the board or on chart paper.

Read aloud the paragraph.

- Tell the children that God's love is so great that he wants all people to be happy with him after they die.
- Point out the pictures of the Saints.
- Ask the children to tell what they recall about each Saint.
- Explain that the Saints are among those who are in Heaven with Jesus.

Discover

Happy Forever

What do you need to do to be happy with God forever?

The Holy Trinity lives in love forever. All holy people who have died are living in love and happiness forever with the Holy Trinity.

St. Joan of Arc

St. Francis of Assisi

St. Jude

St. Martin de Porres

264 Chapter 20

 Quick Tip

Eternity

The concept of forever is a difficult one to grasp by children for whom a week can feel like an eternity.

- Draw a circle on the board or on chart paper, or show the children a circular object such as an embroidery hoop or wedding band.
- Explain that, just as a circle has no beginning or end, people who embrace God's love and laws will live with him forever.

The Way to Heaven

God wants everyone to be happy forever, even after they die. Everyone is invited. Everyone who follows Jesus and God's laws will be in Heaven with God forever.

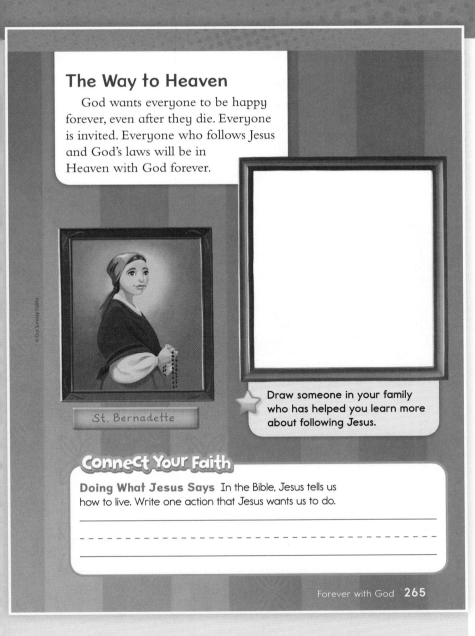

St. Bernadette

Draw someone in your family who has helped you learn more about following Jesus.

Connect Your Faith

Doing What Jesus Says In the Bible, Jesus tells us how to live. Write one action that Jesus wants us to do.

_____

- -

_____

The Way to Heaven

Read the paragraph aloud.

- Share with the children that whenever they show love for others, they get an idea of the happiness that is Heaven.

- Explain that when they live as a follower of Jesus, they are living like the Saints who are in Heaven with Jesus. Everyone who follows Jesus will be in Heaven with God forever.

- ⭐ Have the children draw in the empty frame, a picture of someone from their family who helped them learn more about following Jesus.

Refer to page 320 in the Our Catholic Tradition reference section of the Student Book to learn about praying with the Saints.

 Music Option: Have the children sing, "Do This in Memory of Me," downloaded from **aliveinchrist.osv.com**.

Activity

Point out the Connect Your Faith activity and read aloud the directions.

- Have the children write one action that Jesus wants us to do.

Quick Review

One gets to be in Heaven with God by loving God and others.

Optional Activity

Activity Master 20: The Way to Heaven

Distribute copies of the activity found on catechist page 261E.

- Tell the children to complete the sentences with words from the Word Bank to learn how to get to Heaven.

- As an alternative, you may wish to send this activity home with the children.

Our Catholic Life

Ask: What do we do when someone dies?

- Write the children's responses on the board or on chart paper.

Read the introduction.

- Emphasize that death is not the end. We know that we will meet the person who has died again in Heaven.

When Someone Dies

- Invite the children to listen carefully as you read aloud the list of ways we respond when someone dies.

- Pause after reading each entry, and invite the children to restate the information in their own words.

☆ Have the children place a check mark next to one thing they or someone in their family has done.

- *Ask:* What kind words can you say to a friend when someone they love dies?

Point out the photo.

- Invite the children to tell what they see happening in the photo.

Live

Our Catholic Life

What do we do when someone dies?

When someone we love dies, we are sad. We know that we will miss the person. Since we are followers of Jesus, we know that death is not really the end. Even though we miss the person now, we know we will meet him or her again in Heaven.

Here are some things the followers of Jesus do when someone dies.

© Our Sunday Visitor

 Place a check mark next to one thing you or someone in your family has done.

When Someone Dies

☐ We let ourselves feel sad. We share how we feel with God and with other people we love.

☐ We gather for Mass. We thank God for giving us this person to be in our lives.

☐ We share happy memories with family and friends. We tell stories about our loved one.

☐ We ask God to take care of the person who has died. We ask God to welcome him or her to Heaven.

266 Chapter 20

✓ Quick Tip

Lamenting

Children who are dealing with death and other losses need to know that it is all right to grieve, and to share their feelings of anger, sadness, or fear with God in prayer.

- Tell the children that Jesus cried when his friend Lazarus died. He shared his fear and sadness with his Father in prayer on the night before he died.

- Alert parents or guardians of any child who displays a sad or scary reaction to the discussion.

People of Faith

Saint Emily de Vialar, 1797–1856

Saint Emily was born in France. When she was fifteen, her mother died. She took care of her father's house. She devoted her life to prayer. After inheriting some money, she cared for children who were sick and poor. Saint Emily taught the children that we should always love each other. She also taught them that Jesus wants us to be happy and live with God forever in Heaven.

June 17

Discuss: What makes you happy?

 Learn more about Saint Emily at **aliveinchrist.osv.com**

Live Your Faith

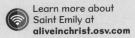

Say a Prayer Do you know someone who has died? This week, say a special prayer for that person.

Dear God,

Please take care of all those who have died,

_____

especially _____ .

Amen.

267

 ## Catholic Social Teaching

Chapter Connections

To integrate Catholic Social Teaching into your lesson, choose one of the following features: Option for the Poor, pages 290–291; or Human Solidarity, pages 294–295.

- Start the Live step of the process by talking about Saint Emily de Vialar on page 267. Then move directly to the Catholic Social Teaching feature.
- Or, to expand the lesson, complete both pages 266 and 267, then move to the Catholic Social Teaching feature.
- Return to Chapter 20 for the prayer on page 268.

People of Faith

Tell the children about Saint Emily de Vialar.

- Invite a volunteer to read aloud the People of Faith story.
- Explain that Saint Emily de Vialar is the foundress of the Sisters of Saint Joseph of the Apparition.
- After she inherited a fortune from her grandfather, she bought a house and moved in with three other women.
- Their ministry was care for the needy, especially the sick, and the education of children.
- Over the course of twenty-two years, Saint Emily saw her order grow from one to over forty houses, most of which she founded in person.
- *Ask:* What makes you happy?

Encourage the children to go to **aliveinchrist.osv.com** at home to learn more about Saint Emily de Vialar.

Activity

As a group, read aloud the directions for the Live Your Faith activity.

- Allow time for the children to complete their prayers.
- Invite the children to silently pray the prayer in their hearts.

Let Us Pray
Prayer for the Dead

Tell the children that the Church family includes people who are alive and people who have died. Explain that today they will be praying specifically for those who have died.

Prepare

Choose a prayer leader.

• Designate Side 1 and Side 2.

 Rehearse "Around Your Throne," downloaded from **aliveinchrist.osv.com**.

Gather

Invite the children to process to the prayer space. Have each child bring his or her book.

• Organize the children in two groups (Side 1 and Side 2) facing each other.

• Explain that both sides pray the sentence marked *All*.

Pray

Follow the order of prayer on the student page.

 Conclude by singing together "Around Your Throne."

Live

 Let Us Pray
Prayer for the Dead

Gather and begin with the Sign of the Cross.

Leader: Those who have died as friends of God are part of our Church family. We pray for them. We ask them to pray for us, too.

Side 1: Lord, our God, we remember those who have died.

Side 2: Bring them home to be with you forever.

Side 1: Gather us all together into your Kingdom.

Side 2: There we will be happy forever with the Virgin Mary, Mother of God and our Mother.

All: There all the friends of the Lord Jesus will sing a song of joy.

From the *Eucharistic Prayer II for Children*

 Sing "Around Your Throne"

We gather around your throne O God.
You are worthy of our praise.
With the saints and all the angels,
in one voice we worship you.
Holy (Holy)
Holy (Holy)
Holy..... are you!

© 2010, Banner Kidd. Published by Our Sunday Visitor.

268 Chapter 20

Liturgy Link

Liturgical Prayers for Children

Point out to the children that the prayer is one said at special Masses for children.

• At every Mass, God's family remembers and prays for those who have died. Direct the children to be quiet and respectful when they pray for people who have died.

 Go to **aliveinchrist.osv.com** for Sunday readings, Scripture background, questions of the week, and seasonal resources.

YOUR CHILD LEARNED >>>

This chapter explains Heaven as the full joy of living with God forever. God wants everyone to live in love and happiness with him.

God's Word

See **Luke 17:20–21** to read what Jesus said about the coming of the Kingdom of God.

Catholics Believe

- Jesus said those who die can have new life with him in Heaven.
- God invites all people to Heaven. All who follow Jesus and obey God's laws will go to Heaven.

To learn more, go to the *Catechism of the Catholic Church* #1023–1025 at **usccb.org**.

People of Faith

This week, your child met Saint Emily de Vialar. Saint Emily had a special love for sick children and taught them that Jesus wants them to be happy here and in Heaven.

CHILDREN AT THIS AGE >>>

How They Understand Life with God First-graders are still forming a concept of Heaven as they struggle with the idea that death is a permanent change and is different from sleeping. If your child has had a grandparent or another family member who died, he or she might have been told that the person "went to Heaven." Children this age tend to think of Heaven as a place somewhere way up in the sky. This can make them also think about life without a parent or caregiver. Because of this, they can be afraid of death and therefore afraid of Heaven. Eternal life, a difficult concept even for us as adults, is fairly incomprehensible for young children. Be careful how you talk to children about Heaven. Even if it sounds marvelous, they may be reluctant in wanting to go!

CONSIDER THIS >>>

What does forever mean to you?

As a child it may have been the time we waited for Christmas or a birthday. As a young adult we may focus on the seeming "forever" of things to come—marriage, family, retirement. The older we get, the more we realize that forever is more than this life. "Every time we attend a funeral vigil or Mass, view a deceased body at a wake, or pass by a cemetery, we are reminded of this simple and profound article of the Creed, the belief in the resurrection of the body. It is a sobering belief, because it reminds us of the judgment yet to come, and at the same time it is a joyful belief that heralds life everlasting with God" (*USCCA, p. 156*).

LET'S TALK >>>

- Ask your child about Jesus' promise to his followers.
- Talk about loved ones who have passed away and what living forever with God means to you.

LET'S PRAY >>>

Saint Emily, pray for us that we may be happy here on Earth and in Heaven with Jesus. Amen.

For a multimedia glossary of Catholic Faith Words, Sunday readings, seasonal and Saint resources, and chapter activities go to **aliveinchrist.osv.com**.

Distribute the page to the children or parents/adult family members. Point out the chapter highlights, insights on how first graders understand concepts, the opportunity for the adults to reflect on their own experience and faith journey, and the family prayer.

Chapter 20 Review

A **Work with Words** Complete each sentence.

Word Bank
- follow
- life
- Heaven
- happy

1. God wants everyone to be **happy**.

2. Jesus said that after death you can have new **life**.

3. You can be happy with God when you **follow** Jesus.

4. You can have joy with God forever in **Heaven**.

B **Check Understanding** Put the events in order.

5. **4** We have life forever with God.

6. **3** We die.

7. **1** We are born.

8. **2** We live.

Go to **aliveinchrist.osv.com** for an interactive review.

Use Catechist Quick Reviews to highlight lesson concepts.

A **Work with Words** Have the children complete each sentence with the correct word from the Word Bank.

B **Check Understanding** Have the children put the times of life in order.

Go to **aliveinchrist.osv.com** to prepare customized and downloadable assessments, send eAssessments, and assign interactive reviews.

Forever with God **269–270**

KEY CONCEPT

Justice, peace, and love are signs of God's Kingdom. Catholics work here and now with God to help his Kingdom continue to grow.

DOCTRINAL CONTENT

- We pray for the coming of God's Kingdom, working together with God as he builds his Kingdom. (CCC, 2818)
- By being forgiving, treating others with respect, and helping those who are hungry and in need, Jesus showed us how to work for the Kingdom. (CCC, 2831–2832)
- When we are kind, share, play fair, and include others, we are spreading peace. (CCC, 2304)

TASKS OF CATECHESIS

Helping children grow in a faith that is "known, celebrated, lived, and expressed in prayer" (NDC, 20).

This chapter focuses on the following tasks of catechesis:

- Moral Formation
- Education for Community Life

Catechist Background

You have been told… what is good, and what the LORD requires of you: Only to do justice and to love goodness, and to walk humbly with your God. Micah 6:8

→ **Reflect** How do you know what is the right thing to do?

Throughout the Gospels, Jesus never directly answered the question "What is the Kingdom of God?" but spoke in parables instead. He compared the Kingdom of God to the small mustard seed that springs up and becomes the largest of plants. (See Mark 4:30–32.) This parable sheds light on the Christian call to hasten the coming of God's Kingdom.

Contemplate a world without crime, poverty, and hunger. Think about what the world would be like if it were filled with righteousness, peace, and joy. These qualities mark the Kingdom that Jesus proclaimed. Though it is easy to get caught up in the fatalistic, "It is impossible" or "I can't make a difference," Jesus calls his followers to believe in the coming of the Kingdom.

The mustard seed was tiny, but little by little it was transformed into a large shade tree. Through the Holy Spirit, Jesus empowers his followers to further the Father's Reign. He calls Christians to participate in his work of transforming the world. As a disciple of Jesus, when you show peace, justice, and love, you bear witness to God's Kingdom.

→ **Reflect** What action can you take in your community to further the Reign of God?

Catechist's Prayer

God our Creator and Father, thank you for calling me to serve young children. Care for them during the summer months. Fill me with faith, hope, and love, always ready to trust where you take me. Amen.

Lesson Plan

Objectives	Process	Materials

Invite, 10 minutes

God's Kingdom Page 271

- ♥ Psalm 145:13–14 Pray the opening prayer.
- 📖 Micah 6:8 Reflect prayerfully on the Word.
- • Discuss What Do You Wonder questions.

🌐 **Optional Activity**
Chapter Poem:
"Signs of Happiness"

Discover, 35 minutes

Love and Peace Kingdom Workers
Pages 272–273

- • Appreciate that we can pray for the coming of God's Kingdom, and work with God for the Kingdom
- • Connect that through Jesus' action of being forgiving, treating others with respect, and helping those who are hungry and in need, he showed us how to work for the Kingdom

- • Explain that when we treat others with love, we are working with God as he builds his Kingdom.
- ☆ Underline what Jesus taught us to pray for.
- • Explain that the good things we do each day help God's Kingdom grow.
- 📖 Matthew 13:31–32 Proclaim "Starting Small."
- • **Share Your Faith Activity** Write one good thing they do every day.

☐ pencils
- • **Optional Activity**
Help God's Kingdom Grow
☐ Activity Master 21 (Page 271E)

Living for the Kingdom
Pages 274–275

- • Recognize that when we are kind, share, play fair, and include others, we are spreading peace

- • **Catholic Faith Words** peace
- • Explain that when followers of Jesus act with peace, justice, and love, they help the Kingdom of God grow.
- ☆ Identify the things that help build the Kingdom of God. Put an *X* next to the things that do not build the Kingdom of God.
- • **Connect Your Faith Activity** Make a membership card.

☐ pencils
☐ index cards

Live, 15 minutes

Our Catholic Life Pages 276–277

- • Recall that God's Kingdom grows whenever people show justice, love, and peace.
- ☆ Draw one way to work for God's Kingdom.
- • **People of Faith** Learn about Saint Pedro Calungsod.
- • **Live Your Faith Activity** Draw a picture that shows a world where everyone worked together for God's Kingdom.

☐ pencils
☐ crayons or markers

Asking Prayer Page 278

- ▶ Rehearse "Right and Just."
- • Follow the order of prayer.

🌐 Download "Right and Just."

Family + Faith Page 279
Point out that the Catholic Families page provides chapter highlights, information on how first graders understand faith concepts, and family prayer.

Chapter Review Page 280
🌐 aliveinchrist.osv.com
- • Customize and Download Assessments
- • Email Links to eAssessments
- • Interactive Student Reviews

ONLINE RESOURCES

 Go to **aliveinchrist.osv.com**

You will find:

- Interactive lesson planning with web specific content and additional activities
- Step by step lesson instruction from printed Catechist Edition for integrated lesson planning
- Custom-built assessments to download and eAssessment links
- Interactive reviews that provide scores and the option to review answers
- Sunday readings with background and questions of the week

 Go to **osvparish.com**

You will find:

- Ask the Experts Q and A
- General Catechist Helps
- Community Connections and Blogs

Sharing the Message with First Graders

God's Kingdom First grade children are familiar with stories, such as fairy tales, that involve kings and kingdoms, and they might think of Jesus' references to the Father's Kingdom in these terms. We can help them understand that Christians cooperate with God to help build his Kingdom here "on earth as it is in Heaven." We will live forever with God in his Kingdom in Heaven, but we also actively work to help God's Kingdom grow by showing love to one another.

Teaching Tip: Point out children who are "working together with God to build his Kingdom" in your room. Whenever someone is kind to someone else, discuss it in this context.

How First Graders Understand

- First graders like ideas and learning new information. Help them understand that they can use what they learn to make a better world.
- All Christians, even young children, are invited to foster and be a sign of God's Kingdom.
- Use realistic stories to inspire children to want to bring happiness into the lives of others through justice, peace, and love.

"I like to help others. Tell me things I can do to help."

Chapter Connections

Chapter Poem

Invite

"Signs of Happiness"

Use this poem to expand the chapter introduction.

- The children will relate the story to their own lives, reflecting on what makes them happy.
- Connect happiness to making someone else happy.

 Go to **aliveinchrist.osv.com** Lesson Planning section for this poem.

NCEA IFG: ACRE Edition

Discover

Moral Formation

- Objective: To be knowledgeable about the teachings of Jesus and the Church as the basis of Christian morality and to understand Catholic Social Teaching

Communal Life

- Objectives: To know the origin, mission, structure, and communal nature of the Church; to know the rights and responsibilities of the Christian faithful

Catholic Social Teaching

Live

 Use one of these features to introduce a principle and engage the children with an activity.

- Call to Community, Pages 286–287
- Option for the Poor, Pages 290–291

Music Options

 Use one or more of the following songs to enhance catechetical learning or for prayer.

- "Right and Just," Live Prayer, Page 54
- "Building God's Kingdom," Discover, Page 273
- "The Tiny Seed," Discover, Page 273
- "Raise Your Voice for Justice," Discover, Page 275
- "Seek Ye First," Discover, Page 275

LECTIONARY CONNECTION

 Chapter 21 highlights Lectionary-connected themes such as justice, conversion, and the Kingdom of God. If your parish aligns its curriculum to the liturgical year, you could use this chapter in connection with the following Sundays.

Year A

Second Sunday of Advent—justice, peace

Fifth Sunday of Easter—priesthood of all believers

Twenty-seventh Sunday in Ordinary Time—justice

Year B

First Sunday of Advent—second coming, conversion

Fourth Sunday of Lent—grace, God's love

Pentecost Sunday—mission

Year C

First Sunday of Advent—Kingdom of God

Thirty Second Sunday in Ordinary Time—Heaven, Hell

Thirty-third Sunday in Ordinary Time—justice

 Go to **aliveinchrist.osv.com** for a complete correlation ordered by the Sundays of the year and suggestions for how to integrate the Scripture readings into chapter lessons.

Name _____ Date _____

Help God's Kingdom Grow

The children in the pictures need your help.
Draw a new picture in each empty box. Show justice, peace, or love.

God's Kingdom

Let Us Pray

Leader: God, you teach us how to live every day.

"Your reign is a reign for all ages,
    your dominion for all generations.
The LORD is trustworthy in all his words,
    and loving in all his works." Psalm 145:13–14

All: God, guide us in working for your
Kingdom. Amen.

God's Word

"You have been told...what the LORD requires of you: Only to do justice and to love goodness, and to walk humbly with your God." Micah 6:8

? What Do You Wonder?

- How do you do what is right?
- When do you bring peace to others?

271

Optional Activity

Chapter Poem: "Signs of Happiness" *Verbal/Linguistic*

Use this poem after the opening prayer, before explaining that God teaches us how to live.

- Read the poem aloud as the children follow along.
- *Ask:* How can you make someone else happy?
- Have the children stand in a circle and sing the song "If You're Happy and You Know It." Have everyone take a turn showing a sign of happiness. Then transition back to the lesson instruction.

 Go to **aliveinchrist.osv.com** for Chapter Poem.

🕐 Invite

❤ Let Us Pray

Invite the children to gather in the prayer space and make the Sign of the Cross. Choose a child to be the leader. Read aloud the Psalm verse from a Bible. Prompt the children's response.

Have the children move out of the prayer space and back to their seats.

Explain that God teaches us how to live.

Say: God teaches us how to live. He guides us every day to live a good life. Listen to a reading from the Bible to hear what God asks us to do.

God's Word

Guide the children through the process of Scripture reflection.

- Invite them to close their eyes, be still and open their minds and hearts to what God is saying to them in this passage.
- Proclaim the Scripture.
- Maintain several moments of silence.
- *Ask:* What did you hear God say to you today?
- Invite volunteers to share.

What Do You Wonder?

Say: God asks us to do what is right, show love, and live in peace.

Invite the children to respond to the questions. Ask what else they might wonder about knowing what is right or being a peacemaker.

Objectives

- Appreciate that we can both pray for the coming of God's Kingdom, and work together with God for the Kingdom

- Connect that through Jesus' actions of being forgiving, treating others with respect, and helping those who are hungry and in need, he showed us how to work for the Kingdom

Love and Peace

Ask: How can you work together with God as he builds his Kingdom?

- Write the children's responses on the board or on chart paper.

Read aloud both paragraphs.

⭐ Have the children underline what Jesus taught us to pray for.

- Emphasize that when we treat others with love, we are working with God as he builds his Kingdom.

- Point out the bulleted list and read it aloud.

- Help the children understand that Jesus taught us with his actions. He wants us to do what he did. He wants us to act with peace, love, and justice.

Love and Peace

How can you work together with God as he builds his Kingdom?

⭐ Underline what Jesus taught us to pray for. Where do you hear these words?

God's Word in Scripture teaches us how to have true happiness. In Heaven, everyone is happy because they are with God. Everyone gets along and loves each other. <u>Jesus taught us to pray that God's Kingdom would come "on earth as it is in Heaven."</u>

When we celebrate God's goodness and treat others with love, we are working to bring peace as he builds his Kingdom.

- Jesus forgave people over and over again. Jesus brought peace.
- Jesus treated others as he would like to be treated. Jesus brought justice.
- Jesus fed people who were hungry. Jesus showed love.

272 Chapter 21

Optional Activity

Activity Master 21: Help God's Kingdom Grow

Distribute copies of the activity found on catechist page 271E.

- Read aloud the directions. Explain that the children will show examples of how we can help God's Kingdom grow.

- As an alternative, you may wish to send this activity home with the children.

The Kingdom Grows

When we love God and others and do even small things to show our love, we work with God to spread the Good News of his Kingdom.

Every day, God gives us many ways to make small, loving choices. The good things we do each day help God's Kingdom to grow.

➡ **How can you spread the Good News?**

 God's Word

Starting Small

Jesus said that God's Kingdom is like a mustard seed. It is a very tiny seed that grows to be a very big tree. It becomes so big that birds can sit in its branches. **Based on Matthew 13:31–32**

Share Your Faith

Think Write one good thing that you do every day to help God's Kingdom grow.

_____

- - - - - - - - - - - - - - - - - -

_____

Share Share with a partner.

273

 Songs of Scripture

Have You Ever Seen A Mustard Seed?

The chorus of this song teaches that God's Kingdom grows through our hearts and through our hands.

- Ask each child to name a way to help our love for God to grow.
- Next, ask them to name one thing they can do to help share God's love (e.g. say something kind to someone, use manners).
- Teach the song.

 Use *Songs of Scripture*, Grades 1–3 CD, Track 9

The Kingdom Grows

Read aloud the paragraphs.

- Explain that the good things we do each day help God's Kingdom to grow.
- *Ask:* How can you spread the Good News?

 God's Word

Proclaim "Starting Small."

- Explain that God's Kingdom started small. God's Kingdom has grown over time and continues to grow.
- Every time we do good things we help God's Kingdom to grow.

Explain that we pray for the Kingdom of God when we pray the Lord's Prayer. To reference the Lord's Prayer, go to the Our Catholic Tradition reference section in the back of the Student Book, page 317.

> Music Option: Have the children sing, "Building God's Kingdom" or "The Tiny Seed," downloaded from **aliveinchrist.osv.com**.

Activity

Read aloud the directions for the Share Your Faith activity.

- Have the children work independently to write their ideas.
- After a short time, have them discuss with a partner.

Quick Review

Jesus began God's Kingdom on Earth. All Christians work for God's Kingdom when they bring more love, justice, and peace to the world.

Discover

Objective

- Recognize that when we are kind, share, play fair, and include others, we are spreading peace

Living for the Kingdom

Read aloud the two paragraphs.

- Show the children a deflated balloon. Blow up the balloon part way. Tell the children that the world would be so happy if everyone worked to be more peaceful.

- Blow up the balloon a little more. Explain that the world would be even better if everyone worked for justice.

- Finish inflating the balloon and tell the children that God's Kingdom grows even more when people show love to others.

- Tell the children to pretend that they are going to be in charge of the happiness in a school.

- Ask the children what they can do to make the classroom a happy place.

- For each scenario, have the children place a check mark next to the things that help build the Kingdom of God. Have them put an *X* next to things that do not build God's Kingdom.

Living for the Kingdom

How can you help God's Kingdom grow?

When followers of Jesus act with **peace**, justice, and love, they help the Kingdom of God grow.

How can children work with God as he builds his Kingdom? How can they share God's love with others?

> **Catholic Faith Words**
>
> **peace** when things are calm and people get along with one another

1. Place a check mark next to the things that build up God's Kingdom.

2. Put an X next to the things that do not build up God's Kingdom.

Some quiet or shy children don't get picked as partners.

☐ Ignore the children that never get picked because they must not be good partners.

☐ Kindly ask one of them to be a partner. This is spreading peace.

274 Chapter 21

Optional Activity

Happiness at Home *Interpersonal, Visual/Spatial*

Ask the children how they could use their suggestions on promoting happiness in school and apply them at home.

- Ask the children to illustrate one of their suggestions.

- Invite volunteers to share their ideas and their illustrations with the group.

Some children don't want to share.

☐ Keep your toys to yourself and don't share them with others.

☐ Share and give others what they need. This is acting with justice.

When the teacher isn't looking, some children are teasing and calling others names.

☐ Show care for others, even if it's hard. This is love.

☐ Join in the teasing so you don't get picked on next.

Connect Your Faith

Make a Membership Card
Write your name in the space below. Talk about ways you can help God's Kingdom grow.

MEMBERSHIP CARD
God's Kingdom
You !
MEMBER
Expiration Date: Never

_____

- - - - - - - - - - - - - - - - - - -

_____

God's Kingdom **275**

Living for the Kingdom,
continued

Have the children work independently or in pairs.

- Have volunteers share their work.
- Have the whole group clap to show their happiness after each presentation is made.

Work with Words
Hold up an index card with the word *peace*.

- Read aloud the definition.

> ▶ Music Option: Have the children sing "Raise your Voice for Justice" or "Seek Ye First," downloaded from **aliveinchrist.osv.com**.

Activity

Point out the Connect Your Faith activity and read aloud the directions.

- Have the children write their names in the space provided.
- Invite them to discuss how they can work with God to help his Kingdom grow.

Quick Review

God's Kingdom is a Kingdom of justice, love, and peace. You work for God's Kingdom by your just, loving, and peace-making actions.

✓ Quick Tip

Justice

Tell the children that justice is a way of acting by which we give God and people what is due them.

- Ask questions, and have the children answer "some people" or "all people." Who should be treated with kindness?
- Who should have enough food to eat?
- Conclude that all people should be treated with justice.

Our Catholic Life

Ask: How can you live in the Kingdom of God?

- Write the children's responses on the board or on chart paper.

Read aloud the introductory paragraph.

- Draw attention to the text on the puzzle pieces.
- Invite volunteers to read aloud the bulleted items on each puzzle piece.
- ⭐ In the empty puzzle piece, have the children draw one way they can live in and show others God's Kingdom.
- Invite volunteers to share and talk about their drawings.
- Encourage the children to do what they have drawn.

To extend the lesson, have the children role play the ways they can work for God's Kingdom.

- Organize the children into pairs.
- Assign each pair one of the bulleted items on the puzzle pieces.
- Have the children create and rehearse a simple skit.
- Invite the pairs to share their skit with the group.

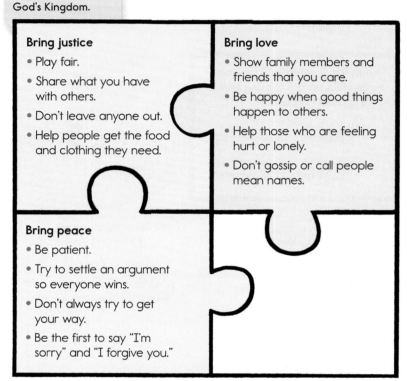

Live

Our Catholic Life

How can you live in the Kingdom of God?

God's Kingdom grows whenever people show justice, love, and peace. Here are some ways you can live in and show others God's Kingdom.

> ⭐ In the empty puzzle piece, draw one way you live in God's Kingdom.

Bring justice
- Play fair.
- Share what you have with others.
- Don't leave anyone out.
- Help people get the food and clothing they need.

Bring love
- Show family members and friends that you care.
- Be happy when good things happen to others.
- Help those who are feeling hurt or lonely.
- Don't gossip or call people mean names.

Bring peace
- Be patient.
- Try to settle an argument so everyone wins.
- Don't always try to get your way.
- Be the first to say "I'm sorry" and "I forgive you."

© Our Sunday Visitor

276 Chapter 21

✓ Quick Tip

Social Analysis

Young children are already sensitive to situations of injustice. Remind the children that they can help work for God's Kingdom when they

- make sure everyone is treated fairly.
- learn about the needs of others, and help meet them.
- get involved to make a positive difference at home and in school.

People of Faith

Saint Pedro Calungsod, 1654–1672

Saint Pedro Calungsod was born in the Philippines. At fourteen he became a lay missionary. Pedro was a painter, singer, and catechist as he worked with the Jesuit missionaries. His greatest desire was to spread Jesus' message of love. He died while protecting a priest from men who hated Christianity. Pedro is the patron Saint of Filipino children.

April 2

Discuss: How can you use your talents to spread Jesus' message of love?

 Learn more about Saint Pedro Calungsod at **aliveinchrist.osv.com**

Live Your Faith

Imagine Draw a picture of what the world would be like if everyone worked together to help build God's Kingdom.

God's Kingdom **277**

People of Faith

Tell the children about Saint Pedro Calungsod.

- Invite a volunteer to read aloud the People of Faith story.
- Emphasize that Saint Pedro Calungsod was only fourteen when he became a missionary in Guam. Missionary life was difficult. Provisions of food did not arrive regularly. The jungles and terrain made life and travel in the area challenging. Typhoons regularly devastated the islands. Despite many hardships, Saint Pedro persevered and he shared his faith with many, many people who became Christians.
- *Ask:* How can you use your talents to spread Jesus' message of love?

 Encourage the children to go to **aliveinchrist.osv.com** at home to learn more about Saint Pedro Calungsod.

Activity

Read aloud the directions to the Live Your Faith activity.

- Allow time for the children to draw a picture.
- Invite volunteers to share their drawings.

Catholic Social Teaching

Chapter Connections

To integrate Catholic Social Teaching into your lesson, choose one of the following features: Call to Community, pages 286–287; or Option for the Poor, pages 290–291.

- Start the Live step of the process by talking about Saint Pedro Calungsod on page 277. Then move directly to the Catholic Social Teaching feature.
- Or, to expand the lesson, complete both pages 276 and 277, then move to the Catholic Social Teaching feature.
- Return to Chapter 21 for the prayer on page 278.

Let Us Pray

Asking Prayer

Tell the children that today they will pray asking God to help them bring peace, justice, and love into the world.

Prepare

Consider assigning the leader parts of the prayer to three different children. If you do so, allow those chosen time to practice.

- Teach the children their responses.

 Rehearse "Right and Just," downloaded from **aliveinchrist.osv.com**.

Gather

Invite the children to process to the prayer space.

- Have the children stand in a circle and invite them to prepare their minds and hearts for prayer.

Pray

Follow the order of prayer on the student page.

 Conclude by singing together "Right and Just."

Live

 Let Us Pray

Asking Prayer

Gather and begin with the Sign of the Cross.

Leader: God, we want to do your will.

All: Help us bring peace.

Leader: God the Father, we want to do your will.

All: Help us bring justice.

Leader: God, we want to do your will.

All: Help us bring love.

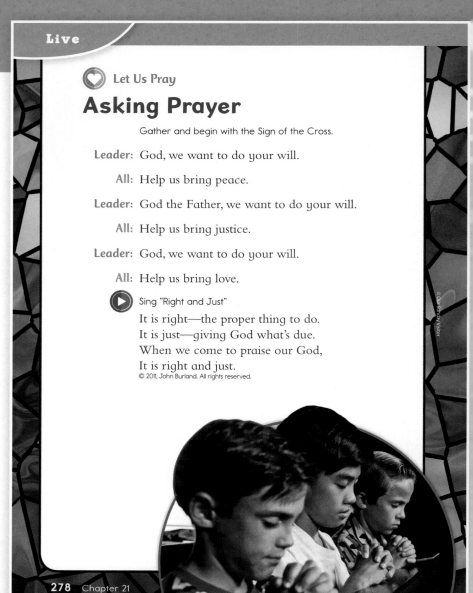 Sing "Right and Just"
It is right—the proper thing to do.
It is just—giving God what's due.
When we come to praise our God,
It is right and just.

278 Chapter 21

 Liturgy Link

Sign of Peace

Tell the children that Catholics share a sign of peace with each other during Mass. People usually shake hands and say "Peace be with you."

- Ask the children how they exchange a sign of peace at Mass and have them practice with each other.

Go to **aliveinchrist.osv.com** for Sunday readings, Scripture background, questions of the week, and seasonal resources.

FAMILY + FAITH
LIVING AND LEARNING TOGETHER

Family + Faith

YOUR CHILD LEARNED >>>

This chapter explores bringing happiness to others and helping God's Kingdom grow.

God's Word

Read **Micah 6:8** to see how God wants us to live so that we can be with him in Heaven.

Catholics Believe

- Justice, love, and peace are signs of God's Kingdom.
- Catholics work here and now with God to help his Kingdom continue to grow.

To learn more, go to the *Catechism of the Catholic Church* #2816–2821 at **usccb.org**.

People of Faith

This week, your child met Blessed Pedro Calungsod, a teenage Filipino catechist who was martyred for the faith.

CHILDREN AT THIS AGE >>>

How They Understand God's Kingdom First-grade children are familiar with stories, such as fairy tales, that involve kings and kingdoms, and they might think of Jesus' references to the Father's Kingdom in these terms. You can help your child understand that Christians cooperate with God to help God's Kingdom grow "on earth as it is in Heaven." We will live forever with God in his Kingdom in Heaven, but we also actively work to help God's Kingdom grow by showing love to one another.

CONSIDER THIS >>>

Without using words, how do we show our children that we love them?

Actions speak louder than words. Making a favorite meal, catching a ball, or wiping away tears as you put on a bandage, are all signs of your love. We make God's life and love present with our words, attitudes, and actions— we manifest God's Kingdom. "The proclamation of the Kingdom of God was fundamental to Jesus' preaching. The Kingdom of God is his presence among human beings calling them to a new way of life as individuals and as a community... It is the Good News that results in love, justice and mercy for the whole world" (*USCCA, p. 79*).

LET'S TALK >>>

- Ask your child what small things he or she can do to help God's Kingdom grow.
- Talk about people who bring peace or share God's love in their daily lives.

LET'S PRAY >>>

Blessed Pedro, pray for us that we may live justice, love, and peace in our family today. Amen.

For a multimedia glossary of Catholic Faith Words, Sunday readings, seasonal and Saint resources, and chapter activities go to **aliveinchrist.osv.com**.

Alive in Christ, Grade 1 Chapter 21 **279**

Distribute the page to the children or parents/adult family members. Point out the chapter highlights, insights on how first graders understand concepts, the opportunity for the adults to reflect on their own experience and faith journey, and the family prayer.

Chapter 21 Review

Chapter Review

A **Work with Words** Fill in the blank with the correct word from the Word Bank.

Word Bank
love
peace
justice

1. When you settle problems with kindness, you bring ____**peace**____.

2. When you care, even if it's hard, you bring ____**love**____.

3. When you give God what he deserves and give others what they need, you bring ____**justice**____.

B **Check Understanding** Put an X by things you can do to help God's Kingdom grow.

4. [X] love your parents   7. [X] pray

5. [X] be a good friend   8. [ ] fight

6. [ ] tease   9. [X] help others

Go to **aliveinchrist.osv.com** for an interactive review.

280 Chapter 21 Review

Use Catechist Quick Reviews to highlight lesson concepts.

A **Work with Words**
Have the children fill in the blank with the correct word from the Word Bank.

B **Check Understanding**
Have the children put an *X* by the things they can do to help God's Kingdom grow.

Go to **aliveinchrist.osv.com** to prepare customized and downloadable assessments, send eAssessments, and assign interactive reviews.

God's Kingdom **279–280**

Unit Review

Use Catechist Quick Reviews in each chapter to highlight lesson concepts for this unit and prepare for the Unit Review.

Have the children complete the Review pages. Then discuss the answers as a group. Review any concepts with which the children are having difficulty.

A **Work with Words**
Have the children fill in the blanks with the correct word or words from the Word Bank.

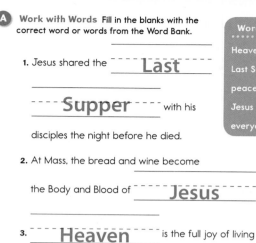

Unit Review

UNIT
7

A **Work with Words** Fill in the blanks with the correct word or words from the Word Bank.

Word Bank

Heaven

Last Supper

peace

Jesus

everyone

1. Jesus shared the _____ **Last** _____ **Supper** _____ with his disciples the night before he died.

2. At Mass, the bread and wine become the Body and Blood of _____ **Jesus** _____.

3. _____ **Heaven** _____ is the full joy of living with God forever.

4. God wants _____ **everyone** _____ to be happy with him.

5. Jesus asks his followers to act with _____ **peace** _____.

Kingdom of God **281**

UNIT 7 Unit Review

B Check Understanding
Draw a line to match the words in Column A with the definition in Column B.

Column A

Column B

6. Eucharist — life after death

7. Jesus' Promise — the Church remembers this meal at Mass

8. God's Kingdom — Sacrament celebrated at Mass

9. Book of Gospels and Chalice — living in peace, love, and justice

10. The Last Supper — used at Mass

C Make Connections
Draw a picture of how you can make others happy.

11.

B Check Understanding
Have the children draw a line to match the words in Column A to the definition in Column B.

C Make Connections
Have the children draw a picture of one way they can make others happy.

Go to **aliveinchrist.osv.com** to prepare customized and downloadable assessments, send eAssessments, and assign interactive reviews.

Live Your Faith
&
Our Catholic Tradition
Reference Section

Live Your Faith

" Let us keep a place for Christ in our lives, let us care for one another and let us be loving custodians of creation. "

—Pope Francis via Twitter, March 19, 2013

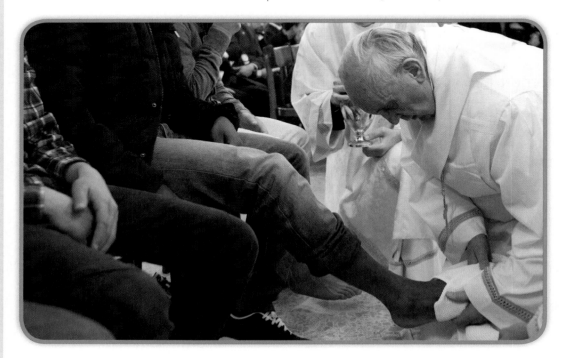

The Seven Themes of Catholic Social Teaching

The Catholic Church's Social Teaching helps build a just society and shows us how to live lives of holiness amidst the challenges of modern society. The wisdom of this tradition can be understood best through a direct reading of Church documents, but here is a synopsis of each of the seven key themes that are part of our Catholic Social Tradition.

Life and Dignity of the Human Person

Each person is created in God's image and all people have rights that flow from their human dignity. The equal dignity of all people means we must work to eliminate social and economic inequalities. We strive to value all people over our personal wealth or possessions.

Call to Family, Community, and Participation

In order for our society to be healthy, we must all make positive contributions to it, bringing to it the light of the Gospels. We can do this by finding practical ways to participate more fully in our own families, in our parishes, and in our communities.

Rights and Responsibilities of the Human Person

Every person has a right to life and the rights needed to live in dignity. The fundamental rights of all people are freedom, justice, and the basic necessities of everyday life. As individuals and as a society, we must work to protect these rights for all people.

Option for the Poor and Vulnerable

God loves all people, and he calls us to love one another as he loves us. In a world where many people live in great poverty while others enjoy great wealth, we must pay special attention to the needs of the poor and reach out to them in Christian charity.

The Dignity of Work and the Rights of Workers

Through labor all people participate in the work of creation and all workers have the following rights that must be protected: the right to productive work, to fair wages, and to pursue economic opportunity. Catholics believe that our work can be a valuable way to serve God and others.

Solidarity of the Human Family

All people—rich and poor, young and old, weak and strong—have equal dignity and rights that flow from that dignity. As part of one human family, we are all dependent on one another and responsible for one another, and must work to reduce social inequalities and provide for one another's needs.

Care for God's Creation

God is the Creator of all people and all that exists in nature. He has given us the bounty of the Earth and its resources and has entrusted us with its care. We are called to respond by protecting and caring for all God's creation for generations to come.

 Go to **aliveinchrist.osv.com** for a complete listing of chapters and Church year lessons correlated to the themes of Catholic Social Teaching.

About This Principle This section presents an overview of the theological foundation of the theme so that catechists have background information at point of use.

Wrap Instruction An easy to follow side column provides catechists with directions and activities for presenting the Catholic Social Teaching in developmentally appropriate ways.

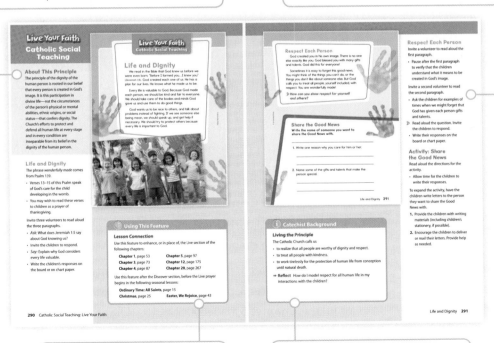

Using This Feature This box identifies core chapters and seasonal lessons to which the Live Your Faith feature is connected.

Catechist Background This box identifies ways the Church calls us to practice the principle and includes a question for catechist reflection.

Live Your Faith
Catholic Social Teaching

About This Principle

The principle of the dignity of the human person is rooted in our belief that every person is created in God's image. It is this participation in divine life—not the circumstances of the person's physical or mental abilities, ethnic origins, age, gender, or social status—that confers dignity. The Church's efforts to protect and defend all human life at every stage and in every condition are inseparable from her belief in the dignity of the human person.

Life and Dignity

Ask: Who made all people?

- Write the children's responses on the board or on chart paper.
- Remind the children that God made people in his own image.

Read aloud the first paragraph.

- Emphasize that God has a plan for each of us. He knows what he made us to be.

Read aloud the second paragraph.

- Emphasize that because God made each person, we need to be kind and fair to everyone.

Read aloud the third paragraph.

- Point out that we need to talk instead of fighting when we disagree with someone and we must always speak up when someone is being mean.

Live Your Faith
Catholic Social Teaching

Life and Dignity

We read in the Bible that God knew us before we were even born: "Before I formed you...I knew you" (Jeremiah 1:5). God created each one of us. He has a plan for our lives. He knows what he made us to be.

Because God made each person, we should be kind and fair to everyone and take care of the bodies and minds God gave us, using them for good.

God wants us to be nice to others, and talk about problems instead of fighting. If someone else is being mean, we should speak up, and get help if necessary. We should help to protect others because every life is important to God.

© Our Sunday Visitor

284 Live Your Faith

🌐 Using This Feature

Lesson Connection

Use this feature to enhance, or in place of, the Live section of the following chapters:

Chapter 1, page 53   **Chapter 6**, page 107

Chapter 3, page 73   **Chapter 8**, page 131

Chapter 5, page 97   **Chapter 9**, page 141

Use this feature after the Discover section before the Live Prayer begins in the following seasonal lessons:

Christmas, page 25   **Easter**, page 38

Pentecost, page 43

The Gift of Life

People live in many different countries. They speak different languages. They have different colors of skin, hair, and eyes.

All people are the same in one important way. God made each one of us. God gave us the gift of his own life and love. God wants us to respect his life in others.

⟩ **What can you do to take care of other people?**

Learn About Others

You can learn a lot from people who are different from you. Answer the questions below.

1. What could you learn from someone who comes from another country?

   _____

   -

   _____

2. What could you learn from someone who has trouble seeing or hearing?

   _____

   -

   _____

Life and Dignity **285**

The Gift of Life

Read aloud the two paragraphs.

- Invite the children to name other ways in which all people are alike.
- Direct their attention to the photograph on page 284, and ask them to tell how the children depicted are showing respect for God's life in one another.

⟩ Have the children discuss the question on the page in small groups.

See pages CE48–CE49 for more information on all seven Catholic Social Teaching principles.

Activity: Learn About Others

Read aloud the directions for the activity.

- Have the children work with a partner. Read aloud the questions, and allow time for the pairs to discuss them.
- Tell the children to write their ideas in the space provided.
- Invite volunteers to share their responses.

To expand this lesson, have the children choose new partners.

1. Supply art materials, and invite the children to draw one special thing about their partners.
2. Ask volunteers to share their work. Have the children give their drawings to their partners to take home.

ⓘ Catechist Background

Living the Principle

The Catholic Church calls us

- to realize that all people are worthy of human dignity and respect.
- to treat all people with kindness.
- to work tirelessly for the protection of all human life from conception until death.

➤ **Reflect** How do you reinforce the lesson of respect for human life in your interactions with the children?

About This Principle

Merely belonging to a family or a community is not enough. A community in which no one participates or works together is simply a collection of individuals. In order to live in the communal relationship God intends for human beings, as Catholics we have to take responsibility for doing our part. We have to give as well as take, sacrifice as well as celebrate. It is also necessary for our survival as individuals that we work together.

Call to Community

Ask: Why does God give us families?

• Write the children's responses on the board or on chart paper.

• Recall with the children that our families are a gift from God. In our families, we learn about God and how to love one another.

Read aloud both paragraphs.

• *Ask:* Why did God give us communities? He knew it would not be good for us to live our lives alone.

Point out that like our families, our parish helps us to learn about God.

Call attention to the picture.

• Ask the children to tell what they see in the picture.

• Help the children see that the picture shows children working together in a community garden.

Live Your Faith
Catholic Social Teaching

Call to Community

God gives us families and communities because he knows it would not be good for us to live our lives alone. In fact, the Bible says that this is why God created Eve to be a companion and friend to Adam. (See Genesis 2:18.)

The Church teaches that God gives us families to help us learn who God is and how to love one another. Our parish community also helps us to learn about God. In families and in parish communities, we work together to take care of one another and to become the people God made us to be.

Planting a community garden is one way we can help take care of each other.

286 Live Your Faith

🌐 Using This Feature

Lesson Connection

Use this feature to enhance the Live section of these chapters:

Chapter 5, page 97   **Chapter 14**, page 199

Chapter 9, page 141   **Chapter 19**, page 257

Chapter 10, page 155   **Chapter 21**, page 277

Chapter 12, page 175

Use this feature after the Discover section before the Live Prayer begins in the following seasonal lessons:

Mary's Birthday, page 12   **All Saints Day**, page 16

Advent, page 20   **Holy Week**, page 34

You Are Needed

What is a family without family members? What is a community without people? What is a parish without parishioners? Every group must have members. No group can continue to live and grow unless its members work together.

Your family, your parish, and your community would not be the same without you. You are needed. You can use the gifts God gave you to help in many groups in your community.

≫ **How do you participate in your family?**

Draw a Picture

Draw one way you take part in your community.

ⓘ Catechist Background

Living the Principle

The Catholic Church calls us

- to recognize that we live in relationship with all members of the human family.
- to break down the walls of selfishness, isolation, and apathy.
- to become fully involved in our families, communities, and world.

→ **Reflect** How are you answering the call to be fully involved in your family, your community, and the world?

You Are Needed

Ask: What does it mean to belong to a community?

- Write the children's responses on the board or on chart paper.

Read aloud the first paragraph.

- Write the word *participate* on the board or on chart paper, and help the children sound it out.

Read aloud the last paragraph.

≫ Discuss the question on the page together as a group.

See pages CE48–CE49 for more information on all seven Catholic Social Teaching principles.

Activity: Draw a Picture

Read aloud the directions for the activity.

- Discuss together how first graders take part in their community.
- Provide time for the children to complete their drawing.
- Invite volunteers to share what they have drawn.

To expand this lesson, have the children create community webs showing their links to communities.

1. Give the children large sheets of paper. Have them write their names in the middle of the paper, and begin the web with their families.

2. Have the children add web links for all organizations, groups, and communities of which they are a part—for example, class, school, parish, city, sports team, etc.

Live Your Faith
Catholic Social Teaching

About This Principle

An American legal aphorism notes that "your individual rights stop at my nose." That's a simple way of summarizing the problems that occur when rights and responsibilities conflict. The rights we have as humans created in God's image are universal but not absolute, because as Catholics, we are also created to live in community, honoring one another's rights and working for the common good. When conflicts arise—as they inevitably will—we are called to use peaceful means to resolve them.

Rights and Responsibilities

Ask: What responsibilities do you have?

- Write the children's responses on the board or on chart paper.
- Point out how chores at home or in the classroom help work for the good of the family, class, or school.

Read aloud both paragraphs.

- Clarify that rights are the things that every person needs or should have, such as food, shelter, clothing, and fair treatment. Responsibilities are our duties, or things we must do.

Point out the picture.

- Have the children tell what they see happening in the picture.

Live Your Faith
Catholic Social Teaching

Rights and Responsibilities

Because God made every person, everyone has rights and responsibilities. Rights are the freedoms or things every person needs and should have. Responsibilities are our duties, or the things we must do.

Jesus said, "You shall love your neighbor as yourself" (Mark 12:31). Following this command means making sure everyone's rights are protected. We also have a responsibility to treat others well and work together for the good of everyone.

© Our Sunday Visitor

288 Live Your Faith

🌐 Using This Feature

Lesson Connection

Use this feature to enhance, or in place of, the Live section of the following chapters:

Chapter 4, page 87	**Chapter 14**, page 199
Chapter 10, page 155	**Chapter 15**, page 209
Chapter 11, page 165	**Chapter 18**, page 243
Chapter 12, page 175	

Use this feature after the Discover section before the Live Prayer begins in the following seasonal lessons:

Christmas, page 25	**Lent**, page 30

© Our Sunday Visitor

Living in Harmony

Have you ever heard a choir sing? Some people sing high notes, some sing low notes. When they sing together, they make harmony, a blend of beautiful sounds.

Each person has rights, things that he or she can do freely. Each person also has to protect other people's rights. When everyone's rights are protected, we live in peace. We make the beautiful harmony of God's kingdom.

≫ **What are some things that keep people from living in harmony?**

Check Your Understanding

Rights and responsibilities are not the same thing. Draw a line from the rights in Column B to the word "Rights" in column A. Do the same for responsibilities.

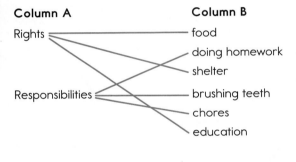

Column A

Rights

Responsibilities

Column B

food

doing homework

shelter

brushing teeth

chores

education

Rights and Responsibilities **289**

(i) Catechist Background

Living the Principle

The Catholic Church calls us

- to recognize and respect the rights of each person.
- to take responsibility for protecting others' rights.
- to resolve conflicts peacefully whenever possible.

→ **Reflect** How can you model for children a commitment to peaceful conflict resolution?

Living in Harmony

Write the word *harmony* on the board or on chart paper, and have the children speculate about its meaning.

Ask the children to listen carefully as you read these two paragraphs aloud.

- Review briefly the comparison between singers in a choir and people in society, making sure children understand the similarities.

≫ Discuss the question on the page together as a group.

See pages CE48–CE49 for more information on all seven Catholic Social Teaching principles.

Activity: Check Your Understanding

Read aloud the directions. Provide time for the children to complete the activity.

- Brainstorm how to protect others' rights, listing the children's ideas on the board or on chart paper.
- Encourage the children to share what they have learned with friends or family members.

To expand this lesson, play for the children recordings of choirs or choruses singing in harmony.

1. Ask the children to listen for the different musical parts working together.
2. As an alternative, invite the parish music minister or choir director to teach the group a hymn with simple harmony.

About This Principle

At first glance, the Church's longstanding practice of the preferential option for the poor may seem "unfair" to young children, who are used to defining justice in terms of strict equality. In truth, we adults sometimes have as much difficulty with this concept as children do. The justice of God's Kingdom calls us to redress the injustices of this world, which means tilting the scales in favor of those most in need.

Option for the Poor

Ask: What can you do to help people in need?

- Write the children's responses on the board or on chart paper.

Read aloud both paragraphs.

- Emphasize that we should treat all people the same way we would treat Jesus.
- *Ask:* What does Saint Rose of Lima mean when she says, "When we serve the poor, we serve Jesus"?
- Point out that the Church teaches that the needs of the poor come first.

Direct attention to the picture.

- Ask the children to tell what they see happening in the picture.
- *Ask:* How are people putting the needs of the poor first? They are volunteering to serve a meal to the poor.

Live Your Faith
Catholic Social Teaching

Option for the Poor

In Scripture, Jesus says that whatever we have done for people who are poor or needy, we have also done for him. (See Matthew 25:40.) We should treat people the same way we would treat Jesus himself. When people need food, drink, clothing, housing, or medical care, or when they are lonely, we should try extra hard to help.

Saint Rose of Lima said, "When we serve the poor and the sick, we serve Jesus." Our Church teaches that we should have special love and care for those who are poor and put their needs first. When we do this, God will bless us.

© Our Sunday Visitor

290   Live Your Faith

🌐 Using This Feature

Lesson Connection

Use this feature to enhance, or in place of, the Live section of the following chapters:

Chapter 6, page 107   **Chapter 16**, page 223

Chapter 7, page 121   **Chapter 20**, page 267

Chapter 13, page 189   **Chapter 21**, page 277

Chapter 15, page 209

Use this feature after the Discover section before the Live Prayer begins in the following seasonal lessons:

Advent, page 20   **Lent**, page 30   **Holy Week**, page 34

People in Need

One day Jesus was teaching a big crowd about God's love. Late in the afternoon, people started getting hungry, but they had no food. Jesus' disciples weren't sure what to do.

Jesus asked who had food. One boy was willing to share his five small loaves of bread and two fish. Jesus blessed the food. There were baskets of leftovers! (See John 6:1–13.)

We are called to be like Jesus and the boy. We should try to share what we have and give to others.

≫ **What do the people in your community need?**

Write a Response

Read the words and write something you could do to help.

1. A friend is feeling lonely. What can you do?

   _____

   _____

   _____

2. A new neighbor has no friends. What can you do?

   _____

   _____

   _____

© Our Sunday Visitor

(i) Catechist Background

Living the Principle

The Catholic Church calls us

- to recognize that all blessings are gifts of God.
- to work for the just distribution of those blessings.
- to defend those deprived of a voice in society.

→ **Reflect** How are you sharing your blessings with those most in need?

People in Need

Ask: What can you give to or share with others?

- Write the children's responses on the board or on chart paper.

Invite the children to listen carefully as you read aloud the story of the feeding of the multitudes, the first two paragraphs.

- Ask the children what the people in the crowd needed, and how Jesus helped them.

Read aloud the concluding paragraph.

≫ Discuss the question on the page together as a group.

See pages CE48–CE49 for more information on all seven Catholic Social Teaching principles.

Activity: Write a Response

Read aloud the directions for the activity.

- If necessary, read aloud each statement and question.
- Allow time for the children to work independently on the activity.
- Invite volunteers to share their work.

To expand this lesson, invite the children to participate in sharing what they have.

1. Encourage the children to donate new or gently used books.
2. Donate the books to a shelter, food pantry, or church or school in a low-income neighborhood.

About This Principle

In our society, people are often distanced from the workers who make their lives comfortable and convenient. The farm workers who harvest the produce we eat every day are often migrants, workers who travel from field to field following the seasons. Migrant farm workers face a number of challenges that flow from their transient status. Many come from other countries and are not fluent in English. Pay rates and working conditions for migrant laborers are often substandard. The Catholic Church calls us to respect the dignity of all those who labor.

The Dignity of Work

Ask: What are some jobs people have?

- Write the children's responses on the board or on chart paper.
- Tell the children that work is part of God's plan.

Read aloud both paragraphs.

- *Ask:* Why are jobs important?

Have the group name three things that Scripture teaches us about workers. Workers should be treated fairly, they should be given fair pay, and they should be able to work things out with their bosses if they are unhappy.

Direct the children's attention to the picture.

- Have the children tell what they see happening in the picture.

Live Your Faith
Catholic Social Teaching

The Dignity of Work

The different jobs people have help them earn money to buy food and other things they need to live. Jobs also allow people to work together with God and his creation. Work is part of God's plan for people, and everyone should work, either in or outside the home.

All adults should be able to have a job if they want one. Scripture teaches that workers should be treated fairly by their bosses. (See Deuteronomy 24:14.) They should be given fair pay for their work. (See Leviticus 19:13 and Deuteronomy 24:15.) If workers are unhappy, they should be able to work things out with their bosses.

© Our Sunday Visitor

292 Live Your Faith

🌐 Using This Feature

Lesson Connection

Use this feature to enhance, or in place of, the Live section of the following chapters:

Chapter 2, page 63   **Chapter 11**, page 165

Chapter 8, page 131   **Chapter 13**, page 189

Use this feature after the Discover section before the Live Prayer begins in the following seasonal lesson:

Pentecost, page 43

Respect for Workers

People work in all kinds of jobs. People work to earn money and to use the gifts and talents God gave them.

Some workers do not earn enough money. Some workers become ill or injured and cannot work at all. The Church teaches that work and workers should be treated well. It should not matter who the workers are or what they do.

≫ **What does it mean to show respect for workers?**

True For You

You are a worker, too.

Read each sentence. If it is true for you, circle the happy face. If it is not, circle the sad face. If it is true sometimes, and you need to do better, circle the question mark.

1. I do my best school work.

2. I do my chores as soon as I am asked.

3. I am proud of the work I do.

4. I thank my family for the work they do.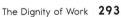

The Dignity of Work **293**

 Catechist Background

Living the Principle

The Catholic Church calls us

- to respect the dignity of all labor.
- to help secure adequate employment for all.
- to reach out to the migrant workers and their families.

➔ **Reflect** How can you learn more about, and show appreciation for, the workers who supply the food you eat?

Respect for Workers

Read aloud the first paragraph.

- Review some of the jobs the children mentioned earlier.

Read aloud the rest of the text.

- Direct attention to the picture, and ask the children to explain how these workers are using the gifts and talents God gave them.

≫ Have the children respond to the question on the page in small groups.

Ask: What kind of work would you like to do when you grow up?

Ask volunteers from each group to list on the board or on chart paper ideas about future jobs.

See pages CE48–CE49 for more information on all seven Catholic Social Teaching principles.

Activity: True for You

Ask the children to suggest ways in which they are workers.

- Share the directions for the activity. If necessary, read aloud the numbered statements and point out the individual icons.
- Have the children work independently. Tell them they may keep their responses private.

To expand this lesson, invite the children to draw themselves as adults carrying out a job or profession that interests them.

1. Have the children write on their drawings a one-sentence description of how their work will help them work together with God and his creation.

2. Display the completed art work.

Live Your Faith
Catholic Social Teaching

About This Principle

First graders have a fairly strong sense of themselves as members of their families and their school class. They may know many of their neighbors, and are beginning to take a stronger role in the parish and in the community. But it is still difficult for six year olds to understand the Catholic concept of solidarity—the understanding that all people are our neighbors, part of one human family.

Human Solidarity

Ask: How are all people alike?

- Write the children's responses on the board or on chart paper.

Introduce the topic. See pages CE48–CE49 for more information on all seven Catholic Social Teaching principles.

Read aloud both paragraphs.

- Help the children to understand that although people are different in many ways, one way we are all alike is that God made us.

- Emphasize that because God made everyone, we should treat everyone with love, kindness, and fairness.

Point out the picture.

- Have the children tell what they see happening in the picture.

- *Ask:* What do all the children in the picture have in common?

Live Your Faith
Catholic Social Teaching

Human Solidarity

People around the world are different in many ways. Our hair, eyes, and skin are many different colors. There are people who are rich, people who are poor, and people who are in-between.

But one way we are all alike is that God made us. We are one human family. (See Galatians 3:28.) God calls everyone to be his children. Because God made everyone, we should treat everyone with love, kindness, and fairness. In the Beatitudes, Jesus says, "Blessed are the peacemakers" (Matthew 5:9). Treating others fairly will help us to live in peace with one another.

© Our Sunday Visitor

294 Live Your Faith

🌐 Using This Feature

Lesson Connection

Use this feature to enhance, or in place of, the Live section of the following chapters:

Chapter 7, page 121   **Chapter 18**, page 243

Chapter 16, page 223   **Chapter 19**, page 257

Chapter 17, page 233   **Chapter 20**, page 267

Use this feature after the Discover section before the Live Prayer begins in the following seasonal lessons:

Mary's Birthday, page 12   **All Saints Day**, page 16

One Big Neighborhood

Who are your neighbors? People who live close to you are neighbors. So are the people who live in your city or town.

Jesus taught that all people are our neighbors. Neighbors can live close by or far away. All humans are part of God's family.

Families and neighbors share good times and bad times. It is important for us to love our neighbors and treat them well.

≫ How can you get to know your neighbors around the world?

Solve the Puzzle

What can you do to help your neighbors? Circle the correct letter in each sentence and write them down to find one thing you can do for your neighbors.

1. Circle the letter that is in L O T but not in G O T.
2. Circle the letter that is in T O N but not in T A N.
3. Circle the letter that is in V A N but not in M A N.
4. Circle the letter that is in B E T but not in B I T.

LOVE

Human Solidarity **295**

© Our Sunday Visitor

One Big Neighborhood

Ask the children to recall the Great Commandment.

Invite the children to listen as you read aloud the text on this page.

- Ask the children for their reaction to the idea that all people are neighbors.

≫ Discuss the question on the page together as a group, listing the children's responses on the board or on chart paper.

Activity: Solve the Puzzle

Read aloud the directions for the activity.

- Have the children choose partners and work in pairs to solve the word puzzle.

To expand this lesson, invite the children to compose prayers for neighbors around the world.

1. Have the children write their prayers on cards.
2. Choose a few cards each session and invite the children who wrote them to lead the group in their prayer.

(i) Catechist Background

Living the Principle

The Catholic Church calls us

- to recognize that we are all children of God.
- to share fully in the joys and sorrows of the human condition.
- to do what we can to extend God's healing love to all.

➜ **Reflect** How can I set a strong example of solidarity for the children?

About This Principle

Technological advancement, with all its positive aspects, can also serve to alienate us from the natural world. As more and more people live in larger and larger urban areas, we lose touch with the wonders of creation. We are more likely to neglect our responsibility to care for the natural world. That's why the Church continually reminds us that all that we have and all that we are comes to us from God as a gift. We are entrusted with creation as stewards.

Care for Creation

Ask: What did God say about everything he created?

- Write the children's responses on the board or on chart paper.
- Help the children recall that God said, "It is good!"

Introduce the topic. See pages CE48–CE49 for more information on all seven Catholic Social Teaching principles.

Read aloud both paragraphs.

- Emphasize that God put people in charge of caring for creation.
- Explain that God wants us to both enjoy creation and take care of everything he made.

Live Your Faith
Catholic Social Teaching

Care for Creation

God created the whole world—the Earth and sky, the mountains and deserts, and all of the plants, animals, and people. When God made these things, he called them "very good" (Genesis 1:31). God put people in charge of the fish, the birds, and all living things. (See Genesis 1:28.) God wants us to enjoy and take care of everything he has made.

Our Church teaches us that God gave us the plants and animals for the good of all people. We need to work to take care of the plants and animals and the places where they live, so everyone can enjoy them now and in the future.

© Our Sunday Visitor

296

🌐 Using This Feature

Lesson Connection

Use this feature to enhance, or in place of, the Live section of the following chapters:

Chapter 1, page 53   **Chapter 3**, page 73

Chapter 2, page 63   **Chapter 17**, page 233

Use this feature after the Discover section before the Live Prayer begins in the following seasonal lesson:

Easter, page 38

Be My Helpers

You can be a good helper. You can help your family at home. You can help your teacher at school.

God asks you to be his helper, too. You can help take care of the gifts of God's creation. You can help by planting flowers and vegetables. You can feed wild birds. You can take care of your pets. You can also help keep parks and playgrounds clean.

≫ Why should you take care of creation?

Be a Good Helper

Draw yourself working to care for God's creation. What are some things you can do to help take care of the gifts of God's creation?

Be My Helpers

Ask: What are the gifts of God's creation?

• Write the children's responses on the board or on chart paper.

Read aloud the first paragraph.

• Ask the children to listen carefully as you read about ways to be a good helper.

Read aloud the second paragraph.

• Invite the children to suggest other ways to help take care of creation.

≫ Discuss the question on the page together as a group.

Activity: Be a Good Helper

Read aloud the directions for the activity.

• Pass out crayons or markers.

• Allow time for the children to work independently.

• Invite volunteers to share their ideas for caring for creation.

To expand this lesson, invite the children to help you create an art gallery to showcase their drawings.

1. Display the completed artwork on a bulletin board titled *We Are God's Helpers*.

2. Invite parents or guardians to come see the artwork.

(i) Catechist Background

Living the Principle

The Catholic Church calls us

• to renew our connections with the natural world.

• to be thankful for all the gifts of God's creation.

• to work for the preservation and care of the natural environment.

➜ **Reflect** How can you maintain a close and caring relationship with the natural world God created?

The Holy Trinity

The Trinity is God the Father, God the Son, and God the Holy Spirit—three Divine Persons in one God.

- God the Father is the Creator of all that is.
- Jesus Christ is the Son of God and our Savior.
- God the Holy Spirit is God's gift of love to the Church.

When you make the Sign of the Cross and say, "In the name of the Father, and of the Son, and of the Holy Spirit," you are showing your belief in the Holy Trinity.

298 Our Catholic Tradition

The Creed

The creed tells the faith of the Church. It brings together the Church's most important beliefs about the Holy Trinity and our Catholic faith.

The Apostles' Creed

This Creed is a summary of the Apostles' beliefs. We sometimes profess it at Mass during the Easter season and in Masses with children.

I believe in God,
the Father almighty,
Creator of heaven and earth,
and in Jesus Christ, his only Son,
  our Lord,

At the words that follow, up to and including the Virgin Mary, all bow.

who was conceived by the
  Holy Spirit,
born of the Virgin Mary,
suffered under Pontius Pilate,
was crucified, died and was
  buried;
he descended into hell;
on the third day he rose again
  from the dead;

he ascended into heaven,
and is seated at the right hand
  of God the Father almighty;
from there he will come to
  judge the living and the dead.

I believe in the Holy Spirit,
the holy Catholic Church,
the communion of saints,
the forgiveness of sins,
the resurrection of the body,
and life everlasting. Amen.

Faith Basics **299**

The Sign of the Cross

Point out to the children that when we make the Sign of the Cross, we are praying to the Holy Trinity.

- Print the Sign of the Cross on sheets of bright paper.
- Print the words *Father*, *Son*, and *Holy Spirit* in trace-over letters.
- Duplicate the prayer and give each child a copy. Have the children trace over the names of the three Divine Persons in one God.
- Pray the Sign of the Cross together.

The Apostles' Creed

Explain to the children that the Apostles' Creed states our Catholic beliefs passed down from the time of the Apostles. The wording in the Student Book reflects the latest English translation, which was revised slightly when we began to implement the Third Edition of the *Roman Missal* in 2011.

- Give each child a prayer card on which is printed:

  I believe in God,
  the Father almighty,
  Creator of heaven and earth,
  and in Jesus Christ, his only Son, our Lord,

- Encourage the children to take their prayer cards home and ask their family members to work with them to help them memorize the words.

The Church

The Church is the community of baptized people who believe in God and follow Jesus. The Church gathers to worship and praise God, especially at the celebration of the Mass.

Each member of the Church has been baptized and welcomed into God's family. Catholics have a mission to share God's message of love with others.

In order to carry out this mission, we receive the gift of the Holy Spirit. Jesus' followers received the Holy Spirit at Pentecost.

The Holy Spirit gave each of the disciples the courage to spread the Good News of Jesus to other people. The Holy Spirit also makes you strong.

Mary, the Mother of God

Mary is the Mother of God. She is also Mother of the Church. Mary is a very special Saint. All her life, Mary said "yes" to the things God asked of her.

At the Annunciation the Angel Gabriel came to Mary to tell her she was going to give birth to the Savior, whom she should call Jesus. Because Mary said "yes," all people have been saved from the power of sin and everlasting death.

Mary is our great role model in the Church. The People of God often ask Mary to pray for them so that they have the courage to say "yes" to God, especially when it is difficult.

Optional Activity

Who Is the Church?

Play the finger game "Here's the Church" with the children.

- Interlock fingers of both hands with palms facing down. Begin the finger play and say, "Here's the church."

- Bring two index fingers to form the steeple while saying, "And here's the steeple."

- Open two thumbs as if opening doors and say, "Open the doors."

- Turn remaining fingers over and wiggle them while saying, "And see all the people."

- Remind the children that the Church is all who have been baptized and follow Jesus.

Optional Activity

The Story of the Annunciation

This Scripture story is often a favorite of children.

- Read aloud the story of the Annunciation.

- Help the children understand that the story's message for us is to show us how to say "yes" to God when he asks hard things of us.

- Provide the children with drawing paper and crayons. Have them draw their retelling of the Annunciation story.

Honoring Mary

The Church honors Mary in many special ways. Special prayers, such as the Rosary, are said. Feast days, such as Our Lady of Guadalupe, are celebrated. We honor Mary at all times, but especially on her feast days. These prayers and feasts remind people that Mary was willing to serve God.

Many countries celebrate Mary in different ways. You can read about a few of these ways on the next page.

Our Lady of Guadalupe

In Mexico, Latin America, and the United States, the people honor Our Lady of Guadalupe. She appeared to Juan Diego on his way to Mass. A church was built on that site. Blessed Pope John Paul II named Our Lady of Guadalupe the Patroness of the Americas.

Our Lady of Czestochowa

In Poland, the people honor the image of Our Lady of Czestochowa. Blessed Pope John Paul II had a special devotion to this image of Mary, who is named queen of Poland. He visited her shrine just after becoming Pope in 1979.

Our Lady of Lourdes

In France, people honor Our Lady of Lourdes. Mary appeared to a young peasant girl named Bernadette. A spring of water flows at that spot. To this day it has healing power. People from all over visit the site.

302

Faith Basics **303**

Optional Activity

A Holy Family Picture Album

Have the children draw a scene that might have been included in a family album of Jesus, Mary, and Joseph.

- Talk with the children about how the Holy Family is a model for every family.
- Provide the children with drawing paper and crayons. Challenge them to consider an event or occasion in the life of the Holy Family that they think might have been included in a family picture album.
- Have the children illustrate one such family album picture for the Holy Family.

Optional Activity

Read the Story

Provide the children with more information about Saint Juan Diego and Our Lady of Guadalupe by reading them a classic version of this story of faith.

- Search online for books and resources relating to this story.
- Show pictures of Saint Juan Diego and Our Lady of Guadalupe and have the children create their own illustrations or retell the story in their own words.

The Seven Sacraments

The Sacraments are special signs and celebrations that Jesus gave his Church. They allow us to share in God's life and work.

Baptism

Baptism frees you of sin and makes you a child of God and member of the Church.

Confirmation

Confirmation seals us with the gift of the Holy Spirit and celebrates his help.

Eucharist

Jesus shares his life with us in the bread and wine that become his Body and Blood.

Penance and Reconciliation

You say you are sorry. Through the words and actions of the priest, God forgives your sins and strengthens you to live as he wants.

Anointing of the Sick

In the Anointing of the Sick, a priest blesses the very sick with holy oil. God gives comfort and peace.

Holy Orders

In Holy Orders God blesses men to be bishops, priests, and deacons who lead and serve the Church.

Matrimony

In Marriage, God blesses a baptized man and a baptized woman to live in love. Married love is the heart of a family.

304 Our Catholic Tradition

Faith Basics **305**

Optional Activity

Attend a Parish Baptism

Provide the children with an experience of Baptism as it is celebrated in your parish.

- If possible, arrange to have the children attend a parish Baptism, whether during a Sunday liturgy or at another time designated for Baptisms at your parish.
- Afterward, talk with the children about what they saw and heard.
- Emphasize how God shares his love and life with us through the Sacrament of Baptism.

Optional Activity

Signs of God's Love

Reinforce that the Seven Sacraments are signs of God's love given by Jesus to bring people closer to God.

- Remind the children that signs of God's love are all around us. The Seven Sacraments are signs of God's love, too.
- Provide the children with paper, glue, and a variety of pre-cut symbols such as hearts, flowers, gift boxes, and so on. On each symbol, print *Signs of God's love are all around me!*
- Have the children create collages with their symbols.

Special Things in Church

Altar

The altar is the table at the front of the church that is used to celebrate the Mass.

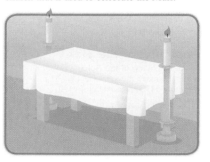

Vestments

The priest wears special clothing called vestments. Some of the vestments that he wears are different colors for the different seasons of the Church year. The priest wears special clothing because he represents Jesus at Mass.

Tabernacle

The Tabernacle is a special place in the church where the Body of Christ, the Blessed Sacrament, is kept after Mass.

Crucifix

A crucifix is a cross with an image of Jesus on it. A crucifix is usually hung somewhere near the altar or is carried in procession as Mass begins.

Optional Activity

Design a Tabernacle

Use this activity to strengthen the children's appreciation for containing the True Presence of Jesus in the Blessed Sacrament in the Tabernacle.

- Challenge the children to design their own Tabernacles.
- Provide them with drawing paper and crayons, and ask them to each draw an illustration of a Tabernacle that would be special enough to hold the Blessed Sacrament.

Optional Activity

Invite a Speaker

Enrich the children's knowledge and understanding of crosses and crucifixes by inviting a guest speaker to the session.

- Consider inviting a parish priest, deacon, or parish staff member to the session to speak to the children about crosses and crucifixes. Consider inviting a person who is knowledgeable about icons.
- Explain to the speaker beforehand that the children are learning about the cross and the crucifix and their role in the Catholic faith. Ask him or her to bring several examples of crosses and crucifixes for the children to hold and examine.

Holy Water

As you enter the church, you dip your hand in holy water from the baptismal font or holy water font and make the Sign of the Cross. This reminds you of your Baptism.

Paschal Candle

At Easter, the Paschal Candle is lit to remind the Church that Jesus is the light of the world. This candle is a very large candle from which many other baptismal candles are lit.

Candles

Candles light the darkness. They are a sign of God's presence. Candles are carried during processions at Mass and are also placed on or beside the altar.

Vigil Lights

Some churches have special candles called vigil lights. They are usually blue, red, or amber. These candles are lit when people ask for special prayers.

Optional Activity

Conduct a Church Tour

Strengthen the children's knowledge of their parish church and its special things by taking them on a tour of the church.

- Make arrangements to bring the children to church for a tour.
- Be the tour guide yourself or invite a parish staff member to guide the children.
- Point out to them the items listed on pages 306–309.

Optional Activity

Sanctuary Lamp

Explain to the children that to show the True Presence of Jesus, a constant light is kept burning near the Tabernacle. Tell them that in some churches this light is a candle, while in other churches this light is an oil lamp.

- Take the children to church to see the sanctuary lamp, or show them a picture of such a light.

The Four Parts of the Mass

1. The Introductory Rites

The Introductory Rites begin the Mass.

- A procession by the priest, deacon, and servers begins the Mass.
- The Church asks for God's mercy with the prayer: "Lord, have mercy. Christ, have mercy. Lord, have mercy."
- A song of glory and praise comes after that.

2. The Liturgy of the Word

The Liturgy of the Word is the first main part of the Mass.

- The community listens to a reading from the Old Testament and one from the New Testament.
- The priest or deacon reads the Gospel and gives a homily. During Mass Jesus is present. Christ is present in:
  - the assembled community.
  - the Word of God.
  - the presiding priest.
  - in his Body and Blood most especially.

3. The Liturgy of the Eucharist

The Liturgy of the Eucharist is the other great part of the Mass.

- Gifts of bread and wine are brought to the altar.
- The assembly remembers Jesus' Death and Resurrection.
- The Church offers praise and gives thanks to God through Jesus.
- Through the power of the Holy Spirit, and the words and actions of the priest, the bread and wine become the Body and Blood of Jesus.
- Before receiving Jesus in Holy Communion people offer one another a sign of peace by shaking hands or hugging.

4. The End of Mass

At the end of Mass, the priest blesses the people and tells them to go forth in peace to share about Jesus.

Catholics serve in the Mass in various ways: as altar servers, cross bearers, singers, readers, and extraordinary ministers of Holy Communion.

Optional Activity

Write a Class Epistle

Talk with the children about the Letters, or Epistles, of Saint Paul. Explain how important these Letters were as reminders of how the followers of Jesus should live.

- Guide the children in writing an epistle to another group.
- Have them include the Christian behaviors that every follower of Jesus should live out.
- When the children's ideas are completed, print the letter on chart paper.

Optional Activity

Make a Mass Mural

Reinforce the children's knowledge of the Mass by having them create a Mass mural.

- Provide the children with a long sheet of butcher paper and crayons or markers.
- Assign small groups of children various Mass parts.
- Challenge the children to draw their images of those parts of the Mass.

Liturgical Seasons and Colors

The Church has many seasons. Each season is marked by a special color or colors that decorate the church and the vestments that the priest wears.

Advent

Advent is the beginning of the Church year and is marked by the color violet. Advent is about four weeks long; it looks forward to the return of Jesus at the end of time, and it leads up to Christmas. It is a time of waiting and preparing.

Christmas

Christmas is celebrated with the colors white and gold. Gold can be used instead of white for special Church holy days. At Christmas the Church remembers the birth of Jesus and celebrates his presence with us now. We look forward to the return of Jesus at the end of time.

Ordinary Time

Ordinary Time celebrates the words and works of Jesus and is marked by the color green.

Lent

During Lent Christians recall their baptismal promises to change their life and act more like Jesus. As a sign of preparation for Easter, Lent is marked by the color violet.

Easter Triduum

The Easter Triduum is the season that lasts for three days and is the most holy season of the Church year. It celebrates Jesus' passing through Death to life. The holy days of Triduum are Holy Thursday (white or gold), Good Friday (red), Holy Saturday (white or gold), and Easter Sunday (white or gold).

Easter

The Easter season starts on the night of Easter Sunday. Vestments are brilliant white for new life because the Easter season celebrates Jesus' Resurrection. Easter also celebrates the new life Jesus' Resurrection brings to all.

Optional Activity

Read the Nativity Story

Children this age really enjoy listening to the story of the Nativity.

- Choose a children's Bible version of the story or one of many trade book versions available at local bookstores or libraries.
- Take some session time to read the story with enthusiasm.

Optional Activity

Loving Lenten Crosses

Talk with the children about the loving sacrifices we make during the season of Lent to prepare to celebrate Jesus' Resurrection at Easter.

- Provide the children with prepared crosses made from white construction paper. Section off each cross with a "stained-glass pattern" of boxes.
- Explain to the children that each time they do a kind or unselfish act during Lent, they are to color in one of the spaces on their crosses.
- Challenge them to fill in each space with bright colors by Easter.

God's Laws

God knows it is sometimes difficult to make good choices. He gave his People the Ten Commandments to help guide them. He wants you to make good choices, too.

The Ten Commandments	What They Mean
1 I am the Lord your God: you shall not have strange gods before me.	Make God the most important thing in your life.
2 You shall not take the name of the Lord your God in vain.	Always use God's name in a reverent way.
3 Remember to keep holy the Lord's Day.	Attend Mass and rest on Sunday.
4 Honor your father and your mother.	Love and obey your parents and guardians.
5 You shall not kill.	Be kind to the people and animals God made; care for yourself and others.
6 You shall not commit adultery.	Be respectful of your body.
7 You shall not steal.	Don't take other people's things; don't take what belongs to someone else.
8 You shall not bear false witness against your neighbor.	Always tell the truth.
9 You shall not covet your neighbor's wife.	Keep your thoughts and words clean; don't be jealous of other people's friendships.
10 You shall not covet your neighbor's goods.	Be happy with the things you have; don't be jealous of what other people have.

314 Our Catholic Tradition

Jesus' Command to Love

Jesus taught that the Great Commandment and his New Commandment sum up the Ten Commandments.

The Great Commandment

"You shall love the Lord, your God, with all your heart, with all your being, with all your strength, and with all your mind, and your neighbor as yourself." Luke 10:27

Jesus' New Commandment

"This is my commandment: love one another as I love you." John 15:12

Faith Basics 315

Optional Activity

Moses

Provide the children with a deeper understanding of the giving of the Ten Commandments by reading to them the story of Moses.

- Choose a children's version of the story or one of many trade book versions available at local bookstores or libraries.
- Read a story of Moses to the children. Invite their reviews.

Optional Activity

Memorize Jesus' New Commandment

Challenge the children to memorize John 15:12.

- Provide each child with the Scripture verse written on an index card.
- Tape the cards to their desk and have them read the verse often until they have memorized it.
- Or you may wish to send the index cards home with the children. Have them place the cards where they will see it often and recite the verse until it is memorized.

Basic Prayers

These are essential prayers that every Catholic should know. Latin is the official, universal language of the Church. No matter what language someone speaks in their daily life, these prayers are prayed in common in Latin.

Sign of the Cross

In the name of the Father,
and of the Son,
and of the Holy Spirit.
Amen.

Signum Crucis

In nómine Patris
et Fílii
et Spíritus Sancti.
Amen.

Glory Be

Glory be to the Father
and to the Son
and to the Holy Spirit,
as it was in the beginning
is now, and ever shall be
world without end. Amen.

Gloria Patri

Gloria Patri
et Fílio
et Spíritui Sancto.
Sicut erat in princípio,
et nunc et semper
et in sǽcula sæculorem.
Amen.

The Lord's Prayer

Our Father,
who art in heaven,
hallowed be thy name;
thy kingdom come,
thy will be done on earth
as it is in heaven.
Give us this day our daily bread,
and forgive us our trespasses
as we forgive those who trespass,
against us;
and lead us not into temptation,
but deliver us from evil. Amen.

Pater Noster

Pater noster qui es in cælis:
santificétur Nomen Tuum;
advéniat Regnum Tuum;
fiat volúntas Tua,
sicut in cælo, et in terra.
Panem nostrum
cotidiánum da nobis hódie;
et dimítte nobis débita nostra,
sicut et nos
dimíttus debitóribus nostris;
et ne nos indúcas in
tentatiónem;
sed líbera nos a Malo. Amen.

The Hail Mary

Hail, Mary, full of grace,
the Lord is with thee.
Blessed art thou among
women
and blessed is the fruit of
thy womb, Jesus.
Holy Mary, Mother of God,
pray for us sinners,
now and at the hour of
our death. Amen.

Ave, Maria

Ave, María, grátia plena,
Dóminus tecum.
Benedícta tu in muliéribus,
et benedíctus fructus ventris
tui, Iesus.
Sancta María, Mater Dei,
ora pro nobis peccatóribus,
nunc et in hora mortis nostræ.
Amen.

Optional Activity

The Sign of the Cross

Tracing the cross on one's own body or the forehead of another has been a common Christian gesture since the early centuries of the Church.

- Take time during prayer to have the children practice this ancient custom.
- Show them how to trace the cross on another person's forehead. Then allow them to do the same.
- Encourage the children to "sign" their family members with the Sign of the Cross.

Optional Activity

Glory Be

This ancient prayer is known as a *doxology*, or as "words of praise." It is part of the Rosary and is traditionally used to conclude the praying or chanting of a psalm in the *Liturgy of the Hours*.

- Teach the children this ancient prayer.
- Use the phrase "as it was in the beginning, is now, and ever shall be" to remind the children that God is eternal.

Personal and Family Prayers

Morning Prayer

Blessed are you, Lord, God of
all creation:
you take the sleep from my eyes
and the slumber from my
    eyelids.
Amen.

Evening Prayer

Protect us, Lord, as we stay
    awake;
watch over us as we sleep,
that awake, we may keep watch
    with Christ,
and asleep, rest in his peace.
Amen.

Grace After Meals

We give you thanks, Almighty
God, for all these gifts which we
have received from thy bounty,
through Christ our Lord. Amen.

Act of Faith, Hope, and Love

*This prayer is often prayed in the
morning to remind us that all gifts come
from God, and that he can help us
believe, trust, and love.*

My God, I believe in you,
    I hope in you,
I love you above all things,
    with all my mind
and heart and strength.

Grace Before Meals

Bless us, O Lord, and these
    thy gifts
which we are about to receive
from thy bounty, through
Christ our Lord. Amen.

Angel Guardian (traditional)

*An angel is a spiritual being that is messenger
of God. Angels are mentioned nearly 300 times
in the Bible. Three important angels are Gabriel,
Michael, and Raphael.*

Angel of God,
my Guardian dear,
to whom his love commits me here,
ever this day (night)
be at my side,
to light and guard,
to rule and guide.

Angel Guardian (contemporary)

Angel sent by God to guide me,
be my light and walk beside me;
be my guardian and protect me;
on the paths of life direct me.

Optional Activity

Morning Prayer

Involve the children in a discussion about the different ways they wake up in the morning and the things they do to get ready for the day. Talk about ways they can make God a part of their first morning thoughts.

- Provide the children with construction paper and crayons.
- Encourage them to draw a picture of themselves saying "Good morning" to God to hang near their beds or where they brush their teeth as a reminder to focus on him each day.

Optional Activity

Evening Prayer

Remind the children that it is important to end each day in prayer, whether using this prayer, one of their own creation, or a combination of the two.

- Provide construction paper, crayons or markers, some yarn, and a single-hole punch.
- Have the children write the Evening Prayer on construction paper, and add their own artwork around the text.
- Punch two holes at the top of the paper; run a piece of yarn through the holes and tie it together to form a loop.
- Encourage the children to hang their prayer cards over their bedposts, on a nightstand, or on a wall near their beds.

Praying with the Saints

When we pray with the Saints, we ask them to pray to God for us and to pray with us. The Saints are with Christ. They speak for us when we need help.

A litany is a prayer with one line that is meant to be repeated over and over again so that those praying are caught up in the prayer itself. Some litanies are to Jesus; others are known as Litanies of the Saints, on whom we call to intercede for us.

Litanies

Christ, hear us.
Christ, graciously hear us.
Lord Jesus, hear our prayer.
Lord Jesus, hear our prayer.

Holy Mary, Mother of God,
pray for us
Saint John the Baptist,
pray for us
Saint Joseph, **pray for us**
Saint Peter and Saint Paul,
pray for us

Lord, have mercy.
Lord, have mercy.
Christ, have mercy.
Christ, have mercy.
Lord, have mercy.
Lord, have mercy.

Prayer of Petition

Lord God, you know our weakness.
In your mercy grant that the example of your Saints may bring us back to love and serve you through Christ our Lord.
Amen.

Optional Activity

Read about the Saints

Read a few Saint stories to the children or show a video on the life of a Saint.

- Choose a Saint whose life will speak to children their age, such as Saint Francis of Assisi or Saint Katharine Drexel.

- Distribute a *People of Faith Saint Card* (Our Sunday Visitor) to each child.

- Pray a Saint prayer. Remind the children that Saints can pray for us and help us pray to God.

Catholic Faith Words

angel a type of spiritual being that does God's work, such as delivering messages from God or helping to keep people safe from harm (171)

Baptism the Sacrament in which a person is immersed in water or has water poured on him or her. Baptism takes away Original Sin and all personal sin, and makes a person a child of God and member of the Church. (239)

Bible the Word of God written in human words. The Bible is the holy book of the Church. (49)

Church the community of all baptized people who believe in God and follow Jesus (153)

Commandment a law that God made for people to obey (129)

creation everything made by God (49)

disciple a follower of Jesus who believes in him and lives by his teachings (186)

Eucharist the Sacrament in which Jesus shares himself, and the bread and wine become his Body and Blood (253)

faith believing in God and all that he helps us understand about himself. Faith leads us to obey God. (118)

free will being able to choose whether to obey God or disobey God. God created us with free will because he wants us to make good choices. (196)

God the Father the First Divine Person of the Holy Trinity (84)

godparents two people chosen by your parents to help you follow Jesus. They are usually present at your Baptism. (241)

grace God's gift of a share in his life and help (239)

Great Commandment the law to love God above all else and to love others the way you love yourself (129)

Heaven the full joy of living with God forever **(262)**

Holy Communion receiving Jesus' Body and Blood in the celebration of the Eucharist **(254)**

Holy Family the name for the human family of Jesus, Mary, and Joseph **(94)**

Holy Spirit the Third Divine Person of the Holy Trinity **(160)**

Holy Trinity the one God in three Divine Persons—God the Father, God the Son, and God the Holy Spirit **(85)**

holy unique and pure; set apart for God and his purposes **(171)**

image of God the likeness of God that is in all human beings because we are created by him **(68)**

Jesus the name of the Son of God who became man **(58)**

K – L

Kingdom of God the world of love, peace, and justice that is in Heaven and is still being built on Earth **(153)**

Last Supper the meal Jesus shared with his disciples the night before he died. At the Last Supper, Jesus gave himself in the Eucharist. **(253)**

Lord's Prayer the prayer Jesus taught his followers to pray to God the Father. This prayer is also called the Our Father. **(139)**

Mary the Mother of Jesus, the Mother of God. She is also called "Our Lady" because she is our Mother and the Mother of the Church. **(94)**

Mass the gathering of Catholics to worship God. It includes readings from the Bible and the celebration of Holy Communion. **(254)**

New Testament the second part of the Bible about the life and teachings of Jesus, his followers, and the early Church **(105)**

obey to do things or act in certain ways that are requested by those in authority **(196)**

Old Testament the first part of the Bible about God and his People before Jesus was born **(105)**

Original Sin the first sin committed by Adam and Eve and passed down to everyone **(218)**

peace when things are calm and people get along with one another **(274)**

praise giving God honor and thanks because he is God **(58)**

prayer talking to and listening to God **(136)**

Resurrection the event of Jesus being raised from Death to new life by God the Father through the power of the Holy Spirit **(221)**

Saint a hero of the Church who loved God very much, led a holy life, and is now with God in Heaven **(171)**

serve to help or give others what they need in a loving way **(184)**

Seven Sacraments special signs and celebrations that Jesus gave his Church. The Sacraments allow us to share in the life and work of God. **(229)**

sin a person's choice to disobey God on purpose and do what he or she knows is wrong. Accidents and mistakes are not sins. **(205)**

Son of God a name for Jesus that tells you God is his Father. The Son of God is the Second Divine Person of the Holy Trinity. **(84)**

Ten Commandments God's laws that tell people how to love him and others **(195)**

thanksgiving giving thanks to God for all he has given us **(61)**

Index

Index

© Our Sunday Visitor

The Subcommittee on the Catechism, United States Conference of Catholic Bishops, has found this catechetical series, copyright 2014, to be in conformity with the *Catechism of the Catholic Church*.

Nihil Obstat
Rev. Fr. Jeremiah L. Payne, S.Th.L.
Censor Librorum, Diocese of Orlando

Imprimatur
✠ Most Rev. John Noonan
Bishop of Orlando
March 26, 2013

For permission to reprint copyrighted materials, grateful acknowledgment is made to the following sources:

Allelu! Growing and Celebrating with Jesus ® *Music CD* © Our Sunday Visitor, Inc. Music written and produced by Sweetwater Productions. All rights of the owners of these works are reserved.

English translation of Glory Be (the Gloria Patri), Lord, have mercy, the Apostles' Creed, Nicene Creed, the Hail Mary, the Lord's Prayer, and Lamb of God (Agnus Dei) by the International Consultation on English Texts (ICET). All rights reserved.

The English translation of a *Rite of Baptism for Children* © 1969, International Commission on English in the Liturgy Corporation (ICEL); the English translation of the Antiphon for the Canticle of Simeon from *The Liturgy of the Hours* © 1973, 1974, 1975, International Commission on English in the Liturgy Corporation (ICEL); excerpts from the English translation of The Roman Missal © 2010, ICEL. All rights reserved. Published with the approval of the Committee on Divine Worship, United States Conference of Catholic Bishops.

Excerpts from the *United States Catholic Catechism for Adults*, copyright © 2006, United States Catholic Conference, Inc.—Libreria Editrice Vaticana.

Music selections copyright John Burland, used with permission, and produced in partnership with Ovation Music Services, P.O. Box 402 Earlwood NSW 2206, Australia. Please refer to songs for specific copyright dates and information.

Music selections copyrighted or administered by OCP Publications are used with permission of OCP Publications, 5536 NE Hassalo, Portland, OR 97213. Please refer to songs for specific copyright dates and information.

Quotations from papal and other Vatican documents are from www.vatican.va copyright © 2013 by Libreria Editrice Vaticana.

Scripture selections taken from the *New American Bible, revised edition* © 2010, 1991, 1986, 1970 by the Confraternity of Christian Doctrine, Washington, D.C., and are used by license of the copyright owner. All rights reserved. No part of the *New American Bible* may be reproduced in any form without permission in writing from the copyright owner.

Additional acknowledgments appear on page 336.

Alive in Christ Parish Grade 1 Student Book
ISBN: 978-1-61278-006-1
Item Number: CU5096

1 2 3 4 5 6 7 8 015016 17 16 15 14 13
Webcrafters, Inc.; Madison, WI; USA; August 2013; Job# 103909

Photo Credits

vi The Crosiers/Gene Plaisted, OSC; **vii** Our Sunday Visitor; **viii** iStockphoto/Thinkstock; **1** Jack Hollingsworth/Photodisc/Thinkstock; **2** RunPhoto/Photodisc/Getty Images; **3** Image Copyright Andresr, 2013 Used under license from Shutterstock.com; **5** (t) iStockphoto.com/eyetoeyePIX; **5** (b) iStockphoto.com/JasonDoiy; **6** Our Sunday Visitor; **7** (bg) Image Copyright Joan Kerrigan, 2013 Used under license from Shutterstock.com; **7** (inset) The Trinity: Father, Son and Holy Spirit. 19th century coloured woodcut/ Universal History Archive/UIG/The Bridgeman Art Library; **9** Image Copyright offish25, 2013 Used under license from Shutterstock.com; **13** Image Copyright Philip Meyer, 2013 Used under license from Shutterstock.com; **14** (l) Image Copyright AISPIX by Image Source, 2013 Used under license from Shutterstock.com; **14** (r) Image Copyright offish25, 2013 Used under license from Shutterstock.com; **15** Image Copyright Zurijeta, 2013 Used under license from Shutterstock.com; **17** Image Copyright Philip Meyer, 2013 Used under license from Shutterstock.com; **18** (l) Image Copyright Zurijeta, 2013 Used under license from Shutterstock.com; **18** (r) RAFAL STRZECHOWSKI/AGENCJA FREE/Alamy; **19** Image Copyright Soyka, 2013 Used under license from Shutterstock. com; **20** Our Sunday Visitor; **21** Image Copyright Philip Meyer, 2013 Used under license from Shutterstock.com; **22** (t) Image Copyright InavanHateren, 2013 Used under license from Shutterstock.com; **22** (b) Our Sunday Visitor; **24** (t) Image Copyright photastic, 2013 Used under license from Shutterstock.com; **24** (b) iStockphoto/ Thinkstock; **25** Image Copyright Philip Meyer, 2013 Used under license from Shutterstock.com; **26** (t) iStockphoto/Thinkstock; **26** (b) iStockphoto.com/goldenKB; **27** Bill & Peggy Wittman; **31** Image Copyright Philip Meyer, 2013 Used under license from Shutterstock.com; **32** Bill & Peggy Wittman; **34** E Simanor/age fotostock; **35** Image Copyright Philip Meyer, 2013 Used under license from Shutterstock.com; **36** (t) Image Copyright Richard Griffin, 2013 Used under license from Shutterstock. com; **36** (b) E Simanor/age fotostock; **38** The Crosiers, Gene Plaisted, OSC; **39** Image Copyright Philip Meyer, 2013 Used under license from Shutterstock.com; **41** Michael Newman/PhotoEdit; **43** Image Copyright Philip Meyer, 2013 Used under license from Shutterstock.com; **44** JJM Stock Photography/Arts/Alamy; **46** (c) iStockphoto.com/ Stephan Zabel; **46** (b) iStockphoto/Thinkstock; **47** Image Copyright privilege, 2013 Used under license from Shutterstock.com; **54** (bg) Image Copyright Joan Kerrigan, 2012 Used under license from Shutterstock.com; **54** (inset) Image Copyright BestPhotoByMonikaGniot, 2013 Used under license from Shutterstock.com; **55** Image Copyright privilege, 2013 Used under license from Shutterstock.com; **57** Image Copyright bumihills, 2013 Used under license from Shutterstock.com; **60** Image Copyright marco mayer, 2013 Used under license from Shutterstock.com; **61** Image Copyright sonya etchison, 2013 Used under license from Shutterstock.com; **62** (tl) Image Copyright Christopher Elwell, 2013 Used under license from Shutterstock.com; **62** (tr) Image Copyright Gayvoronskaya_Yana, 2013 Used under license from Shutterstock.com; **62** (bl) Image Copyright Nattika, 2013 Used under license from Shutterstock.com; **62** (br) Image Copyright Leonid Ikan, 2013 Used under license from Shutterstock.com; **64** (bg) Image Copyright Joan Kerrigan, 2013 Used under license from Shutterstock.com; **64** (inset) Image Copyright eurobanks, 2013 Used under license from Shutterstock.com; **65** Image Copyright bumihills, 2013 Used under license from Shutterstock.com; **67** Jupiterimages/Goodshoot/Thinkstock; **69** Image Copyright leungchopan, 2013 Used under license from Shutterstock.com; **70** Image Copyright Nancy Bauer, 2013 Used under license from Shutterstock.com; **71** KidStock/Blend Images/Corbis; **72** (t) Hemera/Thinkstock; **72** (b) Image Copyright sianc, 2013 Used under license from Shutterstock.com; **74** (bg) Image Copyright Joan Kerrigan, 2013 Used under license from Shutterstock.com; **74** (inset) iStockphoto.com/Murat Subatli; **75** KidStock/Blend Images/Corbis; **80** (c) Our Sunday Visitor; **80** (b) The Crosiers/ Gene Plaisted, OSC; **82** iStockphoto/Thinkstock; **83** iStockphoto.com/Agnieszka Kirinicjanow; **86** Image Copyright Jacek Chabraszewski, 2013 Used under license from Shutterstock.com; **88** (bg) Image Copyright Joan Kerrigan, 2013 Used under license from Shutterstock.com; **88** (inset) Image Copyright bonchan, 2013 Used under license from Shutterstock.com; **92** (t) Image Copyright Elena Kouptsova-Vasic, 2013 Used under license from Shutterstock.com; **92** (b) Anderson Ross/Blend Images/Corbis; **93** Image Copyright oliveromg, 2013 Used under license from Shutterstock.com; **95** iStockphoto/Thinkstock; **98** (bg) Image Copyright Joan Kerrigan, 2013 Used under license from Shutterstock.com; **98** (inset) Alfred Schauhuber/age fotostock; **99** iStockphoto/Thinkstock; **101** Brand X Pictures/Thinkstock; **103** Image Copyright michaeljung, 2013 Used under license from Shutterstock.com; **104** Hemera Technologies/AbleStock.com/Thinkstock; **105** iStockphoto/Thinkstock; **106** (l) ASP Religion/Alamy; **106** (r) Louie Psihoyos/Science Faction/Corbis; **108** (bg) Image Copyright Joan Kerrigan, 2013 Used under license from Shutterstock.com; **108** (inset) Image Copyright Kovnir Andrii, 2013 Used under license from Shutterstock.com; **109** Brand X Pictures/Thinkstock; **114** (c) Image Copyright rmnoa357, 2013 Used under license from Shutterstock.com; **114** (b) Image Copyright Richard Paul Kane, 2013 Used under license from Shutterstock.com; **116** Tim Graham/Corbis; **120** Myrleen Pearson/ PhotoEdit; **122** (bg) Image Copyright Joan Kerrigan, 2013 Used under license from Shutterstock.com; **122** (inset) iStockphoto.com/gordana jovanovic; **123** Myrleen Pearson/PhotoEdit; **125** Gabriel Blaj/age fotostock; **126** Image Copyright alexdrim, 2013 Used under license from Shutterstock.com; **128** The Crosiers/Gene Plaisted, OSC; **129** (bl) iStockphoto.com/Kim Gunkel; **129** (bc) iStockphoto.com/kali9; **129** (br) Our Sunday Visitor; **130** Image Copyright Olga Sapegina, 2013 Used under license from Shutterstock.com; **132** (bg) Image Copyright Joan Kerrigan, 2013 Used under license from Shutterstock.com; **132** (inset) iStockphoto.com/Kim Gunkel; **133** iStockphoto. com/kali9; **135** istockphoto.com/VikramRaghuvanshi; **136** Andersen Ross/age fotostock; **137** (t) Image Copyright Petrenko Andriy, 2013 Used under license from Shutterstock.com; **137** (b) iStockphoto/Thinkstock; **138** Bill & Peggy Wittman; **139** Peter Burian/Corbis; **142** (bg) Image Copyright Joan Kerrigan, 2013 Used under license from Shutterstock.com; **142** (inset) Image Copyright Podriv Ustoev, 2013 Used under license from Shutterstock.com; **143** Andersen Ross/age fotostock; **148** (c) Istockphoto.com/Dimitris66; **148** (b) Image Copyright Samot, 2013 Used under license from Shutterstock.com; **151** Image Copyright Sue McDonald, 2013 Used under license from Shutterstock.com; **152** Providence Collection/Licensed From Goodsalt.com; **153** Image Copyright Pressmaster, 2013 Used under license from Shutterstock.com; **156** (bg) Image Copyright Joan Kerrigan, 2013 Used under license from Shutterstock. com; **156** (inset) Image Copyright Monkey Business Images, 2013 Used under license from Shutterstock.com; **157** Image Copyright Pressmaster, 2013 Used under license from Shutterstock.com; **159** Our Sunday Visitor; **160** Jeff Greenberg/Alamy; **162** (l) The Art Archive/Alamy; **162** (r) Jupiterimages/Polka Dot/Thinkstock; **163** Image Copyright StepStock, 2013 Used under license from Shutterstock.com; **164** Image Copyright Andresr, 2013 Used under license from Shutterstock.com; **166** (bg) Image Copyright Joan Kerrigan, 2013 Used under license from Shutterstock.com; **166** (inset) Istockphoto.com/sjlocke ; **167** Our Sunday Visitor; **169** STUDIO BOX/Photographer's Choice/Getty Images; **171** Perry Mastrovito/Design Pics/Corbis; **174** Comstock/ Thinkstock; **176** (bg) Image Copyright Joan Kerrigan, 2013 Used under license from Shutterstock.com; **176** (inset) Art Directors & TRIP/Alamy; **177** Perry Mastrovito/Design Pics/Corbis; **182** (c) iStockphoto.com/Rosemarie Gearhart; **182** (b) Godong/Robert Harding World Imagery/Corbis; **183** nruboc/Bigstock.com; **185** Osservatore Romano/ Reuters; **187** Image Source/Corbis; **188** Image Copyright Rob Hainer, 2013 Used under license from Shutterstock.com; **189** (l) Leland Bobbé/Corbis; **189** (r) iStockphoto/ Thinkstock; **190** (bg) Image Copyright Joan Kerrigan, 2013 Used under license from Shutterstock.com; **190** (inset) Image Copyright Sergiy Bykhunenko, 2013 Used under license from Shutterstock.com; **191** Image Source/Corbis; **194** (t) Image Copyright homydesign, 2013 Used under license from Shutterstock.com; **194** (c) Image Copyright Elena Itsenko, 2013 Used under license from Shutterstock.com; **194** (b) iStockphoto. com/Christopher Noble; **195** PoodlesRock/Corbis; **196** Jamie Grill/Iconica/Getty Images; **197** Image Copyright michaeljung, 2013 Used under license from Shutterstock.com; **198** Image Copyright auremar, 2013 Used under license from Shutterstock.com; **200** Image Copyright Joan Kerrigan, 2013 Used under license from Shutterstock.com; **201** Jamie Grill/Iconica/Getty Images; **204** Image Copyright altanaka, 2013 Used under license from Shutterstock.com; **205** (bg) iStockphoto/ Thinkstock; **205** (inset) Erik Stenbakken/Licensed From Goodsalt.com; **206** Misty Bedwell/Design Pics/Corbis; **207** Our Sunday Visitor; **210** (bg) Image Copyright Joan Kerrigan, 2013 Used under license from Shutterstock.com; **210** (inset) Design Pics/ SuperStock; **211** Misty Bedwell/Design Pics/Corbis; **216** (t) iStockphoto.com/ oscarcwilliams; **216** (b) Tony Freeman/PhotoEdit; **217** iStockphoto.com/Lokibaho; **220** iStockphoto/jgroup; **221** Bill & Peggy Wittman; **222** Image Copyright pedalist, 2013 Used under license from Shutterstock.com; **224** (bg) Image Copyright Joan Kerrigan, 2013 Used under license from Shutterstock.com; **224** (inset) Image Copyright filipw, 2013 Used under license from Shutterstock.com; **225** Bill & Peggy Wittman; **227** Muskopf Photography, LLC/Alamy; **229** James Shaffer/PhotoEdit; **230** Jupiterimages/Polka Dot/Thinkstock; **234** (bg) Image Copyright Joan Kerrigan, 2013 Used under license from Shutterstock.com; **234** (inset) Image Copyright alephcomo, 2013 Used under license from Shutterstock.com; **235** Muskopf Photography, LLC/Alamy; **237** Istockphoto.com/GreenStock; **238** Nugene Chiang/ AsiaPix/Corbis; **240** (tl) Our Sunday Visitor; **240** (tr) Our Sunday Visitor; **240** (bl) Our Sunday Visitor; **240** (br) Our Sunday Visitor; **241** Digital Vision/Thinkstock; **242** iStockphoto.com/Creative; **244** (bg) Image Copyright Joan Kerrigan, 2013 Used under license from Shutterstock.com; **244** (inset) imagebroker/Alamy; **245** Our Sunday Visitor; **250** (c) Pascal Deloche/Godong/Corbis; **250** (b) Image Copyright Ersler Dmitry, 2013 Used under license from Shutterstock.com; **252** Hemera/Thinkstock; **253** Tony Freeman/PhotoEdit; **254** (l) Tolo Balaguer/age fotostock; **254** (r) James Shaffer/ PhotoEdit; **255** (l) Our Sunday Visitor; **255** (r) Our Sunday Visitor; **256** (t) Pontino/ Alamy; **256** (b) Bill & Peggy Wittman; **258** (bg) Image Copyright Joan Kerrigan, 2013 Used under license from Shutterstock.com; **258** (inset) Bob Daemmrich/PhotoEdit; **259** Tolo Balaguer/age fotostock; **262** iStockphoto/Thinkstock; **263** The Crosiers/ Gene Plaisted, OSC; **266** Image Copyright dotshock, 2013 Used under license from Shutterstock.com; **268** Image Copyright Joan Kerrigan, 2013 Used under license from Shutterstock.com; **269** The Crosiers/Gene Plaisted, OSC; **271** Lou Cypher/Corbis; **272** Image Copyright Stuart Miles, 2013 Used under license from Shutterstock.com; **273** iStockphoto.com/Fertnig; **278** (bg) Image Copyright Joan Kerrigan, 2013 Used under license from Shutterstock.com; **278** (inset) Myrleen Pearson/Alamy; **279** Lou Cypher/Corbis; **284–285** (bg) Image Copyright Heather Renee, 2013 Used under license from Shutterstock.com; **285** (inset) iStockphoto/Thinkstock; **286** Frances Roberts/Alamy; **288** iStockphoto.com/asiseeit; **290** JLP/Jose L. Pelaez/Corbis; **291** Image Copyright Alina G, 2013 Used under license from Shutterstock.com; **292** Image Copyright Tony Campbell, 2013 Used under license from Shutterstock.com; **293** Image Copyright Lev Kropotov, 2013 Used under license from Shutterstock.com; **294** Myrleen Pearson/PhotoEdit; **296** blickwinkel/Alamy; **297** iStockphoto.com/ danwilton; **298** Myrleen Pearson/PhotoEdit; **300** AP Photo/Andrew Medichini; **301** Image Copyright Zvonimir Atletic, 2013 Used under license from Shutterstock. com; **302** (l) Stockbyte/Thinkstock; **302** (r) Jupiterimages/Brand X Pictures/Thinkstock; **303** (t) Franck Fotos/Alamy; **303** (c) Fred de Noyelle/Godong/Corbis; **303** (b) Brian Hamilton/Alamy; **311** Our Sunday Visitor; **315** iStockphoto.com/aldomurillo

Acknowledgements:

English translation of "Morning Prayer," "Prayer Before Meals" (Retitled: "Grace Before Meals"), and "Prayer After Meals" (Retitled: "Grace After Meals") from *Book of Blessings*. Translation copyright ©1988 by International Committee on English in the Liturgy, Inc. (ICEL).

English translation of "Prayer to the Guardian Angel" (Retitled: "Angel Guardian") from *A Book of Prayers*. Translation copyright ©1982 by International Committee on English in the Liturgy, Inc. (ICEL).

Activity Master
Answer Keys

Chapter 2 Activity Master, p. 57E

Chapter 8 Activity Master, p. 125E

1. Say "I'm sorry."
2. Pick up your toys.
4. Pray.
6. Help at home.
7. Go to Mass.
8. Help a classmate who is sad.

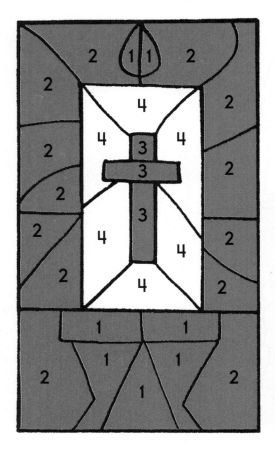

1 = yellow

2 = blue

3 = black

(shown filled in above)

4 = white

Chapter 20 Activity Master, p. 261E

help
share
pray
kind
forgive

Endnotes:

CCC 2559: endnote #2 (2 St. John Damascene, *Defide orth*. 3,24:PG 94,1089C.)